Portfolio Design
for Interiors

Portfolio Design for Interiors

HAROLD LINTON
GEORGE MASON UNIVERSITY

WILLIAM ENGEL
NEW YORK SCHOOL OF INTERIOR DESIGN

FAIRCHILD BOOKS
AN IMPRINT OF BLOOMSBURY PUBLISHING INC

BLOOMSBURY
NEW YORK · LONDON · OXFORD · NEW DELHI · SYDNEY

Fairchild Books

An imprint of Bloomsbury Publishing Inc.

1385 Broadway	50 Bedford Square
New York	London
NY 10018	WC1B 3DP
USA	UK

www.bloomsbury.com

FAIRCHILD BOOKS, BLOOMSBURY and the Diana logo are trademarks of Bloomsbury Publishing Plc

First Edition published 2017

© Bloomsbury Publishing Inc, 2017

All rights reserved. No part of this publication may be reproduced or transmitted in any form or by any means, electronic or mechanical, including photocopying, recording, or any information storage or retrieval system, without prior permission in writing from the publishers.

No responsibility for loss caused to any individual or organization acting on or refraining from action as a result of the material in this publication can be accepted by Bloomsbury Publishing Inc or the author.

Library of Congress Cataloging-in-Publication Data
Names: Linton, Harold, author. | Engel, William (Artist), author.
Title: Portfolio design for interiors / Harold Linton, George Mason University; William Engel, New York School of Interior Design.
Description: New York : Fairchild Books, 2017.
Identifiers: LCCN 2016049852 | ISBN 9781628924725 (paperback)
Subjects: LCSH: Interior decoration rendering. | Design services—Marketing. | BISAC: ARCHITECTURE / Interior Design / General. | ARCHITECTURE / Professional Practice.
Classification: LCC NK2113.5 .L56 2017 | DDC 747—dc23
LC record available at https://lccn.loc.gov/2016049852

ISBN PB: 9781628924725

ePDF: 9781628925821

Cover design: Eleanor Rose
Cover image: Residential Design 3 model, New York School of Interior Design © Anne Aristya
Typeset by Lachina
Printed and bound in China

CONTENTS

FOREWORD BY SCOTT AGELOFF— XI
PREFACE— XIII
ACKNOWLEDGMENTS— XV
INTRODUCTION— XVII

1 OBJECTS & OBJECTIVES— 1

2 THE SPIRIT OF CONCEPTION & CREATIVE PROCESS— 29

3 ORGANIZING PORTFOLIO MATERIALS: WHAT TO INCLUDE— 51

4 FROM CONCEPT TO PROCESS TO LAYOUT DESIGN— 77

5 CAPTURING EXPRESSIVE IMAGES— 105

6 DIGITAL PRESENTATIONS— 133

7 CRITIQUES & CONVERSATIONS— 161

8 RESEARCH & WRITTEN COMMUNICATIONS— 189

9 USING YOUR PORTFOLIO AS A TOOL— 221

10 PORTFOLIO OF INTERIOR PORTFOLIOS— 243

BIBLIOGRAPHY— 269
INDEX— 271

EXTENDED CONTENTS

FOREWORD BY SCOTT AGELOFF— XI
PREFACE— XIII
ACKNOWLEDGMENTS— XV
INTRODUCTION— XVII

1 OBJECTS & OBJECTIVES— 1

Prologue— 1
Portfolios Are Living Documents!— 2
Objects and Openings— 4
Books, Boxes, and Hybrids— 8
Leave Behinds and Teasers— 10
Storyboarding— 10
Going Full Size— 12
Living Sequences— 14
Continuity— 16
Hidden Factors— 18
Patterns of Success— 22
Envision vs. Revision: A Golden Opportunity for a Fresh Approach!— 24
Read between the Lines— 27

2 THE SPIRIT OF CONCEPTION & CREATIVE PROCESS— 29

Stepping Back before Stepping In— 30
Collecting Images for a Form Board— 32
Reading Your Form Board— 34
Inspiration— 37
The Big Idea…Concept— 39
Titles and Problem Statements— 41
Engage— 44
Robust Research— 46
Thinking Out Loud— 48
Preliminary Budget: Testing Materials and Ideas— 48

EXTENDED CONTENTS

3 ORGANIZING PORTFOLIO MATERIALS: WHAT TO INCLUDE— 51

Wish to See— 51
Computer Inventory— 54
Desktop Organization— 55
Fixing Older Projects— 58
Concept Sketches— 58
Comprehensive Design Projects— 60
The Industries— 64
Materiality— 68
Supplemental Categories— 68
Focused Skills— 68
Green Design— 69
3D Interior Space— 72
Allied Interests— 74

4 FROM CONCEPT TO PROCESS TO LAYOUT DESIGN— 77

An Inspired Layout Design— 77
What Do We Mean by Design?— 79
Origins of Concepts— 79
Organization— 82
Designing with Typography— 86
The Role of Design Process— 89
Visualizing the Words— 92
The Umbrella Concept— 92
A Road Map: Typical Conceptual Process for the Layout Design of a Portfolio— 93
Layout and Visualization— 96
Checkers or Chess— 100
Business Perspective: Sketching, Storyboards, and Layouts— 102
Concepts Lead— 102
Juggling— 103

5 CAPTURING EXPRESSIVE IMAGES— 105

Sensing— 105
Expressing— 109
Capturing Images with Purpose— 112
Process: Design Thinking— 112
Lighting and Color Temperature— 113
Materials, Media, and Studio Lighting— 116
Interior Setup— 120
Models— 120
Lighting Studio— 121
Scanning, Photocopying, and Combining Images— 123
Presentation Strategies— 123
Control the Image Editing Process— 124
Understanding Your Strengths— 126
Cultivating Sensibilities: Seeing and Perceiving— 126
Human Factors— 131

EXTENDED CONTENTS

6 DIGITAL PRESENTATIONS— 133
Overview— 133
Preparing Physical Work for Digital Media— 137
Creating Digital Images— 140
Editing Digital Images— 144
Raster Images— 145
Vector Images— 146
Designing the Layout— 149
Exporting for Publication— 153
A Few Final Thoughts— 159

7 CRITIQUES & CONVERSATIONS— 161
Overview— 161
Featured Portfolios— 163
Beyond the Portfolio— 187

8 RESEARCH & WRITTEN COMMUNICATIONS— 189
Summary of Start-Up Interior Design Firms: What Matters?— 189
Resume and Cover Letter— 195
The Interview— 205
Advice on How to Show a Portfolio/Project— 208
General Advice— 208
Design Statement— 208
Meeting with Clients, Design Brief, and Analysis— 211
Concept Boards— 211
Transitions and Evolving New Documents— 211
The Underlying Human Experiences— 216

9 USING YOUR PORTFOLIO AS A TOOL— 221
Overview— 221
Research— 221
Initial Discussions— 225
A New Team— 228
Process Presentation in Your Book— 232
Guiding the Resume— 232
Interviewing (Resume, Portfolio, iPad, Laptop, and URL)— 233
Lead with Confidence— 239

10 PORTFOLIO OF INTERIOR PORTFOLIOS— 243
Alexandra Seager: Successful Layout and Graphic Design— 244
Chad Zumbaugh: Designing within Limits— 248
Kirsten Stover Cessna: Custom Size Books Have Personality— 252
Shizuka Nagaya: Layout Design Reflects Individuality— 256
Kalie Hendricks: Organizing Process and Product— 260
Kelsie Lally: Project Briefs Speak Volumes about Concept and Ideation— 264
Conclusion— 266

BIBLIOGRAPHY— 269
INDEX— 271

FOREWORD

During the past 30 years or so I have examined over a thousand portfolios from prospective students, from students nearing graduation and preparing for their first job search, and from young professionals wanting to take the next step along their career path. While it is no surprise that the format and content of portfolios vary tremendously, it is important to keep in mind these common goals and guidelines:

- Is the overall format and presentation clear and attractive?
- Is everything spelled correctly?
- Does it convey the breadth and depth of your knowledge and skills?
- Does it tell a story about who you are as a designer?
- Is it creative without being weird?

An excellent portfolio can distinguish you, and in the best of all worlds, lead to an interview and a job offer that is a good fit for your background and aspirations. What this book does so brilliantly is help you think through options and choices, avoid pitfalls, and assist you in producing a portfolio that is a positive tool and a good match for you as a designer.

While there is no single recipe for success, here are a few words of personal advice for graduates and young professionals. I prefer a portfolio that is in reverse chronological order and that gets to the point. Show your most mature work first and don't show everything you have ever done. And just because you include a project, you don't need to include every element. Be aware that people who review portfolios look at a lot of them. Chances are that whether or not they like what they see, if the portfolio is too big they will rarely get to the end. The impression you give is created in the first five or six pages at most.

In the end, choose, compose, edit, refine, and publish. And be flexible. In this digital world, it is easy to customize. Be very aware of your audience. You can easily tailor your portfolio so that it relates to the specific audience you are targeting.

Happy Hunting,

Scott M Ageloff, FIDEC ASID AIA
Founding Principal, Ageloff & Associates
Former SVP for Academic Affairs and Dean,
New York School of Interior Design

PREFACE

This book offers an expansive dialog in the form of a conversation between the authors and aspiring interior designers who wish to organize their portfolios for application to undergraduate and graduate programs in design, design competitions, grant applications, academic scholarships, fellowships, design internships, and employment. Our purpose is not to present a how-to or step-by-step prescriptive sequence of assembling an interior design portfolio. Rather, we seek to put forth a well-reasoned and poignant conversation regarding the conceptual dimensions of studio practice and the next steps in achieving your goals for professional development.

Within *Portfolio Design for Interiors* are over 400 images of outstanding interior design portfolio pages in full color that have been gathered from leading schools of interior architecture and design and prominent design firms in an effort to demonstrate creative trajectories and successful portfolio design accomplishments. The evidence of outstanding student design portfolios included in this book is striking in its quality of visual presentation. These innovative print and electronic formats represent a broad range of possible directions and an intended diversity of aesthetic solutions for interior portfolio design. We believe this collection will engage the reader to delve deeply into their own wells of creativity to arrive at a comprehensive and well-planned solution for their own purpose and presentation.

Our survey of leading interior design schools across the country and Canada resulted in a breadth of outstanding portfolio contributions to this expansive study of portfolio design for interiors. We also selected several professional portfolios to illustrate elements of design and photography as well as a few outstanding sample pages from the allied design disciplines. Layout design software such as the Adobe Creative Suite (InDesign, Photoshop, and Illustrator) have become readily available in higher education, contributing enormously to the success of student portfolio designs. Faculty have simultaneously placed more emphasis on the need to prepare students for professional presentation, as witnessed by the growth in portfolio design texts, seminars, and courses around the country. And, new opportunities for portfolio development on the Internet have sparked a revolution in how students are shaping and sharing their work online, how academics are reviewing portfolios for admissions to design programs, and how interior design firms are reviewing prospective candidates for employment.

In support of your professional goals and to help you deal successfully with the organization and design direction of your portfolio, www.portfoliodesign.com contains numerous examples of excellent interior design portfolios. In 2011, the website received an international design award from the Adobe Creative Achievement Competition to be listed among the top new website designs. Here you will find examples of portfolios taken from this book along with discussion of important elements of layout design and multiple pathways to pursue.

The proliferation of interior design websites along with portfolios presented via CD and DVD are now the mainstream. Online publishing houses host a full spectrum of teaser portfolios, sample pages, and full portfolio print presentations. Career day sheets posted online and presented at conferences in various size formats allow a prospective employer to preview design accomplishments including a student's introductory cover letter and resume. Social networks have blossomed into new and exciting instruments for professional introductions and marketing strategies. Design students have taken advantage of online professional networks to connect to the larger world of academics, professional designers, and business people.

The migration from print to digital and online presentations is well underway. The authors corresponded with numerous program administrators, design professors, students, and professionals who unanimously support the shift from traditional print presentations to digital portfolios. The authors communicated with many design students and practicing professionals around the country to discuss the most effective design strategies to organize and present one's work. Along with lectures and workshops, the authors

PREFACE

gathered points of interest from faculty colleagues and established professionals, which have lead us to introduce significant chapters to this volume including "The Spirit of Conception and Creative Process," "From Concept to Process to Layout Design," "Capturing Expressive Images," "Digital Presentations," and "Conversations and Critiques," while also expanding information on the practical dimensions of content in chapters such as "Research and Written Communications" and "Using Your Portfolio as a Tool."

A significant portion of our professional work has been devoted to helping design students and recent graduates organize their work into unified and coherent portfolios with strong graphic sensibilities and an understated elegance. Through the authors' combined lectures at 100+ architecture and interior design schools around the country and abroad, it has been our privilege to meet design students who are eager to explore creative pathways and concepts in relation to the organization and presentation of their projects. It is equally inspiring to meet and work with those students who have the desire to make an immersive product that is philosophically engaging and supported by excellence in the visual elements of design communications.

In compiling your work, consider the purpose of your portfolio and the desired end result. Remember that "all boats rise" when you revise and redesign original content to raise presentation and design content quality. Keep in mind that your work is a reflection of everything that you have learned during your education and experience in design. Give yourself enough time to brainstorm alternative schemes and make mistakes along the way. Test trial layout designs of your work to see how it can be best organized. Do not hesitate to show your work to trusted colleagues and faculty for their reactions and opinions; having an open dialog while designing can be enormously supportive. Similar to the interview process for employment or the application process to graduate school, your portfolio design is an opportunity to rehearse for the next step in your career. Take the full measure of opportunity; do not rush through the process, but allow plenty of time each and every day to react, absorb, and guide what is emerging.

ACKNOWLEDGMENTS

Portfolio Design for Interiors is a collaborative adventure between its authors Bill Engel, Professor of Design at the New York School of Interior Design, and Harold Linton, Professor of Art, School of Art, George Mason University.

We wish to express our sincere appreciation to all of the faculty who responded to our invitation for excellent portfolio examples and also for their exchange of studio observations. We are grateful to all of our student and professional readers and reviewers, authorities in technology, interior design professionals, and specialists in visual communications, design technology, and graphic design for their input and advice along the way.

Many thanks to the administrative help, direction, and support from David Sprouls, President, and Ellen Fisher, Academic Dean, New York School of Interior Design. We wish to thank Becket Logan for support and photography during the process of writing this book and Shelly Zacher for design illustrations. Thank you to Joseph Miranda, our editor at Fairchild Books, for his belief in the longevity and value of this book for students and the profession.

This book represents a survey and discussion of a collection of remarkable interior design portfolios from over 75 students selected by interior design faculty mentors from leading undergraduate and graduate programs throughout the country and Canada. We are thankful to them for working along with us over a two-year period in the development of the project. The trajectory of the students' accomplishments is laudatory. Every student portfolio shown in this book was successful.

This book, of course, could not have happened without the support of numerous others. Thanks to Scott Ageloff for his insightful foreword, which reflects humility, understanding, and keen perception of academic and professional experience. Special thanks are due to several contributors and reviewers including Laura Clary, IDesign Solutions, LLC, architect and technology consultant to the book, for her wisdom, generous advice, and contributions; Laura-Anne Wong, Keith Marks, and Erwin Thamm, for their reviews and critical opinions and especially support with technology. I am indebted to Steven Rost, Professor of Architecture at Lawrence Technological University, who provided material for the section on photography and advice throughout the book.

We would like to acknowledge each of the professional designers who graciously gave of their expertise to review the qualities of five very talented interior design portfolios. You will find these candid reviews of the students' portfolios in Chapter Seven, "Conversations and Critiques." We wish to thank Nancy Kwallek, Professor and Chair, University of Texas, Austin, School of Architecture; Jan Bast, FASID, Founder, McCormack & Wright; Lawrence Chabra, Associate, Robert A.M. Stern, Architects; Vanessa DeLeon and Associates; and Edwin Zawadzki and V. Mason Wickham, In Situ Design.

Thanks to those designers who sent us insightful tips on what not to overlook on your way to completing your portfolio. They're mentioned individually as notes in the margin throughout the book. We wish to acknowledge Diane Fox, University of Tennessee, Knoxville, who teaches an inspired portfolio design course for architecture and interior design students.

Thanks to our family including Bil Wright, Katie Ubl, and Paul Engel, Deeni Linton, and Jonathan and Joshua Linton.

Bloomsbury Publishing wishes to gratefully acknowledge and thank the editorial team involved in the publication of this book:

Acquisitions Editor: Noah Schwartzberg
Development Manager: Joseph Miranda
Assistant Editor: Kiley Kudrna
Art Development Editor: Edie Weinberg
In-house Designer: Eleanor Rose
Book Designer: Lachina Publishing Services
Production Manager: Claire Cooper
Project Manager: Christopher Black

INTRODUCTION

This book has been written for students and practitioners of interior design, interior architecture, and allied environmental design disciplines. William Engel and Harold Linton, co-authors, have taught portfolio courses, workshops, lectures, and seminars for over three decades to students of interior design and architecture. Together with Laura Clary and Steven Rost, colleagues and contributors, we have all enjoyed the conversations involved in working closely with resourceful students, faculty colleagues, and talented design practitioners who collectively expressed enthusiastic support for this book. It is important to note that the content of this book is structured around a broad conversation (similar to design studio critiques) and a multitude of examples that are intended to underscore the most important elements of planning for successful interior design portfolios. The conversation is intended to illuminate successful concepts and discuss them in breadth and depth to help inform the design of your portfolio. We know this will contribute to your exploration of possibilities in order to arrive at a better sense of what works best for your own portfolio. The purpose of representing diverse approaches in visual form is the belief that students benefit greatly from seeing what has come before. When multiple examples with critical opinions are presented, students gain insight because they are able to sift through and review successful strategies in order to reflect upon the possibilities for forming their own principles and design strategies.

The sample portfolios in the 400+ images in this book were created by especially talented and highly recommended undergraduate and graduate students and entry-level professionals. They demonstrate a stunning breadth of fresh design vision and provocative points of view. We embrace a plurality of design aesthetics, a diversity of milestone studio coursework, and the many comprehensive capstone studio design experiences that emphasize research methods and help to tie a ribbon on the undergraduate and graduate degree programs. Building a portfolio based on the representation of design evidence from studio coursework and office projects from employment or internship experiences is also supported with examples of carefully orchestrated projects that clearly reflect the acquisition of professional standards.

The portfolio is the paramount instrument for conveying skills and abilities in all matters of design, planning, practice, and communication. It requires the author to synthesize experience, knowledge, and artistry into a rigorous graphic approach that clearly defines one's knowledge. Successful portfolios require a disciplined plan for layout design to achieve a unified presentation of work that that is both legible and engaging. There are approximately seven main issues incorporated in this process that require careful coordination with each other. These include:

- A creative concept that encompasses the entire book and informs the reviewer of influences, interests, and aesthetic abilities in design
- A visible or invisible grid or spacing structure that guides the positioning of text and visuals
- The formation of a graphic design style that supports without dominating one's design evidence
- The selection of one or two styles of typography along with establishing a hierarchy of point sizes for titles, text, and figure captions throughout the book
- Professional photography and virtual illustrations
- Consideration of paper and board selection and binding methods
- Print quality, which is interdependent with paper selection and the look and feel of the book

It must also be mentioned that effective content is derived from the storyboard process of planning the book.

It is incumbent on the author of the portfolio to pose relevant questions to oneself in review of the most important goals for the representation of design content. How is all of my interior design evidence successfully integrated into effective layout designs for the portfolio? How do students of interior design and allied design disciplines demonstrate their understanding of standards for professional practice?

INTRODUCTION

How and where should I demonstrate design process and the exploration of alternative schemes? How will my portfolio best represent not only studio experience in interior design, but also an understanding of other interests? How will my portfolio integrate and demonstrate many of the issues we explored in the curriculum, such as business courses, design electives, furniture and millwork design, environmental standards, health and safety requirements, sustainability, and more?

Any comprehensive undertaking needs to be broken into its constituent parts in order for one to find meaningful relationships between the parts and the whole. Design students learn not to ignore elements of a problem but to find ways to integrate the needs of the client and requirements of a facility into an aesthetically pleasing and environmentally sensible response. As one progresses in the curriculum, it becomes habit to make notes as to the building blocks of content and standards in each project and course so that one can benefit from a broad range of issues successfully resolved and demonstrated through design accomplishments. Think of the portfolio as both a journal of your education, a training ground, and a rehearsal for an employment interview. Be knowledgeable about your areas of strength and accomplishments in design. As you progress through design studios, be equally cognizant of where knowledge and experience is demonstrated in your work so that you can organize projects and solutions that are reflective of your understanding of professional expectations and integrative of relevant standards of practice.

Junior and senior students in undergraduate design programs and many graduate students begin the process of assembling their work into portfolios typically without experiencing or attending a formal course in portfolio design or development. We wish to offer this book as a companion text for undergraduate and graduate students who require multiple examples to stimulate their thinking about planning for their own presentations. One of several important attributes of strong design portfolios is the idea that it will get you hired. It is important to demonstrate skills and abilities found in your work that are pertinent to generating daily work and production in a small or large interior design office. The interview for an office position begins with a conversation based on the interviewer knowing something of your background exposure, accomplishments, skills, and abilities. The strongest projects in a portfolio are spread apart from one another to illustrate a consistently strong body of work from front to back. A portfolio's first project, last project, and middle project form the "posts" to which other projects called "rails" are connected, thereby building a "post and rail," bridge-like structure throughout the portfolio organization.

Students who have had recent experience assembling their portfolios for submission to undergraduate and graduate schools or in the pursuit of fellowships, competitions, internships, or employment opportunities are smart to undergo a process of review and revision before the loaf is out of the oven. Creating a storyboard serves the designer as a narrative script of page and project sequence. You learn by practice to anticipate layout design problems and how to resolve them satisfactorily. As students learn the basics of portfolio construction and presentation, they begin to recognize exceptional opportunities that arise from a willingness to revise work where needed, which raises the bar of quality throughout the portfolio.

Over the past few decades, professional standards of practice in interior design have been continuously reviewed and upgraded. As the profession grows, the standards for health, safety, sustainability, and other important issues are reviewed and revised. The result has been a more comprehensive and capable practitioner, able to work in myriad design settings with greater control over the process and product, and ultimately with greater benefit to the end user. All of the standards of practice and guidelines for schools of interior design are contained in publications for professional accredited programs by the Council for Interior Design Accreditation (CIDA) at http://accredit-id.org.

The transformation of technology within interior design education contributes to this technologically focused first edition of *Portfolio Design for Interiors*. The technology evolution has enabled most schools to equip labs with the hardware and software necessary for the creation of well-designed portfolio projects. The Adobe Creative Suite has been adopted by the vast majority of design schools in the United States and abroad. The admissions process for schools of interior design and allied disciplines are beginning to require all applicants to present their work for admissions review as uploaded files instead of in print. Although the tide is in favor of the digital approach, there are still many schools that wish to see a print presentation without the glare of a monitor or questions regarding qualitative content.

INTRODUCTION

In working with diverse faculty and students, I have come to realize that many students have widely ranging creative approaches to portfolio preparation, including the design of the enclosing system and all of the samples within. The examples of design portfolios in this collection reflect not only energy and commitment but also much talent and creativity. They offer many insights into today's creative practices of portfolio design, as well as an intriguing look at some innovative forms of enclosure and original strategies for layout and graphic presentation. There is an interesting relationship between a two-dimensional presentation in a book and the three-dimensional world it represents. This is always a helpful attribute for design students to keep in mind: portfolio design requires multiple views of space-form composition in order to best appreciate and understand the fullness of a creative concept.

It is not our purpose to teach the techniques of InDesign, Illustrator, and Photoshop, or the fine points of working with various art materials; rather, our intention is to present an overview of the practices of portfolio design for interiors and environmental design; to present a variety of current portfolios representative of a broad range of aesthetic possibilities and hopefully informative for your development; and to discuss specific technical practices only as they relate to design concepts, execution of the layout, and associated principles of portfolio presentation. We hope that the discussion will provide you with insights into professional presentation practices. The examples have been selected for their clarity, impact, and ability to demonstrate design knowledge. We have tried not to burden the text with technical details but to illustrate a multitude of graphic design alternatives and to show how the most varied strategies can work if informed by an original and creative impulse.

Fresh approaches to developing the visual narrative supporting one's work are leading to greater creative expression and higher quality layout design. A contemporary interior design portfolio may now include high-density CD-ROM or a DVD for full video or multimedia presentation; it may even exist only electronically, on the Internet. For the moment, however, the traditional practices of demonstrating one's abilities in a print format remain strong, but have undergone considerable transformation in attitude and acceptance. Schools and employers are now equally willing to review teaser and full portfolios online or in other electronic formats. In this book, strong attention is devoted to new computer techniques and methods as they apply to portfolio design, with numerous examples included in every chapter.

This book brings together the shared experiences of numerous leading interior design professionals and educators who make comment on the nature of portfolio practices, helping to make this project especially meaningful. Their willingness to critique several student portfolios as well as offer commentary on the elements of planning, design, typography, binding, computer applications, reproduction processes, and philosophy of presentation is an act of faith that is deeply appreciated. The viewpoints of these designers and educators from across the country only serve to emphasize the importance of planning in the process of creating a strong portfolio.

We hope you will find inspiration in this collection and support toward developing your own successful portfolio. We wish to extend our appreciation and great thanks to all the students and design professionals who contributed both work and advice to this project.

1

OBJECTS
& OBJECTIVES

"Designing is a matter of concentration. You go deep on what you want to do. It's about intensive research. The concentration is warm and intimate and like the fire inside the earth—intense but not distorted. You can go to a place, really feel it in your heart. It's a beautiful feeling."

– **PETER ZUMTHOR**, SWISS ARCHITECT AND WINNER OF THE 2009 PRITZKER PRIZE AND 2013 RIBA ROYAL GOLD MEDAL

PROLOGUE

This book of discovery is intentionally overflowing with suggestions, guidance, and abundant examples that will prove to be a useful tool for the design of your portfolio in print and virtual formats. Interior designers need to show their work in an efficient form and demonstrate a diverse range of abilities. Their work must reflect a thorough understanding of the design process and problem solving, and apply the most effective presentation techniques to a demonstration of one's design intentions.

This book is intended to pose significant questions that only you can answer in a way that is fitting and appropriate to your work. Our Socratic method of teaching through asking questions and raising issues is intended to open your imagination to thinking of multiple ideas as the preferred way of conducting design. It is our intention to cultivate your full appreciation of the problem of developing a successful portfolio.

It is not an easy task. There are no simple recipes but some proven principles and guidelines to help you chart your course and make sensible plans. Once you have a framework for designing your book, then and only then is it advisable for you to ignore the rules. The best results blend imagination with excellence in design studio achievement applied to a rigorous understanding and orchestration of theory and practice in graphic layout design.

Within interior design studio education, there are genres of specialization such as projects that emphasize research, conceptual activity, materiality, pragmatics and problem solving, tectonics, lighting, building systems, and more. Faculty hold studio discussions about instant online portfolios, print, and CD portfolios for every stage in a designer's life. Students are preparing to live a life of design. Professional designers wake up making design decisions every day, and they create objects on a daily basis. This is the appropriate time for self-examination and to ask yourself what you desire from a life in design. What do you excel at doing in design? What comprises your palette of skills and abilities that you are comfortable with when requested to produce any form of a design document?

What interests you more and less about design? This book will pique your curiosity and awareness of the areas of your intense interest and other areas for professional improvement. There will always be things you are simply not interested in doing. In this sense, this book is a mirror as well as a guide. The mirror will require cleaning now and again, but will help you as you reflect on your accomplishments and growth, changing and evolving your strengths to become the kind of designer you want to be.

We, as authors, encourage you throughout the process of making your portfolio to be thorough and honest with yourself and with your audience. Among our most important goals is to show you how to work creatively and efficiently within realistic constraints of time and resources. We offer guidance in the photographic documentation of your work and with image development and manipulation using current imaging technology. The discussion includes the exploration of an appropriate selection of design materials for your book. You will learn how to shape, organize, and execute a creative and professional result as well as how to be self-critical in the review of the progress of your work. Most importantly, you will be broader in perspective, better in skills and abilities, and focused on setting and attaining the soundest strategy and result in portfolio design.

1 OBJECTS & OBJECTIVES

Hannah Miles Pierrou

Hannah's portfolio box (figures 1–1 to 1–5) was created during undergraduate studies at Purdue University in fulfillment of the professional curriculum and ultimately to achieve an offer for employment. It was created in Adobe Photoshop and Illustrator and printed on a large format color plotter and laminated to mat board for mounting and presentation. Spray adhesive was used to mount all color prints onto mat boards with the intention of having a firm plate for professional presentation.

All of the parts of the portfolio were contained by a stainless steel box found on the Internet at a cost of $100.00. The entire compilation of work was gathered from courses during the last two years of her undergraduate interior design program. The concept and design of all of the documents, the CD, and the mounted boards required a few months to produce.

The project has been quite successful in finding multiple jobs across the country. Because of the professionalism of her portfolio and presentation, her abilities at critical thinking, knowledge of computer programs, and comprehensive ability to begin and successfully conclude a project were prominent features of her portfolio. Hannah spent a considerable amount of time researching portfolio designs across the Internet. She compares designing a portfolio to designing an interior, "It is like designing a room . . . sometimes it takes looking at all the floor samples, and all the paint colors before choosing the right materials."

PORTFOLIOS ARE LIVING DOCUMENTS!

Portfolios are about living, working, and learning. They are a representation of your interests and accomplishments to date and reflect a sampling of your academic and professional experience along with allied interests that are all part of your origin, history, and understanding. A well-designed portfolio demonstrates a trajectory of growth and, therefore, represents multiple directions of accomplishment with numerous areas of interest useful toward continued exposure and professional development. Your faculty mentors and professional colleagues stand by to help guide you in uncharted waters and have your best interests at heart.

Portfolios, commonly called "books," are often created as a capstone project at the conclusion of an undergraduate or graduate degree program or in relation to applying for an entry-level to advanced position with an interior design firm. They bridge work from an intensive period of studio design production with experience from professional practice. The more exposure students have from working in a business through internships and summer jobs, the richer their portfolios are in relation to representing their understanding and abilities in the setting of office practice.

Here's a TIP:

The creation of a portfolio is an act of faith in taking the next well-traveled step of growing into the design profession. Candidates seeking a position in an office setting should realize they are being reviewed regarding a comprehensive body of work and in a competitive field where design abilities together with breadth and depth of exposure are critical.

Portfolios Are Living Documents!

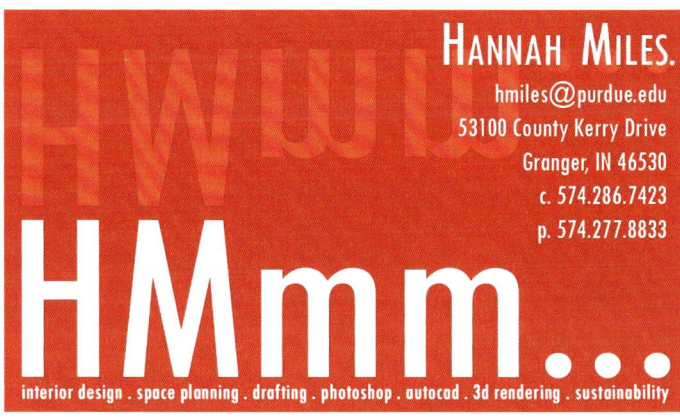

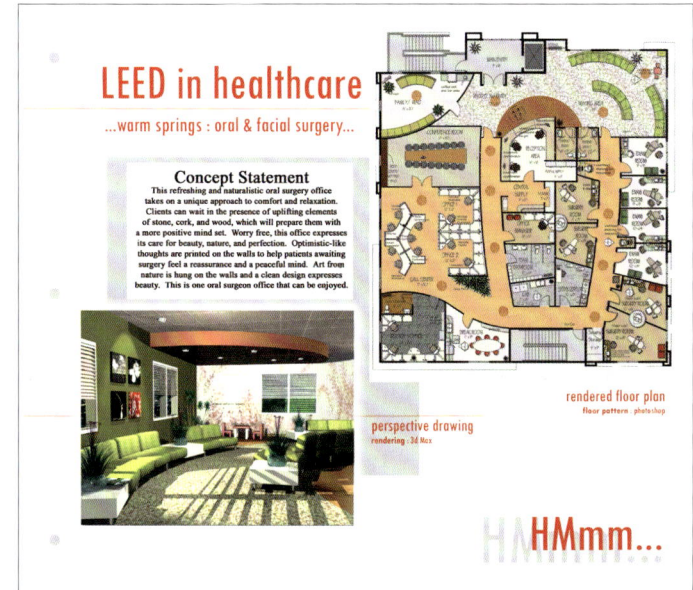
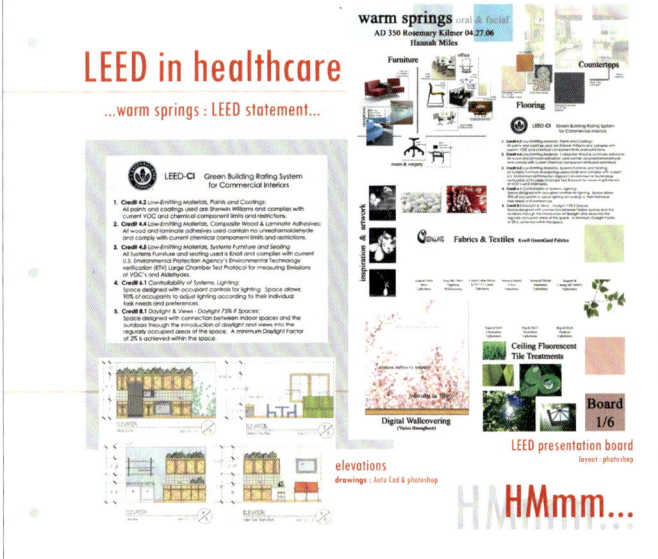

1–1 to 1–5 Hannah Miles Pierrou designed a very cohesive portfolio using color that ties the entities together and an aluminum container that houses her square shapes and serves as a strong package design. She included a CD of her work and printed cards of her individual projects that focused on LEED specifications per project. Her leave behind card is a playful and memorable use of her initials and her honed sense for design humor. Hannah Miles Pierrou, Purdue University, West Lafayette, Ind. 9" x 12".

1 OBJECTS & OBJECTIVES

OBJECTS AND OPENINGS

Your portfolio can be almost any shape and size within reason and industry expectations. Perhaps you are enchanted with a flipbook concept for a teaser, a full portfolio, or as a leave behind. Kevin Wyllie, architect, interior designer, and industrial designer, shared his latest creation with me and I immediately grabbed it and photographed it in the lighting studio (figure 1–6). He notched each page including the Mylar cover to accommodate an elastic band so that the deck of pages printed on card-stock-weight paper can open to spread out or remain contained in a deck for paging through.

Sarah Todd

Sarah Todd created the hard-bound case shown in figure 1–7 to harmonize with a sophisticated double bi-fold page experience of 8" x 8" pages in two stacks, half of which open simultaneously to the left while the others open right, providing expansive design coverage. The reviewer can immerse him- or herself in a comparative unfolding narrative. See samples of both Sarah's undergrad and professional portfolios later in Chapter 1.

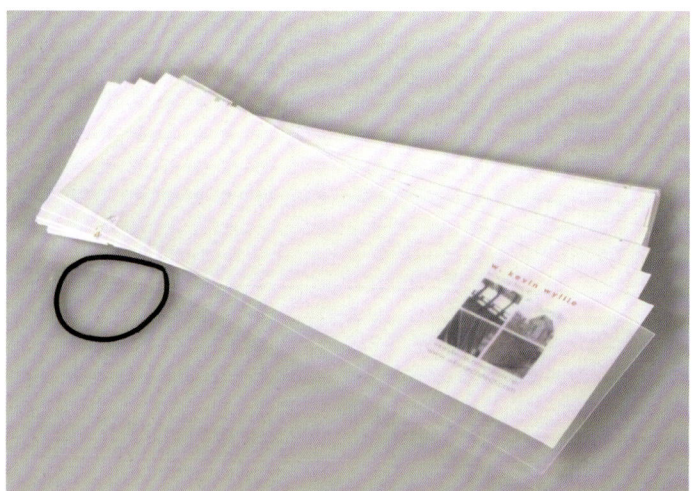

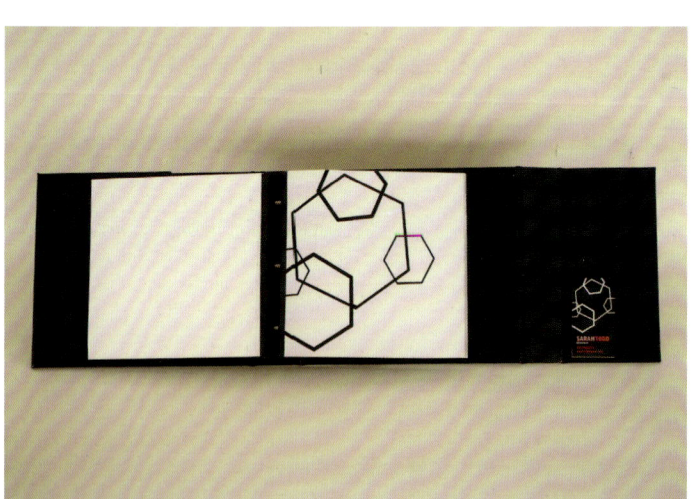

1–6 *(top)* W. Kevin Wyllie, Architecture and Interior Design, Fairfax, Va. 3" x 10"; **1–7** *(bottom)* Sarah Todd, New York School of Interior Design, N.Y., N.Y. 8" x 8".

Objects and Openings

COURTNEY MACDONALD
I BELIEVE IN DESIGNING WITH THE PHILOSOPHY THAT AS HUMAN BEINGS WE HAVE THE RESPONSIBILITY TO LEARN ABOUT OTHER PEOPLE'S CULTURES, RELIGIONS, AND WAYS OF LIFE IN ORDER TO LIVE IN HARMONY. THE OBJECTS AND STRUCTURES THAT WE CHOOSE TO SURROUND OURSELVES WITH ESTABLISH PRESENT MEANING AND FUTURE CONTENTMENT. MY DESIGN PROCESS FORCES ME TO DISSECT EVERY DIMENSION OF HUMAN LIFE, FROM PLANNING FOR WELL-BEING, TO PLANNING FOR AESTHETIC ATTRACTIVENESS AS WELL AS FOR THE UTMOST OF FUNCTIONALITY. I BELIEVE THAT THERE IS A CHALLENGE TO BE EXPECTED WHEN DESIGNING AND THAT IT SHOULD BE MET WITH ENTHUSIASM AND ENERGY.

INTERIOR DESIGN PORTFOLIO

1–8 *(top left)* Callie Ammidon, New York School of Interior Design, N.Y., N.Y. 5" x 5"; **1–9** *(top right)* Courtney MacDonald, University of Wisconsin, Stevens Point, Wis. 8.5" x 11"; **1–10** *(bottom left)* Amanda C. Davis, New York School of Interior Design, N.Y., N.Y. 7" x 11".

Callie Ammidon

Callie Ammidon's 6" x 6" portfolio teaser shown in figure 1–8 is a tried and true winning strategy in the sense that its brief page count with one project per every few pages whets the appetite of the viewer to ask for more (and more). When she hands them the full portfolio at 8.5" x 11", they re-experience those brief out-takes expand to full project presentations and she has the viewer right where she wants them. It comes in a simple paper sleeve that is inconspicuous and yet the vivid color invites you to open.

When you decide to design the cover and/or title page, you may be thinking of a minimalistic approach using just your name and portfolio title on the cover in a type style and composition that harmonizes with the composition inside your book. Courtney MacDonald designed an attractive and compelling cover, shown in figure 1–9, with an opening design philosophy statement and layers of information in strong hues not to be missed. We admire her gusto!

Amanda Davis

Amanda Davis demonstrates a table of contents page in figure 1–10 accompanied by and coordinated with the design of her business card. This begs the position that the cover, design statement, and contents pages can all speak to one's identity through being designed in coordination with each other—simple yet highly effective!

1 OBJECTS & OBJECTIVES

Phylicia Flynn

Phylicia Flynn rounded the corners of her pages, shown in figure 1–11, to soften the impact of the object-ness of a portfolio and drive up the expectation of a tactile experience to come when paging through her book.

Joshua Brewinski

Finally, Joshua Brewinski demonstrates in figure 1–12 the necessary linkage of cover design with each project's opening page. Isn't it fun to see how each section opener is varied yet coordinated with the overall typographic and visual strategy at play?

Many of the skill sets represented in the interior design and interior architecture curriculum are, therefore, appropriate to include in one's portfolio. Evidence of problem-solving, written communications, creative concepts, design process, history and aesthetics, knowledge of building systems, structures and materials, lighting design, space planning, furniture and millwork, visual communications, rendering and drafting, modeling and board presentation, skills in industry software, internships, and office experience are all possible to include.

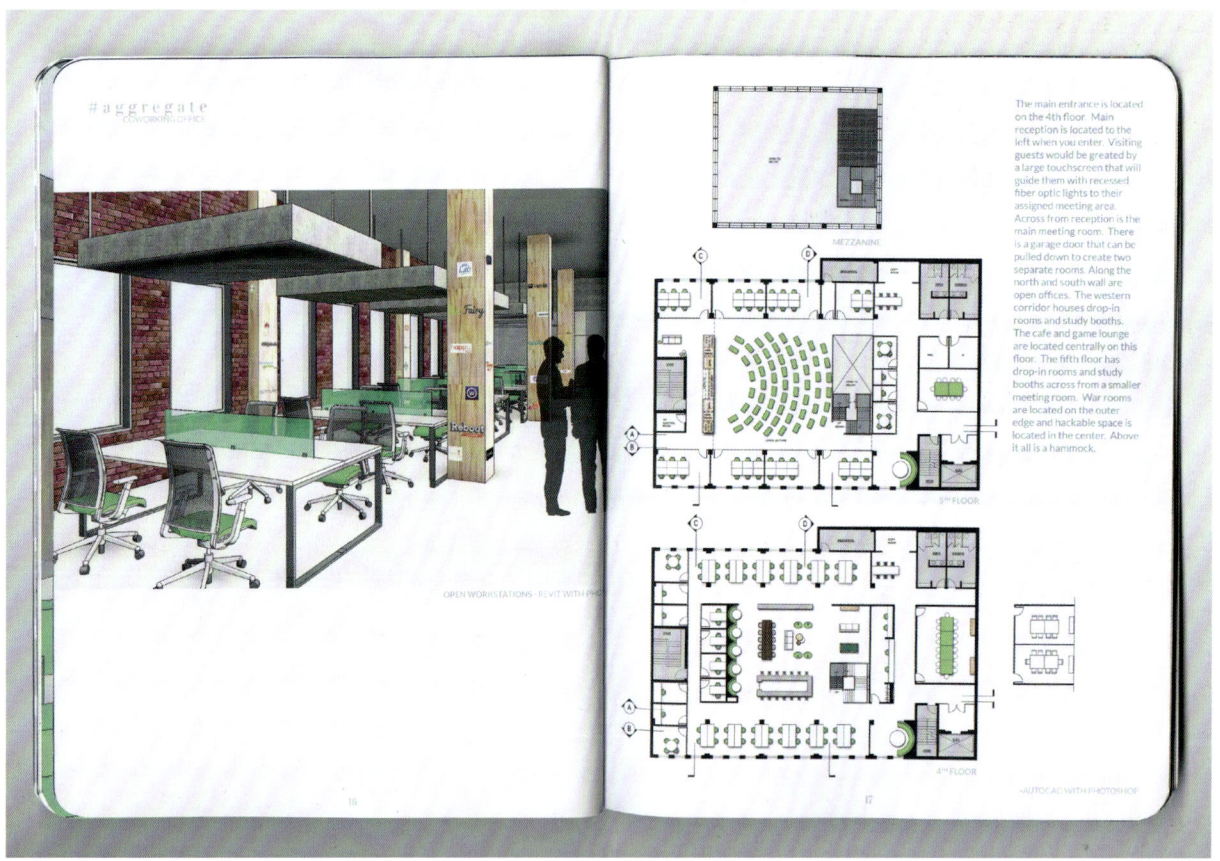

1–11 Phylicia Flynn, 6" x 8".

Objects and Openings

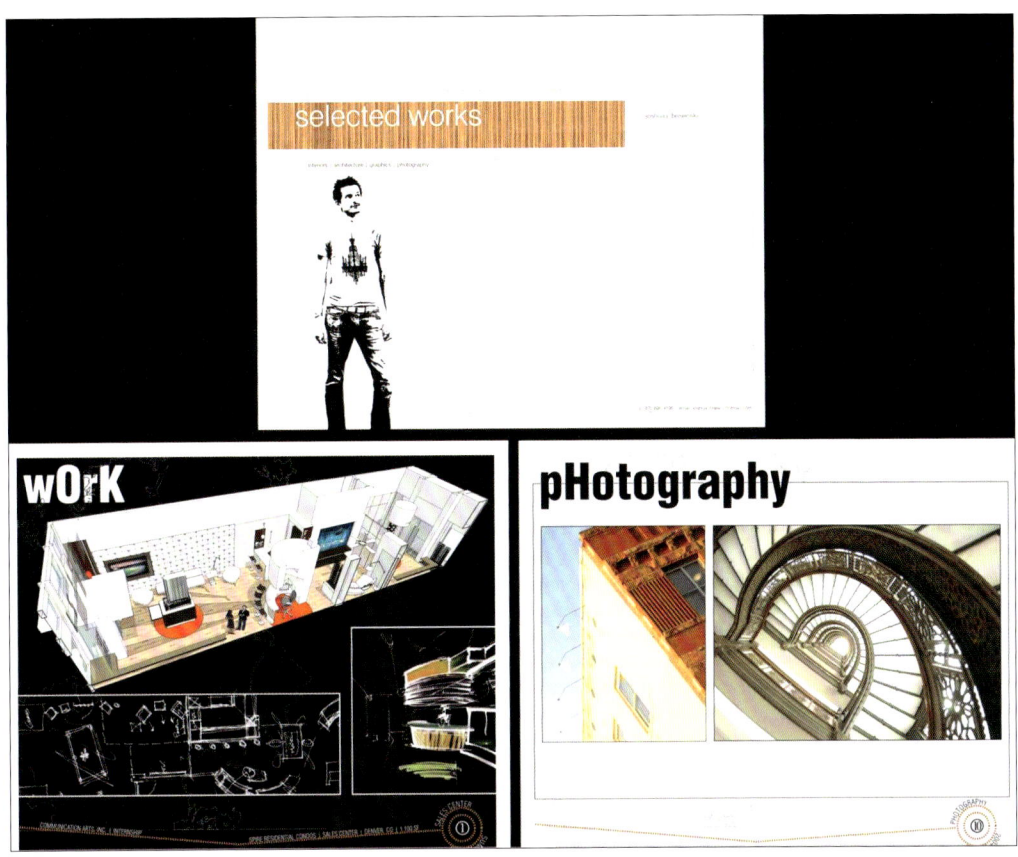

1–12 Joshua Brewinski, Colorado State University, Ft. Collins, Colo. 8.5" x 11".

Additional support comes from accomplishments in competitions, fellowships, scholarships, and awards in fine arts, interior design commissions, and architecture, which constitute the general pool of experiences that are useful to include in one's portfolio. The evaluation of talent is a daily activity in office practice and interior design programs at universities. Students realize they compete in an environment with other applicants who have diverse backgrounds and who collectively wish to make a substantial investment in advancing their education and furthering their career opportunities.

The review process isn't just for those seeking office positions, but also for those looking to use the portfolio document as a tool for obtaining one's clients and managing their business. It is a somewhat more difficult challenge to do this because many new customers will want to see built work completed and photographed, but nonetheless, an emerging designer needs to have something to show, to document, and to demonstrate their professional work as an interior designer.

Professionals use their portfolio as a tool to attract clients. They do, however, rely on sources other than a "book" for exposure. Instagram is a way to expose your work and to connect to other sources and people in the industry, and also to gather connections to future clients and network for business. Twitter will remind people that you exist. Websites always require evaluation and updating. They must be faithful to the company mission statement and direction. Facebook may also prove to update the public and more specifically your friends on daily activities within the professional and personal arena.

BOOKS, BOXES, AND HYBRIDS

Among the most important attributes of designing your book or box is that it suits your purpose as well as supports your work. Bound books of every shape and size are the most attractive and convenient to make and are especially appropriate for applications to design programs in higher education and employment.

Ultimately, digital forms on CD, DVD, and websites online are gaining steadily in use and popularity. Preliminary images are often sent to design offices by email as a PDF before bringing in a printed book. There are also hybrid forms for portfolios such as a box with individual plates and telescoping case designs with booklets per project. Additional variations include unique page sequences with pop-ups, bi-fold and tri-fold pages within bound books and boxed sets, and portfolios that contain both unique print and digital (CD) forms carefully designed as a package presentation together. A comprehensive portfolio design can unite all of the materials of written and visual design into a unified graphic design package including, cover letter, resume, table of contents page, design statement, all design projects, index, and endnotes.

Plate portfolios and boxed editions require more craft skills to make than bound books and are more prevalent in practice as folios for employment purposes. Companies such as Brewer-Cantelmo in New York and the House of Portfolios NYC are available online and known for their high-end portfolio boxes and custom books. They offer state-of-the-art materials for the outside skin of the book as well as material for constructing the shell. They will emboss your name in a variety of types and sizes. There are also numerous hybrid forms for digital portfolio forms carefully designed as a package presentation.

Iryna Carlson

Iryna prepared a cleverly designed boxed set of bi-fold plates to showcase her work from the graduate interior design program (MFA) at George Washington University (figures 1–13 to 1–17). The box is hand-made with a chipboard core covered with orange linen. It is composed of a set of square bi-fold plates (when opened to 8.5" x 17"). The idea behind the organization of content in this collection is especially interesting. On one side of each bi-fold plate are visuals that identify a specific skill set in design and on the reverse side of the same plate is a project that applies that particular skill set in context with a specific design project.

As one views each plate front and back they gain an appreciation for the rich range of abilities and depth of her research. It is also apparent that all the bi-fold plates can be displayed in various ways such as a pinned to a wall surface or standing up as a group of projects in configurations on a table. Iryna added leave behinds, thank you card, resume, career day images in note card format, business cards, and more. She used the Adobe Creative Suite for the layout design of all of the plates. She printed the plates on a semi-gloss lightweight 60 lb paper stock using a Ricoh inkjet printer. She crafted one box but made two sets of all the pages at an expense of $140.00. The container required 5 hours to construct and one month to create all aspects and production of the portfolio. She received consistently strong reviews from faculty and interviewers.

Books, Boxes, and Hybrids

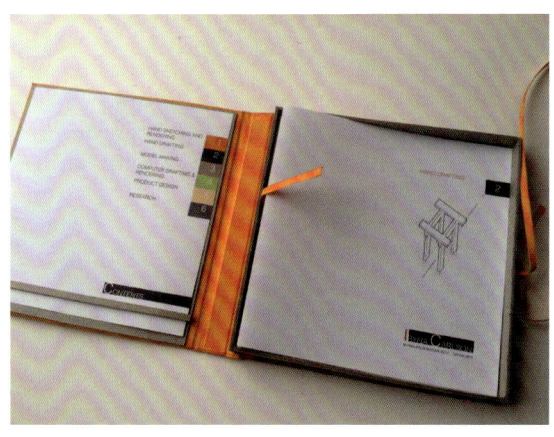

1–13 to 1–17 Iryna Carlson went as far as designing a wonderful container with a material that supports her designs and chose a fresh color to package her work. Her portfolio has an immediate tactile component. It already addresses an important part of interior design and that is touching and feeling materiality. This works well with her drawings as she describes her technique of one rendering that incorporates SketchUp, Podium, and hand work on the drawing. She involves her hand on different levels from the outside container to both drawing and model building. Her design work also includes a series of professional follow-up items such as a thank you card with envelope, business cards, and custom-sized post cards. Iryna Carlson, George Washington University, Washington, D.C. 8.5" x 8.5".

1 OBJECTS & OBJECTIVES

LEAVE BEHINDS AND TEASERS

A most important element in the strategy of portfolio design is to understand the similarities and differences between the purposes and forms of your portfolio, when to show your work, and how much to show at various stages of interviewing. Be prepared when creating a campaign to respond to an advertisement for a position in a firm to only send a small representative sampling of your work. Your response begins with a cover letter, resume, and a few images only as an introduction, commonly called a "teaser portfolio." The teaser is intended to "break the ice" and be a conservative sampling to stir interest. If your package is competitive, you will be invited to come for an interview. At the interview, be prepared to show a full portfolio of your work in print or on your computer. Following the interview, it is the polite form to have a "leave behind," which can include a business card, small folio, or letter-size page with sample images on the front and reverse sides and including your contact information.

Portfolios for employment emphasize office experience in balance with skills in studio design and professional practice. Portfolio collections used for application to undergraduate and graduate degree programs in interior design emphasize research interests, breadth of experience, including employment, along with creative practice abilities. Exploring the requirements for your given portfolio purpose is helpful so that you don't wind up designing multiple portfolios for the same goal when one portfolio could bridge multiple objectives. It is also important to learn how to place emphasis that is appropriate for a single purpose book for academics, employment, competition, or internship.

Career day sheets are another instrument that is growing in popularity and often presented at academic conferences and professional days when design staff attend "meet and greet" events on college campuses or office studios to further acquaint their staff with design programs at universities and develop familiarity with student accomplishments, faculty and administration, and areas of study.

We always explain to our undergraduate students that they should conduct online research at all the graduate schools and offices they wish to apply to as an essential exercise worth its weight in gold. Getting acquainted with the portfolio requirements and expectations of schools and offices for the presentation of your work allows you to accommodate all of the necessities into one book. Along with this exercise, you should create a spreadsheet and record all of the information from each school and office. Also, document all of the requirements for the application form and the portfolio. Portfolio requirements vary widely in content and form from one institution to another as well as the application process and requirements. It is also helpful in understanding yourself and how you fit into an office, or how you might clash, especially with offices that have a very distinct look or design aesthetic.

Some schools require the presentation of a print portfolio while others prefer applicants to upload files of their work directly into their database so they may quickly organize and review the work. Other schools require different quantities of projects or varying numbers of pages as in a print portfolio. Some schools require the book to be no thicker than 1/2" and have no further restrictions such as page count. Other schools set a limit to the minimum or a maximum number of projects and pages in the book. Some schools prefer printing on one side while others accept print on both sides. The best thing to do if you are unsure of a school's requirements is to email the department and explicitly list all of your questions, so you can design one portfolio for all of the schools you intend to make an application.

Schools and offices may suggest preferences and leave the final decision up to you. As an example, your portfolio can be no smaller than a page size of 8.5" x 11" up to a maximum of 11" x 17". They may suggest that an essay or design statement accompany your portfolio that encompasses your interests in design, a summary of your abilities, and an indication of the direction you wish to pursue in professional practice after earning your degree. Often the request to include your resume is optional.

STORYBOARDING

Storyboards, such as the examples from our workshops in figures 1–18 and 1–19, are useful tools for mapping the development of page layout and content in your portfolio. Using a storyboard is one of the single most effective ways to edit and introduce ideas of process and product into your layout design. Most designers who create editorial design work use a storyboard that reflects a double-page spread format at a small hand-held size. They sketch small

Storyboarding

1–18 *(left)* **and 1–19** *(right)* Portrait and landscape storyboards.

cartoon-like images representative of the picture and text appearing on every page. As they go along, they rehearse the meaning and organization of the contents of every section of the book. They visualize and plan the layout design on two pages (right and left) together so they can gain a sense of the overall interest, order, balance, and engagement of the progression of the story or narrative of their work. Nothing is precious on a storyboard—if things don't work, the designer scratches off one page and quickly replaces it with a fresh blank sheet.

Designers are very concerned with how the reader scans an article and the sequence of planning a progression of image, text, and page space. Attention is paid to how the article will engage the reader and progress from left to right, top to bottom, all the while maintaining and developing the story line of the article. Scanning is a term borrowed from advertising where behavior studies were used to verify the patterns of eye movement when reading the text and while observing large and small photographic images. These patterns of eye movement provided insight into how advertising artists and designers might best lay out magazine articles to gain the best response from their readership. Here are some jewels to savor as you reflect upon how to develop an outstanding sense of layout design first in a storyboard version for a portfolio, package, book, box, digital hybrid, or mixed media presentation.

Working with the reduced size of a hand-held booklet (storyboard) provides a convenient and portable easy-to-use sketchpad to which the designer can quickly add or subtract pages and ideas. Keeping the storyboard small allows the designer the ease of "cartooning" hand-drawn ideas at a comfortable size that represent blocks of text, titles, and visual images. Creating the storyboard document is as simple as folding a series of 8-1/2" by 11" pages in half and stapling them together down the crease to form a basic pamphlet. I like to draw freehand in markers while others would rather rule some margins and columns for more studied divisions of page space.

Working within a column structure provides the designer with a pre-described pathway for the organization of text blocks and images. Sizing images to have impact draws immediate attention and engages the reader in the article. Using arrangements of images and text in rows, diagonals, and columns provide a breadcrumb trail or pattern for the reader to follow.

Introducing white or negative space between, above, and below the main visual elements of image and text creates a hierarchy or visual dialog between dark and light, bright and dull, active and passive visual elements on the page. Overlapping images and even diagonal casual arrangements can also be considered at this time. Using rules of proportion in sizing the elements of text and image provides a sense of order and harmony to the design of the spread. As one develops from spread to spread, new patterns or arrangements of form and space emerge, lending contrast and ways to expand the order and organization of spread designs.

GOING FULL SIZE

At some point, however, mocking up the book at full size, no matter how rough or sketchy, will allow you to see groupings of visuals, typography, and details of the layout as they evolve. Even if you just staple the binding at this point so that you can turn the book from page to page, this will kick-start your thinking about the flow of the book and your material. When everything is said and done, the portfolio of your body of work is truly a window into the coming measures of preparation. The commitment and energy invested in the process and the product speaks volumes about the designer and his or her potential in a graduate program or office environment.

Topaz Wong

Topaz Wong (figures 1–20 and 1–21) works with his hands and involves craft and construction in the making of his portfolio. He is interested in ultimately working in sewn leather but this case is a paper simulation of that final leather object. He is also interested in connecting new ways to hold the contents together by investigating buttons that would be sewn into his leather case. The interior page spreads use a dotted line not unlike the sewn stitch of a leather maker to point out features that he highlights in his interior work.

Here's a TIP:

What's up front matters, so open your vision and goals for your portfolio to be as good as it possibly can be.

Going Full Size

1–20 *(top)* **and 1–21** *(bottom)* Topaz Wong's portfolio design is tactile and invites the viewer to touch, feel, and sense the presentation. Velcro was added to the inner faces of the folio leaves to help secure them when closed. Topaz Wong, New York School of Interior Design, N.Y., N.Y. 9" (w) x 6" (h) x 2" (d).

1 OBJECTS & OBJECTIVES

> "The design and content of a student's portfolio is an essential step in their academic development to set the student up for success. I believe that the interior design portfolio is more than a catalog of work, but rather a study highlighting personal design philosophy and brand. The first manifestation of the students' portfolio is an artistic expression and exploration driven by their unique narrative."
>
> – **PROFESSOR THOMAS DANCKAERT**, M.ARCH, KCAD

LIVING SEQUENCES

Do something short and sweet to your book every day as ideas pop into your head. Work on it from day to day. It doesn't happen magically. It is a culmination of hours of patient work, layout, revision, and refinement. Upgrade the weakest links or elements by redrawing, redrafting, re-sketching, or re-illustrating. Think about the role of process in your work versus only the end product. Just because you earned a "B" on a design project doesn't mean you have to stop working on it, especially if you see obvious areas that can be improved and make a positive addition to the overall presentation and design content. Don't be afraid to share your thoughts and ideas with others who design. Be involved in design culture and profession in your office, school, and community and exchange ideas and experiences with others.

Don't be afraid to start over. Lessons learned from previous work are always with you as you re-envision improvements and whole new concepts. Always keep a storyboard close by so you can chart new layout ideas, even while you are working on the emerging concept for a new design.

Not having an idea for the design of your book at the outset is advantageous over those who bring preconceived ideas to the design of their portfolio. Sometimes you find inspiration for the guiding concept for the design of your portfolio by exploring and researching different subjects that may not necessarily be related to design. Portfolios are always exciting when they evolve naturally, tracing the trajectories of imaginative concepts. Portfolios are always boring when they resemble cookie-cutter likenesses of preconceived ideas and content. Demonstrate alternative schemes and solutions.

Nazli Soltani

Nazli created the undergraduate teaser and full portfolio shown in figures 1–22 and 1–23 in fulfillment of a course in visual communications and to apply for employment. She used the Adobe Creative Suite for all aspects of the design. She made an introductory teaser with a CD included and four books bound with a white coil binding. She had four interviews with architects and other designers and received three offers for employment. Nazli remarks on her success, "I learned to be creative, thinking outside of the box, and making a unique project. In the interview I quickly realized how important it is to make your first project something that matches or aligns with the firm's projects and services."

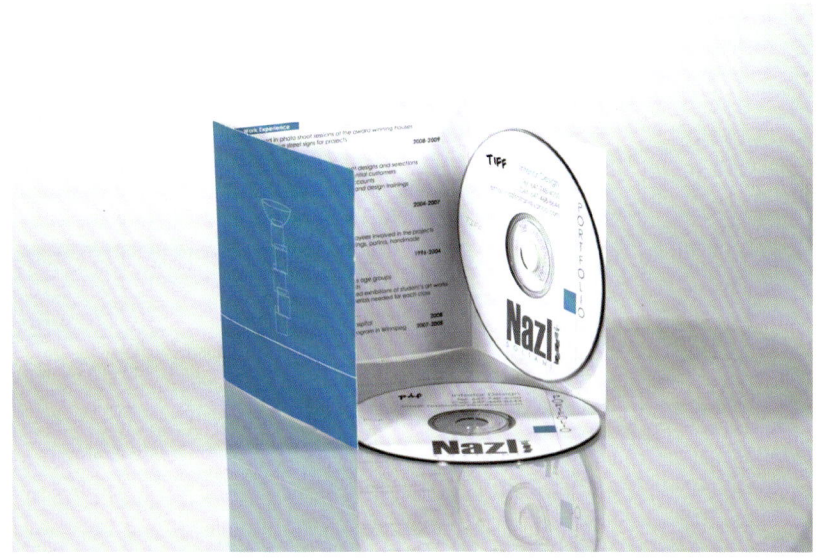

1–22 *(top)* **and 1–23** *(bottom)* Nazli Soltani designed a crisp and clean teaser portfolio that contains resume information printed on both sides as well as her teaser portfolio on two CDs. Along with the teaser, she includes outtakes from her full portfolio, such as the full plate presented here. Nazli Soltani, Algonquin College, Ottawa, Canada. Teaser portfolio 5" x 5". Full portfolio 8.5" x 11".

CONTINUITY

As students progress in design studio experience, they learn to grapple with multiple design issues increasing in complexity and with a greater depth of content. They achieve aesthetically pleasing and conceptually provocative results that synthesize diverse elements of design programs and planning. They evolve in their understanding of standards of practice. The studio breeds the development of expertise in problem identification and real-world appropriate creative solutions. Along with growing technical and visual communication expertise, one's fright of being overwhelmed and consumed by the size and scope of an accredited curriculum subsides as results emerge. Students gain in confidence from repetitive practice but also from research and observation of the work of colleagues, faculty, and visiting design practitioners.

Learn how to wring out a design problem so you cover it from diverse points of view and approaches. Lots of little ideas are like infants learning how to walk—like Frankenstein shifting weight to the left then right, eventually, you see they are going somewhere. It's good not to know right away so you can find yourself someplace new and different. When you master a way of doing something, it's best to abandon it and move on to things you don't know how to handle so that you can figure out a new way of designing.

Learn how to learn from others. Allow yourself to influence others and be influenced by others. The goal here is not to find a "job-job" but to find a good fit with room to grow. Design the portfolio you want to read. Good ideas are simply mash-ups of previous good ideas. Learn how to embrace good work instead of running away from it. A good job owes its originality to being influenced by someone or something.

How do you look at the world as an interior designer? What turned you on about being involved somehow or some way in the profession? Is there such a thing as the right reasons for being a designer—what makes you do it? What draws you to it? I studied to become a designer and had no idea what was involved.

How does your portfolio drip with ideas that demonstrate, beyond talent, that you have the chops to be a successful designer? How do you show business acumen, client communication, work ethic, and an organization of requirements, research abilities, and more in a portfolio? How do you value the opinion of others, colleagues, faculty, professional designers, or design reviewers?

Shiqi Li

Shiqi Li (figures 1–24 and 1–25) created her book as a graduate student as the New York School of Interior Design. She has succeeded in finding internship positions as well as employment. The graphic design was created in Photoshop and printed on a matte finish 80 lb paper using a butterfly format for perfect softback binding at a cost of $80.00 per booklet. The entire design and production required a couple of months to produce the book. Shiqi is in the process of using the portfolio to expand her professional opportunities.

[Here's a TIP:

Thankfully there's more than one right solution to a design problem.

Continuity

Cartoon

Watercolor

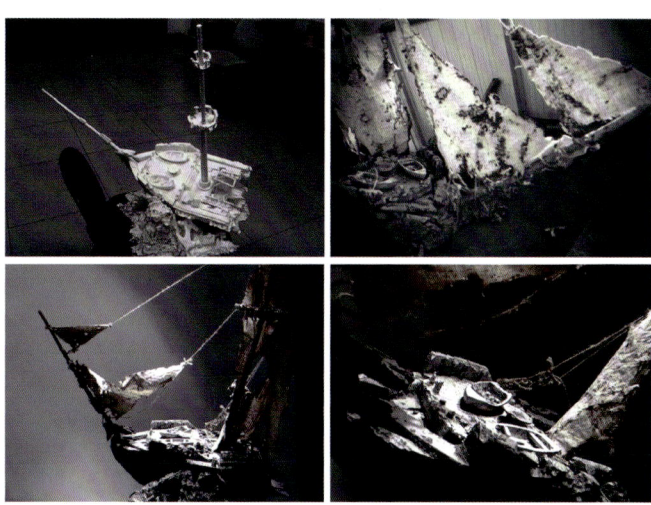
I made a shipwreck from foam with friends, and cast it in aluminum. Then we emphasize the wreckage with tensile structures.

1–24 *(top)* **and 1–25** *(bottom)* Shiqi Li designed a square portfolio with a great deal of creativity and clever artistry. One's attention is easily engaged with the opening pages that collage her studio tools next to a creative typographic composition listing project experiences included in her book. She uses hand-drawing and sculptural artistry throughout the portfolio as well as a fine arts section in the back. Shiqi Li, New York School of Interior Design, N.Y., N.Y. 8" x 8".

HIDDEN FACTORS

There are hidden factors that will most likely never emerge in an interview about your work. Your discussion of the contents of your portfolio plays a central role in the reviewers' appreciation of your effort expressed in a book, box, or hybrid portfolio format. These are the more sophisticated and philosophical attributes to shaping the intentions of your work and the way in which your projects are perceived by the reviewers.

How do you tip a project in a direction that naturally showcases your abilities without missing essential elements of research and content? How do you pull information graphically from what you have illustrated in a design project to showcase? What can you do that will benefit a design office? Don't expect reviewers to make the connection to what you want to do because you have included it in your layout. Remember, they are breezing through your work and making notes about your skills. How do you survey design content (residential and commercial) from one project to the next so that you have represented a full spectrum of the standards of practice and issues of content in the design curriculum and profession? The judgment of faculty or an external body of reviewers that the evidence presented in one's portfolio is representative of a full range of requirements of practice is significant to the designer author's overall abilities and suggests success on many different levels of design experience and exposure.

In teaching portfolio design courses, we have long been aware that many students entering their last years of study or graduating from a four-year degree program do not possess enough exposure to and experience in the portfolio design process. The subject of portfolio design in many interior design schools appears not to be well integrated into the curriculum. Those schools that offer either an elective or required senior course provide a competitive edge on other programs. From surveying design schools for exemplary student work, it appears as though very few schools offer courses in portfolio design. There are some publications devoted to portfolio design for architecture, interior design, graphic design, photography, and applied arts disciplines. We have listed those we feel offer a valuable informational presentation in the selected bibliography of this book. So far as we know, however, there are precious few books that attempt, without being overly prescriptive, to summarize the breadth and depth of layout design expressly for students of interior design and the allied design disciplines.

Aside from the aesthetics of graphic design and presentation, instructors of portfolio design typically have backgrounds in visual communications, architecture, and interior design and can often probe into important areas of professional practice content that should appear in the book.

Here's a TIP:

The search for the creative concept that binds the work into an inspired format, and helps inform the presentation, evolves through a process of inventory of the guidelines of the curriculum.

"In working with our students to develop their portfolios, we first phrase the process in a different way. The portfolio is one component—a major one, of course—of their dossier. The dossier includes the professional package—from the portfolio to the business card, from resume's to stationary for handwritten thank you notes—that effectively brands the student. We emphasize that good design demands a conceptual focus and a rigor that should permeate each decision. The dossier is the first insight a prospective employer—or client—might have into that process. Second, we try to impress upon the student that their time after graduation is not a period where they look for someone to hire them. Instead, it is a bridge into developing mutually beneficial professional relationships. The student should be writing the firm as much as the firm is interviewing the student. Therefore, the dossier becomes an entry into a rigorous self-analysis for the student. What does the student value in design? What inspires the student? What excites the student?

How does their academic work speak to these drivers? And how might one communicate this most effectively?

We also emphasize the importance of acknowledging the digital and analog realms of design. Not having a digitally formatted portfolio and online presence makes little sense, but most people in the leadership of design firms work with physical artifacts. Being able to format and communicate design work in a variety of media—from a printed book to iPad presentation—is essential to the modern designer.

Finally, we expose our students to professionals in the design professions during their dossier design process. They receive input from interior designers, architectural practitioners, and graphic designers. The graphic design critiques are always terribly informative. As designers, we all speak the same language, but the dialect that graphic designers use—in terms of typefaces, spacing, alignments, organization and expression—is so far beyond our tangential information that I cannot fathom developing a dossier without it."

– **ROBERTO VENTURA**, LEED AP, NCIDQ, ASSISTANT PROFESSOR, DEPARTMENT OF INTERIOR DESIGN, VIRGINIA COMMONWEALTH UNIVERSITY.

1 OBJECTS & OBJECTIVES

Hyun Kyu Han

H. K. Han (figures 1–26 to 1–31) believes that social phenomena are directly related to humanitarian design in human habitats. He has a deep respect and desire to be part of this profession because he believes that architecture is at the forefront for innovations influential to better living and working conditions. Having studied interior design at Pratt Institute, Han believes that visual aesthetics are vital to enhancement of nature-inspired designs that will meet the true requirements of modern life.

He believes that interior design interacting with architecture holds the key to achieve the most satisfying modern environments. His undergraduate portfolio from Pratt is highly conceptual and theoretical. He focused much attention on constructing models for his design solutions and then photographing the results. He applied Autodesk, 3DStudioMax, and Revit in producing his book. It was printed on card stock and printed on an Epson color laser printer. He made one book at an expense of $150.00. Han found much support from a portfolio development course at Pratt and working with his various professors. Han found employment with ESI Design in New York.

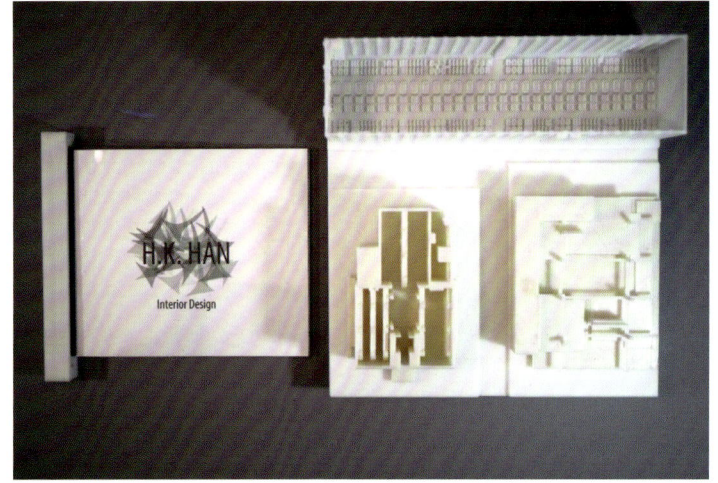

Hidden Factors

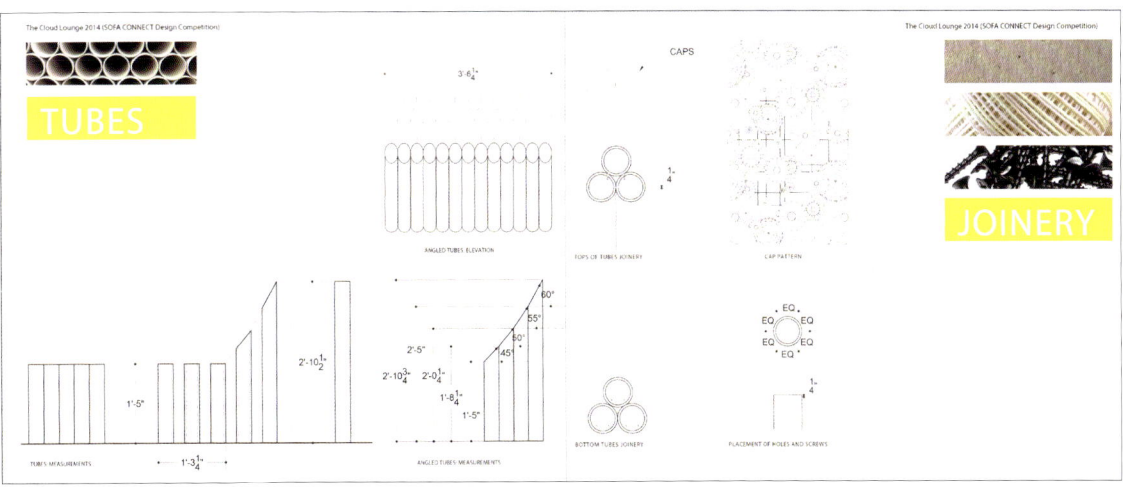

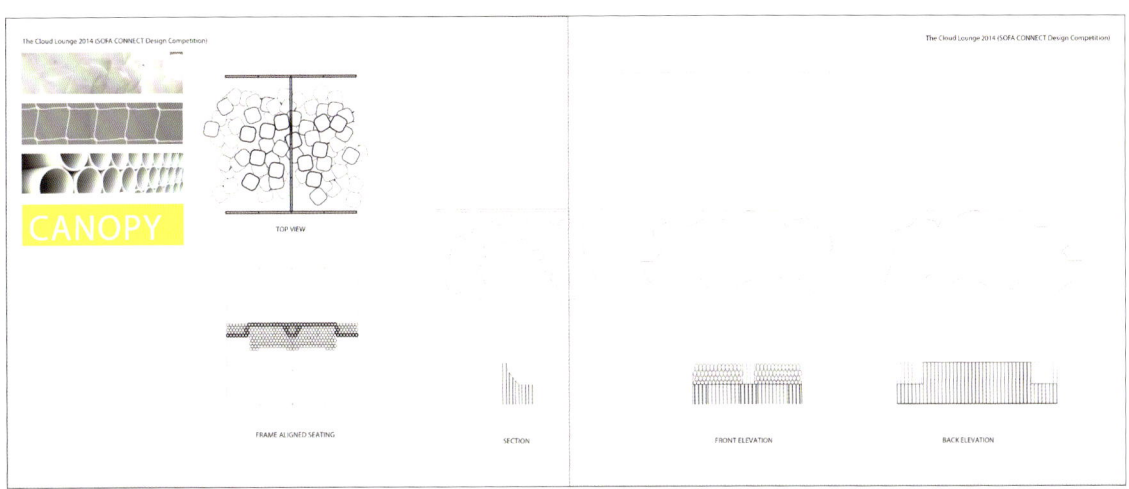

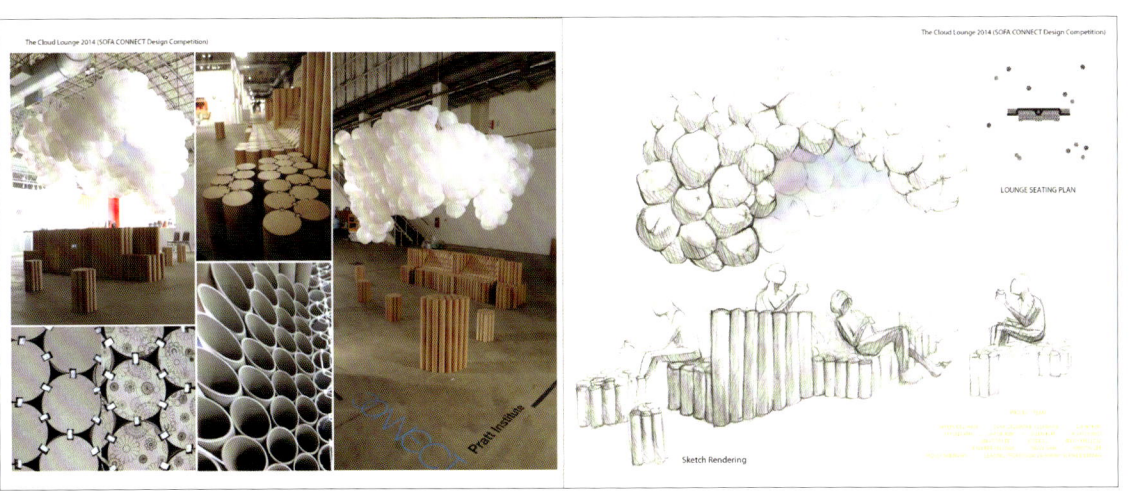

1–26 to 1–31 Hyun Kyu Han has very sculptural layouts throughout his portfolio especially including architectural models to accompany his presentation of drawings and illustrations. In one page spread he utilizes zones of soft color titles to create strong negative white space for the drawings to be exhibited. The exploded axonometrics combined with graphics and program demonstrate his 3D development thought process. He supports his projects with branding analysis and hand drawing. His award-winning sofa competition clearly demonstrates his hand work and built form. Hyun Kyu Han, Pratt Institute, Brooklyn, N.Y. 9" x 10".

PATTERNS OF SUCCESS

If you place your strongest projects at the beginning, middle, and end of the book, you are creating a pathway of consistent strength throughout your book. These are the posts and the rails are those projects that are positioned in between the posts, which often represent shorter and less complex projects, special areas of expertise such as technology, or a section on foundations and fine arts accomplishments.

The guiding concept that informs a comprehensive portfolio presentation is often a simplification of established pre-existing elements. A new format for a portfolio presentation is better found in the simplification or exploration of the elements of design communication. We believe that order succeeds where chaos existed; simplicity is better than complexity; one should minimize risks by communicating in as few neutral forms+color as appropriate; conservativeness outranks opulence; and less is always more!

The successful portfolio design instructor wants the students' portfolios to be real comprehensive representations of the requirements of knowledge, outstanding accomplishments of practice, as well as the quality of graphics, visual communications, layout design, materials, binding, and presentation. A guiding creative concept surfaces in your work as seeds of thematic ideas that upon reorganization and establishment of a clear hierarchy form into a visual narrative and clear way of looking at the presentation of your design experience.

Leah DeVries

Leah DeVries (figures 1–32 to 1–35) created her portfolio as an undergraduate in interior design at the University of Northern Iowa. The central purpose was to seek an internship and eventually a full-time position as an interior designer. She used Adobe InDesign and Photoshop as well as AutoCAD among other software to create all of the projects featured in her portfolio. She then used the online site ISSUU to post her portfolio and gain some attention and hopeful interest.

Having an online presence removed some pressure from being overly concerned with having a hard copy, because the same portfolio would be seen on ISSUU. She did, however, order two copies of her book from peecho.com, which partners with ISSUU. The printed copies have adhesive binding, which gives the books a clean and simple finished appearance. Furthermore, when responding to an invitation for an interview or prospecting in general, Leah sent the link to her interview appointment ahead of the meeting. The total cost for two printed books via ISSUU was $35.00. She spent about 4 months working and reworking the book until she achieved a confident and well-organized presentation.

Having an abundance of helpful suggestions from friends, peers, and faculty, she eventually had to figure out the design by trusting herself. All of the decisions about content, presentation, and overall format-layout were hers and hers alone. She remarks about this, "As long as your portfolio speaks to your own style, goals, and work, it can be successful." At the time she designed her book, she realized there was an abundance of examples and sources to look at. What works for one person won't necessarily work for another and there really are a lot of resources now to explore, which is extraordinarily helpful.

The exploration of a spacing or column structure appropriate to the nature of your design content is necessary so that you can review and experiment with several alternatives before you adopt a particular layout. An important ingredient to the research is whether to use a landscape (horizontal) or portrait (vertical) orientation to the page. Experimentation with how images expand or are contained by the binding method and gutter are chief considerations. Other issues such as page size, orientation, and appropriate spacing structure are important decisions as well as testing multiple ideas in pursuit of logical concepts for layout design.

Patterns of Success

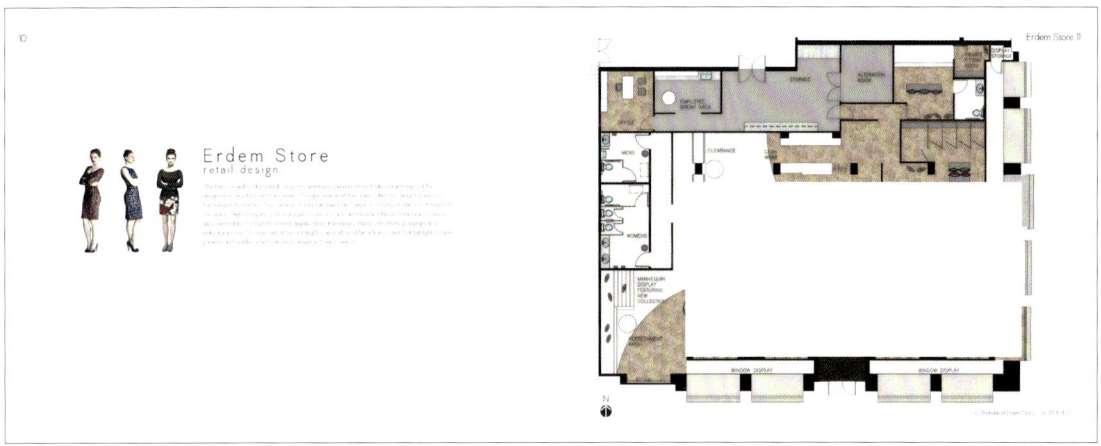

1–32 to 1–35 Leah DeVries chose simple graphics that are clean and crisp as well as a layout book design that is uncluttered and spacious to host her computer renderings. The element that really makes it work are the numbers that are superimposed over the drawings to illustrate the materials and furnishings. It is a simple tool, but very effective. She even gave the company source, making it much more meaningful. This is a no-nonsense portfolio that doesn't have a lot of bells and whistles. The graphics are pure and simple but well chosen. The beauty is in the documentation and research. She is aware that surfaces and furniture are an important part of the interior design portfolio and she highlights them to her advantage. Leah DeVries, University of Northern Iowa, Cedar Falls, Iowa. 8.5" x 11".

1 OBJECTS & OBJECTIVES

ENVISION VS. REVISION: A GOLDEN OPPORTUNITY FOR A FRESH APPROACH!

The portfolio design process is an opportunity to re-envision your work away from the studios, faculty, and colleagues within your own space and natural process of self-reflection. A fresh approach is invaluable to assess what projects should be revised and then how profoundly changes should be carried through. An inventory or audit has documentation or notes on change and upgrade strategies. A new vision should emerge that represents a layout design that allows for the transformation of original work into a vastly more unified, coherent, and clear presentation.

Portfolios (and reviewers) come in various shapes, sizes, and colors. They reflect and demonstrate one's design experience and breadth of knowledge, and contain a snapshot of the larger context of professional abilities, growth, and development. Reflecting the potential for excellence and accomplishment through one's portfolio is no easy task. It requires patient and thorough review of a comprehensive body of work including the interpretation of experience with living and learning, demonstrated skills and abilities, and comprehension of professional standards and knowledge, all within the context of the applicant's background and individual circumstances.

Whether you are making an application for admission to graduate school, submitting your work for a request for employment, or just answering a call for competition, scholarship, internship, or fellowship, your depth of planning and skill in written and visual communications, together with the presentation, are critical steps to success. The total creative concept you bring to your work and the project at hand are among the most critical factors that will determine the outcome of your application. Most schools and employers believe the portfolio is the single most important ingredient in the review process, ahead of grades, standardized exams, written essays, and letters of recommendation.

Here's a TIP:

An excellent place to explore ideas for the organization of your portfolio is editorial design and more specifically magazine and journal formats. Admittedly there are thousands of different types of journals, magazines, corporate reports, and books on diversity in layout designs appropriate to a design portfolio. However, you can narrow the search for inspiration by limiting the field to those magazines, journals, and published works having to do with your subject interests and closely allied disciplines.

Envision vs. Revision: A Golden Opportunity for a Fresh Approach!

Sarah Todd

Sarah Todd's undergraduate and postgraduate portfolios (figures 1–36 to 1–39) represent a fascinating revolution in her thinking and maturity as a design professional. The undergraduate portfolio (figures 1–36 and 1–37) reflects a small format bi-fold approach to presenting her work in a lavish hardbound binder to protect the prints. Both AutoCAD and Photoshop were the chief hardware packages used to create the spreads that were printed on a heavy stock inkjet paper using a commercial-grade plotter. She coordinated the design of a hardbound protective binder with a book-making company, making one portfolio at a cost of $250.00. The time involved from start to completion was 6 to 8 months.

Sarah was frank about the results of her undergraduate portfolio, stating: "I ended up creating an expensive portfolio that I never used because the process to create the individual custom pages took too long. You should think about what you are trying to accomplish in the design of your portfolio. Try to find ways to be creative without reinventing the wheel. Also seek innovative ways of doing things to catch your viewer's attention without costing a fortune."

Sarah's postgraduate portfolio (figures 1–38 and 1–39) reflects a revolution in her thinking and a mature, professional approach to capturing the skills, abilities, and direction of her recent work in design. She conducted

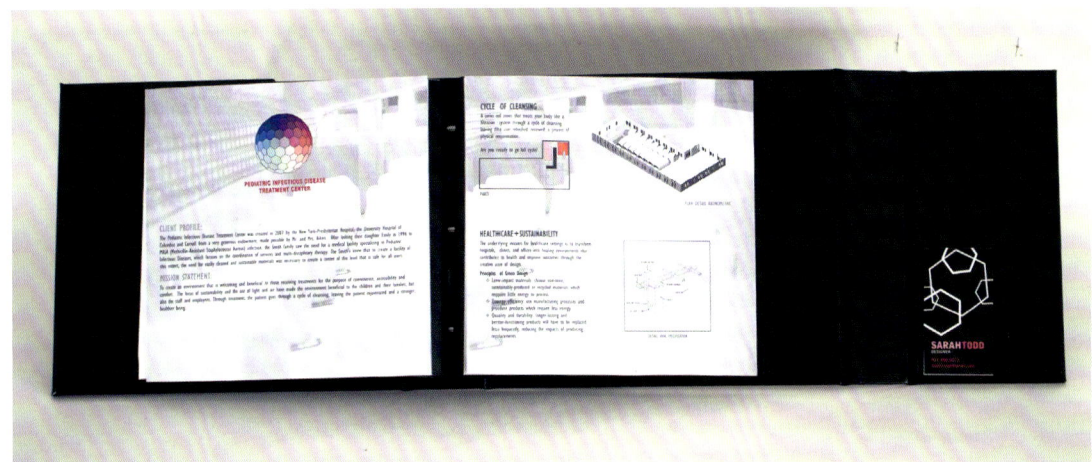

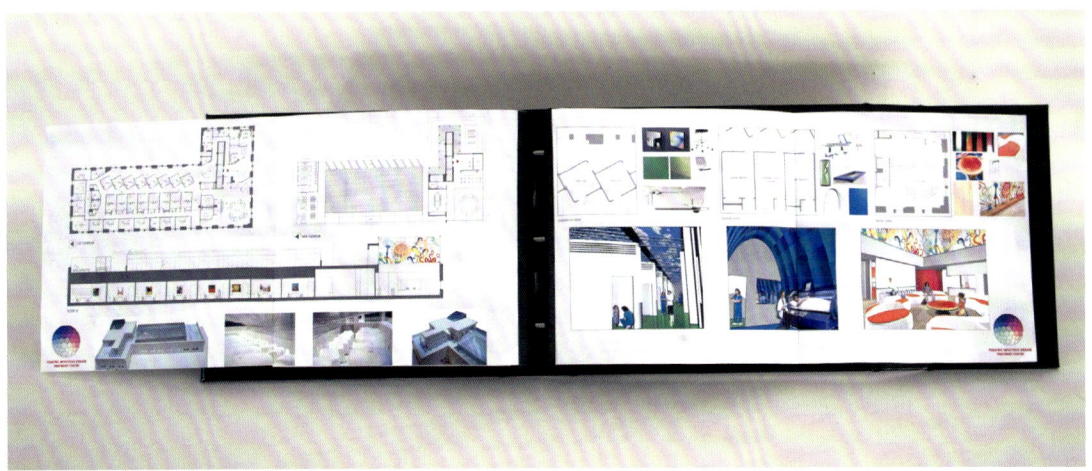

1–36 *(top)* **and 1–37** *(bottom)* Aside from the time element, due to the fact that these portfolios evolved at different periods in Sarah Todd's life, they each have very strong points. We especially like the spatial organization, exuberance, and complexity of the first black book custom portfolio. The bi-fold pages are unique and let you know how layered Sarah is in her thinking and development of an idea within a design problem. She has tied together the business card graphics with the overall design of the portfolio. It is immensely creative and well thought out. Sarah Todd, New York School of Interior Design, N.Y., N.Y. School portfolio 8" x 8".

1 OBJECTS & OBJECTIVES

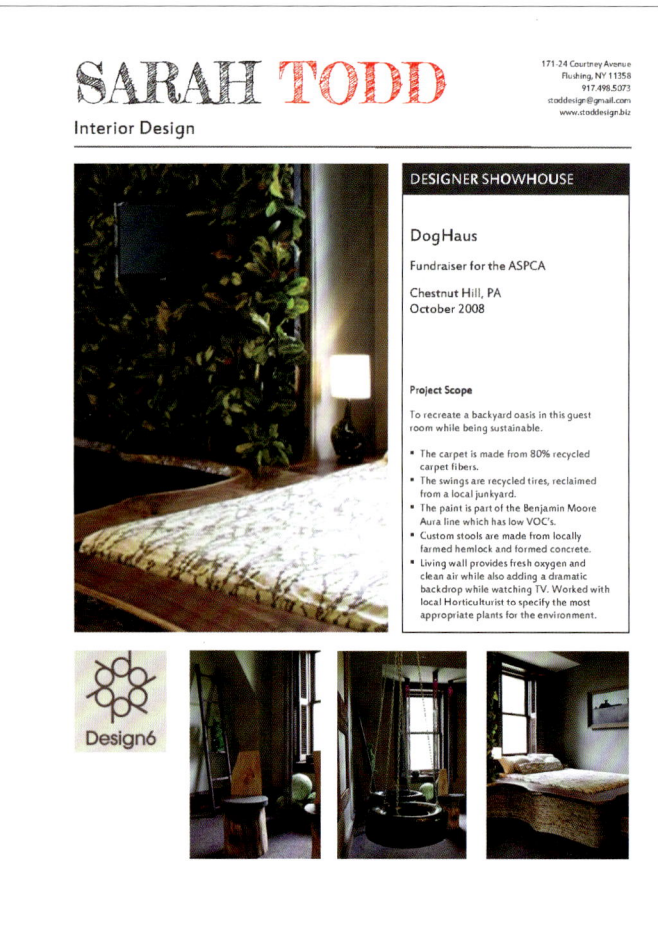

research regarding how to freshen the format so that her book would look more like a seasoned magazine article versus a project display. The cost of her new book was considerably reduced from $250.00 to $50.00 per copy and she designed the entire 20-page presentation within one week. Everyone who saw the new book was impressed with her work and how clean and easy it was to read. She did research to discover how the industry was presenting itself in the marketplace. This was very important to her thinking process and with each page embracing who she was and is as a designer, Sarah feels so much more at home in the new portfolio!

1–38 *(left)* **and 1–39** *(right)* Her second professional portfolio has clear, concise project scope statements that highlight issues of sustainability products used within the design and offer a clear scope of each and every project that she has included. The branding of her name as an image has even become stronger and more confident over time! Sarah Todd, New York School of Interior Design, N.Y., N.Y. Post-school book, 8.5" x 11".

READ BETWEEN THE LINES

Often, design students are unfamiliar with the organizational strategies of the book. They also need to acquire knowledge of portfolio materials and possibilities for inventing the appearance of the book. They may not have previous or any exposure to the requirements for branding and identity and, therefore, do not understand relationships of binding, printing, material possibilities, as well as typographic styles and hierarchy, color, spatial organization, and the orientation of all elements within a page structure from beginning to end.

It is a good lesson to learn that understating the design of your portfolio can mean far more to the reviewer who is easily repelled by embellishments that have no association or connection to the content of your work or the book. The phrase "less is more" has meaning in the design studio; however, it goes double or triple when designing all of the projects for the book and the book itself. The book houses all the substance of each and every project as well as the design of the physical object. Your job is to analyze all materials to find the most elegant, uncluttered common graphic denominator to unify the cover, contents, projects, and support materials.

How do you wish to have your work viewed as a physical and spatial object and experience? Instead of creating bulky figure captions or problem statements loaded with detail, all of the technical information of a project should be organized on a spreadsheet as an index in the back of the book and may include course title, professor, project title, date, dominant materials or software used, image or model dimensions, and page number in the portfolio. In this way, you allow the viewer to first read a general summary at the beginning of the project with important research and content in planning, process, and critical views indicated in simplified captions.

Another interesting thing to do in closing the book is to add a bibliography to the end materials that lists books, seminars, lectures, and workshops that have had a positive influence on your education. A rich bibliography lets the reviewer know you have intellectual breadth and depth. You can also close your portfolio with your resume and contact information.

Portfolio presentations designed with heaping spoonfuls of textures, colors, and imagery might please the designer's taste buds; however, this approach is opposed to what we believe has a better chance to be appreciated for its unity, hierarchy, and integration. The overall design of portfolio graphics should support unity and not conflict with the design vocabulary. The process of design education, in part, is based on learning the elements and principles of 2D and 3D design. Students seek to create original compositions that express understanding of the visual language through creative organization, sensitive use of materials, and integration of form and composition.

Aside from all of the work you include in your portfolio, you will receive different points of view along the way. Understand this is normal and try to sift through advice you receive to find objective opinions that could be advantageous to apply to your own work. Some criticism you will agree with and some you may not. If your portfolio reflects the nature of how you work, it will have a natural affinity to those firms and clients that would be a better fit for you and your career and help identify those firms that might prove incompatible for you. A well-designed and thoroughly organized portfolio will aid you in achieving a place in the industry and a career that embodies a vision that can only be you.

THE SPIRIT OF CONCEPTION
& CREATIVE PROCESS

"Design is the method of putting form and content together. Design, just as art, has multiple definitions; there is no single definition. Design can be art. Design can be aesthetics. Design is so simple, that's why it is so complicated."

– PAUL RAND

Paul Rand was a well-known American graphic designer, best known for his corporate logo designs. Rand was educated at the Pratt Institute (1929–1932), the Parsons School of Design (1932–1933), and the Art Students League (1933–1934). He was one of the originators of the Swiss Style of graphic design. From 1956 to 1969, and beginning again in 1974, Rand taught design at Yale University in New Haven, Connecticut. Rand was inducted into the New York Art Directors Club Hall of Fame in 1972. He designed many posters and corporate identities, including the logos for IBM, UPS, and ABC.

Your portfolio creates a lasting, online or in print, shareable record of hard work. Your approach to each project in your portfolio embraces sensitivity and care; each project's narrative unfolds to reveal inspiring interior design concepts that become a backdrop for living a creative lifestyle. You are a multi-disciplinary "creative" with a diverse portfolio of successful projects. Your alchemy of portfolio design is grounded on the belief that there are numerous approaches to creating design that lead a reviewer to your discovery experience. The role of the imagination in the design process is important to you. You can pick up five rocks on the way to an interview and talk about their color, texture, form, and spatial relationships.

Your imagination is your brand. You have studied a holistic approach to problem solving, together in collaboration with others, and with potentially diverse types of clients. You have established goals to create interior spaces, which stimulate the intellect and enhance physical wellbeing. Your work is an affirmation of the connective tissue between our senses and the user experience.

You can explore alternative paths to problem-solving and design expression by drawing on personal histories and diverse interests, and sometimes a different line of thought. For you, the unexpected inspiration often leads to unusual and perhaps magical design solutions that meet all the criteria for your project.

Your awareness rises to the challenge of engaging portfolio reviewers from both a business and studio perspective. Creative problem solving and innovative design concepts are essential components of your portfolio. A demonstration of studio process and design development experiences reflects your larger abilities to be able to engage clients, communicate objectives, raise concerns, challenge and refine design concepts, and demonstrate excellence throughout your presentation.

Your design process is centered on an intense discovery phase where research is integral to developing informed planning and content. Your education has taught you how to visualize and present design proposals, ensure informed decisions and responsive solutions to achieve performance and design excellence.

In its entirety, this book is a guide for questioning a portfolio. It is not intended to be a recipe book, nor a "how-to." It may not have all of the answers or provide a comprehensive checklist, but it's going to challenge you to respond creatively and imaginatively to defining your portfolio. There are no partial images in our minds or yours. A book of decisions, however, concerns size, shape, color, texture, materials, and ultimately, style. It must be true to your style, intellect, aesthetic, and it must reflect a concept.

Don't let the word "idea" (concept) scare you. In every given design project, you had an idea. Of course, the impetus

2 THE SPIRIT OF CONCEPTION & CREATIVE PROCESS

for that design project was a teacher or make-believe client giving you the program. Now it's your turn to come up with ideas on how best to present your conceptualized design, based on your program, your materials, and your spatial relationships. In a sense, you are both the teacher and student, and you are in control of research and process. It is a requirement to love what you show and that it is your best work at this time and that the message is pertinent to the viewer. At this point, class descriptions have no meaning, nor do class titles, and in fact, you can change the title of the project itself because now you also own that work.

It is time to review your design principles of concept, order, intention, fitting, and editing. Basic principles of composition can be strictly followed or challenged. You may look at the design of this book like a mini movie or a 60 second commercial. It has three main sections, a beginning, middle, and an end. It may even have a climax. It may be predictable, or it may have some surprises. Similarly, the design of your portfolio may take on many alternative shapes and forms.

You will be making decisions as to whether it is read as a horizontal (landscape), or vertical (portrait) format. It may take on other forms and shapes such as a fan deck from an interior paint store, an accordion fold or concertina, or a continuous movie strip. Different formats are enticing, but also, time-consuming. At the beginning of every design you must know not only your budget but also the time you can spend on developing new ideas and new formats.

In the beginning stages it is good to look around and see what has been done, not for the sake of copying, but to determine what appeals to you and what works for the scope of the endeavor. Many students comb through their Pinterest pages for inspiration, but be careful, you are not the only one viewing those pages and layouts. Genuine creativity stems from areas that are unchartered and unseen. This chapter will help you to look at yourself and your style in ways you might not have been aware of.

STEPPING BACK BEFORE STEPPING IN

To begin with, we challenge you to do something that you may have never done before: to design a personal form board before you begin to develop your portfolio. The form board provides you with unique information aside from studio projects you have been involved with during your design education. A form board reflects your "likes" in various areas of the world of art and design and turns them into a responsive design tool to help you to formulate a concept of your portfolio.

Having the perspective to step back and evaluate your personal "form" is crucial to understanding the needs of the portfolio itself. Most important is that you can read the design content of your board and what you have assembled.

Michael Capuano

Michael is enrolled in the New York School of Interior Design MFA program. He wants to work in a high-end residential firm and is not interested in working for a commercial or hospitality firm. His form board (figure 2–1) reflects his involvement with residential materials, objects, spaces, and ambiance. His portfolio (figures 2–2 and 2–3) reflects his focus on residential interior vignette sketches and his ability to put together a professional high-end materials board and design selection for each project. It is important to note that even though many schools of interior design focus heavily on commercial design, healthcare, and hospitality, Michael has focused on the materials and furniture of two particular residential projects so that he could use his portfolio for residential interviews.

Stepping Back before Stepping In

2–1 to 2–3 Michael has included images from a den that he designed while going to school to supplement his portfolio and that is primarily about sketching and computer rendering. It was a wise choice to add that den to his portfolio. Even though it wasn't a class assignment, he made it his own and it is a useful tool for the office and to present to clients he wishes to attract to his practice. Michael Capuano, New York School of Interior Design, N.Y., N.Y. 8.5" x 11".

Manhattan Pied-a-Terre

The intent with this project was to design a hotel suite in an exotic location. This space, in Thailand, is filled with Thai inspired art, and a lattice-work inspired storage piece, as well as finishes that evoke a blend of modern and traditional styles.

Connecticut Condominium Den

For the design of this Connecticut condo, warm colors, and rich finishes fill the space. In the den, shades of rust and terracotta and complemented by warm woods and leather, which evoke a cozy feeling both both day and night. A custom entertainment unit and etending leather table add functionality, while a vintage needlepoint pillow, antique lamp, and a venetian mask add personality to round out the space.

2 THE SPIRIT OF CONCEPTION & CREATIVE PROCESS

> "Imagination is everything. It's the preview of life's coming attractions."
> — **ALBERT EINSTEIN**

COLLECTING IMAGES FOR A FORM BOARD

"Form boards" are created by collecting image samples of designs and spaces you admire from an assortment of clippings taken from magazines, swatch books, journals, collection brochures, corporate reports, and more. Cuttings made from sample materials, color systems, fabrics, typography, and spaces of interest will help you understand what you will need to make design decisions that are relevant to you. You possess qualities that are original and unlike anyone else, which should be reflected in your form board. To discover your tastes, sort through and identify relevant images that have interest for you. These clippings and sample materials reflect your current sense of aesthetics that will continue to evolve and change over time.

Look through Pinterest pages, Instagram photos, and additional source materials and assemble the results into a presentation board format either by hand or digitally. Compose the images in InDesign if you prefer. Don't forget to look at styles of typography and graphic elements of line, shape, texture and color. As you assemble a virtual palette of the visual elements of design, consider evidence in use of hierarchical spatial (grid) systems, intriguing objects, spatial constructs, and displays of new art forms. The door is open to gathering snippets of all your likes and wherever your passions reside.

Before designing your portfolio, you have already identified a field of likes and dislikes on your form board. How are the pictures arranged? Are they arranged casually or are they organized on a spacing structure (grid)? Is there a strong sense of order or gravitational center? What are the characteristics of form that interest you? Will these components of a shape and structure be visible in the design of your book? There are many opportunities to create a book that reflects your particular "likes" based on the way you have made this board.

We are all challenged by having to look at ourselves and how we view the world of interiors. Designers often have a difficult time designing their own homes. While our tastes are broad, our preferences are quite particular. That is the beauty of what constitutes individual style.

Here's a TIP:

Your portfolio is also an instrument in the hands of a gifted designer that enables conversation. There are many approaches to designing this form that we call a portfolio. You are, however, a "creative" who understands a portfolio is never quite complete and is a continuously evolving entity reflective of professional growth and change.

Collecting Images for a Form Board

Audrey Chabaud

Audrey designed a very clean presentation of her work at NYSID using a square format for basically rectilinear projects (figures 2–4 to 2–6). Her layouts echo the spacious design of her form boards and work successfully with color to tie together different projects from different categories of interior design. She employs a balance of full bleed double-page spreads and cropped smaller layouts of renderings and materials. The color-coded diagrams are placed to relate nicely above and around the developed floor plans. The concept statements with justified left alignment are in a soft gray and inform the overall design. Her contact information on the back cover is easy to find and functions as a complement to her cover design.

2–4 to 2–6 Audrey was a graduate student at NYSID and created her portfolio to use for seeking employment opportunities after graduation. She was entirely pleased with the result as it reflected her confidence in composing effective layouts with positive and negative two-dimensional page space. Audrey attributes the success of her book to a professional portfolio design class offered at NYSID and taught by the author, William Engel. She used InDesign to create the spacious layout design and printed it on semi-gloss paper to avoid strong reflection. Audrey Chabaud, New York School of Interior Design, N.Y., N.Y. 8.5" x 8.5".

READING YOUR FORM BOARD

There are many sources, magazines, and online blogs that reflect current trends across all of the design industries today. This exercise is about finding your spirit and style. What you leave out is as important as what you put in. What are your preferences in color on your form board? How was the color placed on the board? Does it create beautiful eye movement? Do you have a preference for chromatic hues or soft neutral colors? Maybe color isn't a great entity at all for you, and that is OK. Your board may even suggest that you design a portfolio that is simply black and white, and what a unique collection that could prove to be!

Are there individual sectors, zones, or spaces on your form board? Are they suggestive of ways to organize and compose design evidence from your search? As you consider your research further, are the spatial configurations found on your board evocative of ways to partition your book or map sections and subsections within the book? Do you mix traditional objects with contemporary spaces? Would you combine classical typography with serifs or is everything streamlined and simple sans serif? If you see that you often mix styles of both old and new, how will that influence the design of the book?

Keep in mind: people will ultimately want to hear what you have to say. The quality of drawing and presentation should be clear and professional. You, however, are the most important part of your presentation. The way you dress becomes part of your portfolio. It is an extension of yourself and your brand.

After you learn how to read your form board and its properties, you will be conscious of an emerging vocabulary of preferential elements in design. Your new vocabulary describes the qualities of things you prefer to experience in design such as unique characteristics of line, shape, plane, color, texture, and space. This new and specialized language is descriptive of your board layout and climate for exposure to the world of design. Writing a few descriptors in words is now helpful when it comes to making decisions based on your style along with your concept.

These practical exercises, even though they may take some time to complete and analyze, will be a very useful experience in contributing to your understanding of your spirit of conception. Form boards are also helpful to execute within a group, as others will see things that you merely take for granted.

Chu Yen Cheng

Chu created her form board leading into her portfolio (figures 2–7 to 2–9) while attending graduate school at the New York School of Interior Design. The chief purpose was to support a search for employment following graduate school. A secondary purpose besides employment was to take advantage of the course time to thoroughly organize all of her design projects and create a complete log of visual evidence for every project, whether it goes into the portfolio or not. What a wonderful thing to do prior to beginning work on the design of your portfolio. Having a record of all work in various categories of process, design development, concept studies, technical drawings, and more serves a variety of critical purposes in addition to using the book for employment, academic reviews, interviews, and related internship possibilities. The results speak for themselves as Chu was offered an internship on the basis of her work followed by an offer of employment.

> **Here's a TIP:**
>
> Learn to objectively and consciously evaluate your style, which is vital to the design of your book.

Reading Your Form Board

2–7 to 2–9 Chu invites you with a strong graphic shape by simply turning the square corner into a device that points you in a direction to open the portfolio. Her exuberant loose marker perspective rendering in the shared kitchen project also invites you into her space by showing materiality in her design. Her overall portfolio uses abundant white space and clean, well-organized layout designs. The corporate logos of each client are predominantly placed at the beginning of each project and serve as titles to separate each and every project. Chu Yen Cheng, New York School of Interior Design, N.Y., N.Y. 8.5" x 8.5".

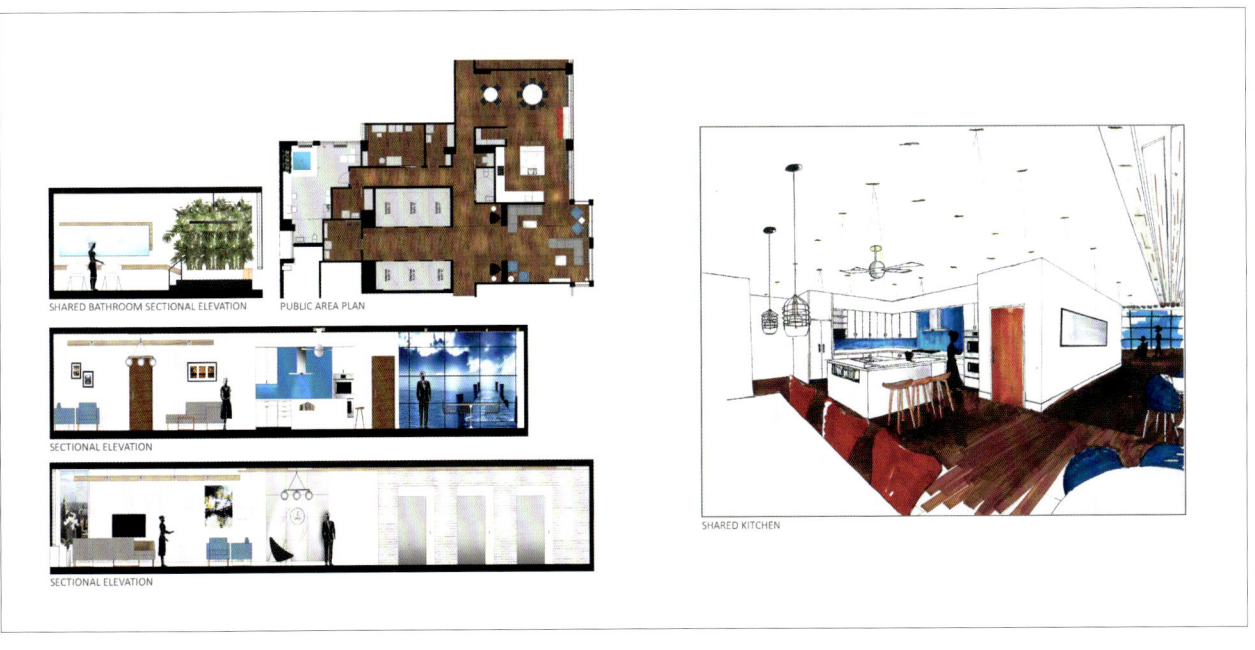

2 THE SPIRIT OF CONCEPTION & CREATIVE PROCESS

Evgenya Epelbaum

Evgenya created her form board and portfolio (figures 2–10 to 2–12) while a graduate student at the New York School of Interior Design. She worked on the project for six months, progressively adding new work as it became available. Her spacious form board resonates throughout her open plan portfolio. Important realizations that echo through her form board and portfolio include that simple is better than elaborate; legible, clear written and visual communication are paramount; and working on the overall big concept of the book takes precedence over getting bogged down with details, especially at the outset of designing the portfolio. Details have a time and place down the road. The main software package used was InDesign in support of layout design. She produced two books for $160.00 and is currently in search mode for a position in an interior design firm. Good hunting Evgenya!

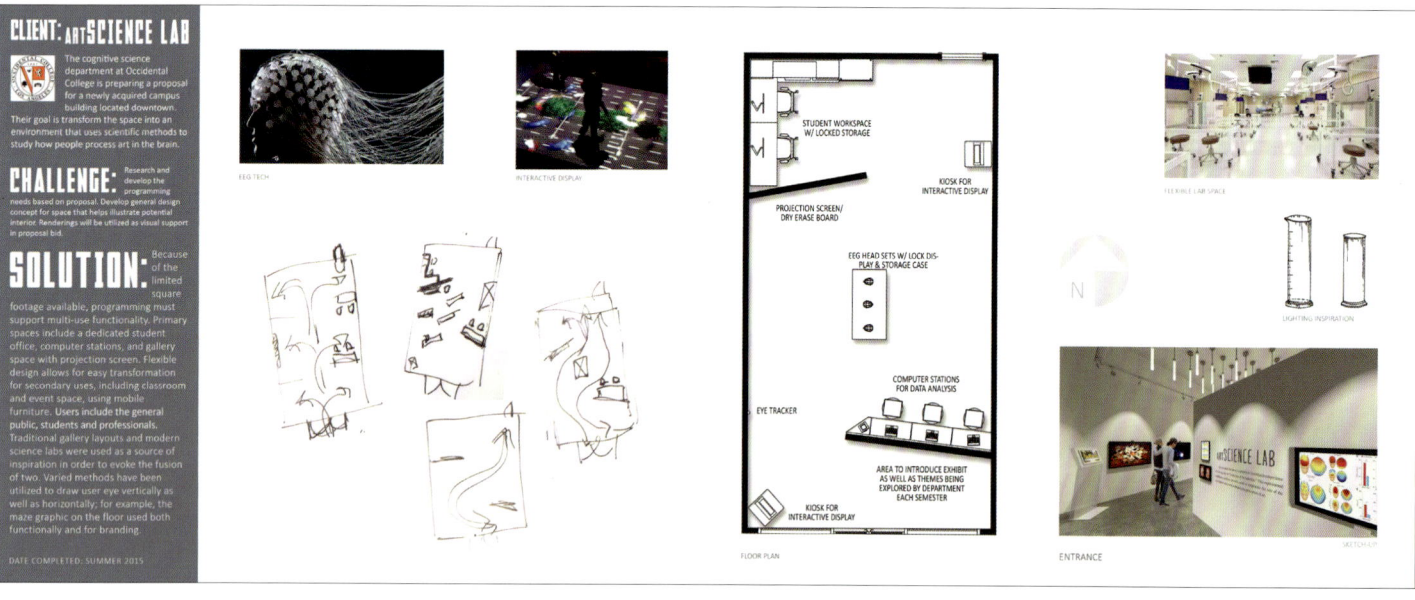

Inspiration

2–10 to 2–12 Evgenya chose a strong stylized font for putting together the graphics of her portfolio. It is an extension of how she thinks and designs. Her parti, diagrams, and perspective drawings within the Wikimedia project pull you into her large dynamic spreads that help to tell the story of how she thinks and how she designs. She allows the viewer to become engaged with her layered design process in the Science Lab project by including a large two-page spread of hand sketching and thinking out loud. The gray zone column at the start of each project was created to introduce important information, to maintain a well-organized text presentation, and to give the viewer a clear understanding of scope and her inspired concepts. Her spacious format supports the passion that Evgenya is bringing to the industry of interior design. Evgenya Epelbaum, New York School of Interior Design, N.Y., N.Y. 8.5" x 11".

INSPIRATION

The creative process is fueled by inspiration, which can drive the design of the portfolio itself. Inspiration is highly personal and relevant to the spirit of conception. Your form board identified your interests and approach to design. Your ability to view new ideas from related sources other than your own is broader than before. There are now multiple sources of inspiration in light and perhaps only one sharp image. One gains fresh insight into the design of any object or interior. There are two areas that inspiration can be especially useful for in developing your portfolio.

What is it that inspires you before you approach design? What gets you thinking and dreaming? Do you watch movies, TV, cartoons, or do you go to a museum? Do you get ideas from an automotive or hardware supply shop? Do you spend hours looking at aquariums? Remember, it is a challenge by itself to discover something out of the ordinary that inspires real growth and imagination.

" Everything you can imagine is real."

– PICASSO

2 THE SPIRIT OF CONCEPTION & CREATIVE PROCESS

> "One of the very special objectives about being a designer is that everything is designed! One may overlook the challenges we face when developing a portfolio, but there is nothing more gratifying than having a beautifully, poetically designed book compiled of all of your favorite works. It is a piece that quickly becomes dear to a designer's heart. The portfolio process should never be 'finished,' it should be an ongoing project alongside all other work. A portfolio is the reflection of who you are as a designer and how you wish to be portrayed to a reviewer."
>
> – **MACY HALE**

Ideas come from unexpected places or experiences, like walks through a park or in meditative solitude. They may arise from an emotional experience such as a dream. They may originate in a research trip to the Library of Congress in Washington, D.C. Allow them to become real and allow them to develop. Don't force yourself to think outside of the box, but rather look inside your box (form board) to see what it is all about.

Preconceived notions of what others do may only hinder what you need to accomplish in the design of your portfolio. It can become a trap by forcing your designs into an awkward format. If you have trouble coming up with inspiration and sincerely don't know where your ideas come from, then just begin with page layout as an acceptable place to start. As with designing interiors, when there is no concept, you just make a floor plan that "works." Assembling a clear and basic portfolio for some people is enough of a challenge. You should always be true to yourself.

Secondly, inspiration is embedded within your work. How do you demonstrate inspirational images within your portfolio? Don't let the inspiration image read as a solution to your project, but rather a tool that shows thinking and process! Inspirational images may be precedents for your design and be positioned at the beginning of a project as critical to understanding the full context of the concept. This doesn't mean that it has to be small in terms of its hierarchy or image size on the page. If inspiration was vital to the development of the project, it actually might occupy a prominent place in the layout of the project. It may even need its own page, and that is up to you.

THE BIG IDEA . . . CONCEPT

After you have read your form board and made notes on what inspires you, it is helpful to formulate a concept. Take time to write about the influences on your thought and be concise. Take more time to edit the idea. It is challenging to narrow it down but best to make it brief.

Developing a concept is a good thing for many reasons. It provides a driver that moves the design of the book forward. Concept comes from within. It can come from combining different images of inspiration, or it can come from something totally unrelated. It can come from a singularity such as color, or even shape. If concept comes from multiple sources, you may want to take the time to develop a concept model that ties different thoughts together. Without a doubt, the model will become something highly original. Your task is to put these images and ideas together to form a new model and new driver for your project and your portfolio.

Know your strengths. If you are a detail person, you may isolate features from within your projects that now become a dominant concept in the layout of your book. You could highlight these details with red circles and zoom in on the details. If you are a process thinker, you could design a book that is laced with sketches and drawings throughout, as a thread. Standard portfolios often show perspectives as the largest image within page layout, but what if your most compelling image is a major detail in black and white? You must keep in mind that this may be the first design project that you have to make that is totally your own. It will have your program, needs, space, scale, and feeling.

Concepts are useful in art and design. They help you answer questions along the way. Every decision made in the book, whether it is about typography, page layout, or even what you wish to include, should honor the concept. Without the concept, you are merely showing photos of your work on an empty stage. The idea drives all your decisions about the book. It distinguishes when you are working within its context and when you are merely decorating your book with superfluous and fluffy "fun" ideas. A cover with a pattern that comes out of nowhere just because you "like" it can only end up confusing the viewer. It may have little to do with your book design or the ideas behind the design. Decorative covers set up expectations from the audience that may have nothing to do with who you are or the actual content of the book. The big idea can engage your audience in ways they have seen before. It allows them to think. It provides a driver, and should not be abandoned at any point in the book.

Here's a TIP:

Look at the history of how you have developed your school projects or past work. What systems of organization were used? Was it oppositional or harmonic? Tension or dynamic organization can drive design. It's not time to abandon those basic design tools. Contrast, value, color, line, plane, point, shape, rhythm, age, sound, weight, mass, and space will all play roles in the development of your book.

2 THE SPIRIT OF CONCEPTION & CREATIVE PROCESS

Michael Rohey

Michael believes that design is meant to inspire and nurture the creative impulse in the viewer. His teaser, shown in figure 2–13, is testimony to a committed designer rising to the challenge of creativity with provocative typographic imagery that only serves to underscore his tenacity for making meaningful designs.

In his full portfolio (figures 2–14 to 2–16), dynamic bold geometries coalesce into creations that have multiple points of spatial viewing. The subject matter is reflective of organic qualities of form found in nature. Organic design intrigues the viewer to recognize that what they see in design is reflected within themselves. When Frankenstein the monster developed his own free will, he ran amok, causing much mayhem. Michael wants to imbue his designs with a capacity to evolve in dynamic ways and form and reform in the mind of the viewer.

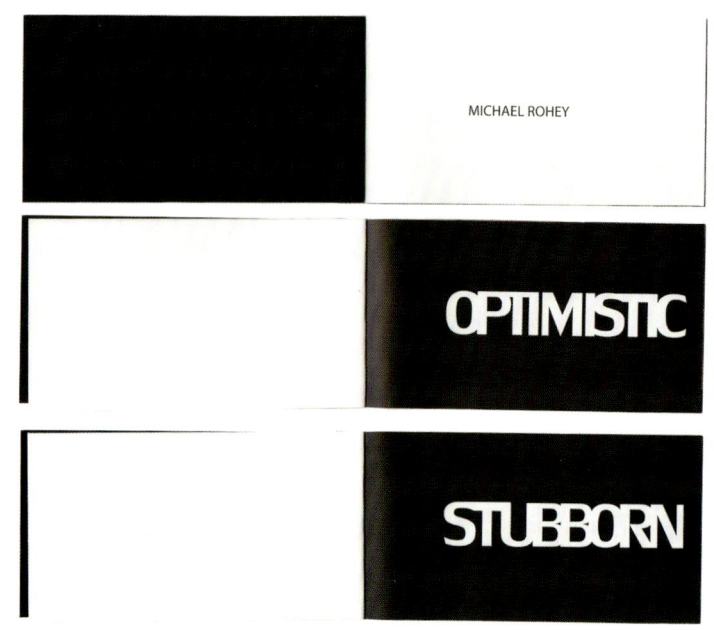

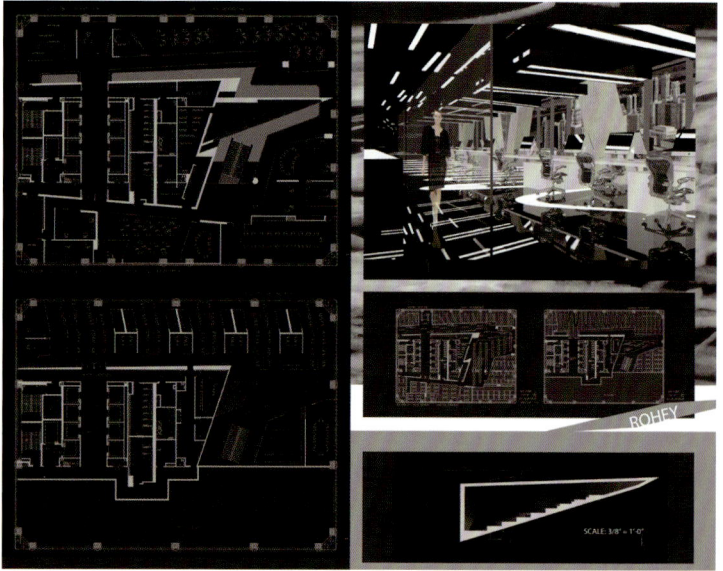

2–13 to 2–16 Rohey's project "Nocturnal" offers an abstract observation of light and shadows in which the space conveys a sense of excitement and curiosity. Circulations expand and contract to force people to interact with the architecture. Areas of refuge are designed to allow people to acknowledge the presence and behavior of people. Michael Rohey, New York School of Interior Design, N.Y., N.Y. 8.5" x 11".

TITLES AND PROBLEM STATEMENTS

Ming Chen Liao

Ming's portfolio (figures 2–17 and 2–18) was both innovative and groundbreaking as a conceptual tour-de-force of professional visual communications design. Each of his projects is contained as folded and stacked translucent newspapers that slide into and out of a vellum sleeve. Each project is beautifully identified in striking typographic titles and unfolds into a multi-image presentation similar to unfolding an edition of six individual newspapers.

Aside from individual titles to your projects, what is the title of your book? Is it your name? Have you introduced a title that is something other than your name but encapsulates the overall concept in your portfolio? For example, "Be everything you are and want to be and more." In this book, the designer has used large amounts of process to spark the reader into participating in his unusual free-hand ways of exploring the design of products. He elegantly communicates his big idea through an honest representation of process studies that reflect what it would be like to work with him in an office setting. The book cover in chipboard and all the materials including hand-stitched binding reinforce this concept of work and his joy in working ideas out through testing innumerable notions of form.

Is there contact information on the front or the back page or outside back page? Is it easy to find you if an employer wants to quickly get in touch with you? Does your cover initiate your overall concept, as previously addressed in this chapter? If so, how does it attract attention? What makes the cover engaging or makes the viewer want to see more immediately? Do you need to use the word "portfolio" on the cover or is it self-evident?

2–17 and 2–18 Ming's portfolio received strong praise by the faculty and exceeded the norm for conceptual portfolio presentation. Soon after graduating from NYSID with an MFA, he was offered a full-time position with the innovative AI Group in Charlotte, N.C. Ming Chen Liao, New York School of Interior Design, N.Y., N.Y. Folded 6" x 9", unfolded 20" x 60".

Do you want to include a table of contents with titles, page numbers, and sections? If you are interested in developing a table of contents for whatever reason, do you also list the parts, such as Hospitality, Contract, Residential, and so on, and then list the right projects within those subtitles? Are you interested in page numbers? Whether or not someone will use any of this information in a live interview, it does show something about your organizational skills.

And when you get to the first page, where do you title the project? How have you considered hierarchy to form sections such as Residential, Contract, Lighting, or Allied Interests, such as photography or painting? Within that hierarchy, how did you title the project and pertinent information that follows?

A design hierarchy is explored in later chapters of this book. Most software design programs allow you to set up default titles with font sizes and even colors or grayscale, so that you can click on that saved heading or subheading to save you the time to redo fonts and point sizes for each project. If you correctly name each collected title, you will be sure not to miss sizing the labels on projects. It helps to polish the graphics of each page in your layout. It will lend continuity to the graphics in your book rather than random chaotic sizes and tones to the labeling of images and project titles.

If the name of your original project was the Johnson Law Firm, and your focus in the project was to demonstrate ADA compatibility, then maybe ADA compatibility is a subtitle to the project. Maybe sustainability was a focus in the project, and that word could be a subtitle in the titling layout. Hierarchy will help the viewer focus on what it is you are trying to convey.

Problem statements should also be placed near the beginning of the layout. They take time to write clearly. They should demonstrate your ability to understand and summarize the given problem and to depict clearly the site and location of the design project. The given problem statement is different than the concept statement. They can be laced together, but they are different entities. The concept should articulate how you are going to develop the solution to the given problem statement. They don't have to be lengthy, but they should be included. They are worth the time to give them thought. Remember, you will be sending your work out online and in an email. People will not know anything about you or the project.

Beverly Clemente

Beverly found strategic ways to use full sheets of vellum throughout the layout as overlays on top of plans and for describing process exploration and design developments. She spent a full year in the design and production of her portfolio (figures 2–19 to 2–23) while also taking a full load of courses. On the basis of a strong portfolio, she received an internship position with compliments on her graphic presentation. Beverly acknowledges that success was due to the many iterations she invested in the process of redesigning her book. Where you begin is not where you end and the product is something she was proud of. Support and feedback were available from her faculty and colleagues. She states, "It is important to remain open to feedback realizing that you don't know all the answers and others with experience can offer sound criticism."

Beverly used white lines over gray tones with subtle colors to open her book. The white lines are similar to the use and understanding of light in every project. Every page includes a pool of light. We like how she overlaps images to tell a story of each project. The renderings are similar to screenshots with rounded corners fleshing out the linear drawings that relate to those individual spaces. She uses line to key certain elements in her designs and chooses earthy natural colors to support her narrative.

2–19 to 2–23 The purpose of Beverly Clemente's portfolio was to design a professional book to represent her as she pursued employment opportunities. She used the Adobe Creative Suite with Autodesk, Revit, and AutoCAD. She created a frosted cover with plexiglass and designed the binding by using a piano case hinge with screwposts. Her pages were printed professionally at a total cost of $130.00 per book. Beverly Clemente, Chaminade University, Honolulu, Hi. 8.5" x 11".

Titles and Problem Statements

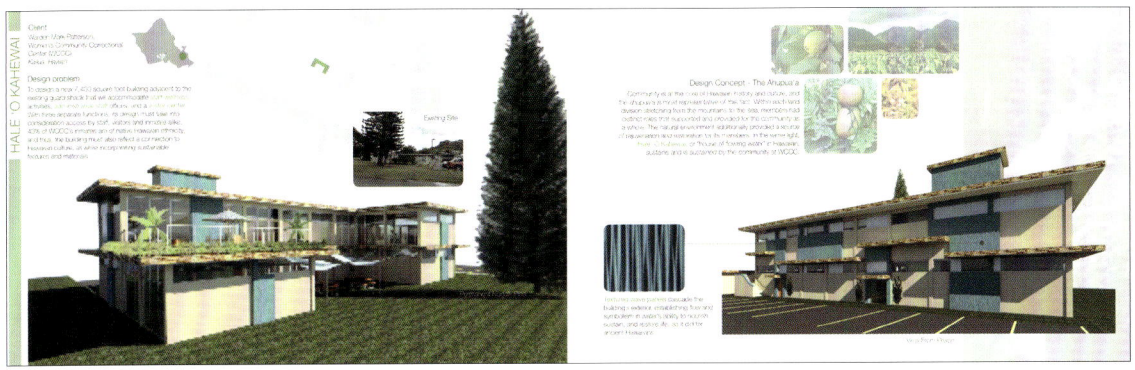
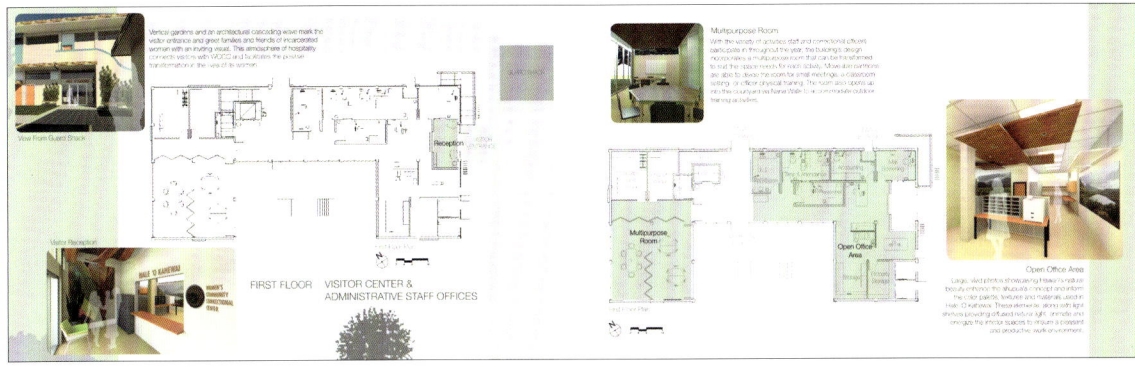
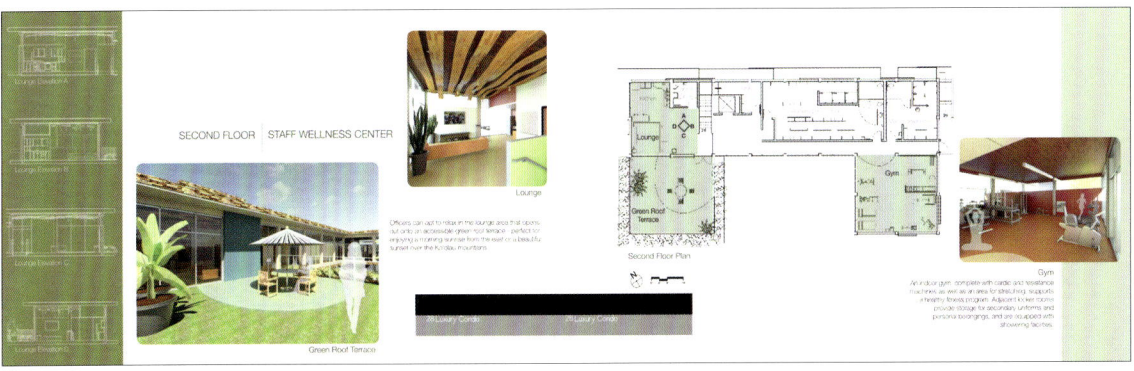

43

● 2 THE SPIRIT OF CONCEPTION & CREATIVE PROCESS

ENGAGE

How does your portfolio captivate your audience? Is it a word, image, material quality, or size and shape of the actual book? It is hard to pinpoint what makes something engaging. It is, however, a valuable attribute of your design concept when it happens and especially when it connects to the book's visual concept or big idea. What makes someone want to read or see more? What draws the viewer into your world of design? If you had a high inspirational image that was a driver for the project, where did you place it and how did it unravel in the design process? If you did execute a concept model, talk about it and use design vocabulary to describe it in your words. Hierarchy doesn't just happen with typography, it happens with image size as well.

Caleb Rempel

Caleb designed a dynamic machine for his portfolio, shown in figures 2–24 to 2–27. His portfolio challenges the formal rectangle and is laced with process and diagramming throughout the book. He has thoughtfully used chromatic color, neutralized colors, and grayscale to complement each project and to give hierarchy to what he wants you to focus on. It is so helpful to see one entire page given to initial thought processes such as adjacency, bubble diagramming, and concept sketching.

Interestingly, Caleb found work before showing his portfolio to his employer. After the first year on the job, he found an opportunity to show his work and received an upgrade to his creative responsibilities. In retrospect,

2–24 to 2–27 Caleb designed his portfolio as an undergraduate student at Algonquin College in the interior design program with the intention to use it to find employment. He used the Adobe Creative Suite along with Rhino 3D and AutoCAD. He viewed the project as any other design challenge to produce a comprehensive and well-designed result. He created two versions, one large and one small, plus a digital version and business cards. The entire production expense was $200.00. Caleb Rempel, Algonquin College, Ottawa, Ontario, Canada. 8.5" x 11".

Engage

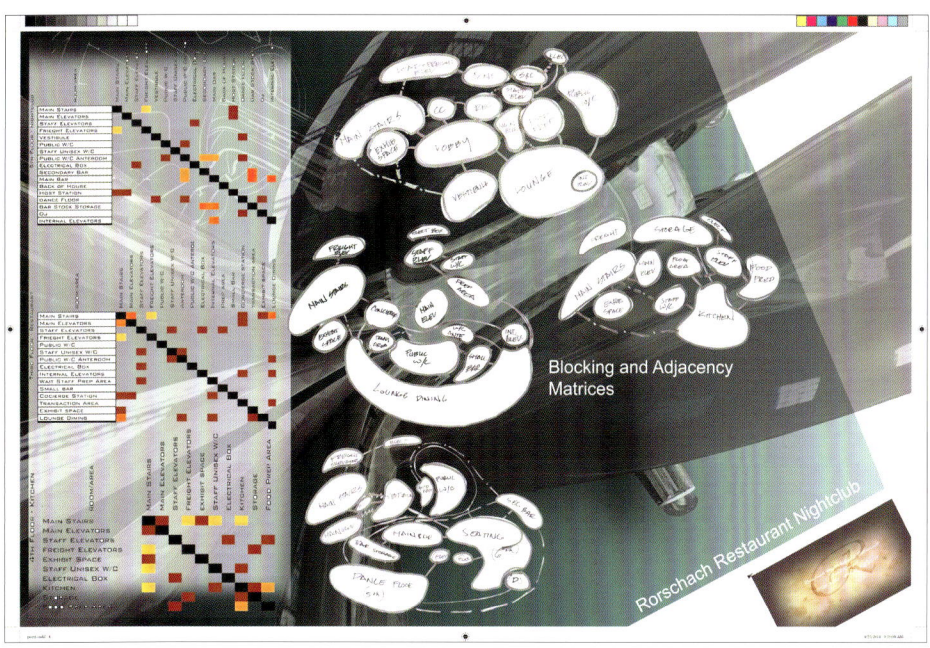

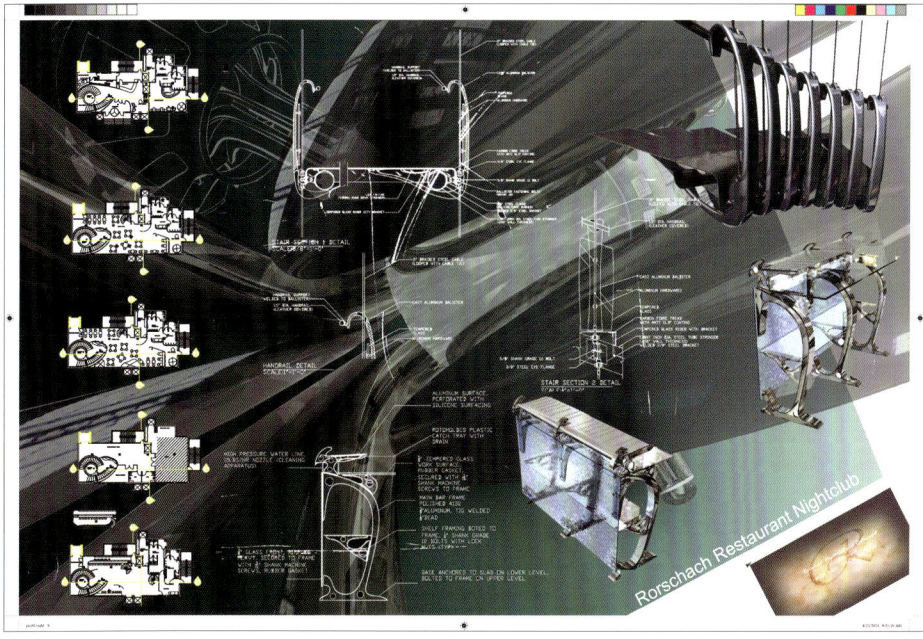

Caleb feels that having additional time is always beneficial to producing a better version—which is always the case. Having the opportunity to take a graphic design course was greatly beneficial to the result of his book.

There are no formulas to achieve an engaging portfolio. If you have designed your portfolio to be specifically for high-end residential, how have you captivated that audience? Was it with materiality? How have you engaged your viewer with the way you have displayed your materiality? How does the paper feel? How have the materials been organized? Remember that just because your assignment required you to put materials into a formal presentation, this does not mean that you need to show them that way in your book. Think about how you want to present them. Photographing them on a beach or a giant rock might be very engaging.

Having a well-drawn narrative may prove to be useful for engaging the viewer. How do you lead them through the project? How did you arrive at that plan? Where did the thought process originate? How did the initial sketches help develop the double height space in your sections?

ROBUST RESEARCH

Research is an important step in creating any portfolio. First of all, you need to investigate the sites of firms that interest you. How are their layouts designed? What are their typography styles? What are their color systems and backgrounds to their images? Not that you should copy them, but you should be aware of what they are showing and what styles they are using.

How would you design your portfolio to look like you would fit in with them, without matching? Look at keywords that each firm uses; this may even help you with developing your narrative. The second mode of research should involve technical process that will build your portfolio. Deciding on a size and method of reproducing your ideas on paper will require some research. Where are you going to have it done? What are their limitations? What kinds of paper do they have, or can you bring your own? Binding issues need review in early stages of development. For instance, some bindings may require you to format the pages 1/4 of an inch to the right or left to make allowances so that the images do not run into the gutter. The gutter is the inside margins or blank space between two facing pages. Sometimes you may design an image that shares both pages, in which case there is no space, but you must carefully plan spacing so that images align according to your intentions.

You could spend hours researching bindings. Perfect binding, plastic, coil, and holes for rings are all readily available. Perfect binding will give you the look of a paperback novel. Coil bindings come in many colors, clear, and metal. It may even become a design element in your book should you choose an intense color. Consider having different ways of connecting the pages in your "book." Perhaps a shoe repairperson or dry cleaning sewing service could stitch your pages together.

If you plan to use online publishing such as Lulu, ISSUU, Blurb.com, or Adorama.com, you will need to see what they require and what they have as options for your design. They have come a long way, and many offer a variety of paper and hardcover options as well. Their products and documents change from year to year, so you have to do your research. A lot of the self-publishing sites have packets of samples you can get at a minimal cost. It is always a good idea to feel the surface and paper.

Carlita Pickett

Upon graduation with a BFA in Interior Design from the Illinois Institute of Art, Carlita's goals were focused on finding employment. The work included in her portfolio (figures 2–28 to 2–31) represent products from her studio design coursework. The portfolio was designed with Adobe InDesign and printed on a Mylar paper stock, then hardbound. She produced two books—one was retained by the school while the other was used for finding employment. The total cost for both books was $200.00 with a local printer. Time involved amounted to a total of three months working continuously several hours per day. Upon graduation, she found employment and feels that the portfolio was instrumental in landing a job. The greatest design challenge of the book was resolving the layouts for each project and still finding a design thread to unify and run throughout the book. She feels the faculty was instrumental in helping her throughout the design process.

2–28 to 2–31 Carlita made the choice to base her portfolio on specific classes she had in school. Her first section on specialty design included branding for a store, a display case, and 2D studies for a sustainable installation for a hotel. In a way, the course descriptions are the program notes for her projects that she has placed in the beginning of each section of her portfolio. Carlita Pickett, Illinois Institute of Art, Chicago, Ill. 9" x 11".

Robust Research

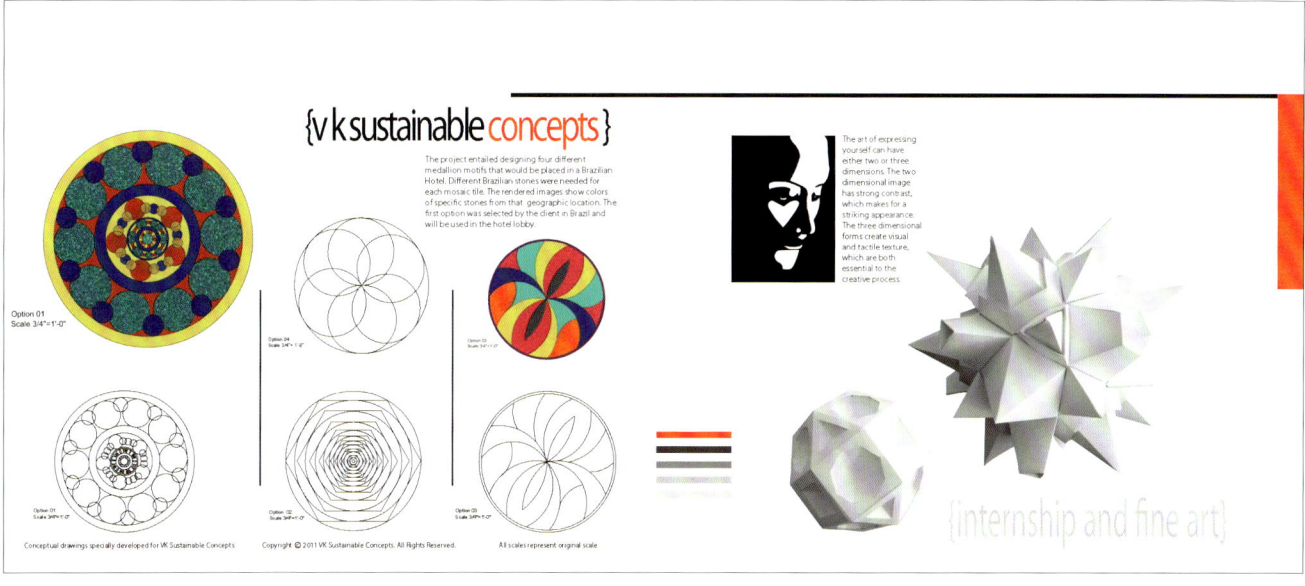

47

THINKING OUT LOUD

A small sketchbook is so helpful when it comes to thinking out loud and developing ideas that flourish because of your concept. Sketching a storyboard sequence will help to illustrate your intentions when exploring different layouts throughout your portfolio design.

The small sketchbook can save you a lot of time. It can help you move from project to project, and it can help you evaluate positive and negative space in a short amount of time. It can even help you edit what you don't want to use, or shouldn't use! It helps you to think out loud. Computers can take a lot of time to place and to move and tend to lock designs and layouts in place too soon, but freehand sketching can allow you to think, to change, and to develop quickly! Just as any interior design project starts with sketching ideas, your portfolio should also take that time and that step. Make several different layouts and compare them. If some design layout comes very easy for you, what is the opposite? The spirit of conception and design process often leads you to places unexplored.

Here's a TIP:

Remember that picking a paper is no different than choosing a material or flooring or surface for a design project. It must relate overall to the concept. Various coated papers will accept the ink in different ways. Some matte-coated papers will make the ink look shiny while others will keep the matte look even in intense dark color fields.

PRELIMINARY BUDGET: TESTING MATERIALS AND IDEAS

If your book idea requires a prototype, I would suggest doing that as soon as possible. If you want your book to have accordion folds or be rolled up similar to a movie thread, you must see what problems there are with these ideas and also how long they will take you to construct. Splendid ideas can sometimes costly and time-consuming to create!

If you are buying paper for your printing, test printing of your color and projects on different papers, like gloss, matte, and satin, is recommended, especially coated and uncoated stock. Do not rely on what you see on the monitor. It takes several days to test the color on the paper. Even after you have decided on the "right" paper, you need to do several tests of different perspectives and rendered drawings on that paper. Most likely it will need to be color corrected in Photoshop. Try not to underestimate how much time it will require to do a good job and to have satisfactory results. We are in a business that is about materials and color, and your portfolio should understand that basic "read."

The last thing you want to present is renderings and projects that are too dark and muddy looking. I am bringing this up early in the development of this book, as it takes the longest time to perfect this area of your portfolio project. What you "save" regarding a file on your flash drive should also be noted as an image for print form rather than screen form. They are two different files. But once you have the corrected file and the perfect paper, if you are doing your printing, you will be able to maintain quality control of that the image and project, provided you are using the same printer and the same computer. A different computer and printer will calibrate the color in a different way. It may not work.

Preliminary Budget: Testing Materials and Ideas

> "Your portfolio is a continuous story. Make it fluid. Be consistent with your spacing. Limit your fonts to a couple of families. Normally, headline, subhead, body text, and caption text should be the same font, weight, and scale throughout. Of course, rules can be broken, just break them thoughtfully. Work on a grid. At the same time, vary the way you place and scale elements onto that grid. There should be a push and pull as you page through the book, through variety of scale, visual weight, technique of rendering, etc. Most importantly, only show your best work, edit."
>
> – **DIANE FOX**

If you take your work to a service bureau to be printed, you will also need to do test sheets before they do the final printing. The self-publishing sites are trickier and harder to test. But the ones mentioned have excellent references. It is also good to know at this point what it will cost, whether you are having someone print your book or doing it yourself. There is no easy answer to any of this. Both will end up costing money. One is more convenient than the other, and that is another consideration. A lot of times, you will need to get your portfolio together for an interview in two days, sometimes even one day. Standard paper sizes help in these situations. Custom-size paper and binding all take time. Always keep that in mind. It doesn't mean you should not pick those custom sizes or specialty bindings, but it does mean you have to allow for the production time.

Know at an early stage what kind of binding you are interested in using. Research what the variables are and how much they cost. Don't just rely on standard default binding. You might explore something that is designed or less ordinary. All of this takes rigorous, robust research! But in the end, is worth every minute of your time. Your research will show in the design and make for an efficient, well-designed portfolio. It will show that you can find things that are unusual. Interior designers specify hardware, and binding is hardware. Remember the Mies aphorism, "God is in the details," which is such a positive anthem that speaks to the poetry of minutiae and the artistic focus and follow-through required to achieve anything of worth.

Now you have identified the evidence that contributes to and supports your inspired concept. In Chapter Three we discuss those important materials to include in your book, what to look for, and how to begin to make selections and organize and prioritize them to represent your projects and full portfolio.

3
ORGANIZING PORTFOLIO MATERIALS:
WHAT TO INCLUDE

"I'm not like most designers, who have to set sail on an exotic getaway to get inspired. Most of the time, it's on my walk to work, or sitting in the subway and seeing something random or out of context."

– ALEXANDER WANG

Alexander Wang is an American fashion designer and the former creative director of Balenciaga. At age 19, he moved from San Francisco to New York City to attend Parsons School of Design. After two years at Parsons, he decided to pursue the launch of his fashion label, which predominantly began with a knitwear collection. In fall 2007, Wang presented a full women's ready-to-wear collection on the New York catwalk for the first time, to critical acclaim.

WISH TO SEE

Many students have a clear idea of those projects they wish to include in their portfolios. You may have received positive feedback on work presented to a school jury of professionals. Your first reaction might be a feeling of flattery. However, that doesn't necessarily mean that including this project is beneficial for your portfolio. It all depends on the purpose of the design of your portfolio. Architectural firms with interior design departments will want to see work that is on an individual scale and style. Your one-room period residential project, even though you like it, even though it received praise from a jury, may not be the most appropriate plan to present for the purpose and given firm in mind.

This chapter is designed to help you select and edit your projects. It is important to create organization using only the most appropriate categories so that you can pick and choose specific work for specific job descriptions. The quality of work should be a top priority in your initial editing. Everything you include should be your best work. One strategy is to sequence projects in chronological order from the first year to your last, or vice-versa. The question of what comes first is not, however, necessarily just about your latest work either. You should consider putting your best work front and center at the beginning of the book, in order to reflect your strengths. In reality, you never quite know how long you have for an interview. You can hope for a formal interview beginning with introductions, a brief discussion of your background, and questions regarding your interests in design, followed by a project-by-project, give-and-take exchange about your portfolio, concluding with the firm's hiring needs. If you save the best project for last, the reviewer may never spend considerable time discussing it. Partially depending on how the interview goes, designers and managers are very busy and their time is valuable and, therefore, brief.

Organizing your inventory, therefore, is good to pinpoint your strongest projects for positioning them up front and in the middle of your book. Sort through all of your work, even if you think you already know what to put into the book. Often, we may forget about something just because it was something we did two years ago. Taking a fresh look at all of your work may lead to a discovery of the right project to add not just because it is good but because it rounds out your book in a way that you hadn't yet considered. By reviewing your inventory, you create a picture of where you are at this stage in your design career. Editing is good at all points in the process of organizing materials, not only from project to project but also within the contents of each and every project.

As you go through your projects, you will want to comb carefully through all of your drawings and information. If something was required for a class, that doesn't mean you have to include that in your book, especially if you didn't spend a lot of time developing it. Reflected ceiling drawings

3 ORGANIZING PORTFOLIO MATERIALS: WHAT TO INCLUDE

(RCPs) are a requirement of some interior projects but are underdeveloped. Sometimes perspective drawings are required but have mistakes on vanishing points and so on. Check those drawings or have someone else who is knowledgeable review all of your work.

Hopefully, you have saved your work on file throughout the years. If projects have included hand rendering, they probably need to be photographed. In Chapter Five, we address making scans and photographs of your work, both 2D and 3D projects, so you have the basics to document your projects. It is helpful, if you have the means or space, to lay them out in one room. It is also useful to have a friend be present when you go into your inventory. Sometimes they will help you to edit a project out or put it in when you are undecided. Find somebody that knows you well. It is time to be very honest. Remember, when you discover an area or document within a project that represents a downturn in quality, single these out for improvement by revision.

Along with various forms of previous employment experience, internships are of high value to prospective employers. If an employer doesn't have to train a new employee from the ground up, the firm's ability to concentrate on projects at hand without interruptions or to assign a mentor to a new employee is enhanced. Employers would like to see more of the following in job candidates:

- Work experience
- Confidence
- Ability to sell oneself and one's work
- Professional appearance and work ethic
- Real language, communication, and presentation skills
- Good people skills
- Realistic expectations/knowledge of career path
- Ability to work with others, team player
- Appropriate sense of accomplishment and humility
- Practical (how-to) design knowledge

Here's a TIP:

Think about what employers and graduate programs wish to see (or wish to see more of).

Mia Zhou

Mia created her portfolio, shown in figures 3–1 to 3–6, during her undergraduate program at Virginia Commonwealth University. Her goals for the design included special attention to the presentation format and its organization with respect to an invisible spacing structure. She used InDesign for the layout and an 80# card stock to print the pages for the book. The use of individual colors per project introduction helped to individualize the presentation. Five copies of her portfolio were created at a cost of $500.00. She worked on the project for one year and the results were a complete success. Her portfolio received a first place portfolio design award from the IIDA competition and she received an immediate offer for employment as a result of her book. She credits two sources of inspiration including *Making and Breaking the Grid* and *Portfolio Design*, 4th Edition, for inspiring her design. She also conducted additional research by searching through architects' published look books and portfolios online, including Tadao Ando and Frank Gehry.

3–1 to 3–6 Mia's cover illustrates her hand at work. It supports the process of hand-rendered interior presentations by its casual splatter moments. Her perspectives are dynamic and invite you in while they demonstrate her ability to understand light and color. It is a very personal portfolio with splashes of color and investigation. Her superimposed entourage also supports her sensitivity to the human side of her design. Mia Zhou, Virginia Commonwealth University, Richmond, Va. 8.5" x 11".

Wish to See

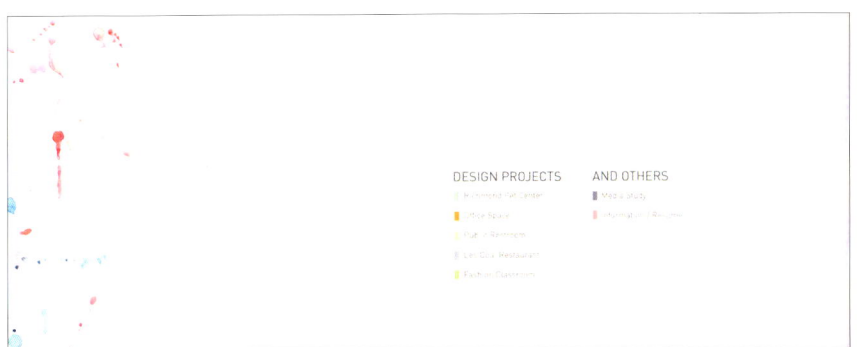

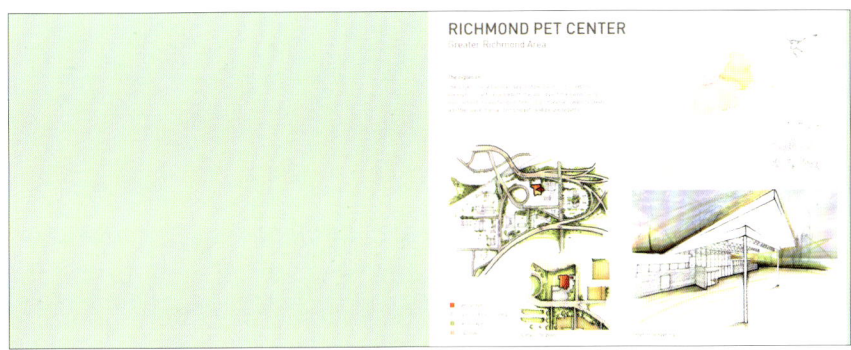

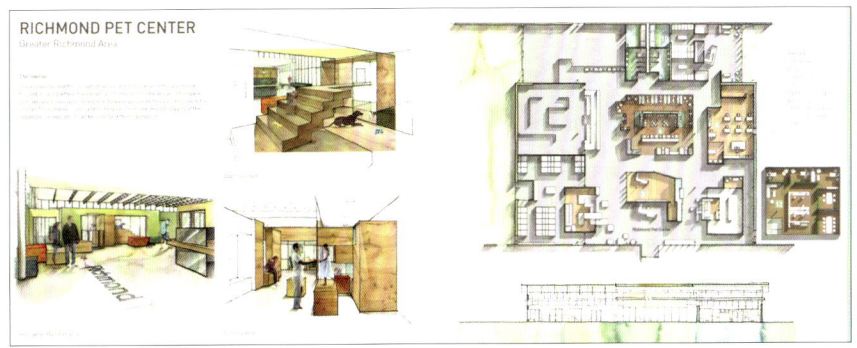

3 ORGANIZING PORTFOLIO MATERIALS: WHAT TO INCLUDE

COMPUTER INVENTORY

Aside from going through all your work, you need to organize your computer software and storage space. I am also sure that by now, that is a relatively straightforward question. Start with what you have on your computer and what you know how to use. What programs do you have (Photoshop, InDesign, etc.)? How much backup do you have (flash drives, external hard drives)? Saving your material and hard work in different locations should be a given. All too often students lose work because they didn't take the time to save it in the cloud or on an external drive. Saving work in different locations is mandatory. You work hard at what you do. Always take the extra time to back up and then back up again. It's impossible to go back and fix. It's too time-consuming, and it never happens. Make sure to mark those flash drives with your inventory. Again, save them in a safe place.

If you are doing your printing, you will, of course, need a printer and plenty of ink for both printing and testing. You should record all work as part of your budget. Ink is costly and adds up fast. Are you using ink or dye? Do you have a 3D printer available or a laser-cutting machine at your school or office? How about a 3D cover printed on a 3D printer?! Keep the laser-cutting machine in mind. It may be able to incise your name or a viewport on your cover. You may need a tutorial on how to use it or what materials can and cannot be cut or engraved on the laser machine, but it is well worth the time and the effort, especially if you are a sculptural thinker and designer. It not only expresses that side of your thinking process, but it also shows that you keep up with technology. The world is always changing and so is design and materiality.

Photoshop on your computer is also essential. White balance, cropping, and general color calibration are relatively easy to correct with Photoshop. InDesign is another great piece of software that is useful for page layout and graphics. Other programs will work. However, these software packages are specially designed for this purpose. The new version of PowerPoint will also work for those that don't know InDesign.

Here's a TIP:

It is worth mentioning at this time that all projects, whether built or not, are real projects. Often, emerging designers prefer to show established projects with real photography. Drawings and renderings, however, are realized, even though not built. You should be proud of them nonetheless.

DESKTOP ORGANIZATION

Organize your projects into folders on your computer. Create folders for paper portfolios and folders for online portfolios. Create folders for resumes and cover letters. It is time to organize. You can even separate those categories into old folders and new folders.

Keep in mind that you will also have to ask permission to use those projects created in an office. A lot of times you will be able to give credit to the firm and also note what part of the job or photograph you were responsible for designing. If you are adding your freelance work, you have to be careful that it is up to the quality of the majority of content in your portfolio. Make the time to carefully photograph those real projects and pay attention to interior lighting. Supplemental lighting is often necessary. Camera angles other than eye level will change the view and the power of the image.

Published work is also something to consider, even if it is in a school catalog. Being published means that someone has thought the work to be professional and meaningful at some level. It gives you credibility. It is a good way to amplify your resume, which may lack work experience. If you have worked on a benefits committee or designed for a benefit, save the publications and any printed matter that includes your work.

Benefits committees include collaborative work, which is also an interesting category or folder that you might consider, especially if you are interested in working in a firm. The ability to show that you work well with others and can come out with attractive design as a result is a good thing. Also, photos of the process might certainly be useful to include. Especially if they are pictures of you working well with others and getting the job done. Whatever the situation, be sure to include the names of the people who worked on the project and give the people on the team credit.

> "Too many applicants struggle to determine how many pieces they should include in their portfolios, or how varied their work should be. These are actually the wrong questions. The better questions are: "Based on the types of projects I would like to do, which pieces in my portfolio best showcase my experience?" and "Which of my pieces best showcase the caliber of work that this firm does?" Because after all, you're not just interviewing to find a place of employment. You're also interviewing the firm to see if it's the right fit for you. When your portfolio showcases only the work that you're passionate about, and that work reflects the expertise of the interviewing firm, your portfolio will naturally stand out from the crowd."
>
> – **JOSH MILES**, FOUNDER AND PRINCIPAL, MILES DESIGN, INDIANAPOLIS.

3 ORGANIZING PORTFOLIO MATERIALS: WHAT TO INCLUDE

Jenna Chambers

Jenna graduated in interior design from the University of Tennessee, Knoxville with ambitions to use the portfolio (figures 3–7 to 3–10) to find an internship and eventually a job. Jenna's process of organization is worth mentioning. The interior program offers an advanced course in portfolio design and requires students to design their own books. The Adobe Creative Suite was her main software design support. She printed the portfolio at the university print center using 100 lb cover stock and matte finish 80 lb paper for the portfolio pages. The print center offers various choices in binding options, so she chose the inconspicuous saddle-stitch binding presentation.

Jenna spent a total of 3 months in organization, design, and production of her portfolio. She began with a rough draft, organizing which projects to use and writing descriptions of the projects. She created a preliminary draft that was presented for reactions at a job fair and took advantage of the feedback to revise and improve the book. All the work invested in the portfolio design was proven worthwhile when she received the response that her book was a strong hiring point from her current employer. She also learned that creating an identity and brand were more involved than previously realized. Jenna says that organizing all projects in files and appropriate formats before beginning to design the book is of great advantage. Sources of inspiration included ISSUU and Pinterest, among other online sources. She was offered two internships that led to employment offers soon after.

3–7 to 3–10 Jenna has a very soft earthy palette of greens, grays, and browns that repeat throughout her portfolio and work. It has a soft delicate touch. We particularly like the circle notation forms on the S.E.E.E.D. Project where she shows how a room setup can be arranged in a different way. This is an important element for students who have modular, changeable designs. You must realize that if you are not around to talk about that important part of the design, your book needs to graphically show the possibilities of what you have proposed. The colors and scale of her woods and materials are well executed and not overdone. The sensitive treatment of materiality in her renderings invites you into her spaces. Jenna Chambers, University of Tennessee, Knoxville, Tenn. 8.5" x 11".

Desktop Organization

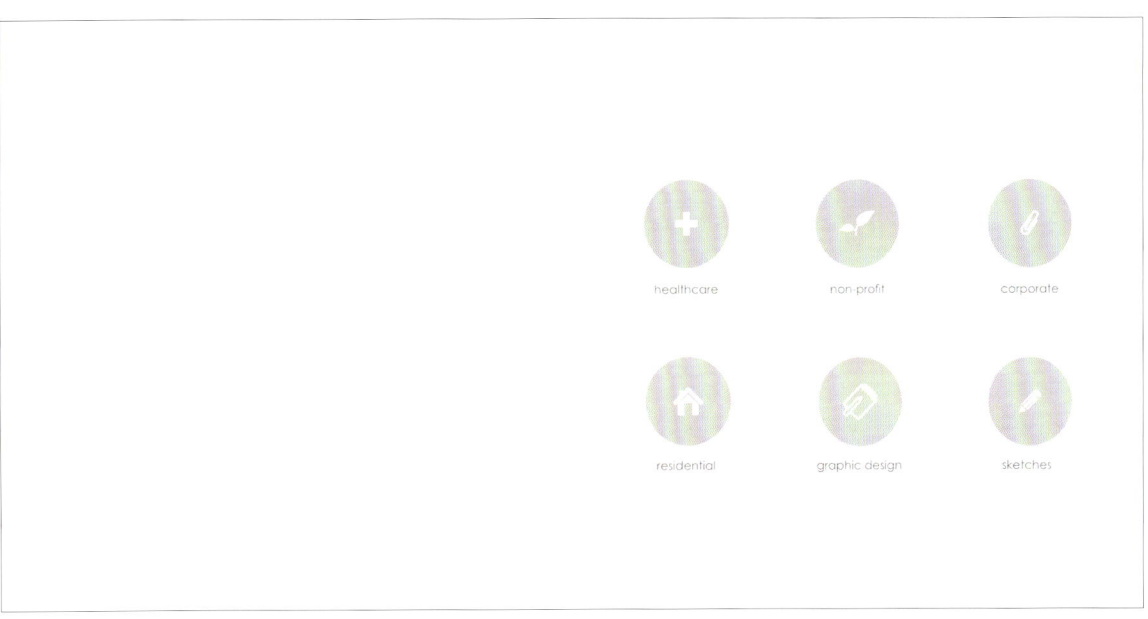

This residential project was based on the exploration of systems found in nature. The swans nest, represents a combination of protection and comfort, much like our own homes. The contrast of its rough exterior and plush- feather lined interior inspired the layout, and finish selections for this home. The project included several design challenges, including minimal use of floor to ceiling walls, and several glass exterior walls that had to remain in the plan.

3 ORGANIZING PORTFOLIO MATERIALS: WHAT TO INCLUDE

FIXING OLDER PROJECTS

You should include a folder on drawings that require fixing or projects that need photographing on your desktop. You will be sure not to forget about these projects as you manage your time. Many students have the desire to form folders to organize design and work projects, however, those folders applicable to work that must be fixed or redrawn are not a priority. Assigning folders for work to be fixed or redone is one of the keys to portfolio success. A student's ability to dedicate enough time to correct problem images is difficult. Many students prefer spending their valuable time applying for the internships and jobs available and making the deadlines for submissions to competitions. It is also challenging to gather the same kind of energy that you had when you produced the project.

While it is good to organize your digital files, you may find it helpful actually to lay out the real projects in your living space. As you go through your boards, check them for obvious mistakes or problems that were pointed out in a critique. Be realistic as to whether or not you will be able to fix problems or to redo a drawing that had misinformation or was just drawn incorrectly. It is also time to edit your work ruthlessly.

CONCEPT SKETCHES

While going through your work, collect concept sketches for each project. Employers want to see how you think. It is best to show the development of design projects. Too often process drawings don't make it to the final presentation. It is important to save process examples. Often the idea sketches that were discarded were more impressive than the finished presentation perspectives.

Students often wish to focus on their latest and best project, their design thesis. If the project was outstanding and a culmination of what you have learned throughout your design education, an entire portfolio could be dedicated to the thesis project, especially if it is truly comprehensive on many different levels. This is a decision you will have to make. The thesis project could become a book unto itself, and that would not be wrong. The other projects you have accomplished may be organized in another subsidiary book that accompanies your thesis portfolio book. But be careful, it may be limiting. Many of the projects throughout a school curriculum are designed to approach different areas of interior design. For those who have not taken a thesis class, there are many things to consider when choosing what to include in your portfolio.

> "A well-designed portfolio is single-handedly the most important document any design-related graduate across the world needs in order to acquire the best job possible. It needs to be a comprehensive collection of your best work. Do not conform to what other designers are doing. Your portfolio is exactly that—*yours*. It should represent you as a designer and a person, always evolving."
>
> – **JOHN F. XAVIER MCHENRY IV**, NEW YORK SCHOOL OF INTERIOR DESIGN

Concept Sketches

Iryna Carlson

In figures 1–13 to 1–17, a previous demonstration of Iryna's plate portfolio reflects careful orchestration of drawing skills applied to various sketching and rendering projects. Similarly, in figures 3–11 and 3–12, her model-building skills are presented on one side of a bi-fold plate and applied to a studio project on the reverse side of the same plate.

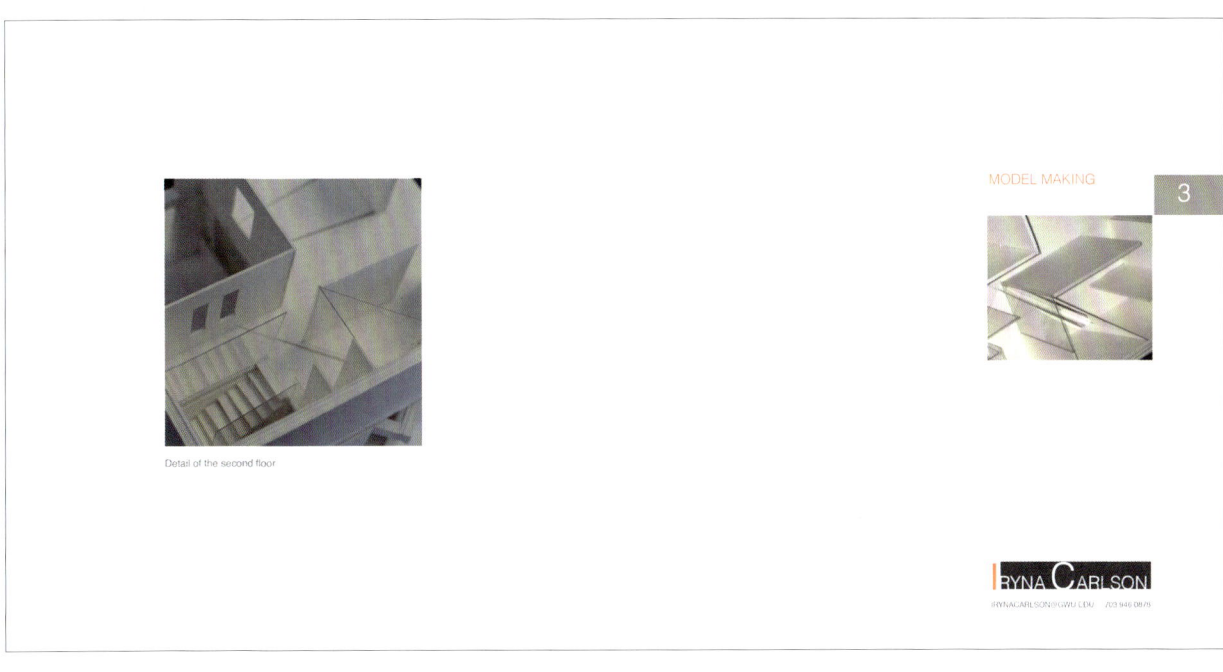

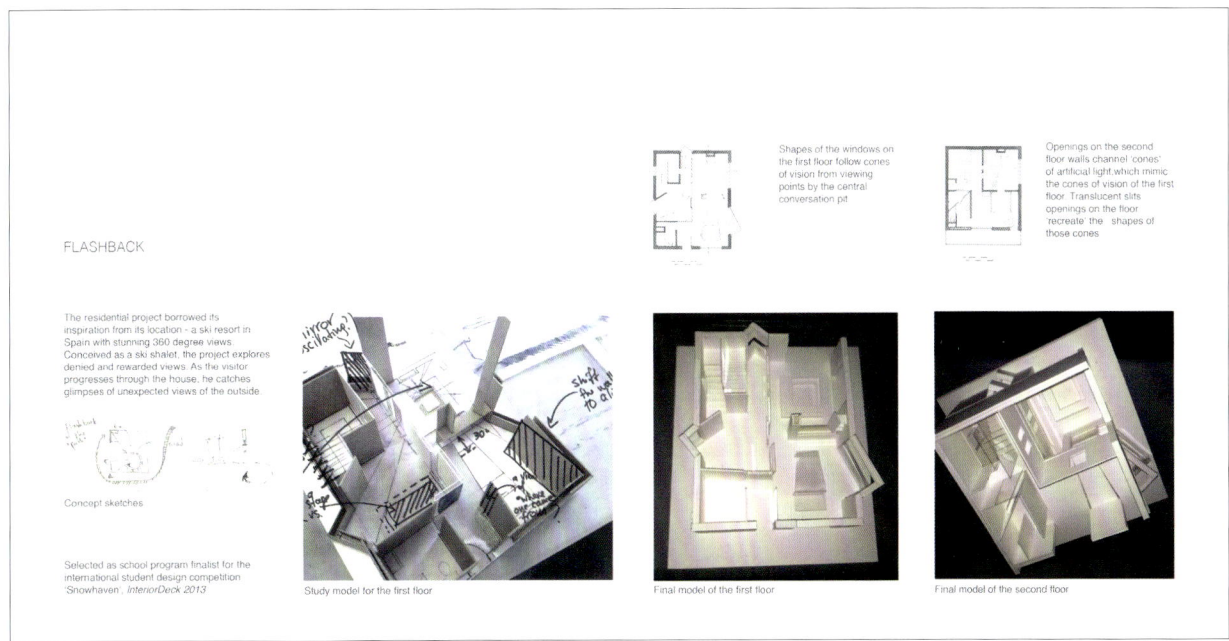

3–11 and 3–12 Iryna Carlson, George Washington University, Washington, D.C. 9" x 9".

3 ORGANIZING PORTFOLIO MATERIALS: WHAT TO INCLUDE

COMPREHENSIVE DESIGN PROJECTS

Review your strengths within the categories you have created. What do you want to emphasize with your audience in mind? Undergraduates in associated arts degrees will have a smaller pool of projects. You may only have residential designs and associated classes in design, art history, and textile furnishings. Portfolios do not have just to include full design projects. You may want to focus on the smaller residential rooms you have created, along with a full sampling of materials, room layouts, and color. You may even wish to show some of the period history classes and your knowledge of them. In a small residential design firm, this would be highly desirable. Many companies may even want to know your knowledge of paneling in many different periods and styles. Even traditional contract offices that do lobbies and hallways will want some knowledge of paneling and forms.

Show that you understand what types of fabrics are used for different programs. Materials for restaurant contract designs are different than specified material for residential sofas or chairs. Show a clear understanding of ratings and codes. Make notes of those codes and how you used them throughout the smaller projects in your portfolio. There is no such thing as a little project when exhibited well in your portfolio. Minor design projects can show rigorous thinking and designing! If you have created a custom banquette or piece of furniture for the project, show its detailing and its materiality. Package the project well. Make it a client presentation. Make it personal.

Even students with one-year BID degrees and two-year associate degrees can produce a comprehensive design portfolio. You need to be creative with how you show what you have accomplished. You may have to add additional material to the design project that wasn't assigned or part of the program. In the end, it will show that you understand the business and are qualified to become an intern or part of a smaller residential design office.

If you are a BFA or MFA student, you will probably have some larger thesis project that will include case studies and thesis prep. Do you have a book of research that was required for that course? How will you show some of that research? Will you pick and choose certain ideas, findings, and data that are pertinent to someone in the industry? Will that information be placed near the beginning of the project along with the title and problem and concept statements? How much of it will you include? You might even consider having that research book separate from your primary portfolio, as a subsidiary document.

As discussed, concept sketches will no doubt be a part of any comprehensive design project. What is your ability to draw and convey ideas that you have in the development of that project? They don't have to be works of art, but they should carry some thought process. Most employers will appreciate those sketches and the ability to think out loud with your hand.

Reut Ravhon

Reut, an interior design student at the Fashion Institute of Technology, created the portfolio shown in figures 3–13 to 3–16 in order to have a well-organized record of his work. Five months was devoted to the complete process of organization, design, and production of his book. One of the advantages of producing a portfolio is the benefit of having much in place to build upon in the future. The process of designing one's portfolio never ends. There will always be more work to add and change. Support and design advice came from faculty and friends. The portfolio found success as part of an application to graduate school. Reut employed AutoCAD, AutoCAD 3D, Revit, SketchUp, Lumion, Photoshop, Illustrator, and InDesign. The large format book, 11" x 17", was printed using an Epson inkjet printer. Reut used creative resources in the design of the cover: a laser-cut template and spray paint with acrylic sheets front and back. He made one book at a cost of $170.00.

Here's a TIP:

Too often students discard those initial drawings and ideas and race to the finished perspectives and rendered elevations. Sometimes they feel a bit sterile, and the fast sketching can help to make it more personal and add feeling to your overall portfolio.

Comprehensive Design Projects

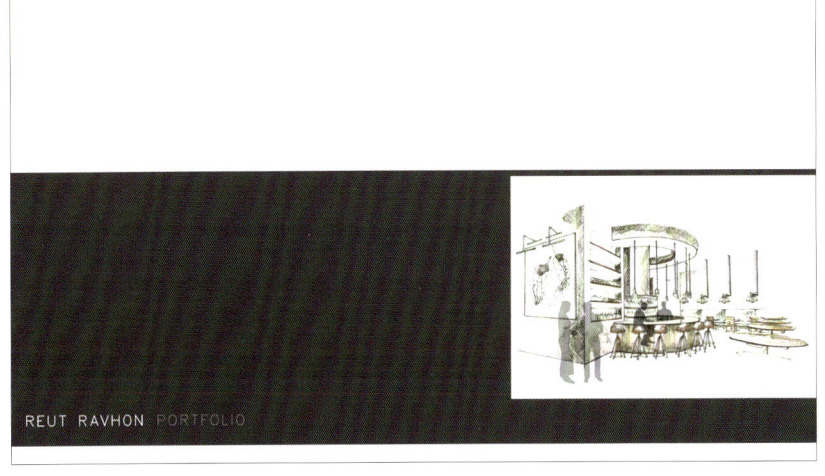

3–13 to 3–16 Reut has designed a rigorous interior design portfolio that is based on concept and a thoughtful process. His layouts of positive and negative space emphasize his drawings and materiality. His graphics, though understated, are supportive of the sophisticated projects that he has designed. The inclusion of his sculptures emphasizes his attention to detail throughout his design projects. Each rendering carefully addresses not only natural light but designed light and surface. They are sensitive and welcome you to immerse yourself into his world of form-making. Reut Ravhon, Fashion Institute of Technology, N.Y., N.Y. 11" x 17".

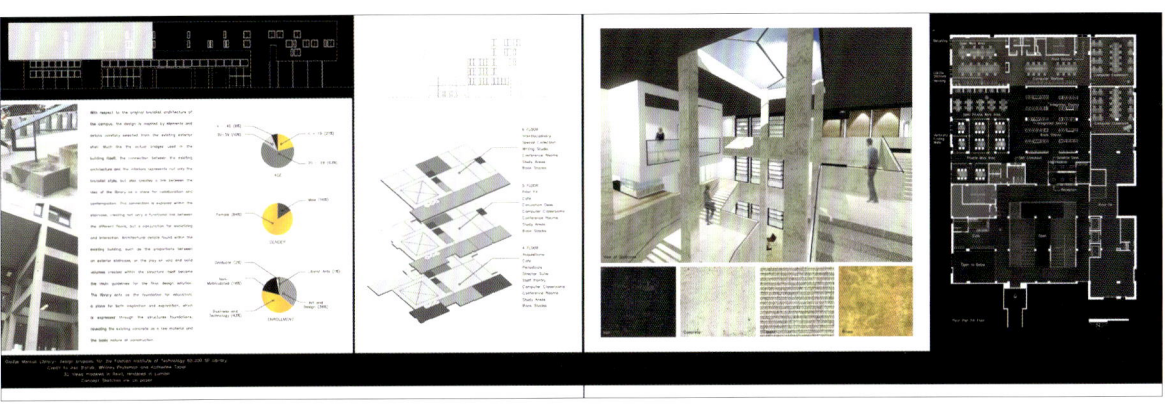

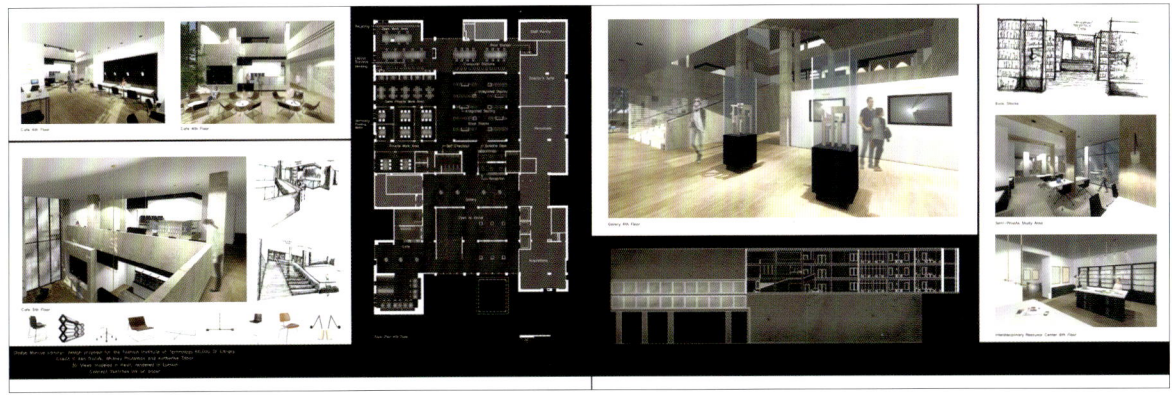

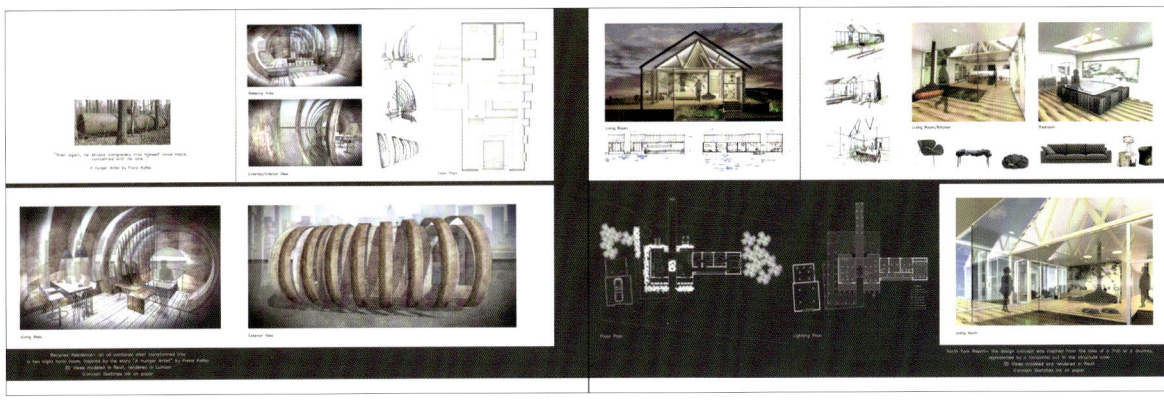

3 ORGANIZING PORTFOLIO MATERIALS: WHAT TO INCLUDE

Amanda Klein

Amanda designed her portfolio (figures 3–17 to 3–21) in the final semester during her senior year at Kendall College of Art and Design with the purpose showcasing her work and personality while using it to interview to find employment. She used a variety of software packages including AutoCAD, Revit, InDesign, and Photoshop. She created one book with a walnut veneer case and screw-post binding and one corresponding website for a total cost of $50.00.

During the process and following graduation she received constructive feedback from student colleagues, faculty, and professionals, which helped drive revisions into a better product. Although she feels like the packaging could be more creative, she benefited enormously from being disciplined and well-organized entering the design process. Her initial idea of packaging the book in an industrial designed wooden case is still a goal she will strive to achieve to refine future iterations of her book.

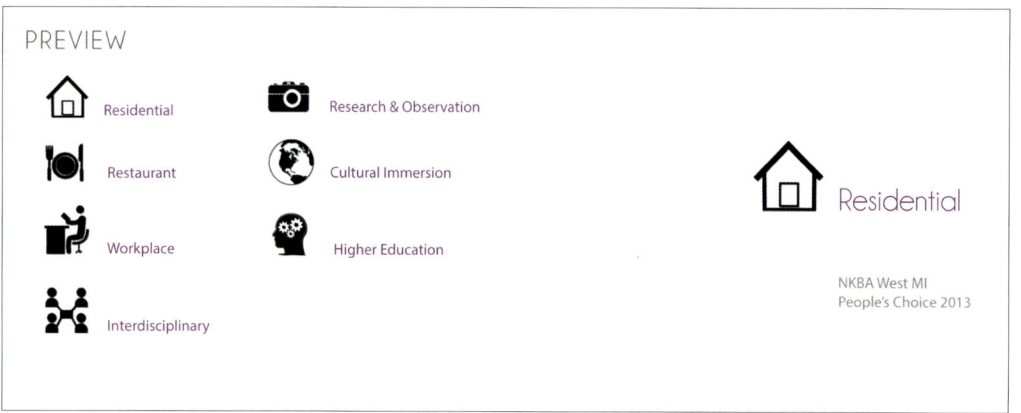

3–17 to 3–21 Amanda has taken the time to work with design icons for her table of contents. They repeat throughout her book and orient you to the type of project you are reading. She includes concept sketching and bubble thought processes with every project. You gain a clear sense she does her research and enjoys the process of design and thinking. Her materials and finishes are well documented so that you are not just looking at a great rendering, but can understand the materiality and relationship of textures and forms. Her observation and portfolio includes cultural research in the Dominican Republic. She opens doors of understanding through her design and use of the portfolio as a tool to explore creative and sensible work. Amanda Klein, Kendall College of Art and Design, Grand Rapids, Mich. 8.5" x 11".

Comprehensive Design Projects

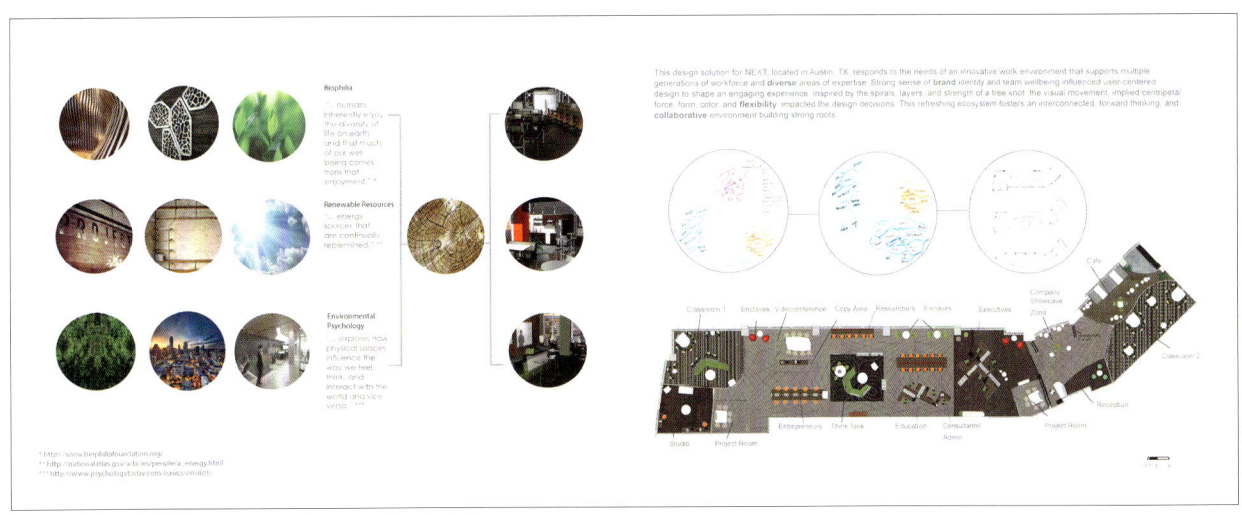

3 ORGANIZING PORTFOLIO MATERIALS: WHAT TO INCLUDE

> "Being able to see the process illustrated is an important part of a portfolio. Include the influences and your path to the solution, not just glamour!"
>
> – **TARA MCCRACKEN**, NCIDQ, IIDA, IDEC, LEED AP, ID+C, CHAIR, INTERIOR DESIGN PROGRAM, ASSISTANT PROFESSOR, KENDALL COLLEGE OF ART & DESIGN, GRAND RAPIDS, MI.

THE INDUSTRIES

If you are interested in the larger healthcare industry, which has grown tremendously over the past decade, make sure that you include healthcare projects that address healing, sustainability, and psychological aspects of furniture space, color, and lighting in interior design. How will your design and thinking impact that industry and, more importantly, the patient?

If you are focused on hospitality, focus on restaurants, hotels, concierge, lobbies, and areas that pertain to that industry. How does the art affect and work with space? Again, show a clear understanding of materiality and codes when specifying certain fabrics for certain public areas. You may even want to demonstrate that you know that the wall materials have connections that are detailed. These additions will bring your interior design portfolio to a higher level.

If your focus is functional kitchen and bath, show what makes your design unique. You can even create diagrams of traffic and flow in these smaller spaces. Demonstrate that you understand movement. This category of focus should include working drawings and detail, reflected ceilings, and lighting schedules. The working drawings should remove the scale notations since you are placing the pictures in a new format and size. It is necessary for the sake of the book. Sectional cuts should be properly notated on the plan as well and should refer to the elevation sections.

There are some ways to align the views to ensure the drawings relate to each other.

Do not forget to include appliance schedules, door schedules, and paint schedules as well. Show that you understand the countertop surfaces and why you chose them. Are you interested in recreational design such as sporting facilities, entertainment, or cultural institutions including education and museums? Make sure you include the site and location. It is important to note that the ski lodge is in Aspen rather than in NYC!

Think about the type of firm that you are applying to or the kind of client you are interested in working for. Make sure that you are showing them what they need to see as well as the creative side of you! Demonstrate that you understand how and where you fit. Be a professional on every level.

It is important to understand that even though you are interested in high-end residential, but only have healthcare or contract projects from school, this does not mean you cannot put together a portfolio that means something for a residential firm. You can still focus on areas of the contract projects that relate to a residential apartment or house, such as materials and furniture or lighting. And vice versa, there are areas of residential that relate to contract interior design. You have to be creative and know what you need to emphasize, but it can be done.

The Industries

Shunsuke Hashizume

Shunsuke Hashizume's undergraduate portfolio layout has a clear, precise structure that ties together his plates into multiple formats for presentation. The 11" x 17" plates were stacked in a vertical format for studio or client presentation. The vertical format gave power to the already dynamic presentations of his projects. The plates also became a book with binding across the top similar to a calendar presentation. The color/tone zone to the left side of his layout clearly organized the progression and narrative of his design process.

A carefully organized series of plates are presented in figures 3–22 to 3–25, demonstrating how a large-format studio presentation can be reduced in size for application to a portfolio plate or book presentation. The unifying graphic design maintains a text block for project titles and explanation flush left with ample open space for the organization of plans, perspectives, and conceptual and technical drawings.

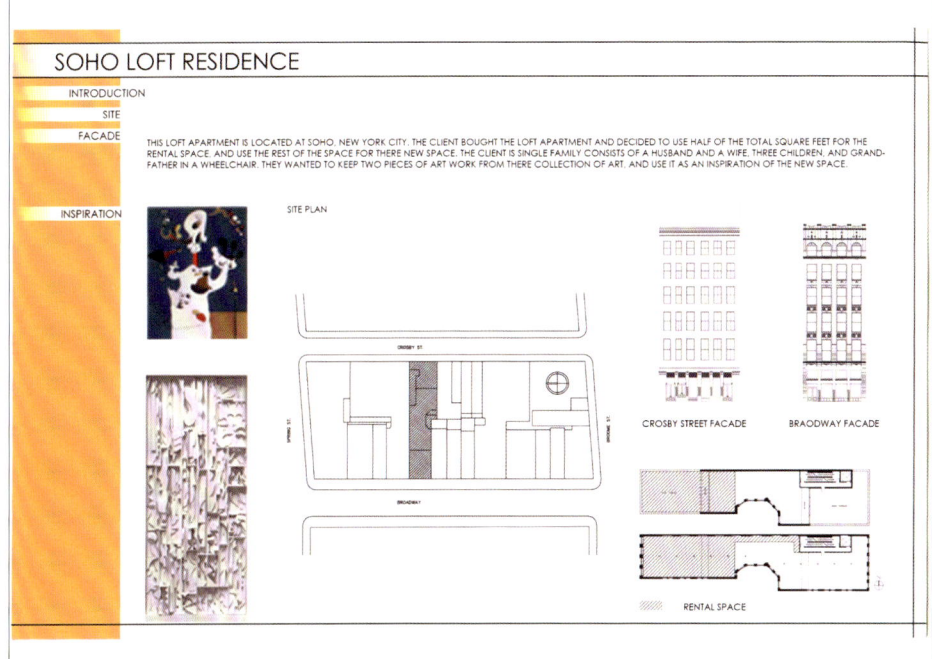

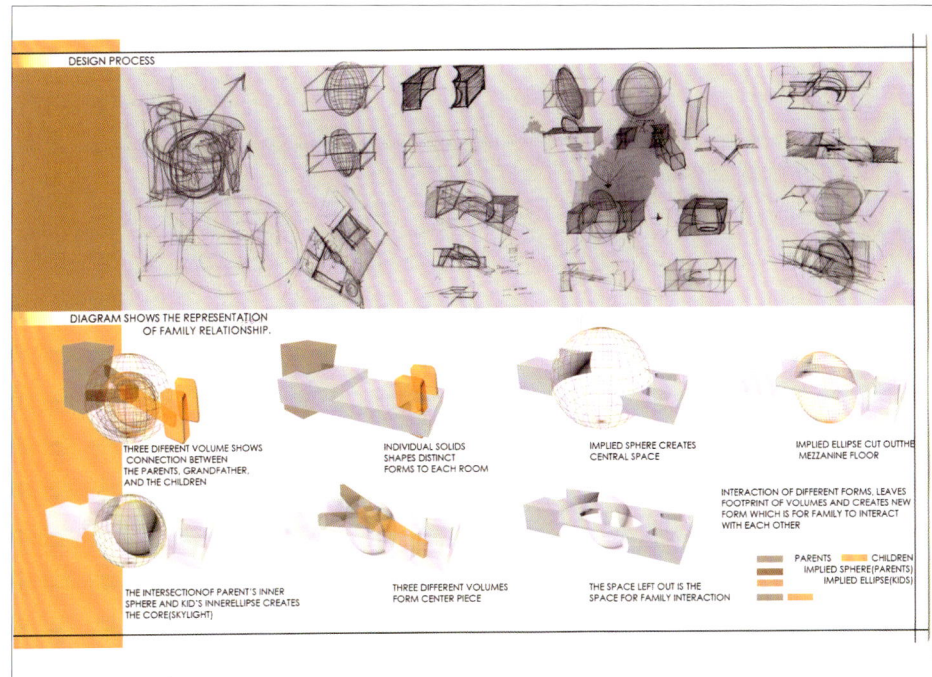

3–22 to 3–23 Shunsuke Hashizume's undergraduate portfolio layout. The concept of Hashizume's design process cuts through the middle of this vertical two-page spread with a strong zone of rigorous design sketching. The graphic sensibility of color and value contrast supports his design and informs the reviewer of his role as a team player in this project. Shunsuke Hashizume, New York School of Interior Design, N.Y., N.Y. 11" x 17"

3 ORGANIZING PORTFOLIO MATERIALS: WHAT TO INCLUDE

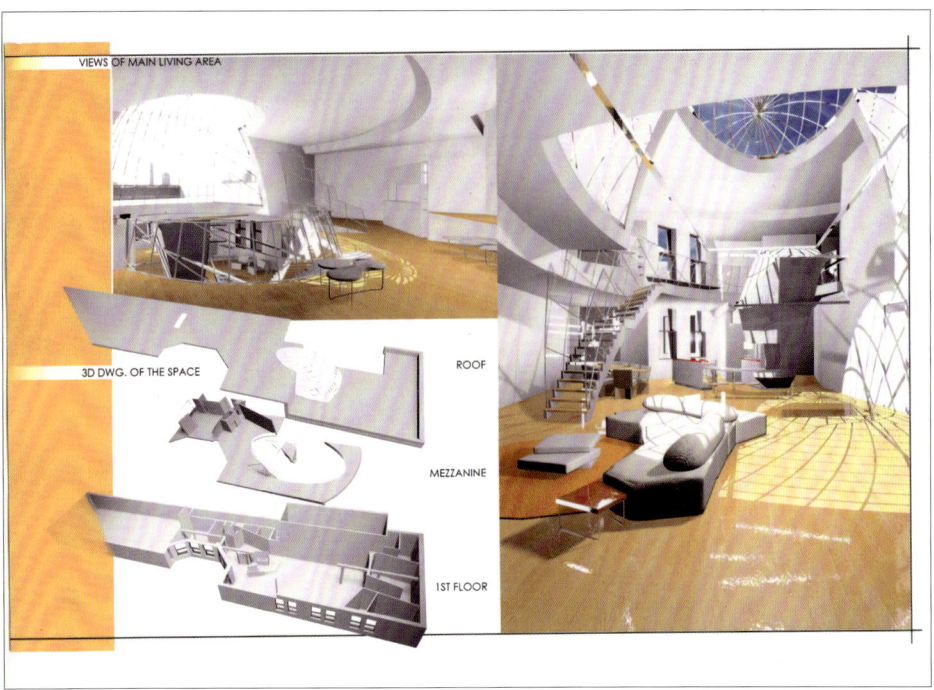

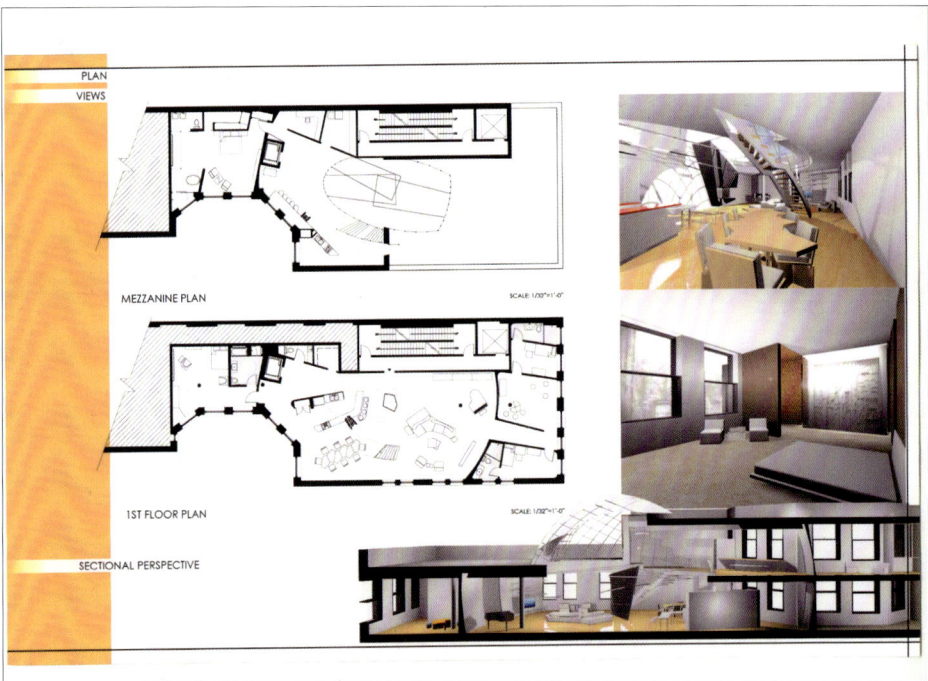

3–24 to 3–25 Shunsuke Hashizume's undergraduate portfolio layout. The concept of Hashizume's design process cuts through the middle of this vertical two-page spread with a strong zone of rigorous design sketching. The graphic sensibility of color and value contrast supports his design and informs the reviewer of his role as a team player in this project. Shunsuke Hashizume, New York School of Interior Design, N.Y., N.Y. 11" x 17"

The Industries

"A portfolio is finding your best work, the work that you are most proud of, but most importantly work that expresses your personality in a snapshot of only 32 pages."

— **CARLITA PICKETT**

Joe Hynn Yang

Yang's pop-up teaser portfolio in preliminary planning (figure 3–26) is intended to magnify those architectural precedents important to his interior space concept. His rough draft features several inspired and historic forms, such as a colonnade, which become significant ideas surrounding and supporting the concept for transitional spaces between inside and outside, such as a loggia.

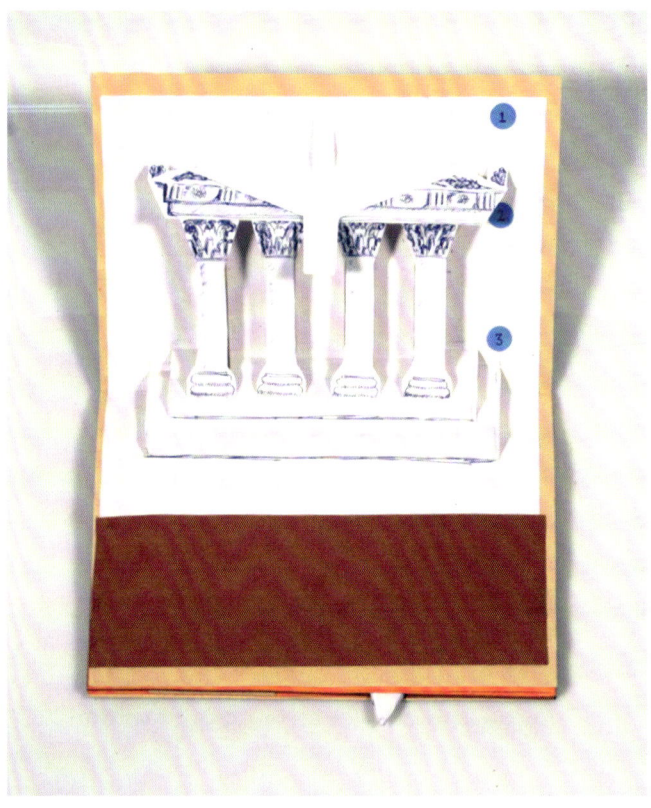

3–26 Yang's pop-up teaser portfolio in preliminary planning. Joe Hynn Yang, New York School of Interior Design, N.Y., N.Y. 4" x 7".

3 ORGANIZING PORTFOLIO MATERIALS: WHAT TO INCLUDE

MATERIALITY

As discussed, materiality is so important in any interior design portfolio, whether it is a small residential portfolio or large contract project. Spend the time to photograph and scan material samples. Make sure that you take the time to graze them with light to emphasize the texture or surface. Scanning often obliterates or washes out the textures and makes them read on a flat surface. Dark materials should be used sparingly only because they often print or read as black. Make color adjustments in Photoshop so that the output is correct. It takes time, but it is worth it. Consider changing the scale of materials depending on usage or size and scale in the project. Maybe floor samples could be larger than pillow fabrics, for instance.

If they were assembled on a board, consider photographing them in a setting that will help the viewer understand the design intention. The beach, a large rock, and floating on water are all ways to reset the materials in a way that supports your design and concept. Allow yourself to take the components of your design out of context and into the new context that we call the portfolio. The book then becomes a container for your ideas and your materials and not simply a placeholder. When you are opening your portfolio, you are opening the world, an interior of your ideas and your forms.

You may even use real materials, such as textured papers or photographs, or scan materials that will serve as sectional dividers to your design projects. Materials can be addressed in the design of the book, as well as the palettes and surfaces that are included in your individual design projects. It helps to create a form that supports your work and your thinking. You may need to do some shopping for papers, veneers, or even a design mart where materials can be photographed or scanned.

SUPPLEMENTAL CATEGORIES

Last but not least are categories such as competitions and teamwork. You may want to include work that you have created for design competitions, whether you have won or not. They are actual design projects that you have executed based on physical parameters and real budgets. If it was a group project, list the team players. If it was an installation in a benefits event, show the process of designing the facility. Consider showing photo examples of you working on the team. These are important additions to your portfolio. Interior design is collaborative. Demonstrate that you work well with others.

FOCUSED SKILLS

Research the skills you will need for each job within every firm. What will they require you to know and how have you adequately shown that in your portfolio? It might be a section in your book that shows a definite knowledge of those skills, or you may highlight drawings within each design project included in your book. Either way, make sure that what you say in your resume is visual within your book. AutoCAD, Revit, Rhino, Adobe Creative Suite, SketchUp, laser modeling, 3D printers, and even the latest PowerPoint all fall into this category. Remember that to say you are proficient requires a certain number of hours using that software. Be honest when you state something.

3D printers and laser cutting machines have changed the presentation of interior projects and even the portfolio design. Placing these skills in your portfolio is similar to the sketches and finished presentation drawings. The highly detailed laser cut models are useful to set against the general study models that are made out of foam core. One shows development and one shows a more finished presentation. They are both skills, and both are highly desirable in the interior design portfolio. You can even use the laser cutter to cut out your name on the cover of the collection or maybe even a sharply cut window on a chipboard frame within the portfolio. Keep in mind the portfolio design can show skill in the design of the book! Remember, the person interviewing you knows nothing about you or your skill level or design for that matter. Your portfolio is such a useful tool to show your scope and that you are immersed in the world of design.

Keep in mind that if you display a lot of hand rendering as a skill, and you don't want to do hand rendering anymore, don't assume that your reviewer will understand that. Whatever you include, you should be happy with not only the result but also the process of getting there!

GREEN DESIGN

Are you sustainable in the way that you approach interior design or do you just use bamboo as a default to addressing this growing need to save our planet? Is green design a thread throughout your design projects, or do you simply have one or two projects that have addressed this need? It is another time, to be honest. You can't make something out of nothing, especially if you haven't discussed it. If you have addressed it, how will you show that the materials used are green? Will it be a separate column within each project or a zone that is highlighted in some way or another? Is it in the problem statement at the beginning of the project?

If the furniture was made with a particular process that was eco-friendly, your portfolio should show that, especially if it was important to you when you chose that particular object or surface. You can't assume that someone will know about eco-friendly processes in every interview.

The following statement is taken from the ASID website and demonstrates their commitment to helping designers understand basic green concepts and also to connecting people to designers who care about the environment and about controlling climate warming. As you will see, they even have areas to click on to get immediate help. For those who will be using their portfolio specifically to work with designers that are green-based, this site and paragraph will prove helpful.

> "Green design is a design that goes beyond being just efficient, attractive, on time and budget. It is a design that cares about how such goals are achieved, about its effect on people and on the environment. An environmentally responsible professional makes a commitment to try regularly to find ways to diminish design's impact on the world around us. It is also a smart way of doing business: sustainable design is the fastest growing segment of our industry."
>
> — **ASID**, MINNESOTA

3 ORGANIZING PORTFOLIO MATERIALS: WHAT TO INCLUDE

Courtney Wierzbicki

Courtney studied interior design at the Kendall College of Art and Design and created her portfolio, shown in figures 3–27 to 3–32, with the purpose of seeking employment following graduation. Her approach to emphasize horizontality to the layout design solved a substantial problem with many portfolio designs, which is how to conduct the narrative or manage telling a story about one's work and how to sequence images one upon the next. By emphasizing horizontal page design, the reader follows the designer's lead, anticipating change and story development to move left to right across the spreads. Courtney created her book with the Adobe Creative Suite and printed the book on matte finish non-glare 60 lb large-format paper with a coil binding. She spent a full semester working on revisions and testing multiple layout possibilities.

COURTNEY WIERZBICKI
LEED Green Associate, Student IIDA
courtneywierzbicki@yahoo.com
616.745.8020

TABLE OF CONTENTS
Next Office Design
Roots Bistro
NKBA Kitchen
Chairmania: Case Studies
Woodhouse Condo
90 Acres Restaurant
KCAD Facilities: Communication Office
Higer Education

3–27 to 3–32 Courtney has included *real* short studies and designs in her portfolio. The layouts of materials are easy to understand and the renderings and photographs do tell the story. Her cover page addresses her interest and involvement as a LEED green design associate and the opening paragraph of her first design project calls out an honorable mention as an award. These are both good attributes to mention front and center in your design portfolio. Let the industry know your commitment to the trade and to the profession. Courtney Wierzbicki, Kendall College of Art and Design, Grand Rapids, Mich. 8.5" x 11".

Green Design

NKBA KITCHEN

CHAIRMANIA

HIGHER ED

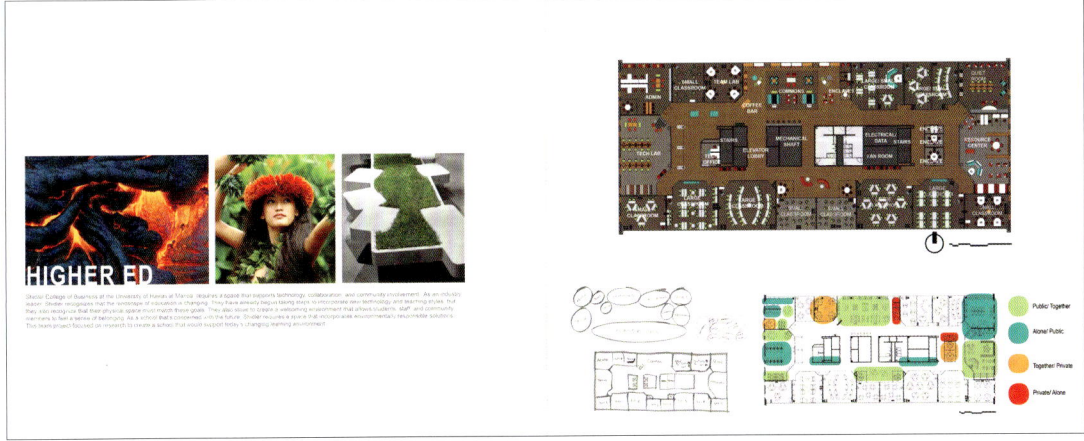

3 ORGANIZING PORTFOLIO MATERIALS: WHAT TO INCLUDE

3D INTERIOR SPACE

Color and light are important aspects of all interior design. What projects demonstrate your ability to conceptualize space as light and color? Color board studies, color classes, and color renderings all explore and demonstrate your understanding of light and color. If your color class work had you research figures in history or color plate theories, think of ways of showing that knowledge and research. If you class involved painting, show a page of process and color mixing. Get your camera out and photograph your working table. Keep in mind that a balance of finished projects and working process is desirable. Again, it shows that you are living a life of design and are immersed in the subject.

Including projects that are 3D models will add so much to your portfolio. Interior design is the study of containment on so many levels. Do light and color affect the space and human aspect of design? How will your portfolio show that study of light, color, and space? How have you used color within the design of the book and collection? What about the value of how you use materials and color? Looking back on your personal form board will clue you in to how you typically use dark tones, medium tones, and light tones when designing an interior project. Maybe the portfolio could address dark, medium, and light tones throughout the book!

Lighting projects that show studies of surfaces affected by luminaires and color temperatures will greatly enhance your understanding of materiality and the colors chosen to design that particular project. For some designers, color is a driver and should be organized in the book with that in mind. For some, light is a driver. Don't underestimate the power of value and light in the design of the portfolio.

She used the Adobe Creative Suite for the design of her portfolio and printed it on an oversize heavyweight matte finish paper (80 lb) at a nearby FedEx Kinkos. She then trimmed the pages to establish the bleed running to the edge of the paper and bound the book with a black coil binding. Numerous versions were created in a flurry of design revisions and redesign. Five different books were finally created that led to two final versions. Altogether, she spent $300.00 on the entire process and production and spent a full month on the job around other priorities at school.

The layout design transferred to PDF format very well so that she could mail it along with her resume in pursuit of employment. She carried a hard copy to interviews. She credits test printing as integral to the success of the book, so she could make adjustments in the output. Then came a website based on a well-structured print version—the transfer to a grid online was a smooth process. Inspiration for her book came from exploring allied disciplines such as automotive design portfolios at cardesignnews.com/portfolios. One of the attributes of these books was their spacious layout that provided an open composition for a demonstration of process drawings, which connected with the build-up of her projects.

Jennifer received multiple job offers on the basis of her strong, thoughtful book. Over the past few decades, there has been steady growth in students creating websites for posting their own portfolios, as well as portfolios posted on social networks and hosted on allied design websites, and PDFs, are transforming the need for a traditional printed portfolio.

Jennifer Kasick

Jennifer studied at The Ohio State University, Department of Design, BSD Interior Design program, where the importance of professional development is well-integrated in the curriculum and all students produce portfolios near their senior year in preparation for seeking internships, employment, or application to advanced academic programs. As an undergraduate she created the book, shown in figures 3–33 to 3–37, in anticipation of seeking employment following graduation.

3–33 to 3–37 Jennifer created a strong comprehensive portfolio. We like her bold graphics and titles that are sometimes vertical and not stacked! The straight vertical and bold typography also supports her undulating forms that investigate the materiality of skin shape and structure. It is a bold portfolio that combines interior design with a sculptural sensibility. Her three categories of medium, execution, and objective are well written and make each project and scope easy to understand. The black zones that she has created for text also work well sculpturally. They make the white space even stronger and they support the dynamic shapes that she creates for interior spaces. Her focus on 3D models also supports her understanding of interior design as a container that is seen and experienced from many different views. Jennifer Kasick, The Ohio State University, Department of Design, BSD program, Columbus, Ohio. 9" x 12".

3D Interior Space

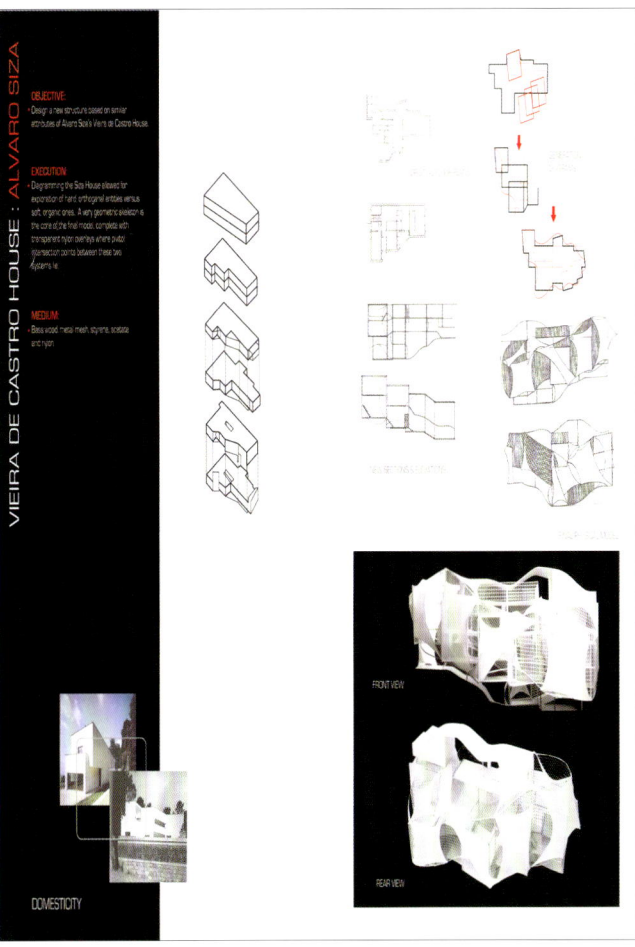

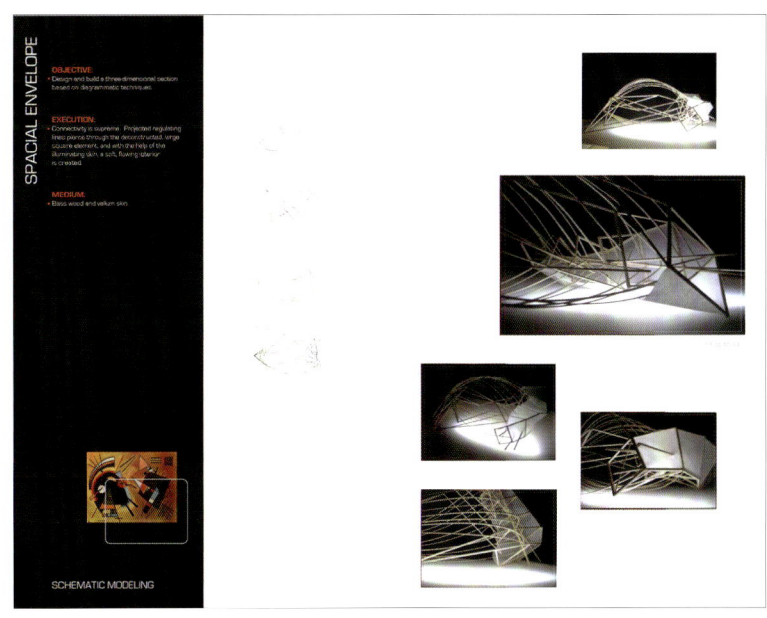

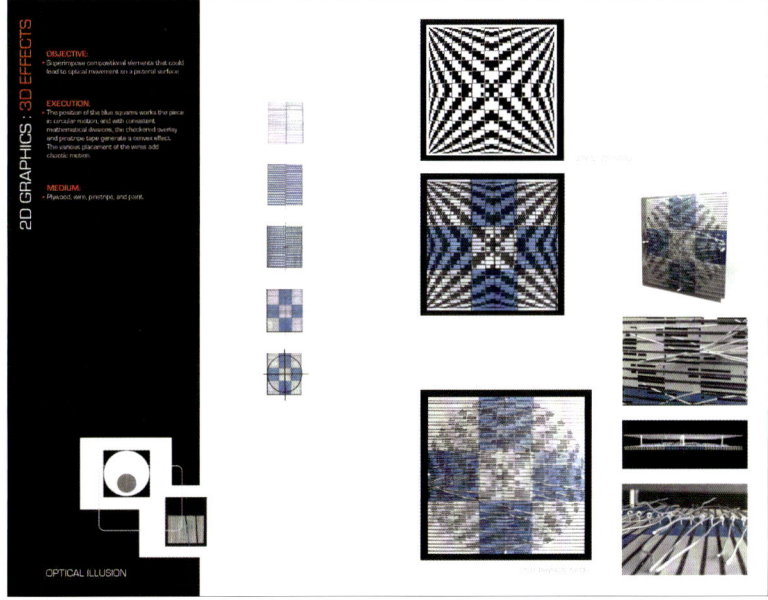

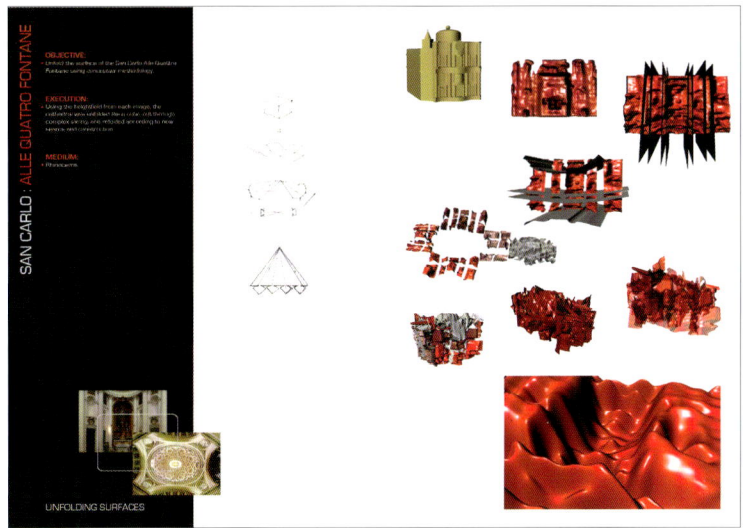

● 3 ORGANIZING PORTFOLIO MATERIALS: WHAT TO INCLUDE

ALLIED INTERESTS

What do you do in the arts that would supplement your work as a designer? How do you live the life of a designer on different levels? While this shouldn't be the focus of any design portfolio, it does demonstrate that you are a well-rounded individual who is passionate about things that are visual and sensual in daily life. Form making is always significant, even if it is a different material and genre.

The role of allied interests may not be intense and lengthy, but it may give insight as to who you are and where you grew up. Painting, photography, ceramics, pottery, sculpture, and drawing all demonstrate that you are immersed in the visual arts. Anything that shows your take on composition and form could be included in this category. Placing these images can be strategic throughout your book, or you can just put them in a section toward the end of your book.

If you do a lot of traveling and have many personal, cultural experiences, you may want to include a photography section that shows this experience and knowledge within your portfolio. Many firms ultimately have employees do a lot of traveling. Photography can easily demonstrate this experience. Remember to list your languages when writing your resume. Along with a hardcopy object, portfolios can be produced with online websites such as behance.com and crevalo.com.

Sarah Elena Cuellar

Sarah Cuellar produced the portfolio shown in figures 3–38 to 3–43 while in the MFA program at NYSID. She had a strong concept that involved lacing the individual projects with her travel experience and expertise in photography to document her international travel experiences. The entire portfolio makes strategic use of the umbrella concept to demonstrate her design thinking and thought process. The cover abstraction of an urban street grid and the project postcards serve as a clever introduction to each studio project in her book.

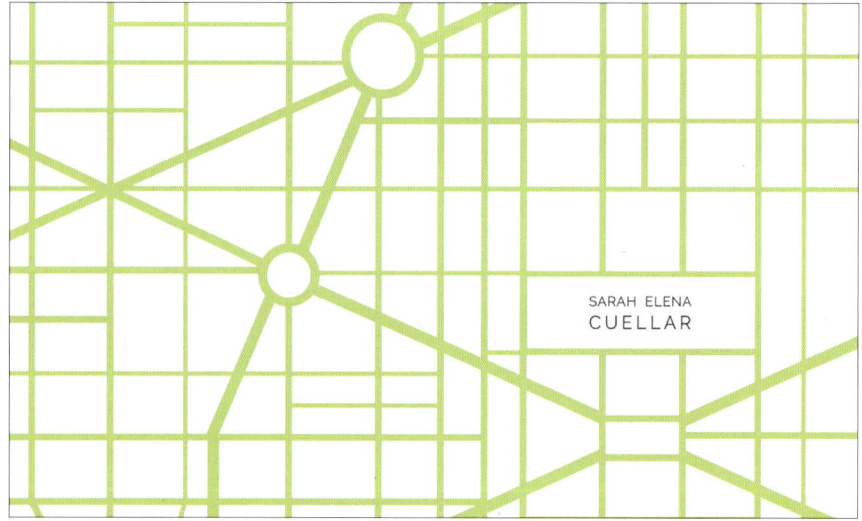

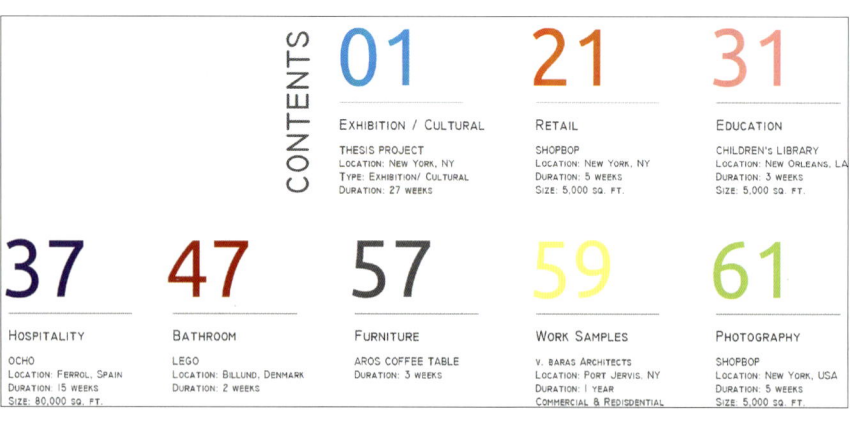

3–38 to 3–43 Sarah Cuellar's portfolio is a brilliant merging of her allied interests of photography and design. She used her portfolio as a tool to show her vast traveling experience. The cover is a grid of a city and the introductions to each project are postcards with address lines used to title the separate projects. Another creative detail is the design of mini-logos for the stamps that reiterate the essence of each design and follow each design project. This format supports her language skills and international experience, bringing her resume to life. A simple white spiral binding allows the pages to lay flat. She also chose an unusual elongated proportion for the layout, column structure, and page designs. She is truly an original designer and this portfolio supports her thinking and passion for interior design. Sarah Elena Cuellar, New York School of Interior Design, N.Y., N.Y. 8.5" x 11".

Allied Interests

THESIS: Design a museum for the Latin American author, Gabriel Garcia Marquez

MGGM
70 Madison Avenue
New York, NY

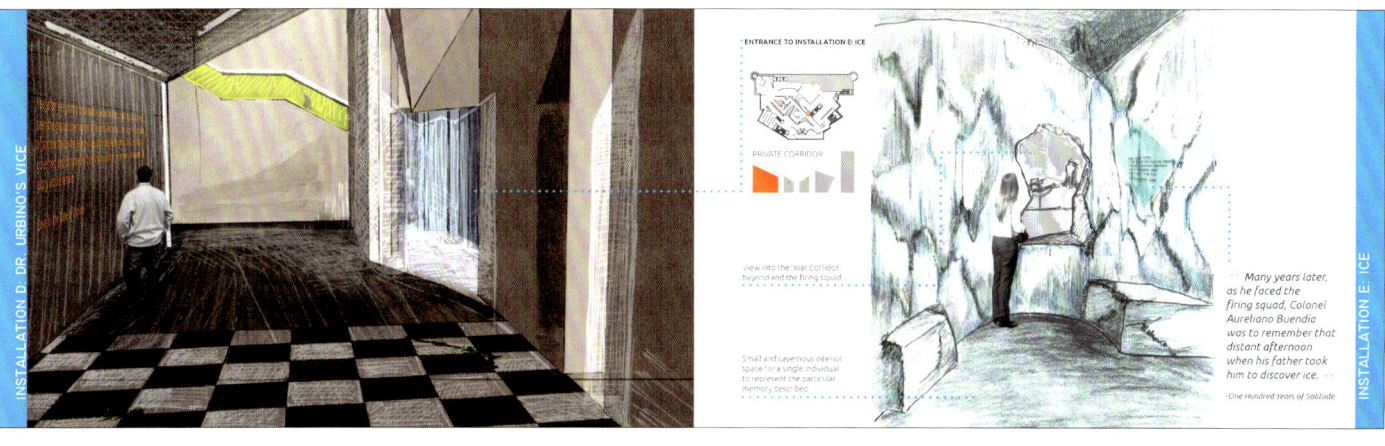

INSTALLATION D: DR. URBINO'S VICE

INSTALLATION E: ICE

"Many years later, as he faced the firing squad, Colonel Aureliano Buendia was to remember that distant afternoon when his father took him to discover ice."
—One Hundred Years of Solitude

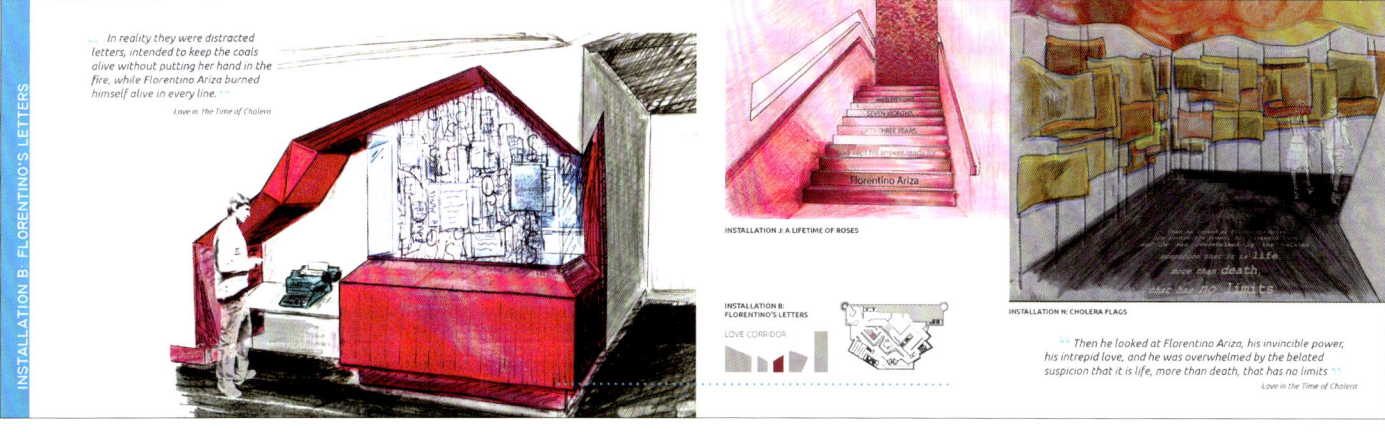

"In reality they were distracted letters, intended to keep the coals alive without putting her hand in the fire, while Florentino Ariza burned himself alive in every line."
—Love in the Time of Cholera

INSTALLATION B: FLORENTINO'S LETTERS

INSTALLATION J: A LIFETIME OF ROSES

INSTALLATION N: CHOLERA FLAGS

"Then he looked at Florentino Ariza, his invincible power, his intrepid love, and he was overwhelmed by the belated suspicion that it is life, more than death, that has no limits."
—Love in the Time of Cholera

INSTALLATION O: THE TOWN SQUARE (VIEW FROM -1)

"Before reaching the final line, however, he had already understood that he would never leave that room, for it was foreseen that the city of mirrors (or mirages) would be wiped out by the wind and exiled from the memory of men at the precise moment when Aureliano Babilonia would finish deciphering the parchments, and that everything written on them was unrepeatable since time immemorial and forever more, because races condemned to one hundred years of solitude did not have a second opportunity on earth."
—One Hundred Years of Solitude

INSTALLATION O: THE TOWN SQUARE

INSTALLATION O: THE TOWN SQUARE (VIEW FROM 0)

4
FROM CONCEPT TO PROCESS
TO LAYOUT DESIGN

"Light is a magical ingredient in a portfolio that makes its presence known through the most subtle effect of gentle persuasion."

– ROBERT KANER

AN INSPIRED LAYOUT DESIGN

The overall goal of your layout is to express the excitement, energy, and vitality of your work, reflective of excellence in advanced technical skills and broad industry knowledge. Your portfolio will demonstrate how you move a space from concept through design and into reality. The industry requires that you have reached a deeper level of problem solving, a demonstrated ability in time management, and a focus on skills and abilities in technology.

Your layout design is all about plausibility and opportunity—imagining a real space in which people can live, work, and play. Interior designers consider people, their safety and well-being, and how they react to the spaces they live and work in. Your living-working environment has been a source of inspiration and discovery. You enjoy the experience of diverse culture, art, and industry that inform your work. Your best layouts reflect an exploration of imagination. They demonstrate the way visuals occupy page design, and all kinds of visuals, blocks of text, and white space is maintained and manipulated in a dialogue that teases and invites the eye to look again.

Crucial to all strategies for layout design of any publication, but especially design disciplines, is space. An interior design portfolio lives and breathes with the dialogue created by the invisible grid structure (vertical and horizontal) and how specific form and areas of blank white space populate it. Considering the composition across the full width and height of a double-page spread means carefully planning the way the eye is engaged from top to bottom and left to right. This reading of the elements and spaces is called "scanning." Areas of greatest importance (image size and contrast) attract the eye and then direct one to secondary factors to discover the pattern and direction of similar-sized and smaller elements.

Not only does a portfolio display your work and style, but it also shows your ability to organize work in efficient ways. Your decision to use a set of plans and elevations for a given problem demonstrates your ability in drafting (AutoCAD and Revit). Another project may focus on 3D interior renderings. A third project could focus on lighting and a fourth on furnishings or atmosphere and materials. The diversity of projects in your portfolio underscores your full abilities that you bring to an office. A variety of work means that you can be selective in what you show and how you show it.

Invariably, you will choose projects for your portfolio from an assortment of photos, designs, and sketches that demonstrate your ideas, style, and present and past design projects. Photos or drawings should be high-resolution and professional, showing your concepts in sketch theory or practice. While multiple images of one project are excellent, change your organization to show your work from different points of view. Diversity is key, even if you specialize in one type of design. Most designers compile all of their project evidence into a book format. Today, working with publishing software is best to create a professional and finished printed product.

"BE WHAT YOU SEEM TO BE" (figures 4–1 to 4–4) is a devil-may-care lighting design catalog produced by Ango, Bangkok, Thailand. This is just the sort of spirited marketing instrument that catches youthful readers' attention

4　FROM CONCEPT TO PROCESS TO LAYOUT DESIGN

while offering abundant visual delights to peruse. The catalog's excellent photography, exceptional light-hearted illustrations, chipboard front and back covers, and cream, 80# dull enamel stock are just enough delight to respect simple resources and lift the reader up to the plateau of thinking "affordability.". This project should be on every design student's must-have design book list. If you ever wondered what it takes to design a book with the utmost humor, this is what you have been dreaming about now realized and in the flesh. See more at www.angoworld.com.

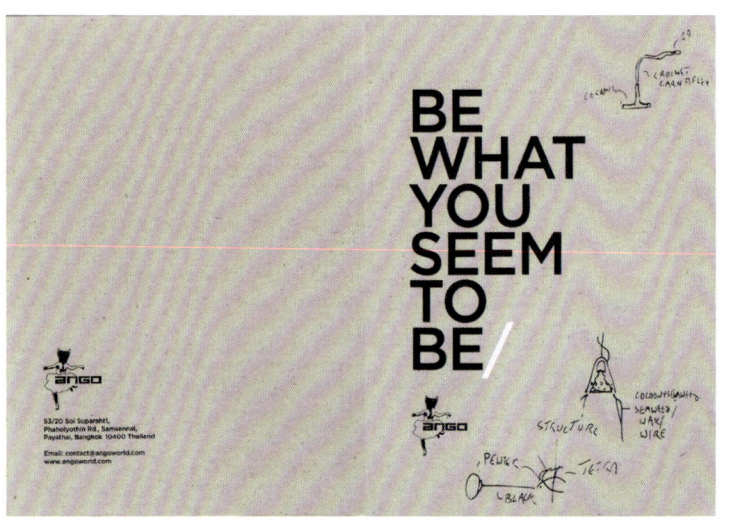

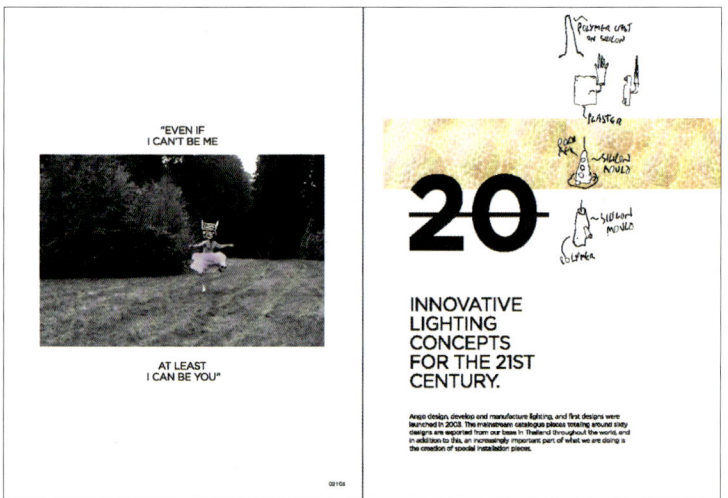

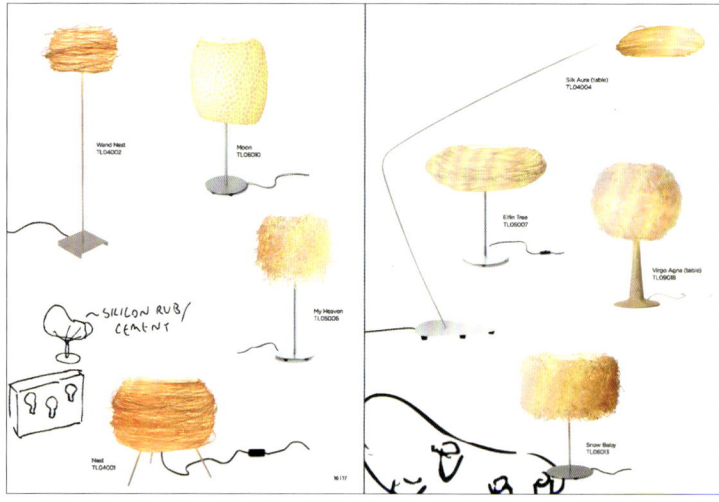

4–1 to 4–4 The "BE WHAT YOU SEEM TO BE" lighting design catalog from Ango plays with an irreverence toward chi-chi design. Ango turns their genius toward marketing with a provocative slap-in-the-face attitude regarding how lighting products enhance and illuminate one's individual personality. Playful, to say the least, the design team focused attention on a light-hearted graphic design with emphasis on sophisticated lighting fixtures and related products that redefine and transform your living and working environment into one that is playful, practical, and beyond the pedestrian. Graphic Design Credit: Apple Chutitanawong (Project No.143). Photography Credits: Remix Studio, New Brain Studio, Surapan Tanta.

WHAT DO WE MEAN BY DESIGN?

The design is original work! The problem is to be resolved using careful research, thorough problem review, planning for an engaging creative experience, construction of form in a model and drawing in two and three dimensions, and realized in analog or digital means.

Creativity and self-expression should be apparent throughout the portfolio and the use of selected materials and formats. Your portfolio tells a story that demonstrates design results and creative concepts and serves as a demonstration of your academic background, office experience, and related experience in the field of interior design. In the next chapter, we explore how to capture images through photography and with other imaging technology to produce your concept and strategy for efficient layout design.

ORIGINS OF CONCEPTS

The tiniest kernel of a sensory experience can kindle our urge to describe a stimulating creative thought. A conversational sketch on a napkin or an odd scrap of paper folded into a 3D model can lend enough information to record an experience and what it felt like.

Design concepts are the embodiment of actual experiences people feel when they enter a doorway, proceed through a passageway, and enter the main space. We document sensory experiences in an attempt to describe new environments composed of the visual elements of light, color, movement, pathways, 2D and 3D forms, and space. A design concept might be inspired by the experience of transparency and the sense of sunlight passing through layers of leaves in a gentle breeze.

A simple concept is hard to forget. Just like working with a lump of clay, design ideas, composed and recomposed in different ways, can be applied to more than a few circumstances. Inspiration is formative. Designers who have the creative urge and willingness to strip away preconceptions and prejudices are able to direct their instincts toward a frontier of new creations. Design concepts are all about ideas—and good designs begin with interesting concepts!

Here's a TIP:

Concept and process are like conducting an orchestra where some instruments take center stage at times or remain in the background and supportive roles. You need to score your portfolio as a rehearsal of what is to happen along the way. Formatting a grid structure to follow can get the job done, but creating a more inspired concept is more challenging and adds "something" that only you can do.

4 FROM CONCEPT TO PROCESS TO LAYOUT DESIGN

Åsa Bollvik

Hailing from Sweden, where a colder climate and seasons of limited light emphasize the importance of a well-designed interior environment, Asa Bollvik carefully takes such matters into consideration when designing interiors as well as her portfolio (figures 4–5 to 4–10). Asa's interior projects differ in scope, spanning cultural, retail, and residential, yet together they represent and demonstrate an approach where she allows function to initially control the aesthetics. The characteristic Scandinavian aesthetic is highly influenced by nature with open layouts, muted colors, and natural materials, all used to mimic their unique landscape and create a timeless design allowed to age beautifully.

Asa created this 11" x 17" format undergraduate portfolio while studying at the Fashion Institute of Technology. Her goal was to present her skills and sense for aesthetics in a legible and cohesive design. She used InDesign for the layout design and PowerPoint to support the visuals, and printed the book on a standard inkjet printer. She used standard binding materials. The total expense for one book was $180.00. Asa's portfolio was created in one semester in a special portfolio course at FIT. She learned the importance of page layout and balance as well as the artistry important to telling a story. She looks forward to using her portfolio in search of employment, and custom-designed variations of it for applications to graduate programs.

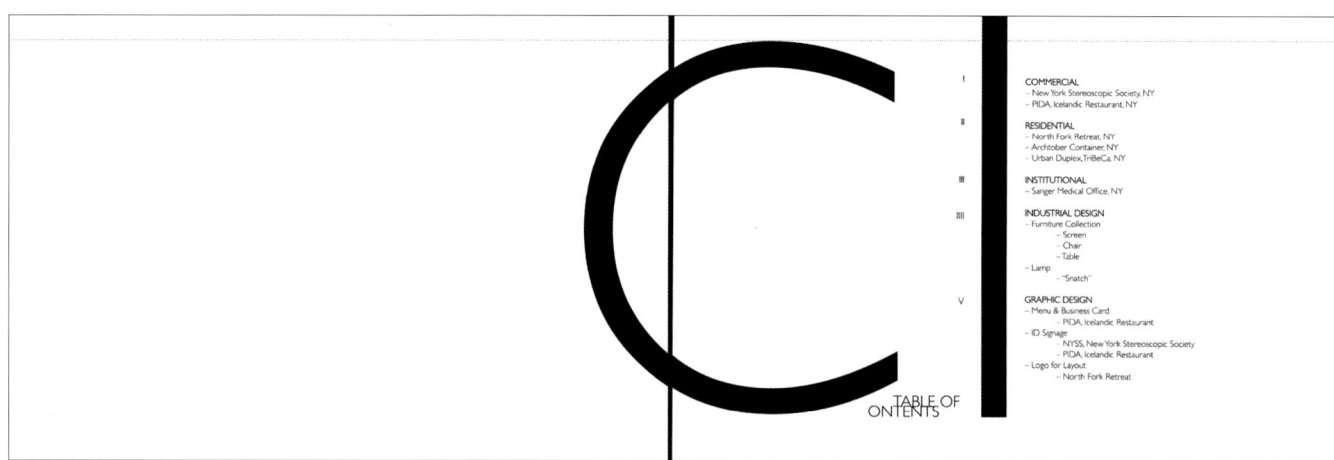

4–5 to 4–10 Asa's portfolio exhibits a strong interest in graphic communications, and her portfolio design supports that with strong opening shapes to signify sections. The black color and strong shapes still allow the warm tones and colors of her projects to remain important. She treats the two-page spread as a total canvas, allowing shapes to overlap the center column in a good way. Asa Bollvik, Fashion Institute of Technology, N.Y., N.Y. 11" x 17".

Origins of Concepts

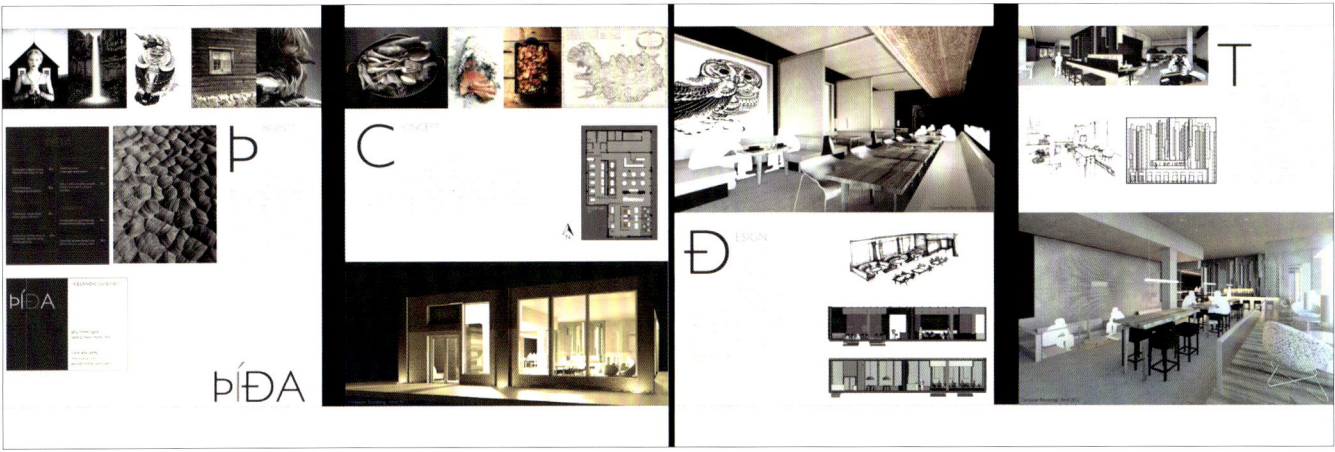

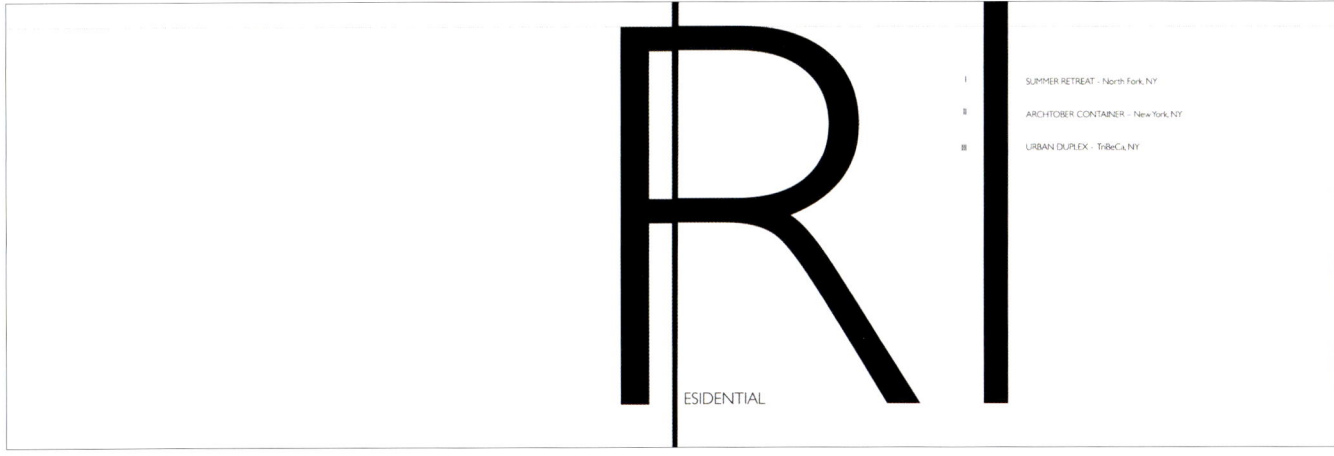

R | SUMMER RETREAT - North Fork, NY
II | ARCHTOBER CONTAINER - New York, NY
III | URBAN DUPLEX - TriBeCa, NY

ESIDENTIAL

ORGANIZATION

The organization of an idea evolves with the vocabulary of design, such as shape, color, texture, and composition. As an aesthetic evolves, a composition emerges that becomes the framework for further action. Aspects of abstraction become more legible as everything gains focus. Your earliest visions are now a framework for making accurate decisions about the experience, shaping and defining its form and composition.

Portfolio design is an unfolding transformative and compelling experience. The individual written portions in a portfolio, such as a design statement, resume, project statements, solution statements, and figure captions, support and serve the overall aesthetic of the book as an object as well as an unfolding spatial experience. Initial elaboration of your schemes offers the gist of your design concept for your portfolio without much detail. They lead, however, to a means of visualization that brings them quickly to the light and to life.

The display of the design of your portfolio might be a particular image or color scheme. It might be an idea to use geometry prominently. It might involve the grid and the play of positive forms/blocks and negative space. Visual concepts tend to be more concrete than writing. Interesting qualities of form and space in your project evidence can often be the seed of thought for the layout design of your portfolio. Tying these things together is like the discovery of a thread that runs through your work and informs what to test with graphics and layout. The visual is about how you'll communicate the verbal.

It's all about a process. Decisions are made based on concept and layout is the realization of those questions that you address along the way. A portfolio, as we have said earlier, is a work in progress. It will change from interview to interview and also as you create new work and replace older projects. As you grow and develop new skills and greater aesthetics over time, the whole concept of process finds interwoven positions within the layout, for they continually overlap with one another.

While concept addresses the big idea that drives the form we call your book, the design will develop your ideas and place them on a blank canvas. Sometimes it is an overwhelming decision to decide what size or shape your book should take. All too often we impose forms that have nothing to do with our projects and our given subject matter. Look at your projects and the shapes that you have designed. That will help you decide what shape will work best for your images. The two must work together. Sometimes, however, forcing the given work into something entirely different can bring about a wonderful layout, such as long projects within a square or even a round shape imposed within that square.

Joe Hynn Yang

Joe Hynn Yang is a graduate student at the NYSID and an authority on Asian art at Sotheby's in New York. He is used to rapid note-taking and visualizing multiple schemes in sketch form. These two pages, shown in figures 4–11 and 4–12, exemplify his extemporaneous visuals and notes taken from a lecture on storyboarding in portfolio design class at NYSID.

Organization

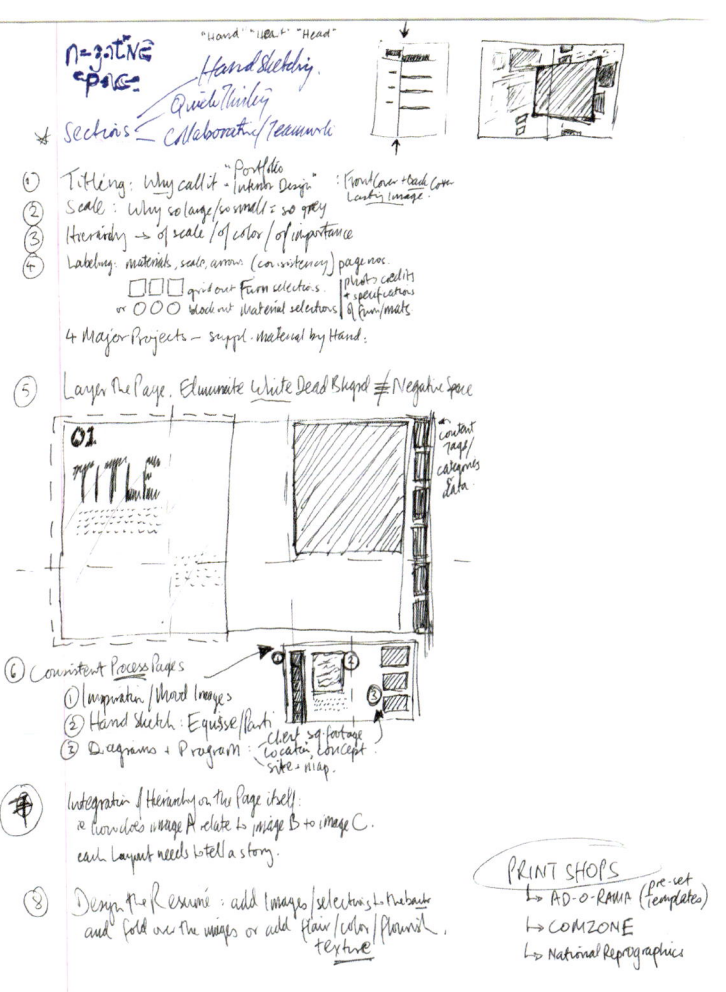
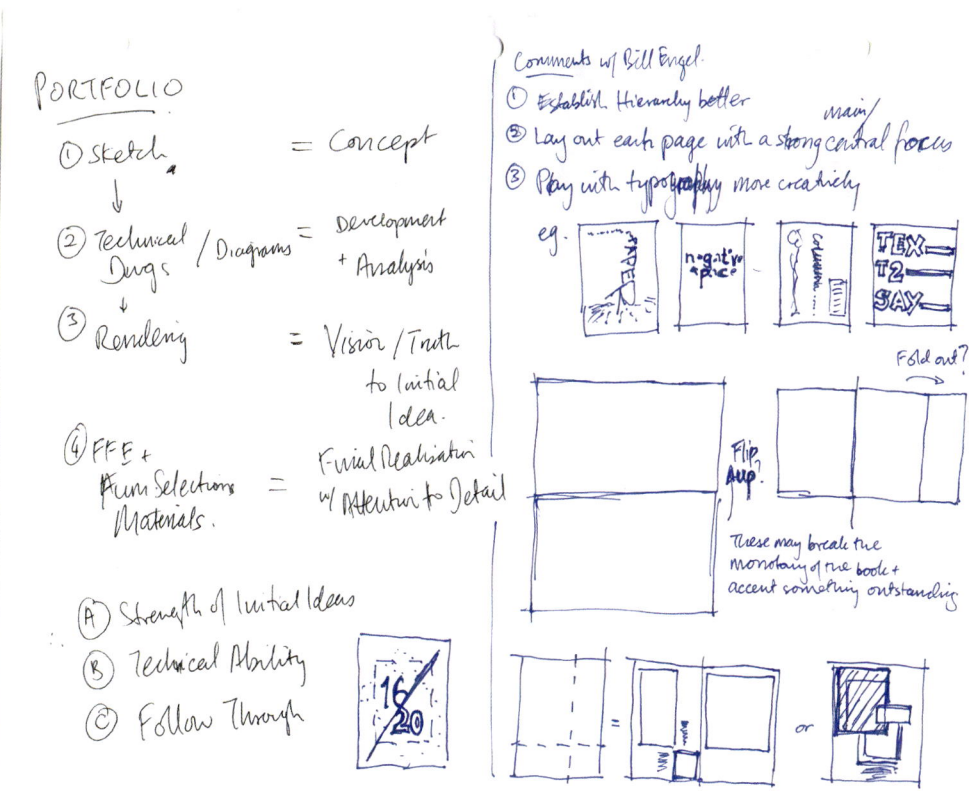

4–11 to 4–12 Rapid storyboard sketching and note-taking. Joe Hynn Yang, New York School of Interior Design, N.Y., N.Y. 8.5" x 11".

4 FROM CONCEPT TO PROCESS TO LAYOUT DESIGN

Stephanie Betesh

Stephanie created the well-disciplined presentation shown in figures 4–13 to 4–18 during her undergraduate years 2 and 3 in the interior design program at the University of Texas-Austin School of Architecture. Her purpose was to showcase skills developed at the university as well as personal projects to create a broad picture of her own abilities. It was equally important to carefully orchestrate each problem so that the viewer would understand the concept that drove each project and its solution. She used the Adobe Creative Suite for the organization of the layout design, refined quality of photographic images, and clarity of illustrations.

The book was printed full bleed on an 80# weight paper stock at a local printer in Austin. The book was bound with a silver coil wire binding that was the least conspicuous solution for the book's aesthetics. She made two different versions: one was the full portfolio to take to interviews and the second was a slimmed down version as a teaser and take-away portfolio to leave behind for potential employers. Especially intriguing about Stephanie's process in designing both books is the way she developed the portfolios as her work progressed in school. Instead of designing them late in her senior year, she began the process knowing how important it would be at the beginning of her sophomore year and then evolved the design as new work came in but also in response to inspiring changes coming to her about the book's layout design! This truly represents the principle of a portfolio as a living and evolving document.

What did Stephanie learn along the way? She responds, "I learned the importance of hierarchy—not making every image the same size, white space is just as important as image, and references like ISSUU are great sources to view the competition."

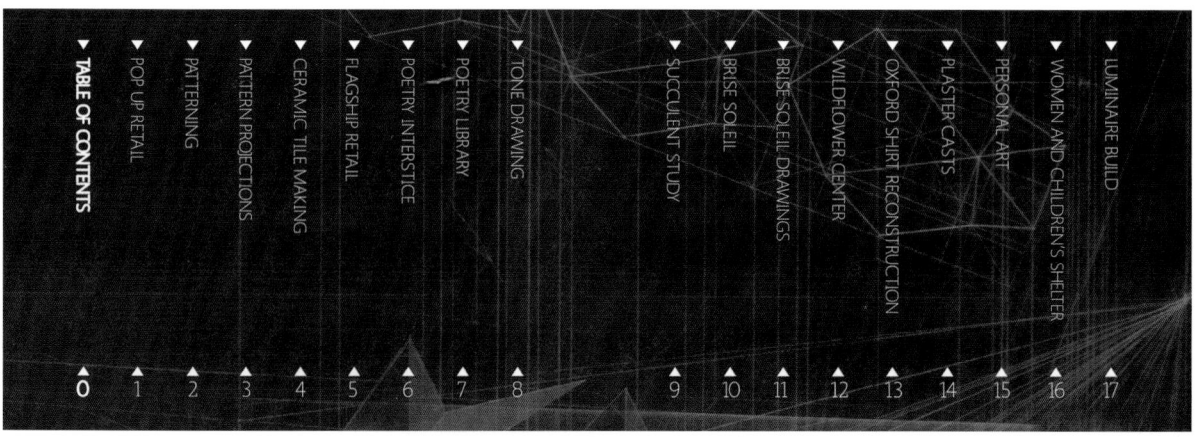

4–13 to 4–18 Stephanie created a very strong portfolio of positive and negative space with bold forms and amplified texture. Her use of vertical typography as if it is descending from space works as a poignant counterpoint linear element imposed over bold shapes, which she uses appropriately throughout many of her page layouts. The structure of her cover page supports her work on the inside of the book. She clearly engineers space not only in her well-drawn perspectives and models but in the overall design of the book. Stephanie Betesh, University of Texas–Austin, Austin, Tex. 8.5" x 11".

Organization

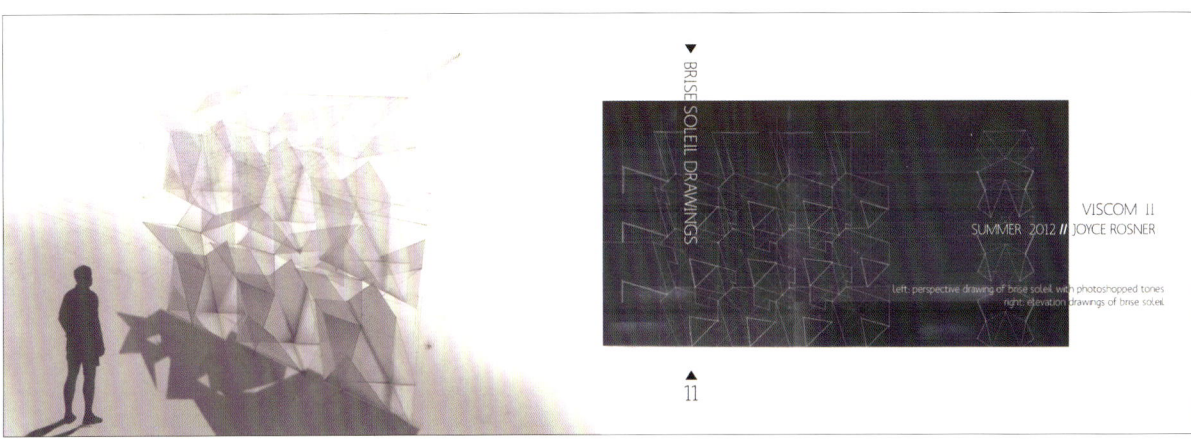

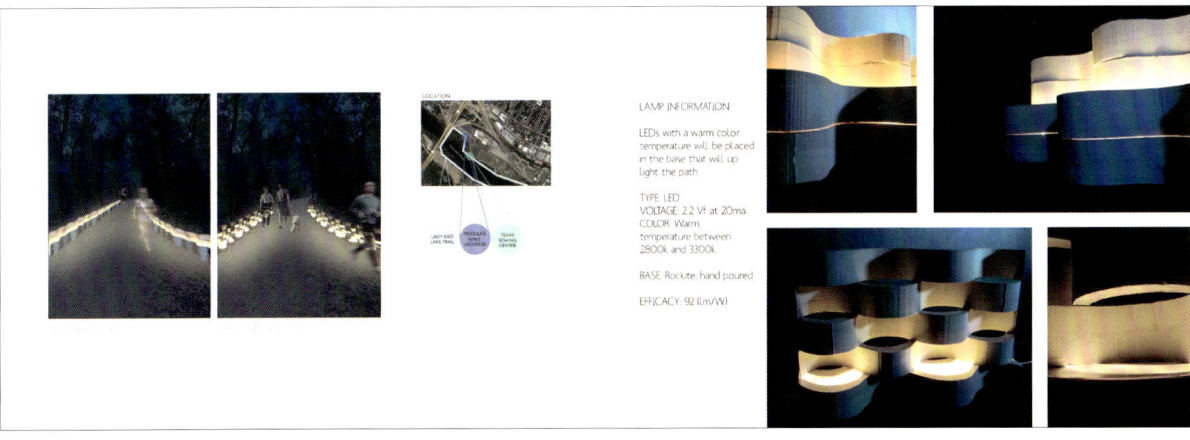

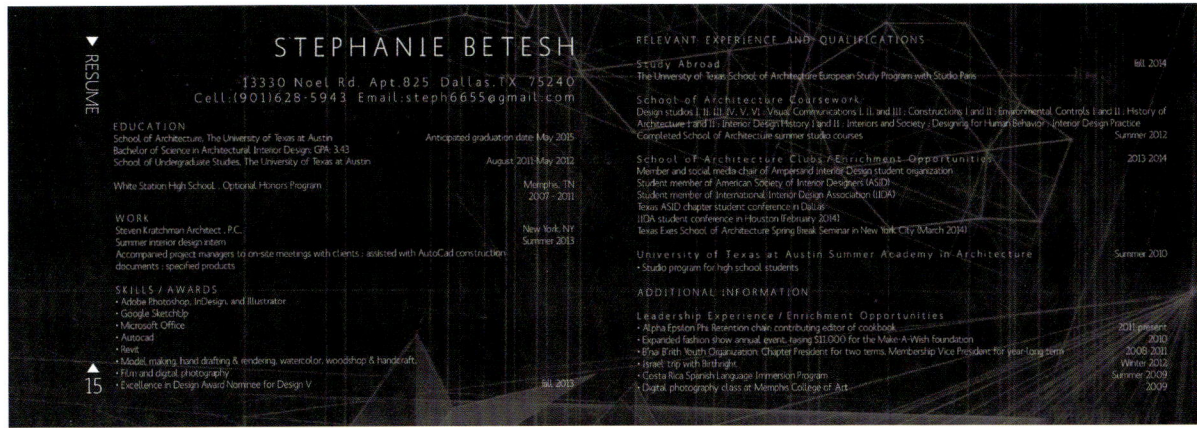

85

4 FROM CONCEPT TO PROCESS TO LAYOUT DESIGN

DESIGNING WITH TYPOGRAPHY

A successful page layout is achieved through the use of both typographic and spatial elements in combination (figures 4–19 to 4–25). Understand what to include, such as headings, subheads, body text, pull quotes, listings, column headings, as well as other visual elements. Use the portfolio inventory list to develop a typographic hierarchy. A sample list is shown in the example of a hierarchy.

Focus on the presentation of content that initiates where to look, and in what sequence. The styling and placement of all elements—both type and images—should guide the viewer through the content in order of importance.

CONTENTS ⟶ **WORK** to be included ⟶ **ELEMENTS** in each
categories, e.g.,   in each category   project, e.g.,

Cover   List projects and   Location
Table of Contents   other work   Inspiration
Professional projects   Concept
Student projects   Program
Other work/skills, e.g.,   Drawings
   Renderings   Sketches
   Construction documents   Materials/Finishes/
Allied interests   Furniture/Lighting

4–19 *(left)* Taking stock of what is useful to include in your portfolio involves a careful inventory of design evidence to determine what best represents design content and how you wish to use it. Portfolio inventory development is a three-phase comprehensive planning outline that enables one to be quite thorough too!

4–20 *(bottom)* Page folds and binding methods. Page folds—Top: Half-fold, gate-fold, tri-fold, Z-fold, accordion-fold, double parallel fold. Binding methods—Top row options result in flat pages: saddle stitch, coil, comb, ring binder, lay-flat. Bottom row options create curved pages (as the last image demonstrates), which require more inner margin to accommodate the gutter: post binder, perfect (soft cover), case wrap (hard cover).

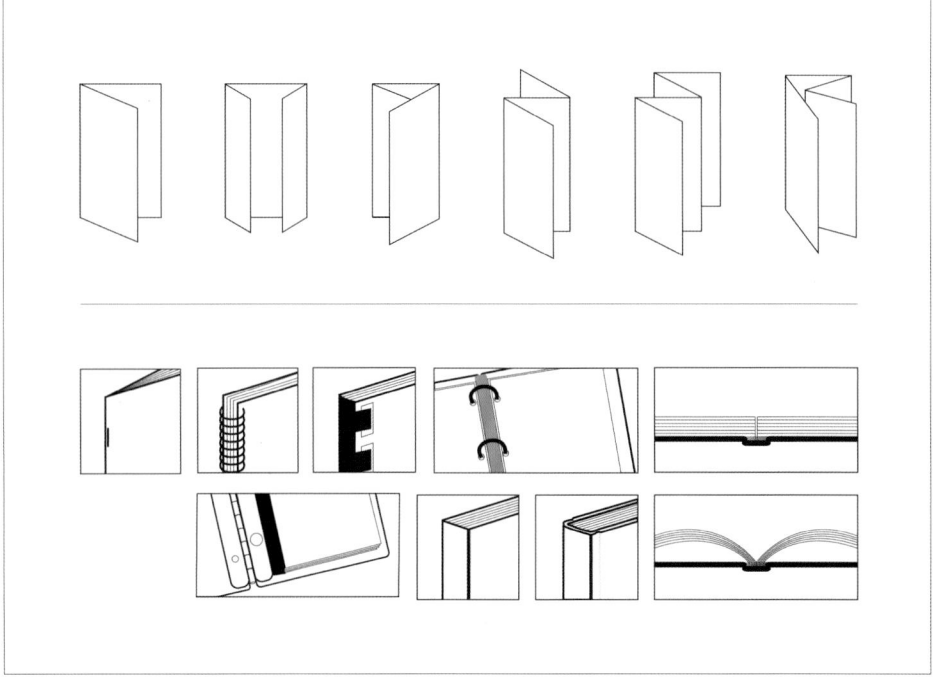

Designing with Typography

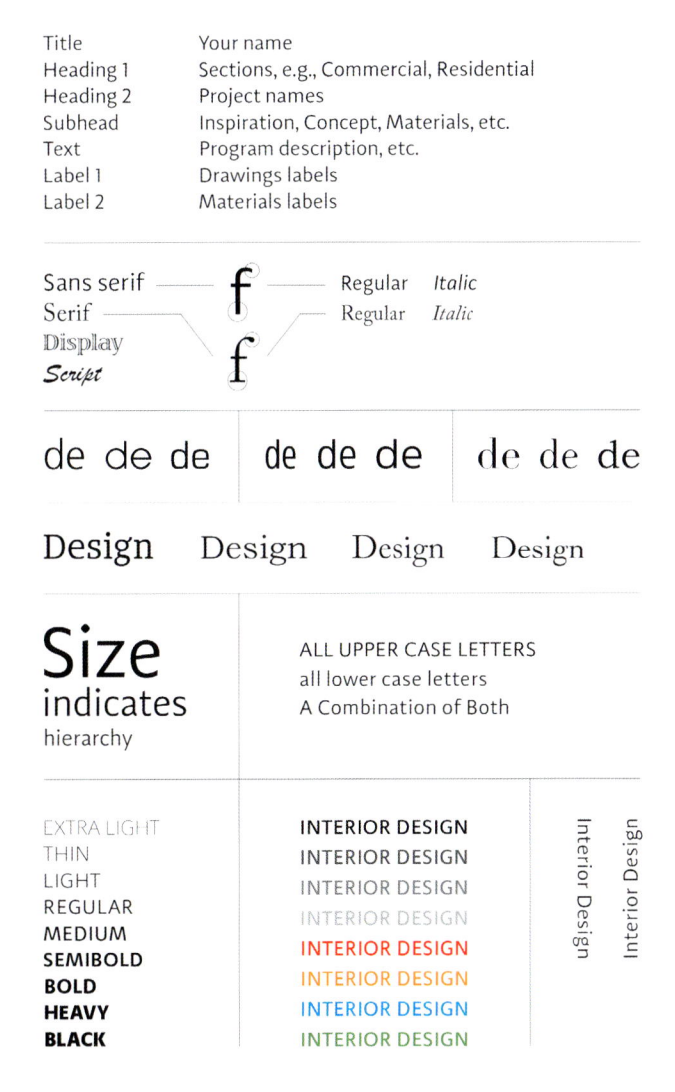

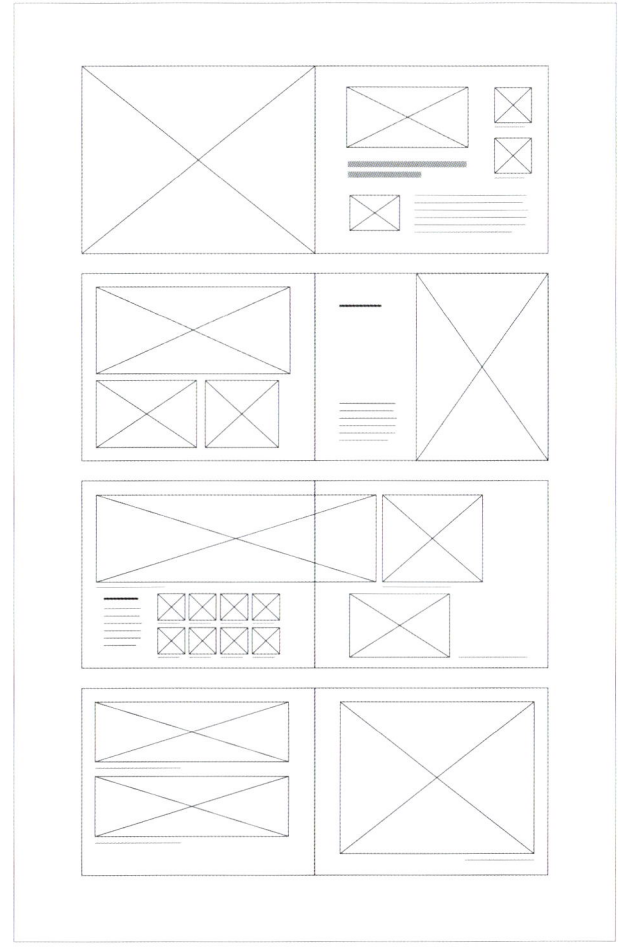

4–21 *(top left)* These studies show front and back covers with facing pages between. Use any number of additional spreads as needed.

4–22 *(top right)* There are innumerable ways to use column structures (vertical divisions) and rows (horizontal divisions) to compose page designs. Explore how images and text (and a portion of negative white space) can lead to a harmonious grouping of elements that can vary from spread to spread and yet retain a thematic or structural sense of organization.

4–23 *(bottom left)* These are the characteristics to consider when choosing typefaces and establishing a hierarchy. Row 1: Establish a strong *typographic hierarchy*. Row 2: *Type classification and style*. Typefaces fall under these four categories. Sans serif and serif are most legible, which makes them useful for much of the content in this application. They are usually available in both regular and italic styles. Row 3: Left—*Shape*. Some typefaces are more oval, round, or square. Center—*Proportion*. Vertical to horizontal. Right—*Contrast*. More or less contrast in stroke thickness. Row 4: *Proportion*. Height of lowercase letters in relation to uppercase letters (X–height). These examples are all the same point size. Row 5: Left—*Size*. Right—*Case*. Row 6: Left—*Weight*. Center—*Color-tint and hue*. Right—*Orientation*.

4 FROM CONCEPT TO PROCESS TO LAYOUT DESIGN

4–24 *(left)* **Letterspacing** can be tight or loose, as can *line spacing*, creating degrees of change in reading speed, which affects overall legibility and comfort when reading. *Paragraph alignment* generally includes flush left, ragged right; flush right, ragged left; justified; and centered.

4–25 *(right)* The organization of major image, supporting images, and text blocks including heading, subhead, problem description, and labels provide a useful practice exercise to work with on the way to designing an active layout for your portfolio. A more formal adherence to the grid above and a looser approach that challenges the grid below are both valid and can even be used in combination within the portfolio.

THE ROLE OF DESIGN PROCESS

Before you decide about whether you will show process studies at the outset of projects in your portfolio, consider the reason why process is important to a reviewer. Process studies demonstrate how well you think things through in the context of problem solving, design communication exercises, and creative team settings. As a tool or skill, the method and media for sketching vary as per the design process, the end product, and the client's expectations.

Sketching throughout the design process is beneficial for large and small projects. Sketching advances from loose, which shows fundamental concepts, through developing detail and definition. Compositions or layouts are refined with detailed sketching and digital visualization. Rapid sketching is also an excellent way to explore ideas quickly. You can resolve multiple design issues and solutions to a design problem at hand; this is an essential step in the design process. It saves time to work through concepts on paper before going to the computer. Searching for the best presentation of design content and layout ideas means making small studies within a double-page spread format, working quickly, and generating a multitude of possibilities in a relatively brief period.

S. Laura-Anne Wong

Laura-Anne created a provocative portfolio with several extensive projects from the graduate architecture program at the University of Michigan. Her interests were in the theory of urban design and emphasis on shaping spaces for living and working. Her abilities in defining provocative concepts and exploring pathways for shaping interior space are well-matched by an extraordinary facility working with software for layout design and 3D imaging, such as the Adobe Creative Suite, Rhino, Maxwell Render, and V-Ray, among others.

The design of her book, which is shown in figures 4–26 to 4–32, was a vision of light including light-sensitive grays, muted tertiary hues, and minimal reflection. Her book was produced in its physical form at Lulu.com. She used a gloss cover stock for paperback production with dull-enamel paper stock, and perfect bookbinding. She made two copies for $30.00.

> " Your portfolio is a golden opportunity to show not only what you have already accomplished, but to chart a new trajectory of what you want to do in the future."
>
> – **LISA LEAGUE**, NCIDQ, LEED GREEN ASSOCIATE.

4 FROM CONCEPT TO PROCESS TO LAYOUT DESIGN

Among the many lessons one can learn from this book are that designing with subtle weights of gray lends a cohesive visual theme to the project while grounding the graphics throughout the presentation. Another notable strategy in the creation of the portfolio was that it takes less time to design the book than the time required to assemble all the work files and make sure they are of a consistent professional level for final layout design. Deadlines sometimes are very helpful in squeezing time into managing priorities. You also discover that some decisions regarding details along the way definitely don't matter as much as the goal of your vision in the end. The result was a successful product that communicated content in a simple and elegant manner. She received several offers for interviews and employment from well-known firms across the country.

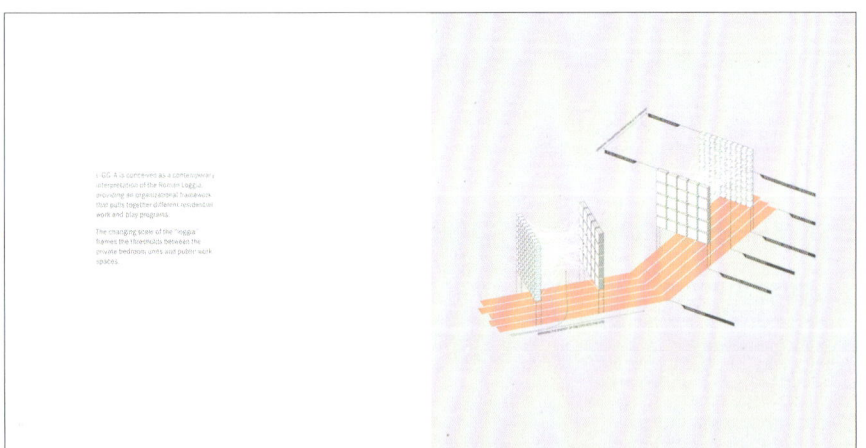

4–26 to 4–32 Laura has a unique way of showing her work throughout her graduate portfolio. Axonometric drawings reveal her design process while providing understanding of spatial relationships that breathe and float on the white space throughout the portfolio. It is an important study of the flow of space for residential and work domains and her graphics and site drawings demonstrate that not only is it a clear concept but that it works on so many levels of visual communications, problem solving, spatial analysis, planning, and eventually graphic design. The gray typography is another elegant and understated element that remains a secondary support role to her drawings and the elegant entourage about the human factor in architecture and interior design. It just doesn't get much better than this! S. Laura-Anne Wong, University of Michigan, Ann Arbor, Mich. 7.5" x 7.5" paperback.

The Role of Design Process

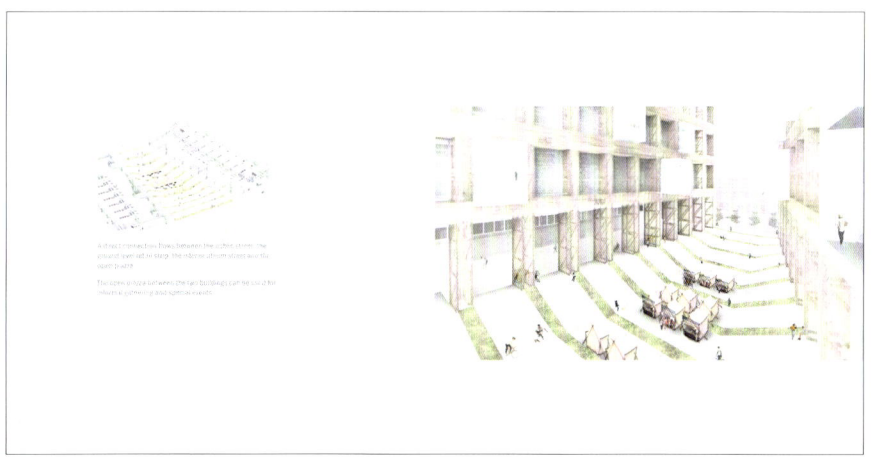

4 FROM CONCEPT TO PROCESS TO LAYOUT DESIGN

VISUALIZING THE WORDS

A string of written thoughts that inform the reader about the core of your visual thinking is necessary for either your design statement or as a solution statement to each project—and perhaps both. The purpose of the opening design statement near the table of contents is to introduce yourself not just in terms of a biography but also to include a concise, single-page narrative regarding your interests, abilities, and direction in interior design. Just like writing a composition, honing the outline before embarking into prose is advantageous toward thoroughly understanding the breadth and depth of an opening design statement or a written concept that introduces a design project later in your book.

Students should take this opportunity to develop their writing in context with their work because it speaks volumes to a prospective employer or academic review committee regarding the articulation, organization, and priorities of a potential applicant. More than this, well-written documents throughout the portfolio are integral to your narratives. They are like lily pads allowing the reader to follow your research, creative trajectory, and practical abilities, plus your business sense and planning.

Here's a TIP:

You might find, as I do, that getting away from actively developing a concept and letting your inner mind work on the problem leads to the best results. Your form board may be influential to arriving at an idea for the layout design of your book. It is a collection of thoughts about precedents, current trends, and influences. Form boards are equally appropriate to include at the beginning of an interior design project in your portfolio as inspiration for a given design studio project.

THE UMBRELLA CONCEPT

The best designs start with an exciting concept. Your concept is how you'll solve the problem of communicating your perceived purpose for the portfolio's design. While there is no one way to implement a concept, the first necessary step is gathering information. You collect information in a number of ways, such as through your intellectual research of portfolio examples from the history of visual communications, interior design, and architecture, and, from pre-modern art and design periods (19th and 20th century) until the present. The more information you have the better you'll be able to create different concepts for the layout design both verbally and visually. They all help to determine how you'll convey that message. Knowing the visual elements that support your idea is helpful because they contribute to defining the problem and your potential best approach to the layout design.

Concepts emerge from almost any source, sometimes in words or visual images and sometimes from other sensory experiences like touch, smell, and sound. Words descriptive of the senses are often what people think and feel when reviewing a project or visiting a site. It's part of the experience you want them to have. Design elements need to be in harmony with the concept, communicating the same message.

A ROAD MAP: TYPICAL CONCEPTUAL PROCESS FOR THE LAYOUT DESIGN OF A PORTFOLIO

Research, Programming, and Schematic Design

- Determine the primary purpose(s) of the portfolio and its requirements.
- Determine what can be retained from existing school projects and office materials.
- Develop basic grid concepts and decide what will work as an overall schematic for the book.
- Prepare and test a few different preliminary page layout strategies.
- Review for feedback with a trusted faculty mentor or experienced colleague.

Design Development

- Test at least three different layout design schemes, including page orientations of portrait or landscape.
- Finalize selections of typographic styles, text blocks, and images from your library.
- Sketch various compositions of the flow of text and visuals together.
- Finalize the selection of projects to be included as representing all requisite abilities and design knowledge.

Review Important Professional Documents

- After final approval of all critical documents, prepare appropriate documents to save in folders per project.
- Consult with any other professionals as necessary regarding structural specifications and legal documents.
- Demonstrate documents such as bid specifications for furnishings, built-ins, and so on.
- Prepare a budget for the creation of one or more books.
- Review plans, specifications, and budget with a trusted and experienced colleague or mentor.

Publication and Online Planning

- Obtain competitive bids for more than one print/web service.
- Review all bids from printers and online suppliers.
- Arrange for timely commencement of work.
- Schedule test pages and work sequence to enable a rapid completion of the project.
- Review print tests and online versions of work for the portfolio.
- Supervise completion of work.

4 FROM CONCEPT TO PROCESS TO LAYOUT DESIGN

Jennifer Jenkins

Jennifer graduated in interior design from the Art Institute of Austin. Her purpose was to organize her portfolio (figures 4–33 to 4–38) to reflect her interests and her desired trajectory in practicing professional design. Moreover, she wanted to underscore her commitment to design in various ways, including concept development and design process. Her hope was to draw attention to her passion, intentions, and background preparation by making sure visuals and technical work were clear and well presented.

She used Adobe InDesign, Photoshop, and Illustrator as well as AutoCAD and Revit for technical work. She printed the portfolio on a large format printer using card stock to lend a substantial feel to the book. The parts included cover letter, resume, mailer inserts, and design objective statement. She made twenty mailers and used about half of the production before finding a position. The work included in the portfolio was created during her three-year program at the Art Institute. Jennifer believes the whole project was successful. Most importantly, each component represents who she is as a person and designer. The most important lessons learned were the critical importance of evolving a concept for the book and all supporting parts, including branding and strategy. Among the inspiring sources she explored was Simon Sinek's TED Talk, "How Great Leaders Inspire Action."

Jennifer received several offers but found a dream job with CTA Architects and Engineers in Austin where she is learning a great deal about the allied design disciplines while making important contributions to the office and community with confidence. With ambitions to eventually go to graduate school in a few years, she is busy building the next leg of her journey.

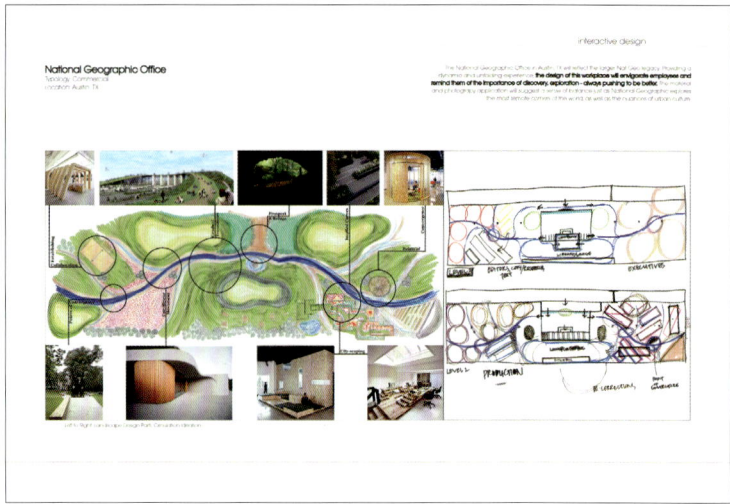

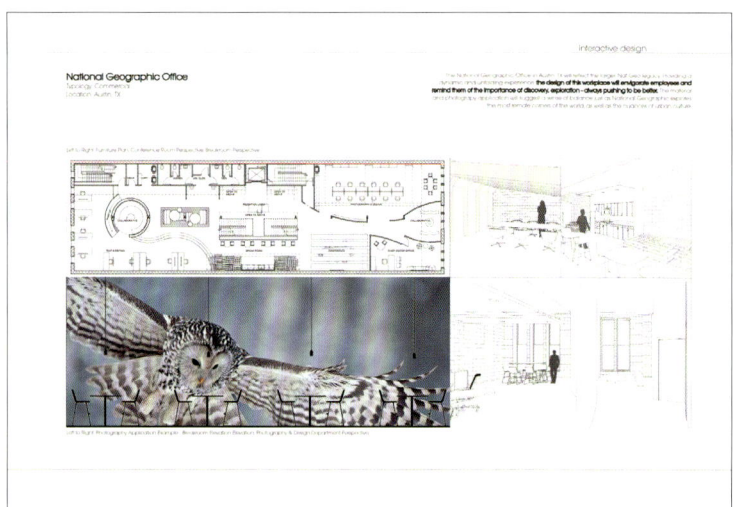

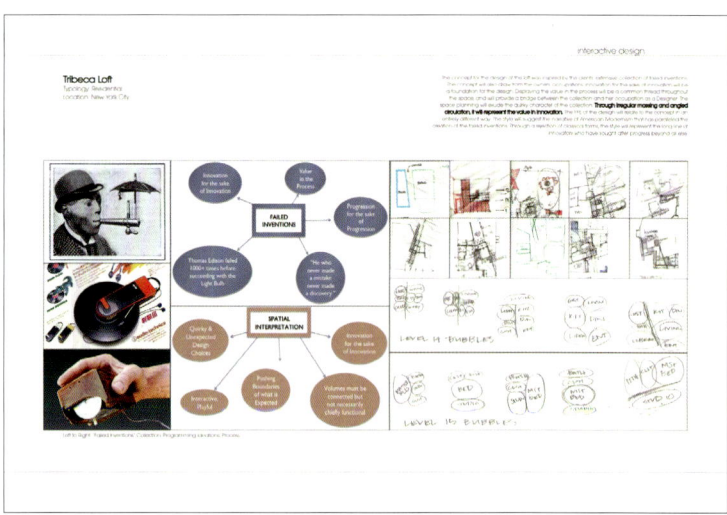

4–33 to 4–38 Jennifer chose to portray the process of design and her thinking throughout this portfolio. She also shows skill in hand drawing that is uniquely tied to her computer graphics and rendering. Spatial bubble diagrams and interconnected planning process is highlighted. We think this is a good example of what many employers ask for across the board, and that is the ability to show thinking and process and not just finished slick renderings. The parti ideations study of written documents will probably not be read by any employer simply because of time, but nonetheless shows that this designer can do research and gain in-depth understanding of a problem. We think this is a great attribute of any design portfolio. Jennifer Jenkins, Art Institute of Austin, Austin, Tex. 11" x 17".

A Road Map: Typical Conceptual Process for the Layout Design of a Portfolio

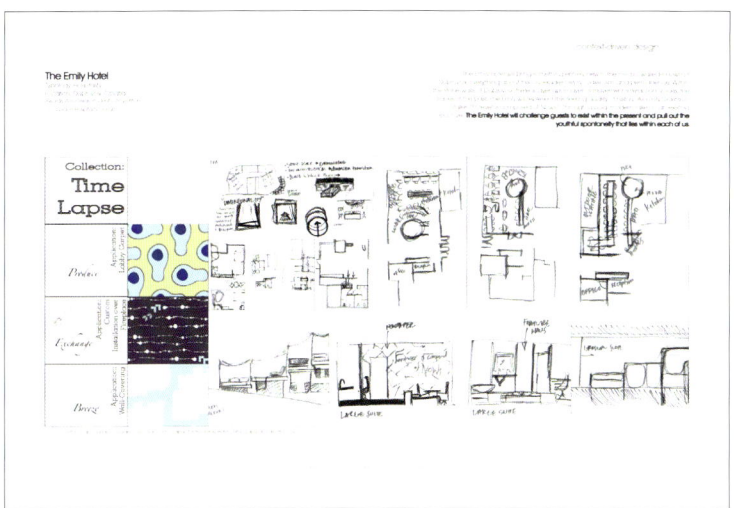

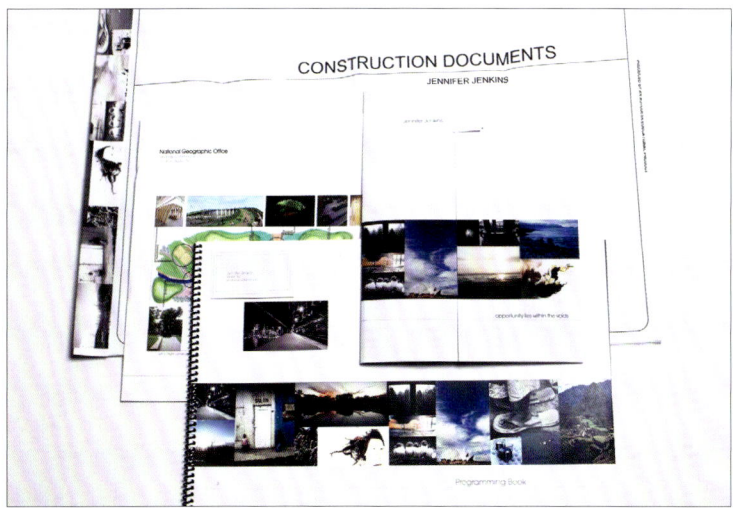

LAYOUT AND VISUALIZATION

Creating a design or illustration refinement involves many stages of visual communications. Following several rounds of design sketching, a digital designer moves to the computer. The process of sketching then moves into digital drafts. The importance of sketching in any given project is well understood. In today's office practice, designers must know how to go seamlessly to software such as Revit, Studio Max Pro, and Photoshop. As the project progresses, client corrections are requested for approval. Interior designers often prefer digital solutions at almost every stage of design development. The designer decides which media (illustration, virtual or physical models, or multimedia) will get the job done in the most efficient and inventive way as a deadline looms. The layout for an interior design portfolio can begin with a single page with a brief biographic design statement that describes your interests, abilities, and direction in design.

1. Start with an Interesting Statement

A design statement is about you as an emerging designer. An effective design statement at the beginning of your portfolio includes two or three relatively brief paragraphs about who you are, your accomplishments, skills, and abilities, your passions, and your goals for the future. Summarize your design career with a focus on experience, preparation, and future aspirations. Another approach to discussing your background is to introduce your experience and accomplishments in tandem with each project statement throughout your portfolio so that the evidence of your abilities is shown in context with your work.

2. Maintain a Group of Successful Projects in Your Portfolio

Select a group of approximately eight to ten projects that represent a range of skills and are reflective of your goals and the position you wish to achieve. Too many projects and you begin to water down the strength and distort the focus of the book. Locate your best projects at the beginning, middle, and end of your book. Every page has two sides—a front and back. So when we talk about the page count being between 20–25 physical pages, we are actually speaking about printing on both sides, meaning 40–50 faces of information.

3. Choose Recent or Relevant Projects for Your Portfolio

Projects in your portfolio should be as recent as possible, unless a past project supports where you want to go and the quality of the project is good. Give priority to commercial work over concept or schoolwork. When making the representative selection of work to include, consider removing older projects so that the work appears as a whole to be recently completed in the last couple of years.

4. Ensure Your Portfolio Represents Your Across-the-Board Accomplishments

The portfolio has a purpose. The purpose of each project in your portfolio is to form a palette of abilities that represents a broad range of your skills. The work orchestrates the use by demonstrating all of your capabilities. What a project lacks, another should include. The compilation of all the work represents a picture of you in the context of finding a rewarding position suitable to your realistic potential on the job.

5. Include Teamwork

Describe your role and responsibilities in a team/group design project. Be as clear as possible in describing your role in that project. Collaboration is the nature of professional practice.

6. Direct the Composition of Your Portfolio to Focus on the Job You Seek

A variety of projects and presentation styles help make your portfolio relevant to a broad audience. If you can include projects that you know are unique to the nature of work of a firm, the reviewer will have an easier time assessing and understanding your fit for their practice.

Layout and Visualization

> "It is imperative that portfolios be prepared today in digital format as well as hardcopy. Consequently, we have introduced a course that teaches Adobe Suite as part of the core curriculum. These skills are also helpful in the daily work of a designer."
>
> – **RACHEL HAGNER**, PROGRAM DIRECTOR, INTERIOR DESIGN, BERKELEY EXTENSION, UNIVERSITY OF CALIFORNIA, SAN FRANCISCO, CA

7. Know What You Want to Do as a Designer

It takes time in school to evolve into your work and discover what type of design you want to do. Sometimes one creates a broad representation of design in their book because that has been the nature of their education and response to studio projects. There are various exceptions to this point, such as a portfolio filled with outputs from renderings, plans, elevations, sections, details, lighting plans, and a range of basic model studies. The combined strength of these documents can result in a position on a design team doing what you were doing in school but on an advanced level. Take the time to determine what you want in your design career. Gaining an initial position will expose you to the full operations of a practice and allow you to find your way in honing your future goals and aspirations.

8. Use Your Portfolio as a Living Document

A portfolio should always be evolving and living in beta or a testing state. Update your book twice a year, or at the very least, update it annually. Do not allow for work or documentation to go missing, because a job opportunity might arise that could leave you scrambling to get things organized before the submission deadline. The Scout's motto applies here: "Be prepared."

9. Create a Killer Portfolio

A good way to get started is to create a template by using the grid technique (popular with graphic designers) and populate your design work from there. It is always tempting to over-style your portfolio, especially if you have a high octane personal brand, but at the end of the day, the best thing to do is keep your layout design simple. You don't want the background or portfolio layout to overshadow your design work.

10. Decide on Digital vs. Printed Portfolio

The new means of digital communication is replacing print portfolios and becoming standard. Don't discard your book, though; the honesty and tangibility of the hard-copy print medium could be winning factors that enable you to find your next design job. It is still important to design for the medium. An excellent layout for a printed portfolio will require revision to work on a laptop screen or projector.

4 FROM CONCEPT TO PROCESS TO LAYOUT DESIGN

Ilijana Soldan

Ilijana's portfolio (figures 4–39 to 4–43) was created in her final semester of undergraduate study at the Virginia Commonwealth University School of the Arts. Her intention was to showcase the progression of her work throughout undergraduate study both in terms of design development and graphic communication. The layout design was completed entirely in InDesign. A wide assortment of software went into the creation of all the projects inside of her book including AutoCAD, Revit, Illustrator, Rhino, and SketchUp, along with hand-rendering and hand-modeling.

The portfolio was produced at a local print shop using laser printing nearby her school. In order to avoid transparency and images ghosting through from behind the paper, she chose a slightly heavier stock (32 lb paper stock) in a semi-gloss finish rather than typical copy-weight 20 lb or 24 lb paper. In addition, she selected vellum papers for overlays to bind with the book as floor plans and circulation diagrams were appropriate. Occasionally, bifold pages were also inserted to open when detailed large format presentations were required. She bound the book with an inconspicuous white metal ring.

She has made individual portfolios throughout her education for various purposes. Having spent time in revising her work and assembling presentations for course reviews and applications for employment, she is quite adept at working with grids and layout strategies. She added her senior thesis project to her basic portfolio and spent a substantial effort (approximately 25 hours) customizing her book for each graduate program throughout the country. Altogether, she spent a full semester of 100+ hours including portfolio workshops and critiques creating several books.

The product was completely successful. Ilijana remarked, "A portfolio represents the core of who you are as a designer. Everything you believe should be reflected within these pages. Having a portfolio that truly represents you sets the initial impression about you with anyone looking at it. For me, our graphic design students helped enormously with countless questions and suggestions." With the help of her portfolio and resume as a branding package, she was able to find employment quickly after graduation as well as acceptances to the all of the graduate schools she made application to.

4–39 to 4–43 Ilijana Soldan's portfolio is a fine example of the rigor of design communication with an underlying structure and order—the grid can be inferred after a few spreads, which indicates an interest in and practice with rational systems and relates to her design work. The text and graphic devices are simplified, lending weight and emphasis to her projects, which belies a sensibility about honesty and integrity in design; there are few places for the designer to camouflage poor work with eyewash and distractions. Confidence is one of the strongest attributes of a good designer, and this portfolio communicates security and self-assuredness. Ilijana used her name to become a concept. Like the great Louis Kahn statement "Order is," we have Ilijana's "Design is," formed of course from her initials, but supported by the work in her book. Her book is laced with sensitive watercolor renderings. She tops that by adding a full-page collaborative project with scale models and follows up with a full-size model of an ergonomic chair she designed. Ilijana Soldan, Virginia Commonwealth University. Richmond, Va. 8.5" x 11".

Layout and Visualization

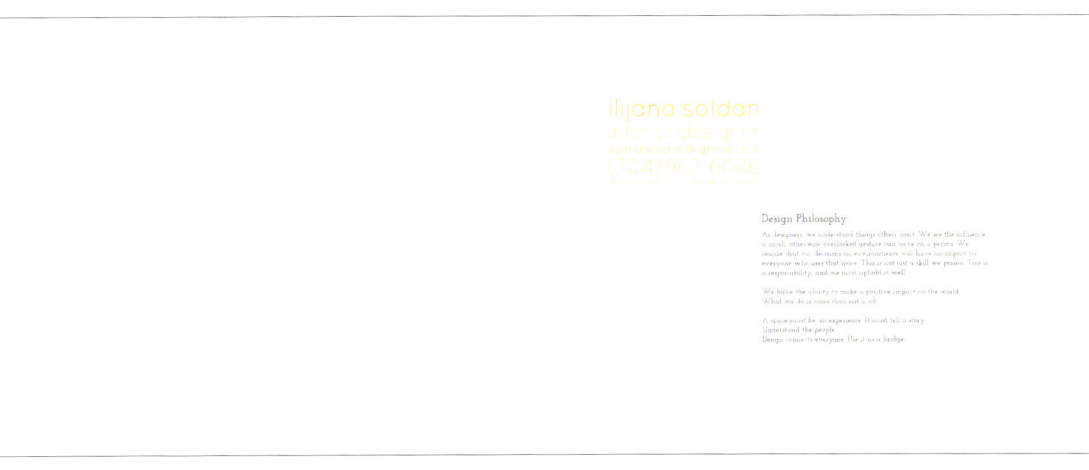

CHECKERS OR CHESS

Long ago, my dad was a pro-am chess player. He enjoyed playing exhibition games in department store lobbies open to the passerby to stop and watch the games (and shop)! He lost matches infrequently. When you interview for a design position, you are competing against numerous designers with the same purpose. Your concept needs to be better than the competition. The rigor of being a designer is about keeping your finger on the pulse of the profession. Know the conventions of portfolio design and what is typical of a fair presentation. Then figure out how to best the conventional display. That by itself gives you plenty to investigate and think about to gain a leg up.

Your search to discover an exciting concept for your portfolio is intended to bring something of a surprise and unexpected ingredient to the idea for the book. Perhaps you wish to use chipboard for the front and back and pack the book full of the process with the theme in mind that you are a maker and, therefore, your work concerns industry and materials. Your goal is always to discover something truthful and interesting about yourself and make that relevant to all who review your book. Chelsea Stafford put herself on the line with her presentation for redesigning the corporate offices of Red Bull.

Chelsea Stafford

Chelsea graduated from the Kendall College of Art and Design with a major in Interior Design. Her portfolio (figures 4–44 to 4–46) demonstrates skill in hand drawing as well as growing abilities in layout and design. Her project for Red Bull has a good sense of contemporary office space organization and this works well with her computer illustration abilities. She worked on the portfolio project during a full semester with other coursework. Chelsea used InDesign and Photoshop to create the book's layout design and adjust image color and lighting. She felt that the entire project was as challenging as any other project in her curriculum.

4–44 to 4–46 Chelsea included a photo of herself on the cover of her portfolio. She presents herself smiling, as someone you want to get to know, and not simply a mug shot on a driver's license. She artfully crops the forms around her image that support the shapes in the portfolio and interior design. Chelsea Stafford, Kendall College of Art and Design, Grand Rapids, Mich. 8.5" x 11".

Checkers or Chess

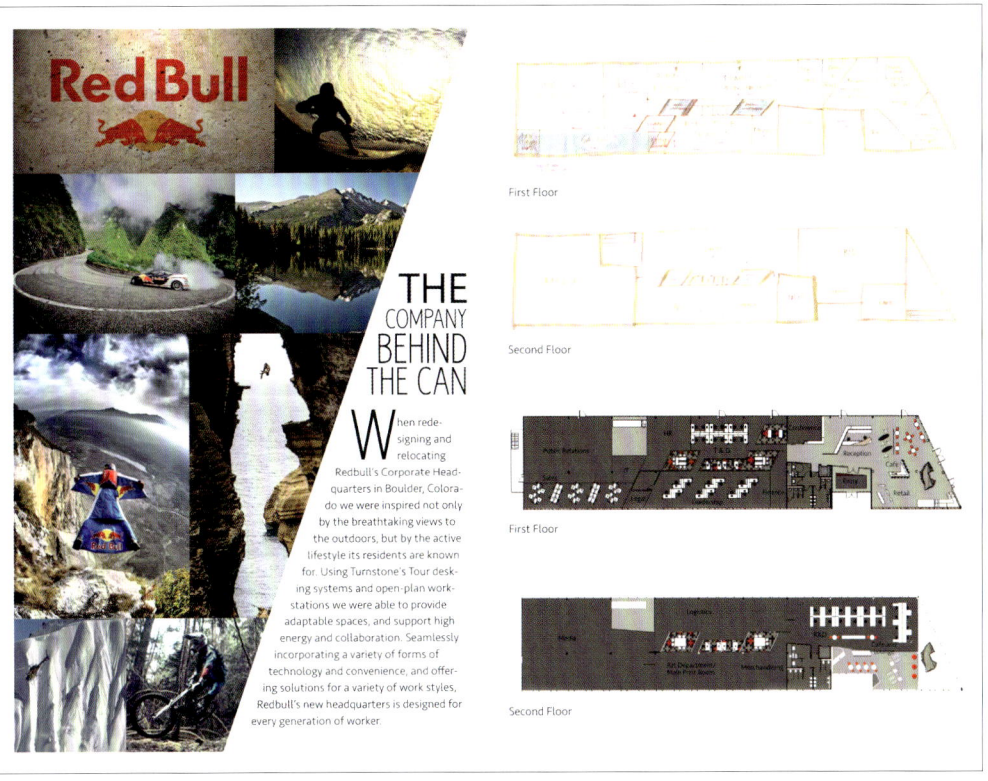

THE COMPANY BEHIND THE CAN

When redesigning and relocating Redbull's Corporate Headquarters in Boulder, Colorado we were inspired not only by the breathtaking views to the outdoors, but by the active lifestyle its residents are known for. Using Turnstone's Tour desking systems and open-plan workstations we were able to provide adaptable spaces, and support high energy and collaboration. Seamlessly incorporating a variety of forms of technology and convenience, and offering solutions for a variety of work styles, Redbull's new headquarters is designed for every generation of worker.

First Floor

Second Floor

First Floor

Second Floor

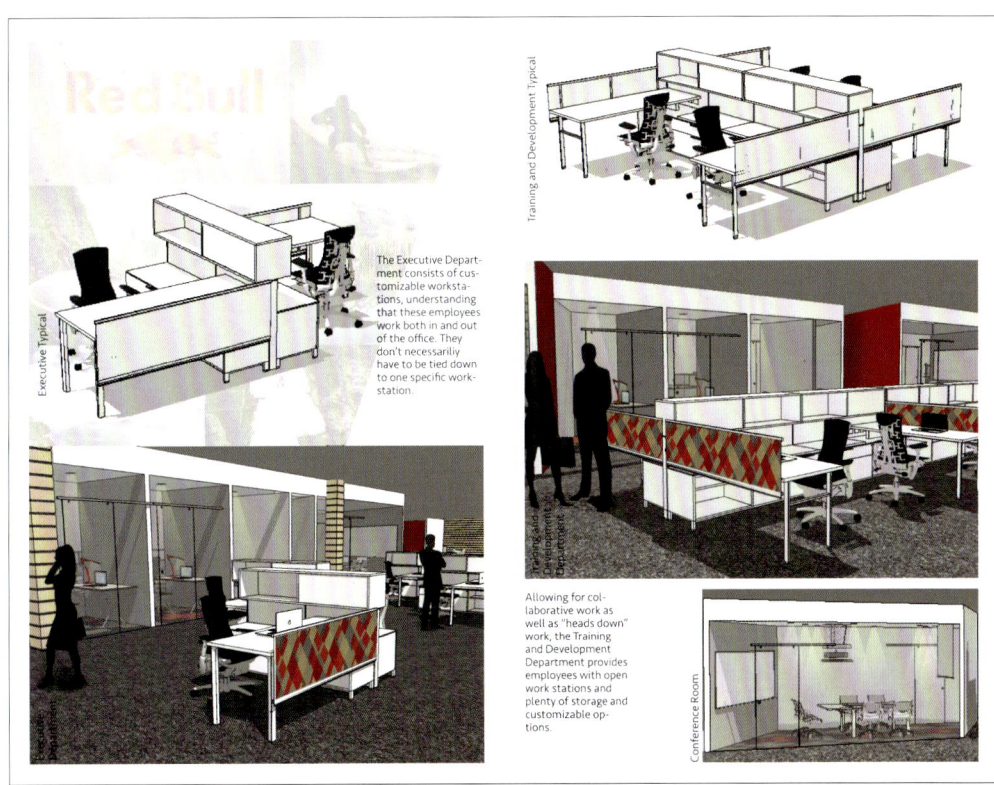

The Executive Department consists of customizable workstations, understanding that these employees work both in and out of the office. They don't necessarily have to be tied down to one specific workstation.

Allowing for collaborative work as well as "heads down" work, the Training and Development Department provides employees with open work stations and plenty of storage and customizable options.

101

4 FROM CONCEPT TO PROCESS TO LAYOUT DESIGN

BUSINESS PERSPECTIVE: SKETCHING, STORYBOARDS, AND LAYOUTS

Showing thumbnails or rough compositions in a portfolio demonstrates your understanding of how business progresses with a client in an office setting. Quick, simple sketching saves an enormous office time. Make sure the customer is in agreement with your choice of design before moving forward to invest hours in designs. Request thumbnail approvals from clients as a standard part of the illustration and design multi-stage process. It is especially common on broad and complex interior design projects and other architectural projects as well. Consider the design of your portfolio to be a large complex job. If your sketching has clarity and sensitivity to line and value, it can be quite a bonus for a design firm to have you on board. If your sketching has an architectural feel and you can bring context and set into your drawings with simple graphic conventions and reference to the setting for the project, the client will be better educated regarding the stream of drawing conventions and what to expect from the firm and design team regarding visual communications. Including these drawings in your portfolio in sequence with a portfolio project or printed on vellum as an overlay on a plan expands the context and value of preliminary drawings.

Storyboards are frame-by-frame visuals of an unfolding event or project. They are useful to chart the subsequent development of content in your book project by project but also visual by visual. Storyboards are used informally as a journaling activity to record and explore your interests on many subjects. It can be used to explore multiple options you could take in a particular design.

A storyboard for a portfolio is concerned with how image and text are utilized in every project. In addition, it has a strategic advantage in rehearsing what kinds of process investigations will accompany each project and to what extent they will unfold within other materials in that project. They could look like horizontal or vertical small film strips, overlays on vellum of free-hand drawing, or carefully orchestrated studies within a grid structure guiding position and placement.

Aside from storyboards, free-hand drawing and sketching are often used to facilitate design research in multiple fields of industry and design; these can make for a powerful concluding section in one's book. In the sketch area of a portfolio, the goal is to visually explore topics germane to the subject at hand. A well-drawn storyboard can be carefully organized and included in the back section or end materials of your book.

CONCEPTS LEAD

Think of graphic design as a way to couple your concept with an application of a grid design in subtle and understated ways. Testing various ways that unify and create harmony between your content and page layout should take the lead in your layout design process. If your concept is one of luxury and formal elegance, you know right away that you need to use more white space to suggest luxury through clarity and simplicity. Similarly, individual color schemes are sometimes the result of market focus and therefore a specific range in palettes would be preferable over others.

Here's a TIP:

Your concept will show you where to go with specific layout design decisions. It's the roadmap you come back to again and again throughout the design process. If something isn't working, it's probably because it doesn't fit the concept. If nothing is working with your layout, you might want to explore a different idea.

JUGGLING

As you explore graphic concepts for the design of your portfolio, realize that you are organizing a layout with at least seven unresolved design questions in the air: layout design, typography, design content, paper, printing, photography, and binding, just to name a few. Recognize the fullness of the problem and the individual parts. Keep your mind open and allow each of the parts to find each other. Allow the process of designing the book to focus on trial studies. Experimentation will lead you to a more integrated and especially well-orchestrated production. Know your purpose! Research your competition. Learn how to persist in your design vision as you work with the issues mentioned above toward an interesting result.

There's no right way to generate an idea. What works for one designer won't necessarily work for another. However, there are parts of the process that everyone should go through. You can't solve a problem without knowing what that problem is. Before developing a concept for a website or portfolio, you need to answer questions about your book's purpose, the possible expectations of the reviewer, market competition, and your goals for the web page or book. Your process should always begin with the seven items mentioned above, understanding the purpose of the book and researching the interior design firm or graduate program you wish to attend.

Wei Tsun Lin

Wei Tsun Lin's portfolio design concept, shown in figures 4–47 and 4–48, embrace the idea of a remix, a different version of a musical recording produced by remixing. His playful portfolio concept serves as the basis for conceiving each project in the book to be an individual record with its own dust jacket and design content. In his case of several projects, each design is revitalized and transformed by the designer developing a new conceptual basis for each project and then designing original packaging for the portfolio.

4–47 to 4–48 Music album remix concept design for each project and collective packaging for the entire portfolio. Wei Tsun Lin, New York School of Interior Design, N.Y., N.Y. 8" x 9".

5

CAPTURING
EXPRESSIVE IMAGES

"Sensing is a way of looking at the people, places and things around us. Have you ever tried to view the world from someone else's perspective? A designer's vision reflects their awareness that our surroundings are the result of creation, and the necessary artistry that goes into the process."

– LAWRENCE CHABRA

SENSING

This chapter addresses the potential of photography to describe design projects created in the studio by interior design students. We explore the advantages of digital image making through the means of process and production. It is meaningful to note that during the pre-digital age of photography, there was a certain trust in the believability of the photographic image. While it is true that all photographic images are, by definition, transformed by the tools associated with photography, such as the lens, lighting, and composition, for the intent of this chapter, these images are manipulated to suit the designer's purpose. Upon the arrival of digital photography and the various processes by which such images are transformed, the status of photographs' truthfulness has changed. Photographs are no less impressive for that change—they just have a different way of communicating.

When you begin to document your work directly by taking and manipulating photographs, you will need a digital camera and software packages, such as Adobe Creative Suite, which includes Photoshop. With these tools and basic studio lighting lamps, a tripod and copy stand, you will begin to photograph your 2D and 3D interior design projects. Most two-dimensional works are either scanned or directly imported from your digital files. Study models, finished models, sculpture, furniture designs, and constructions, including industrial and any other three-dimensional objects, are photographed in a lighting studio.

Although we are concerned about making a single object image, you will see this has as much to do with design as does the project's intent in your interior design portfolio. The ambition, insight, and drive you bring to the photograph will extend the process from simply a document to a design statement. This undertaking, therefore, raises recording interior design three-dimensional studio coursework in ways that only digital imagery allows.

5 CAPTURING EXPRESSIVE IMAGES

Robert Kaner

Today, Robert Kaner's office overlooks the High Line and Chelsea's art district of Manhattan. Light and materiality are both important dimensions of Robert Kaner's design sensibility and sensitivity. Full bleed screen images on his website, www.kanerid.com, give power to his mastery of all of the aspects of interior design (figures 5–1 to 5–3). The website is easy to navigate from one project to another and has a clear concise paragraph that explains concept and intention without being laborious but offering salient information to the overall project. The bars that pop up on the bottom of the page easily disappear so that the full bleed image reads as a movie screen.

His online portfolio provides an uncluttered window into the clean aesthetic of his high level professional practice. Every photo is carefully organized and placed in an order that moves you through multiple variations of his residential and commercial style. As a master of design, his practice is often retained to select and consult on modern and contemporary art that works well with the interiors.

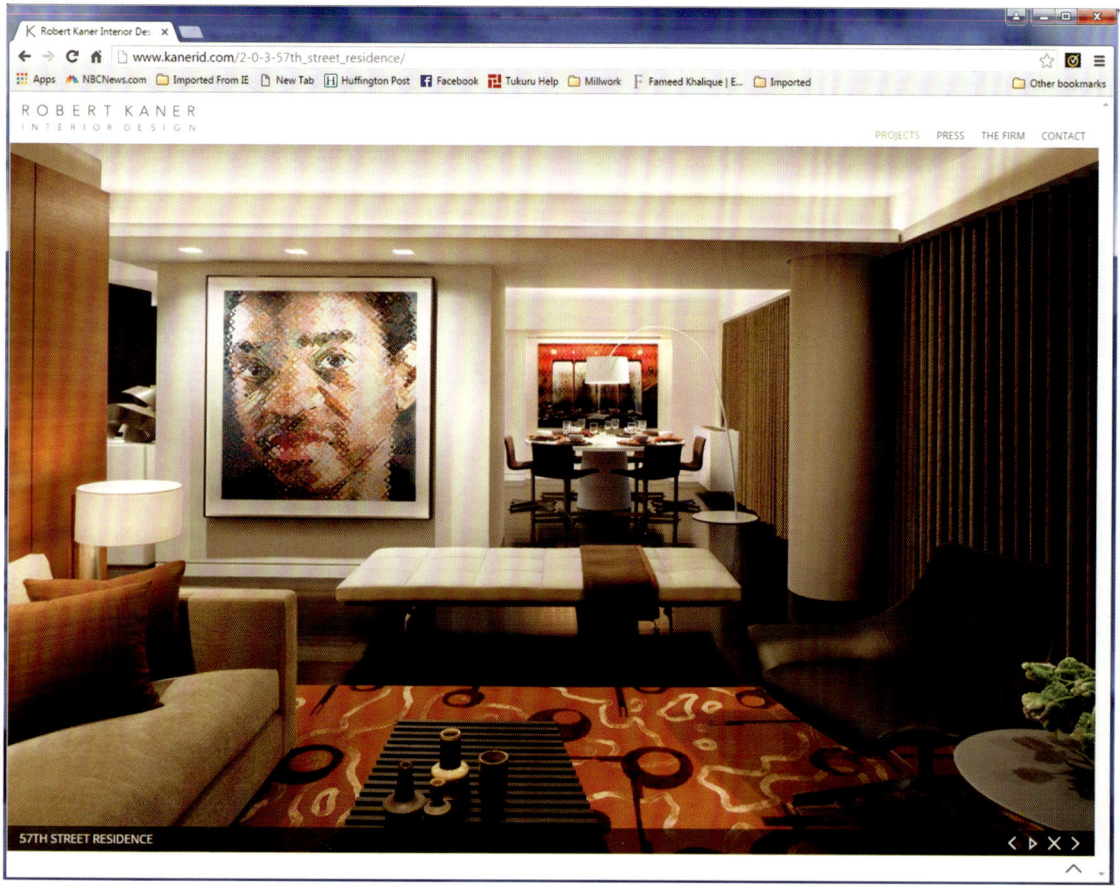

5–1 to 5–3 Interior projects from the website of designer Robert Kaner, www.kanerid.com.

Sensing

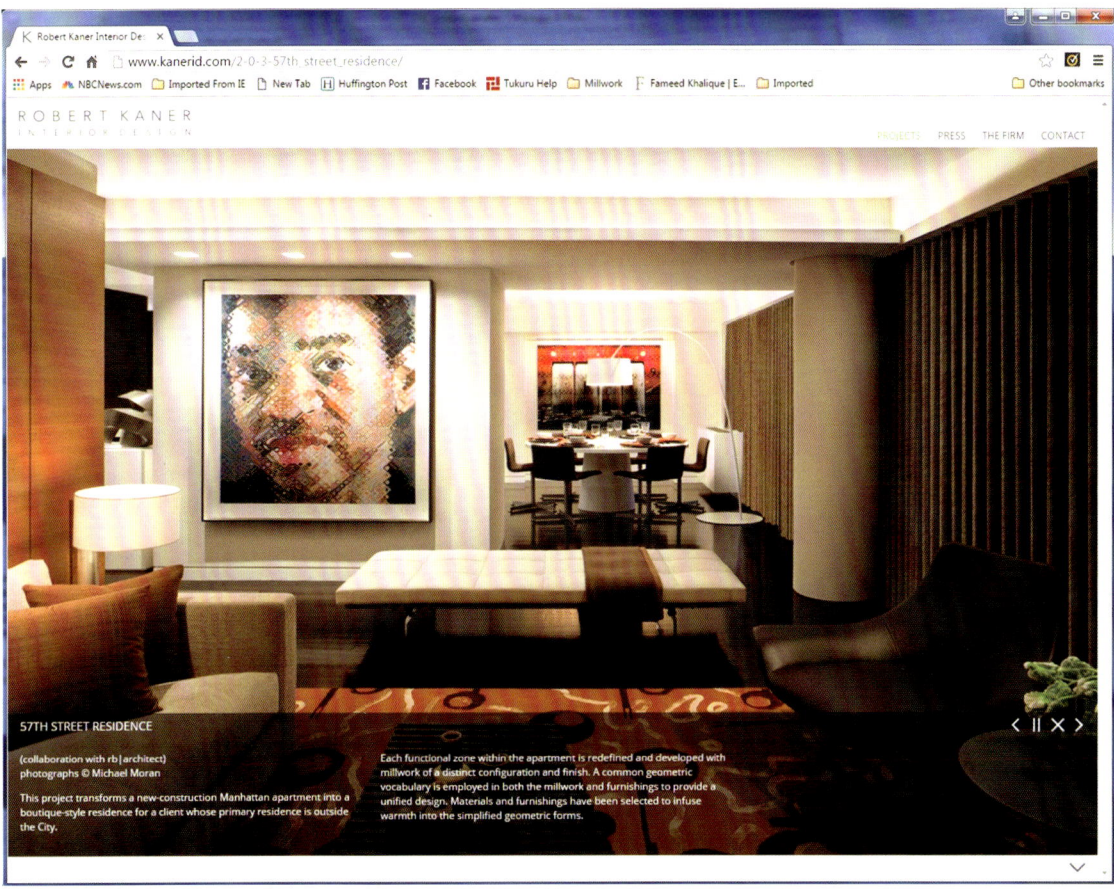

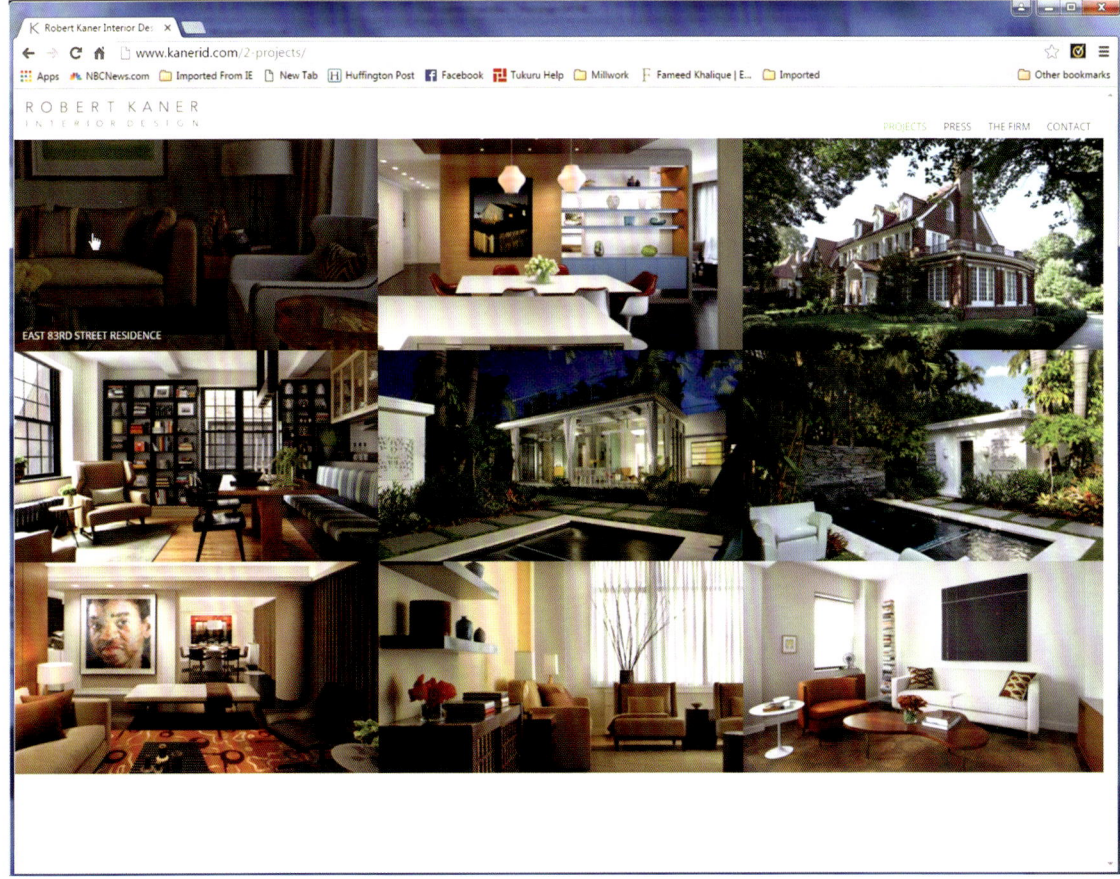

5 CAPTURING EXPRESSIVE IMAGES

Capturing images of your work for use in your portfolio incorporates the methods of photographic and digital reproduction. Digital and analog photography embrace a greater perception of how you see the world and your ability to orchestrate how images need to appear. Every interior designer brings a unique perspective to a project and engages the world in familiar ways. With a fresh perspective on their surroundings, artists observe, inform, and inspire their work, often in unexpected yet sensitive ways. In addition to their powers of visualizing novel solutions that inspire us, they are especially adept at sensing opportunities for change and then expressing that change by manipulating materials and visual elements to effect that change.

In this chapter, we focus (pun intended) on the selection and documentation of images that go into your portfolio; however, we also wish to equip you with the broader perspective of design vision. You need to develop studio know-how so that you recognize the necessary steps to capture a professional and evocative image using the most appropriate and available photographic tools and techniques. You need to become acquainted with various methods of image capture and manipulation to make the wisest decisions as to the best method to document your work. It is equally important to visualize how to manipulate your images artfully to achieve the desired results for all of the artifacts you have collected for your portfolio.

What bells go off when looking at the array of design evidence you have collected during all the years of your design education? Perhaps a project created in the junior year was entirely successful in the studio, but a few images (drawings, renderings, models) are not as high a priority as most of the others. A golden opportunity is to infuse, strengthen, and support the portfolio with your design vision.

Innovation involves making decisions about what to express and how to do it, from the central idea to the fine details of implementation. Sensibilities not only guide these decisions but they also ultimately influence how people experience the resulting product, service, or brand. Will customers just end up getting something that "works," or will they make an emotional connection with it—one that involves personal and cultural relevance and inspires future loyalty?

Here's a TIP:

Reassess all of your work to embrace and better express your vision, which will help raise your confidence and make your work more consistent, so there are no significant dips along the way.

EXPRESSING

Expressing is a means of creating change by exploiting one's visual perceptions. By valuing and sharing observations just because they seem beautiful, intriguing, offensive, or amusing, designers enrich their intuitions. Their subjective awareness of how particular attributes evoke a sense of beauty, intrigue, fire, or amusement contributes to how best to express those qualities in any given design. In using their sensibilities, designers connect to our sensitivities and enrich our experience. Most professionals readily recognize the practical benefits of a product or service, but they often overlook the less-apparent qualities of an experience from which they derive pleasure, identity, and meaning. Design thinking entails much more than applying methods. Methods must be employed together with design sensibilities to create value.

Your portfolio is a collection of process and product, functioning as a summary of thinking skills, drawing skills, and developing strategies. It also reveals the designer behind the work. Your sensitivities to space, light, materials, philosophies, and technical skills are all laid out in these pages, in a sequence, to tell your story as an interior designer. The collaboration between the design content and the graphic design form with which you tell your story is important, since it will offer your audience access to you and your work.

Managers schooled in analytic and rational decision making may find the idea of relying on their visual acuity uncomfortable. Design sensibilities, however, create the experiences and outcomes upon which successful businesses capitalize: clear distinction from competitors, lasting market impact, and customer loyalty.

All of your design evidence has specific identifiable visual emphasis. As you invest time in planning each project for the pages of the portfolio and establishing a hierarchal visual system, the type of interior design should be considered. The portfolio should allow your thinking, planning, and visual design skills to flourish. These qualities will occur with careful planning and good graphic design and photography skills. Whether the images are fabricated/illustrated in a particular software package or photographically documented with a camera, they need to represent your awareness of the character of the place and space. The quality of light, in both exterior and interior spaces, is critical to all types of projects. In conjunction with light, the "camera perspective" or point of view plays a significant role in creating a suspension of fiction for a project's presentation. When capturing images to be used in your portfolio's graphic design, allowing your audience clear and unfettered access to each and every visual is an essential element of storytelling.

"Educators must both allow and encourage students to design portfolios that will ultimately lead them to their career ambitions. Like a house with character that sells for more than the neutral home, a well-designed and purposeful portfolio creates careers, not mere jobs."

— **NADIA S. PIDGEON**, PROGRAM COORDINATOR, INTERIOR DESIGN, ART INSTITUTE OF AUSTIN, AUSTIN, TX.

5 CAPTURING EXPRESSIVE IMAGES

Lillian Bakhash

Lillian believes that any portfolio finds success only through patient and exacting work. The premise of her undergraduate portfolio, shown in figures 5–4 to 5–7, was to form the book as a platform to communicate various attributes of design process, planning, and communication, such as hand drawings, concept development, and demonstrations of methodology. She acknowledges the portfolio class at NYSID as being supportive of her work and portfolio creation. She views the portfolio as a way to take advantage of the expertise of the school to support the trajectory of growing her own business. She used PowerPoint and Photoshop to create the design of her portfolio for both print and for online distribution and by mailing a CD. She continues to update and present her work as new accomplishments accumulate. She has included a page (figure 5–7) of professionally photographed work by important interior design photographers in the design and editorial industry. Her portfolio shows that a transition from academic to professional can exist and work together!

Sun Factory
Two adjoining units at a former 1950's motel were converted into a modern summer getaway, communicating the concept of "Sun Factory" by layering radiating color over industrial finishes.

Driftwood on the Ocean, Montauk, NY

5–4 to 5–7 Lillian's portfolio is a great example of exuberant hand rendering that is an effective tool for color exploration and form in interior design. It captures an emotion that takes average computer modeling a bit further. She successfully shows school work in conjunction with built projects. The hotel has a beautiful composite board that exhibits professional photography while clearly demonstrating the concept of color within the rooms that comes from the paintings displayed in the hallways. The concept of design comes from the paintings instead of the paintings being put in at the end of the project. Her hand work throughout the portfolio supports this idea and the titles of the projects, such as the Sun Factory, treat the problem with life and light. Lillian Bakash, New York School of Interior Design, 11" x 17".

Monochrome
A collaboration with In Situ Design, a 33 room Extended Stay Residence mimics a livable 3-dimensional painting, immersing guests in visceral color palettes that vary from floor to floor – blue, teal, pink, green and orange and coat the ceilings, wall, carpets and bed linens.

The William Hotel

Expressing

Exploring color as a painter would, the goal was to reach past fashion and personal likes and into the depths of unapologetic color.

The William Hotel

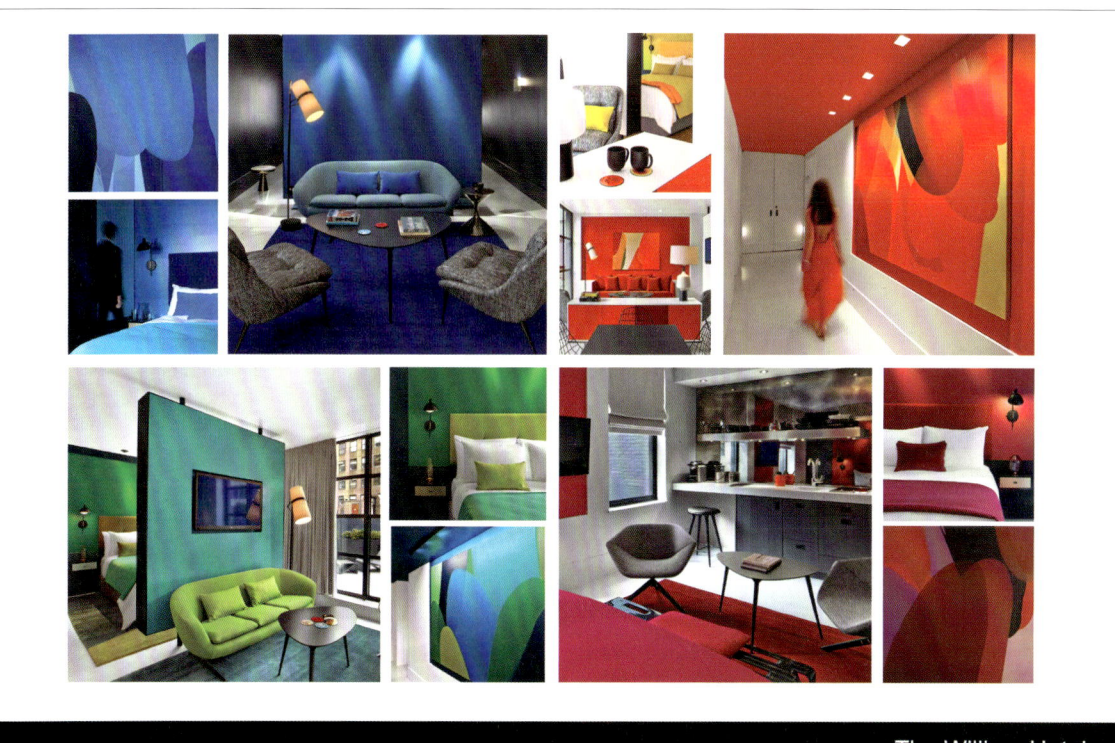

The William Hotel

CAPTURING IMAGES WITH PURPOSE

When considering the organization, collection of projects, design, and use of a portfolio you should think about those predominant factors that contribute to distinguishing your interior design portfolio from those in the allied disciplines such as architecture, urban design, or industrial design. Perhaps some of your projects have affinities to those in other disciplines allied to interior design. With most interior design projects, however, interior designers embed their work with an in-depth understanding and expression of the psychology of place and purpose. When choosing elements to include or emphasize in a project, consider how to best highlight this important aspect of the design. When photographing a model, think of the effect lighting, shadow, and perspective might have on communicating the psychology of space. Other photographic techniques, such as the use of depth of field, have an impact on how one thinks about an interior space. Considering these things can help you establish a hierarchical set of ideas for communicating that an image has importance or dominance.

PROCESS: DESIGN THINKING

The impact of the photographic technique on the "reading" of the design process is an interesting subject. A formal approach to photographing an image suggests a unified and complete thought. Your idea is called a "money shot" or a resolved conclusion. If, while leading up to the final image, you create images with various techniques, such as copy machine, scanner, and collage, in contrast, these images suggest a process that is evolving.

The creative composition originates with a deliberate sense of casualness in the setting up of the photograph. Cardboard study models are non-precious examples of the evolution of a design process. Photograph these study models and final models in your design or lighting studio. Look for a range of artistic elements in found objects like a beehive or a seashell in a desk setup. The tools used to create the drawing, model, or view of the site/context for the design project can produce an atmosphere of investigation or inquiry, which contributes to the design of the final image and lends it considerable importance through the contrast of technique.

"Only make something if it's both useful and needful. But if it is both useful and needful, do not hesitate to make it beautiful."

– SHAKER PROVERB

LIGHTING AND COLOR TEMPERATURE

Principles of light and temperature also play a significant role in establishing and communicating the visual concept that the interior designer wishes to offer. Foundation principles of color and light, as well as all of the elements of design, require control and finesse to achieve your vision. When photographing, be sure to use proper color temperature bulbs (lighting) for the settings on the camera or "fix" this with your photo editing software such as Photoshop. Cold temperature light suggests one thing, while warm light suggests another. The materials/finishes that are in the design will be affected by the type or color of light. These issues surface when photographing design boards and existing interior/exterior space and when using other photomechanical tools such as a photocopiers and scanners.

White balance needs to be corrected when shooting anything with the camera. You can usually correct white balance by simply hitting the autocorrect tab on Photoshop, but you can't always rely on this. There are other options for making color and contrast adjustments in Photoshop. You have to know if the incandescent tungsten lighting needs to be more blue or if the blue natural daylight needs to be more yellow. These are both problems adjusting white balance, which is one of the major problems in creating an image for a portfolio and one that students need to understand. The other autocorrect tabs that help in restoring a real image are auto-levels and auto-contrast. Often, hand-drawn lines of perspectives need greater contrast and sometimes enhanced brightness in Photoshop. You will find an adjustment category in Photoshop. For shooting your work, you should be using a 35 mm SLR camera that shoots reliable professional images as opposed to your phone camera. The better digital cameras will read the color or will require less adjustment in Photoshop than what your phone camera will do!

As with all areas of design, human factors such as comfort design, functional design, and systems need to be a central concern when representing your ideas and work. The use and implementation of graphic design principles and strategies for photographing, scanning, studio setting, lighting, and dealing with human factors of size and scale should all be orchestrated to demonstrate your acute awareness and control of the visual elements of composition.

5 CAPTURING EXPRESSIVE IMAGES

Mark Sanchez

Mark created the large format (11" x 17") portfolio shown in figures 5–8 to 5–12 as an undergraduate at Algonquin College in search of a summer internship. He used Adobe Creative Suite and a laser printer for print production on cardstock-weight paper. It was then spiral bound for a professional presentation. Mark made one portfolio at a cost of $35.00. He was very successful in finding a 4-month internship in London, England. He mentions, "I did read John Maeda's 'Laws of Simplicity' which was an especially insightful book and I learned the importance of simplicity when presenting my work." Next time around, Mark plans on researching other binding options as well as formatting possibilities.

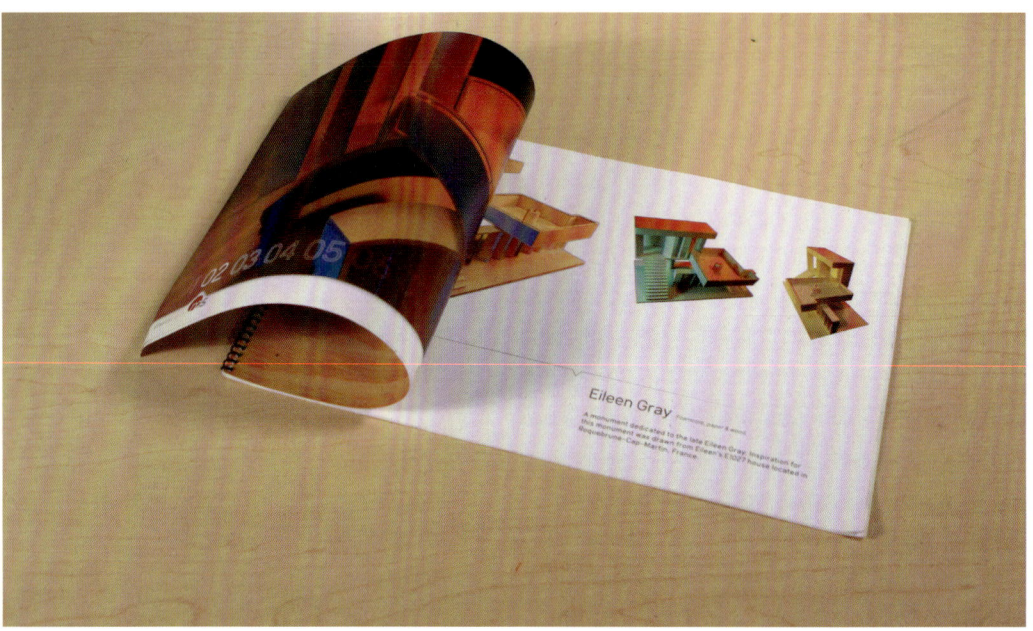

5–8 to 5–12 Mark introduces his book with materiality, texture, and strong graphics. It invites you to see the rest! He consistently shows you what his hand produces, from mixed media rendering to hand-built models. He has included his life drawing as well, and such a great addition this is, since all interior design revolves around the human factor! He has neatly organized a page on innovation and collaboration. All interior design is about collaboration, and we feel this is an important addition to his book. His schematic thought processes are also important to understanding how he approaches a design so that the portfolio does not rely only on the finished products. Mark Sanchez, Algonquin College, Ottawa, Ontario, Canada. 11" x 17".

Lighting and Color Temperature

Cliffside Spa – *Residential Space Modeling*

Cliffside Spa 3ds Max, Photoshop & Markers

The objective of this project was to design a residential space, model it in Sketchup, and then render it using 3ds Max.

I envisioned a Japanese retreat tucked into a rocky cliffside, resting high above a lake.

Loft Design – *Scaled Model*

Loft Design Foamcore, illustration board & acrylic

This project first began by developing plans for a loft that included a mezzanine and vertical circulation. These plans were then used to create scaled model.

Scale: 1/2"=1'-0"

Changing Seasons – *Healthcare Design*

Rehabilitation Centre AutoCAD and Photoshop

These sections are from a rehabilitation centre that I designed as an answer to the need for a modern approach to healthcare. The centre meets the clinical needs of the patients, while also offering therapeutic programs as well such as aqua and physio therapy.

115

5 CAPTURING EXPRESSIVE IMAGES

MATERIALS, MEDIA, AND STUDIO LIGHTING

In the previous chapters, you discovered the importance of establishing a strategy for creating a voice to reflect you and your work. Upon successful review of your work, it is appropriate to plan for the graphic design implementation. It is a good time to begin editing and storyboarding. Here you will discover the value of the storytelling that best suits you and your quest. It is also the right time to gather the appropriate photographic tools to assist in documenting your work. These "discoveries" will bring together techniques that you are familiar with through your education as well an updated list of software, hardware, and documenting methods appropriate for your particular needs.

Let us assume that you will implement 21st-century technology so that your portfolio is laid out in a digital manner. We do not presume there is little value in the hand or mechanical approach to laying out your work. Hiring a professional photographer is one approach, but is costly. Be sure to establish an agreement on cost for services rendered plus the expectations of preparedness. The goal might require works on paper mounted on foam core before photography and will impact the budget. Extra mounting is expensive, and your production schedule must also be a consideration. However, with the accessibility of a good camera borrowed from schools, rental services, or personal contacts, or just owning a camera personally, the interior designer can take ownership in the process of documenting the work both in 2D and 3D.

You need to be familiar with photographic equipment including cameras, lighting, tripods, copy stands, plain walls and backdrops, and the space where you are working. Your space should be clutter free and have a tabletop clear where you can store and review the work. It is best to be aware to avoid damaging papers and models that might be delicate from aging or special techniques. A blank wall such as Homasote to pin work on is ideal. Most schools with design programs will have these types of walls available in studios or critique spaces. Otherwise, a lumber yard will carry that material in 4 x 8-foot sheets. Because most works on paper will fit within a 4-foot square area, these sheets can be cut in half and then applied to an existing wall with drywall screws. Pushpins, clips, or drafting tape should be available for temporarily mounting the work on the wall. The use of repositionable foam tabs is also useful since it isn't another visual element on top of your drawing to deal with, such as pins or tape that would need editing and Photoshop to remove them afterward. Large rolls of seamless paper called photographic backdrop paper, which come in different widths in a variety of background colors from a photography shop or set shop, will prove invaluable.

Lights—the source of light and lighting—are a critical aspect of the process of documenting your work. A light that renders your project(s) accurately should be controllable, whether it be natural light or studio lights. Digital camera sensors read the color temperature of the light source. The most up-to-date cameras will have an "averaging" setting for types of lights sources. Image-based software such as Adobe Photoshop will also allow for changing or correcting for color shifts that may have resulted due to incorrect color temperature light sources. What is most important is that your images best represent the desired intent of your work. The white paper is white (not yellow or blue), and your color renderings are true to your purpose.

Choosing to photograph your work with the aid of a copy stand or setting the camera on a tripod will allow for an accurate and consistent compositional framing and a stabilized image. Some other decisions include whether you are documenting 2D or 3D work, the size of the artwork to be documented, the availability of equipment, and the size of the studio. Equipment decisions will include type of tripod, lighting, copy stand, camera, and lenses.

Again, if we assume you are using a digital camera, we can discuss the advantages of a 35 mm DSLR (digital single lens reflex camera) over a point and shoot. Both cameras will do the job, but with the DSLR you will be able to choose an appropriate lens. Most important when documenting 2D work is to avoid distortion (warped edges) and avoid parallax problems. Simply stated, this occurs when what you see in your viewfinder is not composed identically to what your sensor or recording device records. And finally, be sure that your viewfinder (or screen) shows that your image fills the frame. Some viewfinders show more, some show less of the object than what gets captured on the sensor. I will expand on these three areas.

Lenses, whether they are built into the point-and-shoot variety camera or are interchangeable like on the DSLR, are designed for a variety of viewpoints. They are measured in millimeters and range from wide angle (peripheral vision is expanded) to telephoto (drawing long distances forward)

Materials, Media, and Studio Lighting

"A portfolio is the definitive opportunity to reveal your design character. It's not a collection of work, rather, it should be seen as your best design project to date. Its unique presentation is the best way to make a great first impression, and to help you stand apart from your competition."

— **NADIA VOLCHANSKY**, IDEC, LEED AP, INTERIOR ARCHITECTURE AND DESIGN, THE GEORGE WASHINGTON UNIVERSITY.

with points in between. The wide-angle lens ranges tend to cause distortion and will be visible along the edges of the paper you are photographing. The telephoto lens range will limit your ability to focus on close objects and limit the camera's ability to step back far enough to capture the image. The recommended range of focal length is 50 mm to 105 mm to avoid these problems.

When documenting artwork, you are going to want the best resolution possible. Start with the fullest composition and viewing field. Many digital cameras will allow you to view the subject matter through both the viewfinder and on a screen that is on the back of the camera body. A word of caution is worthwhile at this point in the discussion. Viewfinders may or may not provide you with the image that is recorded on the sensor and, therefore, the ultimate image that you will use. It is best to review and take note of this during your first experience with the camera. Make the proper adjustments with your zoom lens or by moving your camera closer or further away from the subject.

If an original piece of art/design work needs to be enlarged to fit a design layout, there is a possibility that the new image size may be grainy or pixilated. The result will likely be image deterioration and degradation. Unless this is a quality that is part of the concept for the design of the page or portfolio, it is best to heed the advice provided moments ago, when determining the size of the picture on the page.

Another setting in control of the photographer that affects the quality of the image about readability is the ISO, or the control that sets up the sensitivity of the camera's sensor. The more sensitive to light a sensor is, the more "visual noise" will be recorded. Many cameras will have an "automatic" setting. Other, more sophisticated cameras will allow the photographer to make an educated decision. An international standards organization established the numbers and, therefore, they are consistent throughout the world and shared by every camera in existence.

Parallax occurs when parallel lines are askew. If, when photographing a rectangular or square object such as a piece of paper or board, the edges of that paper are not parallel within the viewfinder, this will cause concern when laying out the object on the portfolio page. The goal is not to distract the viewer during their review. When setting up the camera in front of the object, pay careful attention to the following:

- Attach the paper/board at all four corners to the surface being used so not to allow the paper to curl away or toward the camera.
- When using a tripod set the height of the camera to the center of the art/design work (both right and left as well as up and down).
- Set the lens zoom to a range between 50 mm and 105 mm or 35 mm to 85 mm for DSLR, to avoid the warping previously mentioned.
- Tilt the camera so that its body is parallel to the surface "holding" the art/design work.

Many students now use the skew option under the edit and transform tab in Photoshop to correct non-parallel lines that occur when using lenses and cameras. For studio photography, you need to control the camera exposures by using a gray card, bracketing, shutter speed, aperture, and ISO settings. With digital photography you can control the bracketing with simple digital light adjustments on programs like Photoshop without spending much time on multiple camera bracketing.

5 CAPTURING EXPRESSIVE IMAGES

Interior Photography: Lisa League, NCIDQ, Interior Design

As an interior designer, Lisa has practiced for many years working on both residential and commercial projects. She was senior designer and project manager for boutique hotel developer The Kessler Collection and part of the team at the world's leading design consultant in the hospitality industry, WATG. Through those experiences, she gained a unique insight into the challenges and rewards of working as an interior designer.

These experiences lead her to found Qpractice (https://www.qpractice.com/), the first online training company to help interior designers pass the NCIDQ exam, a professional exam for certification and licensing in the United States and Canada. Besides her NCIDQ and LEED credentials, she is a licensed interior designer in Florida and has an MS in Interior Design.

Her professional brochure, shown in figures 5–13 to 5–15, was created to serve as a professional presentation of projects and skills for potential clients. The book was created with Adobe InDesign, Photoshop, and Acrobat Professional. The overarching purpose was to serve as a digital portfolio with an online presence, however, several versions were produced by both Office Depot and Blurb (http://www.blurb.com/).

One of the most challenging attributes of the book's fully photographic content was to adjust the color contrast for different paper qualities from glossy to matte and maintain the color as true as possible. Editions of ten or more books were created and then expanded as new work was completed and helped to redefine the range of her experience and accomplishments. The results from her portfolio book and online presence have been a continual stream of commissioned work. Lisa found the online resources to be inspirational in many ways as work is continually posted and updated on Blurb, Lulu, and ISSUU. Versions of her portfolio were responsible for every job she has received.

5–13 to 5–15 Lisa has put together an impressive bold brochure type portfolio of realized projects with strong real photographic images in lavish color saturation, light, and style. Her boards and materials are highly developed and also carefully arranged. She truly packages herself and her brand in a unique way. We appreciate her choice of light gray typography to underscore each project; it is sophisticated and highly professional. By looking through her sketches, large renderings, and materials and furniture layouts, you get the sense you are in the hands of a real designer. The inclusion of entourage supports her design and understanding that these are spaces to be used by people. See www.lisaleague.com.

Materials, Media, and Studio Lighting

CONCEPTUAL DRAWINGS

SPACE PLANNING

CONSTRUCTION DRAWINGS

FINISH SPECIFICATIONS

PLUMBING AND LIGHTING SPECIFICATIONS

CUSTOM MILLWORK DRAWINGS

LOBBY FF&E

GRAND BOHEMIAN HOTEL & RESIDENCES

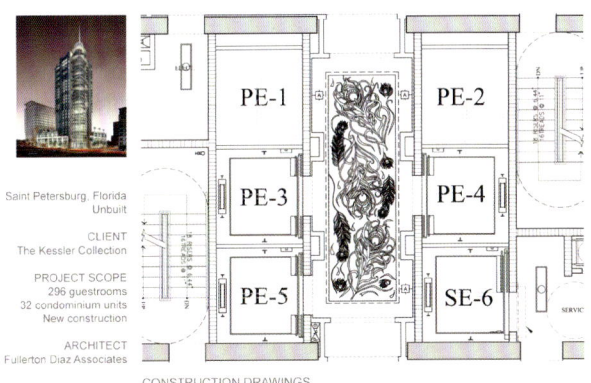

Saint Petersburg, Florida
Unbuilt

CLIENT
The Kessler Collection

PROJECT SCOPE
296 guestrooms
32 condominium units
New construction

ARCHITECT
Fullerton Diaz Associates

CONSTRUCTION DRAWINGS

FINISH, PLUMBING, LIGHTING AND APPLIANCE SPECIFICATIONS

MEP COORDINATION

CUSTOM MILLWORK DESIGN AND DRAWINGS

CUSTOM PATTERN DESIGN

PRELIMINARY FF&E BUDGET

Inspiration: Modern Asian Fusion

"She has always demonstrated not only the utmost talent and design capabilities, but also the ability to consult/coordinate with the other disciplines with great ease and professionalism.
I highly recommend Lisa and look forward to our next collaboration."

Florentino Mas
Project Manager,
Fullerton Diaz Architects

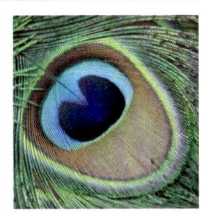

119

INTERIOR SETUP

Actual rooms that either students or professionals photograph require acute attention to setup and preparation and they make excellent additions to your portfolio. Using real spaces as vignettes could be supplemental to the main body of work shown in a book. As in the professional industry, a decision to show built work is up to the interior designer entirely based on the actual room designs. The inclusion of these spaces in your portfolio could be supplemental to the speculative work typical of a studio design outcome and offer a detail that could be appreciated by viewers.

Using proper wide-angle lenses and positioning yourself to include the full point of view that matters most to the design are the goals you should set. At the same time, make sure that the camera is pointed in the proper direction so that reflective surfaces, mirrors, and windows are at an angle where there will not be glare that is disturbing to the overall image. White balance, value, and intensity are adjusted in Photoshop. After a picture is created, cleaning up the image or making it more chromatic is easy. It takes considerable time, but is very worthwhile in the end.

Being detail oriented is valuable. One must anticipate having to clean surfaces, straighten pillows, stack blankets, and hang towels as time-consuming tasks. All of the detailed information in the interior has to be completely professional. Styling components are finally added to make an interior appear natural.

Robert Kaner Interior Design creates highly individualized interior spaces that reflect a modernist sensibility suffused with warmth and comfort. Through a careful analytic and aesthetic approach to design, each project takes on a distinct character reflective of the client, context, and lifestyle. The Kaner website, http://www.kanerid.com, is an especially efficient use of professional photography to attract clients to their firm. Kaner works with soft fabrics, warm paint tones, and dark rich woods that photograph well under natural light and offer the audience an insight to his design aesthetic.

Tsao & McKown have built their eclectic practice on distinctive ways of thinking rather than a trademark style. Their website home page (http://www.tsao-mckown.com) is an interesting arrangement of striking color photographs of office projects designed with a minimalist menu to ease navigation through a substantial range of interior design accomplishments. The global experience is quite evident on the home page as images of design projects appear and dissolve allowing new ones to emerge into view.

Lisa League is a successful designer with interests in the education of aspiring interior design students, and also a wealth of professional expertise and myriad accomplishments and awards in hospitality design. Her website home page (http://www.lisaleague.com) offers an introduction to her work with rich visuals while serving as an introduction to her print portfolio under "Portfolio" on the menu. The office portfolio has an abundance of beautiful full-color photographs designed almost like an album of memories with large images arranged tastefully and smaller detailed images beneath.

MODELS

One of the challenges of photographing interior space is to record the atmosphere and lighting intent of the design while at the same time providing enough light for the camera sensor to read the area. An associated challenge is to provide points of view that are critical to understanding the intended movement through space.

LIGHTING STUDIO

The lighting studio at the School of Art, George Mason University, Fairfax, Virginia (figure 5–16) is equipped with 12' wide rolls of photographic backdrop paper in various tones and hues for shooting studio sculpture, furniture, and models. Portfolios (as objects) are generally photographed on this steel table with curvilinear translucent white acrylic sheet on top that provides a soft, neutral, and unobtrusive background.

Photographing an original interior requires a wide-angle lens and conditions of all natural light or supplemental lamps. The photographer plans how the reader will view the area and can vary from eye level to aerial and several other points of origin. Images often require editing in Photoshop to polish the final composition via cropping, color, illumination, and glare. Photoshop can also "fix" the askew images relatively quickly. Photographing student (architectural)

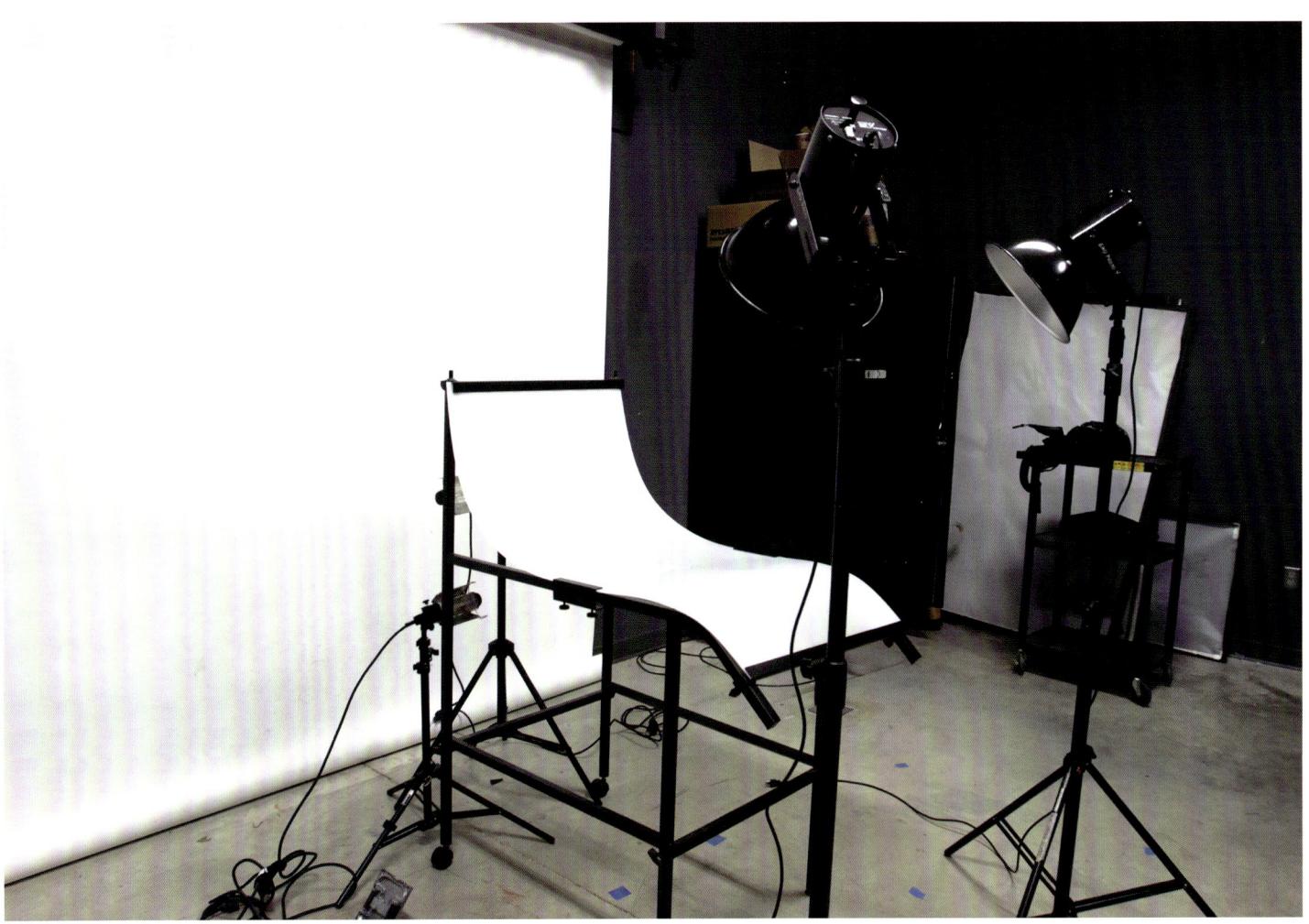

5–16 Within the lighting studio at George Mason University, there are various neutral white and gray backgrounds for photographing various 2D and 3D projects.

models has particular challenges. The design student as the photographer needs to look at space in the context of both artificial and natural lighting to determine how to capture the most appropriate condition of light in context with the intended purpose of the interior.

Many students documenting their design work prefer a lighting studio setting to photograph models of all kinds because the studio environment offers the most control of lighting and environment. Lighting studios, especially those in photography programs, are typically equipped with individual lamps, seamless backdrops, high-end quality cameras, and a variety of lenses to capture the quality of a model in its most advantageous illumination.

When lighting studios are not an option or within budget, you can easily photograph models using a macro lens and several flashlights held at strategic spots in your design to enhance the overall spatial effect. Of course, you will need several hands to do this, but it is a way to get several fellow students involved to participate in the design process and offer their suggestions for improvement along the way.

Flashlights are helpful in that they can easily graze surfaces of materiality to enhance the surfaces as well as space!

In the lighting studio, designers take the time to test quality and quantity of light to become familiar with their specific effects, for example, shadows, color, and atmosphere. Positions of the camera are rehearsed to determine the potential results of taking close-ups, overviews, and unique detail photographs. Different kinds of lamps include natural sunlight, overhead soft-box light (overhead light that gives the general effect of sunlight), key light (strobe), bounced light (indirect), and diffused or modified light (light passing through a translucent umbrella).

If the designer prefers a particular quality of light on the subject, these effects are most achievable in a lighting studio. The use of seamless backdrop paper creates a neutral setting or point of contrast for the subject. Backdrop papers come in rolls of approximate size 6', 8', and 12', and in black, white, light gray, blue, and brown. Lighting studios typically have these rolls mounted against a wall and controlled by hand or electronically.

"A good portfolio demonstrates many things, including the presenter's personality which is the professional product of effective skills, creative thinking, logical organization, and who they are as a designer. The intentional use of technology should highlight and promote understated evident skills and abilities rather than be a tool for presenting 'pretty images' that are lacking in substance."

– **JEANNEANE WOOD-NARTKER**, PH.D., PROFESSOR, PROGRAM DIRECTOR, INTERIOR DESIGN, CENTRAL MICHIGAN UNIVERSITY, MT. PLEASANT, MICH.

SCANNING, PHOTOCOPYING, AND COMBINING IMAGES

Other methods of reproduction include scanning, photocopying, digital altering of original drawings, or collage and combining images into new compositions of enhanced reproducible images. While reviewing the inventory of projects in your digital files or storage space, you might find work that has relevance to your current design process. There are a variety of mechanical and digital methods to creating images. Lens media is not limited to the use of a camera.

The scanner has few controls; however, when a scanned image is imported into picture control software such as Adobe Photoshop, the designer can make adjustments similar to those found on a camera. Additionally, the designer can control contrast, color, and density of the image to give the illusion of transparency. The scanner acts like a camera as it records objects not limited to flat, two-dimensional objects such as drawings. Scanners have a very shallow depth of focus. The depth of field is the illusion of space recorded by the camera. Focusing a camera on the surface of the subject matter is referred to as the critical focus. The aperture of the lens controls the depth of field (the discussion as to why or how is not appropriate for this text). Shallow depth of field suggests a particular focus. A great depth of field allows for a three-dimensional object or space to be fully in focus.

Here's a TIP:

Determine a design strategy and be honest about the project's original intent.

PRESENTATION STRATEGIES

Photographing your projects has a significant impact on your approach to the layout design of portfolio pages and sequencing images or views of each project. With a clear understanding of importance placed on the process of design within your book, documenting those elements that contribute to a holistic vision for that project is important. Each photograph plays a role in this process. And each image follows the plan for the graphic design of your portfolio.

The projects that you have selected to include in your portfolio have been carefully culled with a particular strategy in mind. That approach, founded on the principles of securing an overview or history of the work, has been created over days, months, and years of education, hard work, and discovering your passions. It is at this point in the process when designing that includes ordering systems, layout, sequencing views, typographical choices, format, and binding (to mention a few) comes into play. An overall and unified presentation is achieved through a careful application of design skills and strategy to the unfolding story. Storytelling gains momentum by its imaginative delivery and the orchestration of a plan for all of the visual elements of its content(s).

5 CAPTURING EXPRESSIVE IMAGES

CONTROL THE IMAGE EDITING PROCESS

Before you decide to share your skills with others, you will make several critical decisions about how you document and use visual images of your design content. Typically this goes hand-in-hand with organizing your portfolio's content to match the its purpose, that is, to direct your work toward a given goal. Portfolios are malleable and purposeful. Visual communications have many purposes. To pursue your aspirations, you need to recognize the nature of the requirements of your chosen goal and assemble your work based on the kind of opportunity you wish to pursue. Your design evidence requires careful planning and execution to meet the expectations of experience, abilities, and rigor inherent in the academic program or type of design firm in which you wish to work, including properly capturing it for print or digital presentation.

Know the strengths of your projects and which of them best express design confidence. You hope to convince a reviewer that you know how to design. Therefore, making a portfolio is tantamount to rehearsing for an interview. It requires a kind of honesty with yourself and your work that leads to redoing elements of projects, revising process evidence, and perhaps even redesigning a project because you know the result will be significantly better.

Renee Struthers

As a requirement of studio projects in the graduate program at the University of Manitoba, the portfolio shown in figures 5–17 to 5–22 was created at the completion of the term. It was also a means to summarize and review the work produced throughout the full-term graduate studio. Renee developed a consistent graphic language to coincide with a very specific design concept and typology. Furthermore, Renee learned how to represent a full-term studio in a comprehensive manner. She confesses that if she were to change something, she would have added more written description throughout the presentation. Renee used Adobe CS5 for the design of the full portfolio. It was printed in full color by a laser printer.

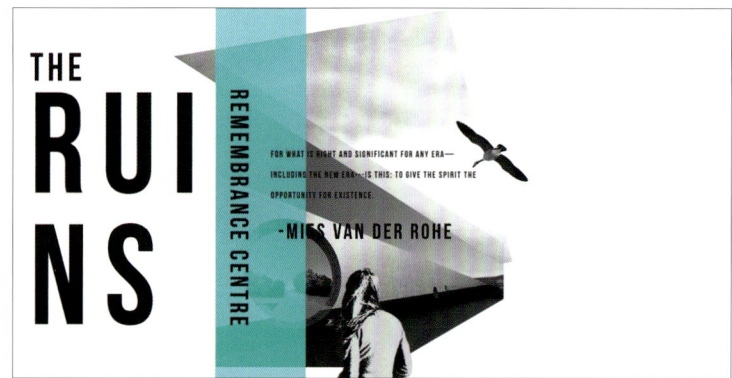

5–17 to 5–22 Renee Struthers presents a comprehensive term-long project from a graduate studio entitled, "Belief and Spirituality in the 21st Century: In Search of the New Sacred." This portfolio exhibits her ability to organize thought processes as a tool to arrive at a solution with a strong concept. It was also useful as a presentation aid as well as a portfolio for a course submission. The portfolio served as a means to summarize and review the semester's work. It was not intended as an instrument to search for employment. Renee learned how to create a consistently unique graphic language that coincided with a specific design concept and typology. Renee Struthers, University of Manitoba, Manitoba, Canada. 8.5" x 17". See http://www.reneestruthers.com.

Here's a TIP:

Knowing your work is knowing yourself.

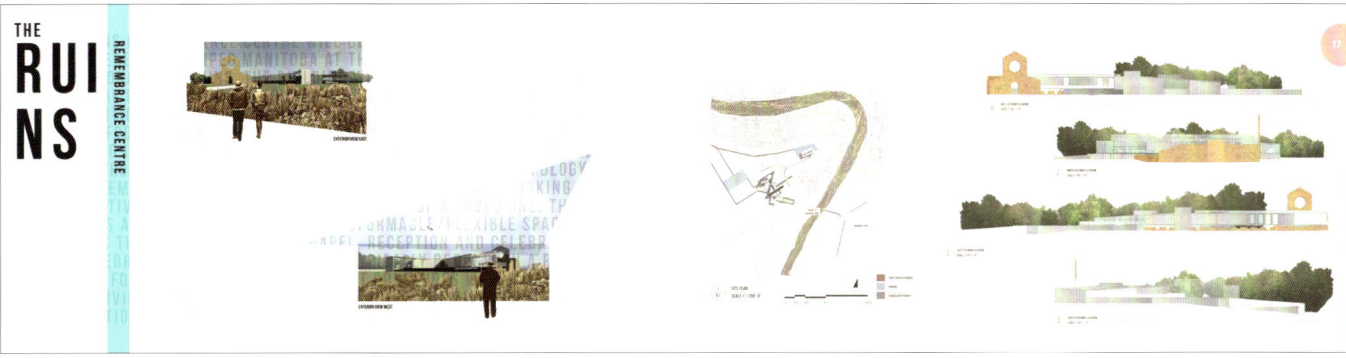
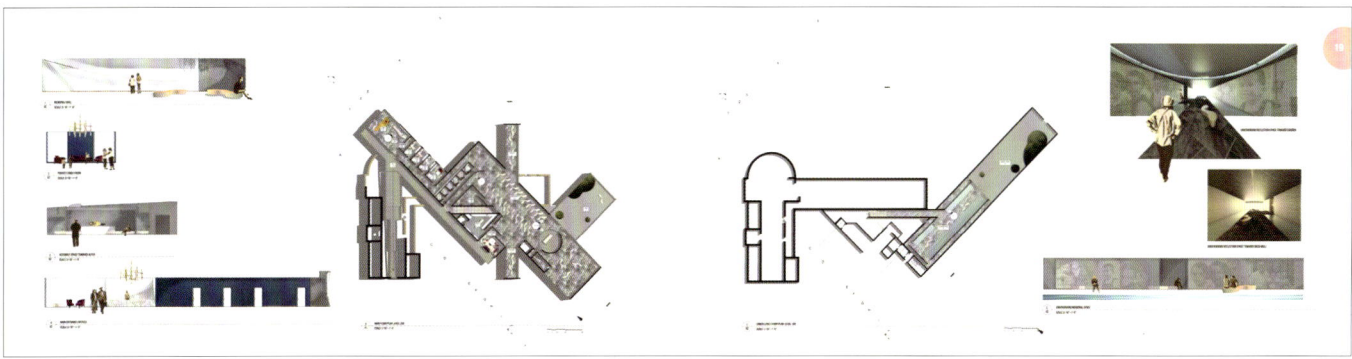
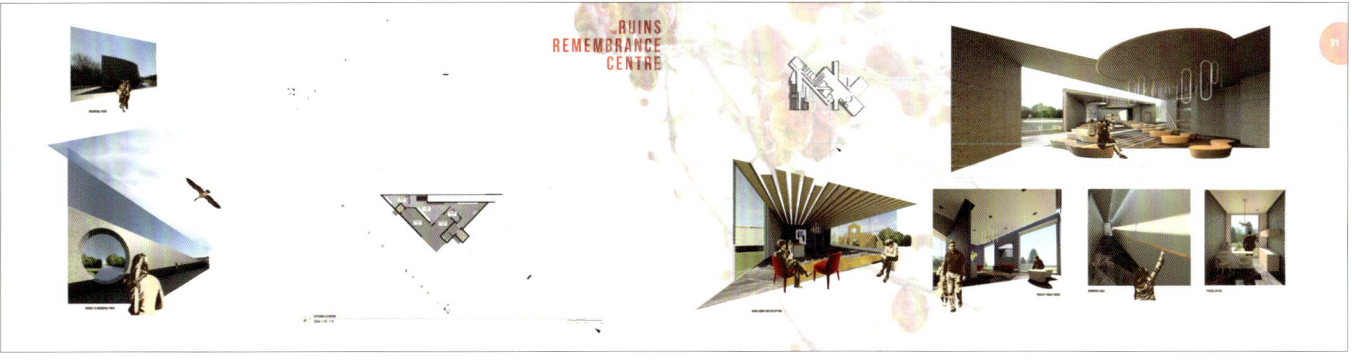
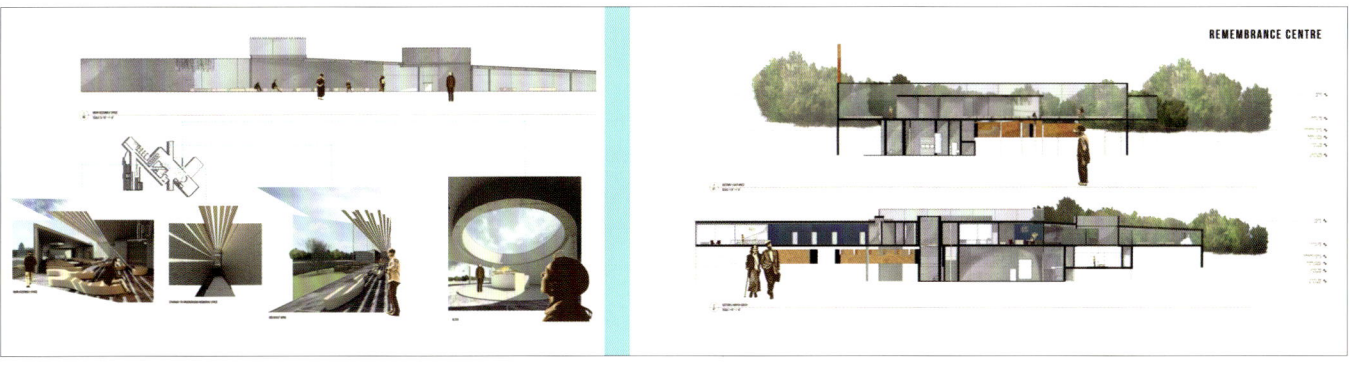

UNDERSTANDING YOUR STRENGTHS

Your designs have multiple applications to office practice. Preparing the groundwork of a portfolio for career development is an organizational task to add to your breadth of experience. This will help you form a qualitative presentation and represent your multitude of abilities in the discipline in a way that demonstrates confidence and myriad skills in design and visual communications. You will also be able to package the presentation with an understated but professional unified layout design.

Are you a Jack (or Jill) of all design disciplines? Are you motivated to focus your design content in a particular direction or genre in order to achieve your purpose? You should adopt a strategy to select, document, and apply your work to your portfolio. Remember, an active layout design is critical because you will continually reinterpret its structure spread after spread. Eventually, it is reviewed by either an academic program faculty member representing an admissions committee, or an office manager or associate principal who already has ideas of who and what he or she is looking for and whether you match the needs of the firm.

CULTIVATING SENSIBILITIES: SEEING AND PERCEIVING

Capturing images of your work for use in your portfolio is not limited to the methods of photographic and digital reproduction; you can use images to embrace a greater perception of how you see the world and to show your ability to perceive of all the essential ingredients. Every designer brings a unique perspective to the table and engages the world in familiar ways. With a fresh perspective on their surroundings, artists and designers observe, inform, and inspire their work, often in sensitive ways. In addition to their powers of visualizing novel solutions that inspire us, they are especially adept at sensing opportunities for change and then expressing that change by manipulating materials and visual elements to effect that change.

Here's a TIP:

Embrace the passion you had when creating the original project. Capture the enthusiasm you had when you collected images of inspiration that ignited the thought process behind your plans. Be careful of temporary emotions when creating the book. While they can be eye candy for developing a portfolio, they can also distract from the intention of the individual projects.

Jun Hong

Jun has made a set of rules to follow in his portfolio design. First, he decided to limit his projects to two pages only. The first page would always have five concept images along with a concept statement; he loosely brands the separate projects by using different typography styles. He has ruthlessly edited the second page to captivate his audience with the entire design and project development (figures 5–23 to 5–28).

Understanding your place in time is essential for the development of your book. Whether it is futuristic in its vision, contemporary in form, or only focused on historic preservation, your book can embody time, materiality, and form. Typography and layout designs can support and define a component of form reflective of an era of design culture. Design throughout history, from the industrial revolution to the present, has very different qualities and evokes different emotions. Age, new or old, is a quality that can resonate on many levels of portfolio design down to the choices of paper, binding, and branding.

Cultivating Sensibilities: Seeing and Perceiving

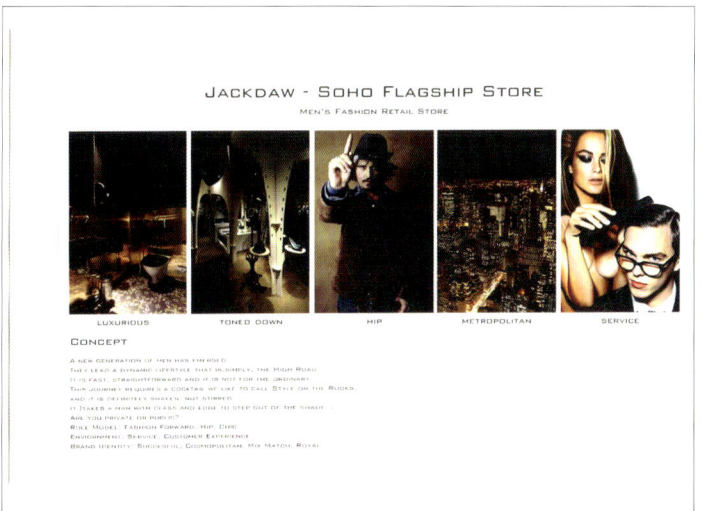
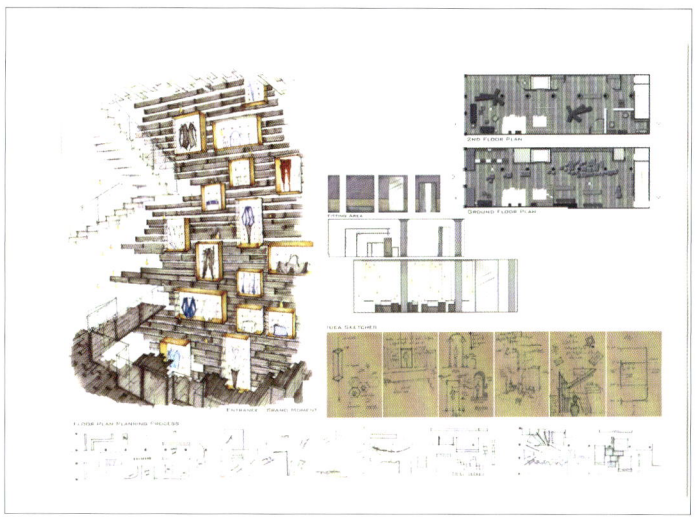

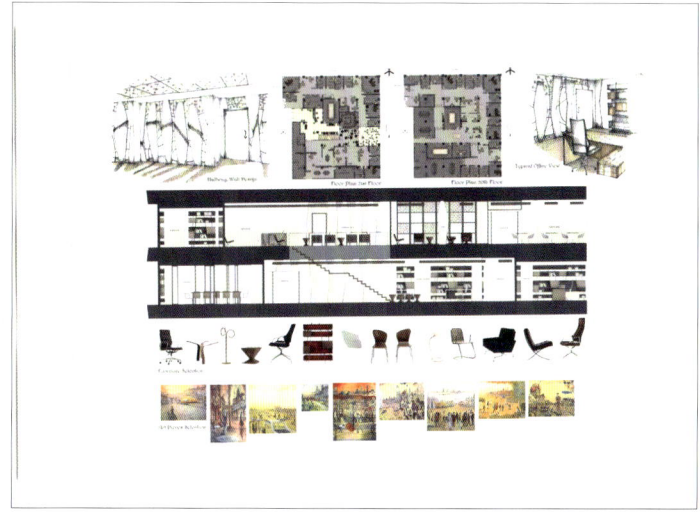

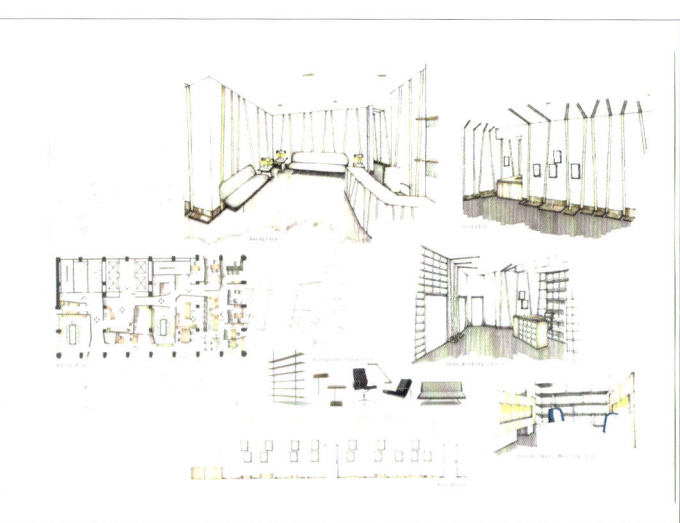

5–23 to 5–28 Pursuing a graduate degree affords the opportunity for advanced research in design and new portfolio strategies. Jun Hong, Sung Kyun Kwan University, Seoul, South Korea. 8.5" x 11".

5 CAPTURING EXPRESSIVE IMAGES

Perhaps it's a product package whose form and material contradict the verbal message it is trying to convey about nature or purity. Perhaps it's a restaurant that intends to welcome guests at their dramatic fountain entrance and provide a soothing experience. Designers may reframe experiences in Victorian theatrical themes or sleek contemporary genres. Be open to rethinking your approach and carrying through on a promise in a more useful and positive way.

The second design responsibility—expressing—is a means of creating change by exploiting these perceptions. By valuing and sharing their observations just because they seem beautiful, intriguing, offensive, or amusing, designers enrich their intuitions. How do you evoke a sense of beauty, intrigue, fire, or amusement? How do you express tactile qualities of form in any given design? Do designers connect their sensibilities to ours? How do they enrich our experience, even when we're not consciously aware of it? Most professionals readily recognize the practical benefits of a product or service, but they often overlook the less-apparent qualities of an experience from which they derive pleasure, identity, and meaning.

Tarah Spohn

Tarah created the undergraduate portfolio shown in figures 5–29 to 5–33 with a dual purpose of completing a course requirement and seeking employment following graduation from the New York School of Interior Design. The Adobe Creative Suite was instrumental in the layout design and preparation of visuals for her portfolio. Tarah used a local professional print center for the production of her book. She used full bleed images to maximize their impact and selected a white glossy paper and gray card stock for the cover. Binding was created with a black linen tape. She made a total of four copies, including a revised version after graduation.

Her portfolio development course at NYSID was an effective resource to help her develop her ideas for her book. She spent two months working on the portfolio and received numerous compliments especially on the clean layout design and quality of her sketching and visuals throughout the book. Naturally the best results come from more time invested in the process of design. Also, time invested in gathering the opinions of respected sources is instrumental in building the book and then revising it over and over. The majority of feedback springs from Tarah's book design and how she integrated sketching and graphic design devices into an overarching, well-organized portfolio presentation. She benefits from showing how adept she is with design software. The graphic design skills in her book show her design savvy, a key skill for rising interior designers because firms want professional presentations to clients in business meetings and design developmental sessions.

5–29 to 5–31 Tarah's skills of hand rendering and full color sketching are positioned throughout her book. She created a unique color/material group on the bottom right of each two-page spread. She labeled them and they serve as a clear palette for the design of each project. Her drawings are dramatic and the perspectives pull you into her spaces with a focus on materiality, shape, and light. Because she alternates two-page spreads between hand drawing and computer rendering, she has created a book that shows versatility and the ability to think of and execute design solutions. She also breaks the middle of her book with a dynamic representation of her furniture design in a 3D model form, also with strong materiality. All in all, it is a thoughtful and energetic book to page through. You sense her passion and involvement with design on so many levels. Tarah Spohn, New York School of Interior Design, N.Y., N.Y. 8.5" x 8.5".

Cultivating Sensibilities: Seeing and Perceiving

tarah spohn
tarahspohn@gmail.com
203.909.2729

Ferrol Spa Retreat and Hotel

Hotel, spa, and yoga retreat located in Ferrol, Spain, drawing from the influence of the surrounding ocean and naturally weathered elements

Revit, 3DS Max, Photoshop

Public Spaces

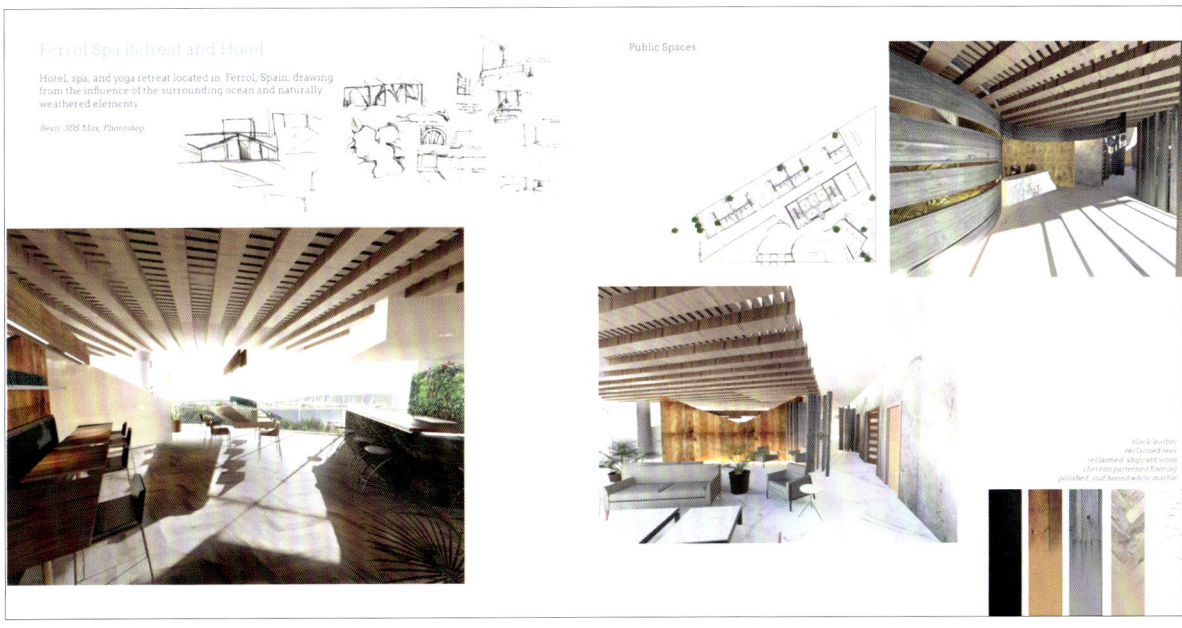

Guest Rooms

5 CAPTURING EXPRESSIVE IMAGES

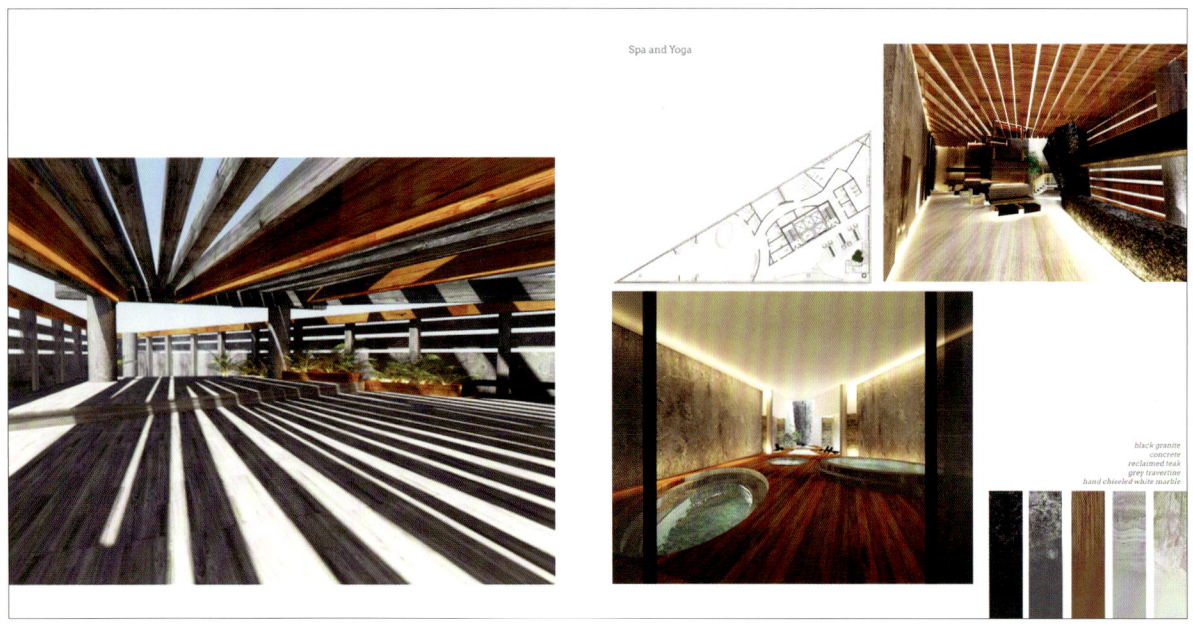

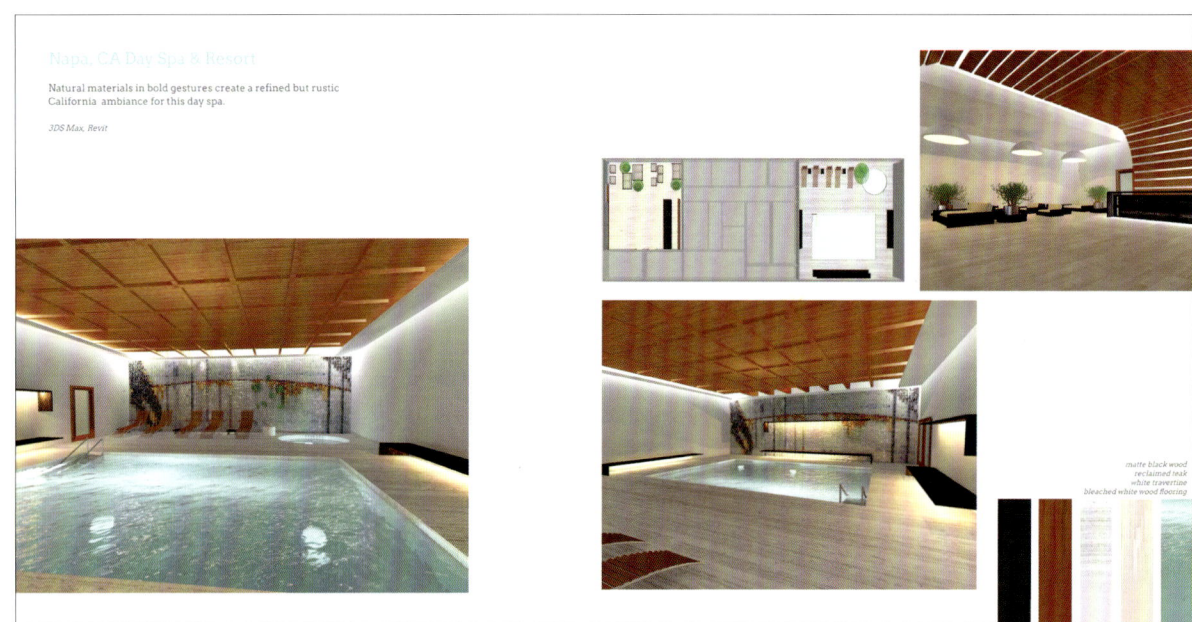

5–32 to 5–33 Tarah's skills of hand rendering and full color sketching are positioned throughout her book. She created a unique color/material group on the bottom right of each two-page spread. She labeled them and they serve as a clear palette for the design of each project. Her drawings are dramatic and the perspectives pull you into her spaces with a focus on materiality, shape, and light. Because she alternates two-page spreads between hand drawing and computer rendering, she has created a book that shows versatility and the ability to think of and execute design solutions. She also breaks the middle of her book with a dynamic representation of her furniture design in a 3D model form, also with strong materiality. All in all, it is a thoughtful and energetic book to page through. You sense her passion and involvement with design on so many levels. Tarah Spohn, New York School of Interior Design, N.Y., N.Y. 8.5" x 11".

HUMAN FACTORS

Health, safety, and welfare are the watchwords of the professor of interior design. Depending on the type of design project and the engagement of the design elements, portfolios can appear at first to be quite similar, however upon closer inspection, nuances regarding the human condition (health, safety, and welfare) may be impressive attributes of a design solution. Human factors in the interior design of space can add significant importance to the designed environment and separate you as the designer from others. When photographing your work, pay particular attention to the nuances of design evidence, such as graphic elements and color sensibility, so that the work is faithfully rendered.

It is up to the designer to emphasize or draw attention to the elements that define design process from the outcome. The photograph addresses certain details that the interior designer has established through a hierarchical system of imagination and communication. Layout, sequencing, lighting control, and graphic design elements in tandem with the picture, either photographic or graphic (drawing), are all realized.

As demonstrated throughout this chapter, you can see how inextricably interwoven your vision is with meaningful relationships between documentation and technique, visual layout, and the concept of the portfolio. The time invested in developing thorough experience with the many ways of creating and manipulating images in context with your intent is invaluable to the creative process.

How do you distinguish your design evidence from the other applicants in the field? Your understanding of and ability to create meaningful and appropriate images of your work in proper context within your portfolio is vital to the larger appreciation of your job. Excellent collections of design work establish clear parameters for the inclusion of different kinds of images in support of the story behind the work.

Whether you intend to submit your book for employment or as an application for graduate school, your work will be reviewed in competition with others. In the next chapter, you will consider multiple versions of a basic plan for your book for print and also digital, for uploading when applying for employment, internships, or graduate school admissions.

In the following chapter, we outline techniques surrounding digital media. We discuss these tools at length for their "operative nature." Knowing precisely when to deploy these tools and technology is vital when developing your body of work. Ultimately it is the combination and hybridization of these various skills that begin to shape your portfolio and that have the power to show both personality and professional/academic prowess as an interior designer.

6

DIGITAL
PRESENTATIONS

"Digital media break narratives into fragmented bits of information and strip away the inherent human meaning, intimacy, tactility and sensuality of things."

– JUHANI PALLASMAA

OVERVIEW

Contradiction, as this passage may suggest, should be our liberation, not our constraint. Intended to dare rather than proclaim, this quote merely poses a challenge to the contemporary interior designer and should spark a holistic approach when wielding technology as a means of generating creative works. Digital media is just another tool, which when leveraged correctly can embody the very qualities this quote wishes to dismiss. This chapter merely attempts to shed light on the various processes involved in this art in order to fully render a body of work with all its magic and intent.

Digital media is a fundamental and powerful tool for the interior designer today. It presents a more efficient means of creating and editing work, as well as producing material for presentation and communication. Although software used in professional practice and education has similarities, it is important to note their key differences due to projects' various timelines and end goals. In professional practice, the time allocated for design is much less than it is in education, and in education, more emphasis and time is given to the aesthetic of the visual representation. Technology is developing at a rapid rate, increasing the range of design software available for use in studio practice. The portfolio examples included in this chapter and throughout the book were created with software that provides for flexible methods of ideation, editing, and refinement for presentations online and in print formats. Cultivating one's understanding of what is possible using digital means opens new pathways for the comprehensive development of a project, publication, portfolio, and online variations such as a website, promotional instruments, CD/DVD, or social networks.

Unlike other means of disseminating creative work, the interior design portfolio presents an opportunity to explore the hybridization of digital tools. Generative works in a variety of media are brought together and integrated into one cohesive piece. For our purposes, this creates an incredible foundation to begin the conversation about the use and combination of digital media.

Digital means for producing one's portfolio offer flexibility in design communication, consistency of output quality, and ease of dissemination, making the use of digital media essential in portfolio design. Multiple versions can be produced and modified to meet different criteria for portfolio presentations, for example, applications to undergraduate or graduate schools, grants, internships, or competitions. It is important to be aware that different presentation formats and layouts could be very useful for one submission and not so for another. Working back and forth in multiple software programs will be integral to refining the content of your graphic work and layout design strategies. As you master multiple software programs, you will hone techniques for effectively improving and strengthening your project results, coordinating the various features of your work into a unified portfolio. Learning how to manipulate multiple programs can be difficult initially, but with persistent use and advice from those more experienced, the benefits will soon be reaped. Online tutorials and videos are readily—and freely—available, and studio environments are an excellent source of insider tips and techniques.

6 DIGITAL PRESENTATIONS

Vivi Rosenberg

Vivi designed her portfolio (figures 6–1 to 6–5) as an undergraduate student at the New York School of Interior Design for the purpose of seeking employment after graduation and also as an important method to organize and prioritize her work for the record and future use. She found InDesign for layout design and Photoshop to correct visuals to be the best software for the design of her book. Vivi did a rehearsal portfolio at full size to gain a feel for the project and its design. She simply stapled it together without worrying about the exact binding method so she could turn the pages and gage the layout, flow, and sizing of text and images. Her portfolio was printed on a satin finish 80 lb non-glare paper with only slightly reflective properties. The cost to print and bind one copy was $37.00. She spent about 5 weeks to create her book. She felt that the book was successful; even though the projects are quite different from one to another, they work nicely together as a bound collection. In the future she may revisit to add more

6–1 to 6–5 Vivi has a nice balance of computer-generated images and fine watercolor renderings in the second half of her book. Her materials are dramatic and oftentimes dark. She printed many images as tests to make sure the color read as a material and not a black image. Sometimes what she saw on screen was not what she saw on the printed book. She had made a starter book with all of her images on clean white space simply stapled to help understand the flow and progression of the book. She even tested different sizes to make sure the images were strong and the right scale. Process was important and she treated the book as a real design project. The result is clean and powerful with nice hierarchy in the typography. Vivi Rosenberg, New York School of Interior Design, N.Y., N.Y. 8" x 10".

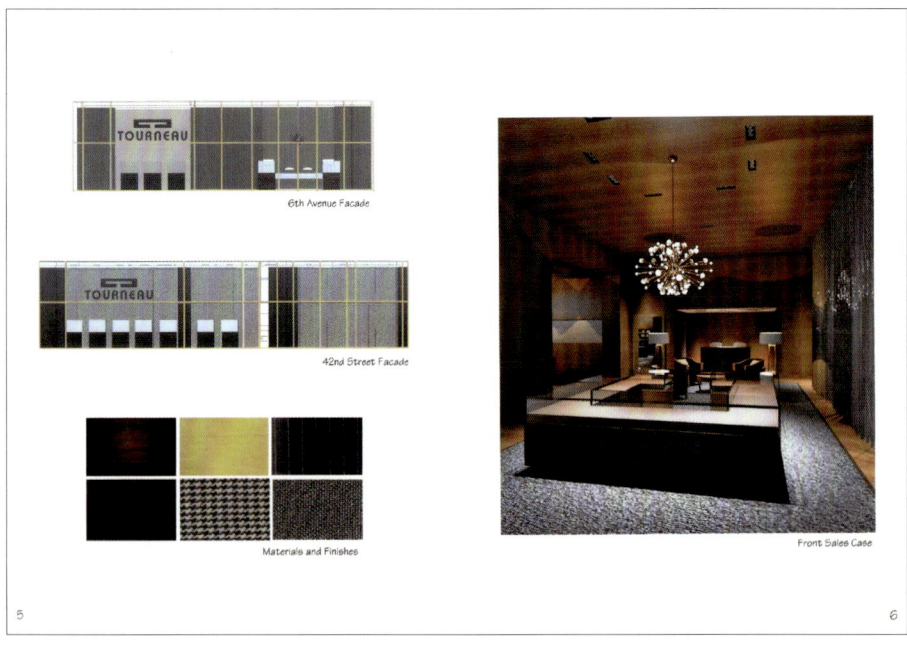

Overview

Sales Floor

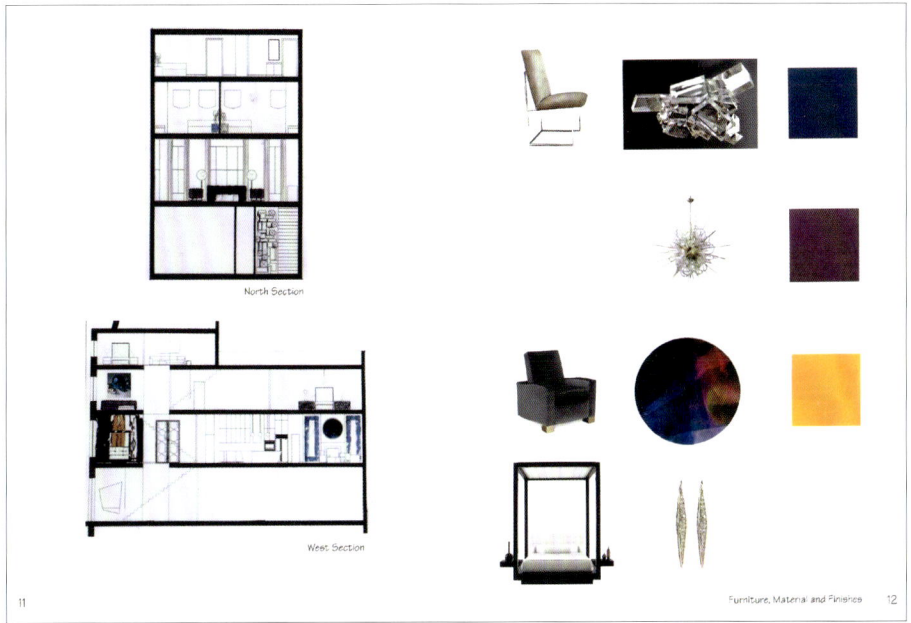

North Section
West Section
Furniture, Material and Finishes

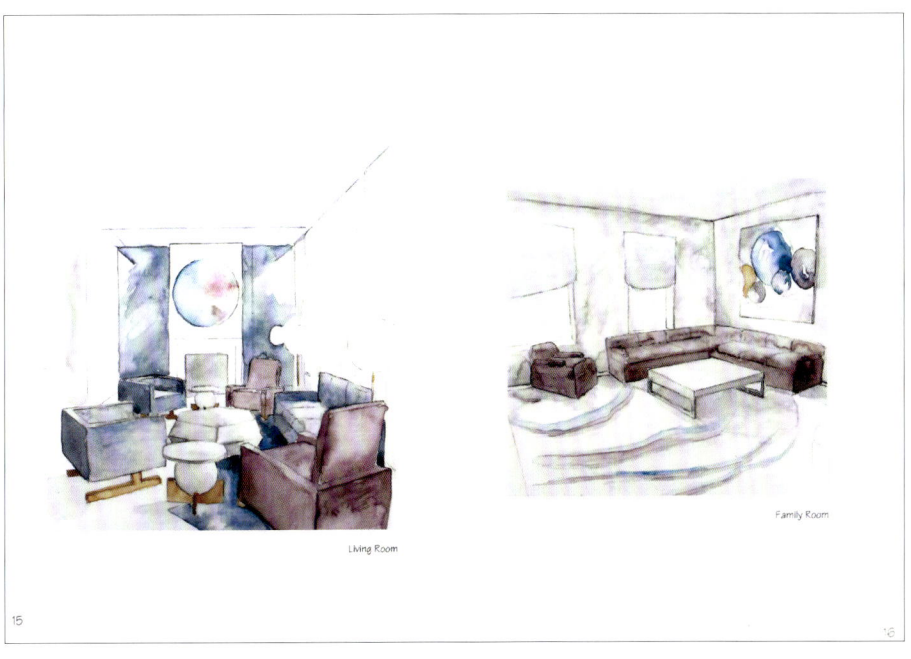

Living Room
Family Room

6 DIGITAL PRESENTATIONS

> **Here's a TIP:**
> The portfolio should be approached as an act of design, existing on the same creative tier as its content.

work. She found inspiration in a Chanel coffee table book. She was impressed with the clarity of the images and content of the work. It came as a boxed set of separate bound booklets, which might be a way to organize, collect, and maintain collections as a record of her work.

If you are designing an online published hard copy book as Vivi Rosenberg has done, you will need to research which places suit your requirements and which offer the best proportions for the finished book. The online publishing sources mentioned previously have come a long way in the past couple of years. Vivi produced a cheap bond paper, stapled image layout of the design, which is an important step prior to uploading images to adorama.com. The stapling of the prototype book helped her to page through and see how the pace and images flow together or apart. She also needed to meet the individual requirements of the online publishers to upload her images properly so that they will not be pixilated, blurry images that will prove to be unprofessional or unreadable. Most of these sites will immediately tell you if the image is too small or the file is incorrect when you upload the image.

You will still need to make many design decisions when producing your book. You will have paper weight options and paper sizes to choose from. Some publishers will even offer flat lay books that are glued together as perfect binding. This is a big plus for students who wish to have full two-page spread images that bleed into one another without a roll occurring at the gutter of the binding. Adorama does offer this option and it makes a big difference. The online process of producing a portfolio is convenient and cost effective, especially if you are planning on producing many portfolios to send out to different cities throughout the country. But you need to do the research of what these different sites not only offer but also what their requirements are for uploading images and producing your two-page spreads.

Traditionally the portfolio is the first handshake between academia and professionals, acting as a surrogate to both personality and artistic aptitude. Time should be taken to reflect on the overall intent of the portfolio and what the interior designer wishes it to express regarding his or her body of work. Once you have outlined a storyboard and layout design with an organizing framework, you can now consider implementing it in a digital format. In this chapter, basic methods for preparing the work and presentation digitally will be presented. You should then set aside a decent amount of time for creating, critiquing, and modifying the presentation layout to achieve the most visually compelling portfolio. Designing your portfolio is a challenging and time-consuming process, and sometimes multiple options need to be tested before deciding on a final one.

The advantages to the use of digital media are the ability to save multiple versions of the work, which is incredibly helpful if you later decide that you prefer an earlier design. It is also useful to note that digital files can become corrupted for various unknown reasons, so saving multiple files as the design progresses, and backing up your work on different hard drives or online is essential. Including number dates (yyyymmdd) in your file names helps to organize your files in chronological order for easy searching later on. It is important to remember that digital media is a powerful tool and like any other tool requires the same amount of rigor while executing. Organization, clear intent, and a constant iterative development are fundamental while producing the portfolio.

PREPARING PHYSICAL WORK FOR DIGITAL MEDIA

There is a somewhat theatrical performance that occurs amongst the analog and digital characters of work. The two all but kiss briefly, flirtatiously rousing their intrinsic qualities from this encounter. They will never share in a symbiotic relationship, holding to the same qualities as they did in their medium, however, it is this tension we must capture: a provocative dance the interior designer must learn to choreograph. The transition between mediums has always frustrated the interior designer. It is a process that has been viewed by most as detrimental to the work, but it is this limited view that cripples its possibilities. The transformation between mediums, physical to digital or digital to physical, should be thought of as an introduction to a larger conversation within the work that would otherwise lay dormant. The processes and methods to follow begin to shed light on the ways this conversation may occur, offering a glimpse into an otherwise unchartered terrain awaiting discovery. Let these methodologies reveal new trajectories within the work to inform and strengthen the story you wish to portray.

Physical project work is converted to a digital format in a variety of ways, but depending on the original medium that the work is in, some methods are more appropriate than others. You will want to emphasize the most interesting aspects of your work, the character you wish to portray, and the act they will serve, so take this into consideration as you choose a method of documentation.

Flat, two-dimensional images are best documented using a flatbed scanner. Unlike taking a photograph, the scanner helps to reduce any distortion in perspective, and a high resolution for the scanned image can be set to the full and correct scale. Scan your work at a minimum resolution of 300 dpi (dots per inch).

Large images or reliefs that are too big or too thick to fit on a scanner bed will need to be photographed using a high-resolution digital camera. The work should be mounted either horizontally on a copy stand or vertically on a blank wall. The copy stand can position the camera directly perpendicular to the work, minimizing distortion in perspective. Arranging the work horizontally can also reduce any unevenness of the cast light, especially if the copy stand has lamps directed down onto the work. If you mount the work vertically, however, more care will need to be taken to achieve a good photograph. The camera will need to be carefully positioned central and perpendicular to the work, at a distance far enough away to capture the work with minimal distortion in perspective. A camera stand or flat surface should be used to prevent any movement of the camera, which can cause blur in the photograph. Be aware that any fixtures used to attach the work to the wall should not be seen. Also, most spaces are typically lit from above, which will cause the work to be subtly lighter at the top. This effect is so common that it is not usually noticed unless

"A portfolio should show everything you can do and do well. One can assume you won't show what you cannot do. So, show the reviewer everything as it is better to be over-prepared than under-prepared and always have the 'piesta resistance' in the ready."

– **JIM KENNEY**, PROFESSOR OF INTERIOR ARCHITECTURE, CALIFORNIA STATE UNIVERSITY, SACRAMENTO, CA.

the lighting effect is unintentionally reversed, so make sure that the work is always oriented the right way up, and place other lights in the space to balance out any unevenness in the lighting. Whichever method is chosen, be careful that the work is lit brightly enough to prevent any noise (due to low lighting) in the photograph, but not so bright that part of the work becomes washed out. Especially when shooting work with more three-dimensional elements, remember that some carefully considered shadows could work well to emphasize the form of the relief.

Three-dimensional models or sculptures will need to be captured with a high-resolution digital camera. The context in which the work is mounted or positioned should enhance the work, and not distract from it. Typically, blank, muted backgrounds with minimal contrast are best. White backgrounds can wash out work that is white or lightly colored, while black backgrounds are quite harsh, and can be overpowering for more delicate work. Depending on the work, brightly colored backgrounds could work well, or they could overtake the work and dominate the photograph. Concerning the angle of the photograph, you will have to experiment with multiple angles. It is best to make numerous photographs, from different perspectives and orientations, as sometimes the photograph you prefer at the time might not be so useful when reviewing them later. Some aspects of the work may require a close-up photograph, so make sure that the lens can focus properly on the detail and is not blurry.

Desirable distortion, though advised to be executed sparingly, is another means of capturing physical work. Contemporary photography and digital processes continue to reveal new ways of documenting our physical world. These examples are prevalent in any text or website regarding contemporary photography. It is to the interior designer's advantage to become familiar with these artists and techniques to generate new means of capturing work. There are numerous professions, such as automotive design, industrial design, and photography, that execute and push imaging techniques every day and provide grounds for exploration. The means of image capture is used with control and thoughtful execution to achieve the desired outcome. The processes described above all create a type of digital image called a "raster" image, and understanding the nature of this image type will help determine which software to use for additional editing and is discussed in more detail in the "Editing Digital Images" section.

As previously mentioned, the translation of your physical work into a digital format is not always smooth, and further editing will always be required. It is important that we continue to capitalize on this unevenness and agitation. The techniques outlined in this chapter only represent a small, but active, portion of contemporary techniques available to the interior designer who is experimenting with both digital and analog modes of representation. Reveal rather than cloud, instigate rather than distract, and most of all allow this translation to affect the work!

Jillian Schultz

Ordinarily, boxing text and graphics by outlining their forms with borderlines is considered to be an unnecessary treatment in page design because it establishes a redundant and extraneous layout that often conflicts with other elements on the page, such as freehand sketching and illustration. However, Jillian has found a softer approach that works beautifully with her content due to the use of light values, thin lines, and soft color treatments (figures 6–6 to 6–9).

Jillian weighed all of these layout decisions carefully over the period of a semester, and she found a way to work harmoniously between the elements and process of designing her book. InDesign and Photoshop were the most important software packages used in her design. She used an Epson Workforce laser printer with ultra-premium matte paper along with a Pina Zangaro screw-post portfolio case purchased from the Internet. She made one case for a cost of $30.

6–6 to 6–9 Jillian's portfolio displays a strong sense of organization and clear thought process. You can easily understand her thought process throughout a design project. She successfully uses soft light colors against neutral white and sometimes gray backgrounds. Colors in line create zones or linear box shapes that highlight her concept and program notes without competing with design content and serve to tie together the entire project. Jillian Schultz, Villa Maria College, Buffalo, N.Y. 8.5" x 11".

Preparing Physical Work for Digital Media

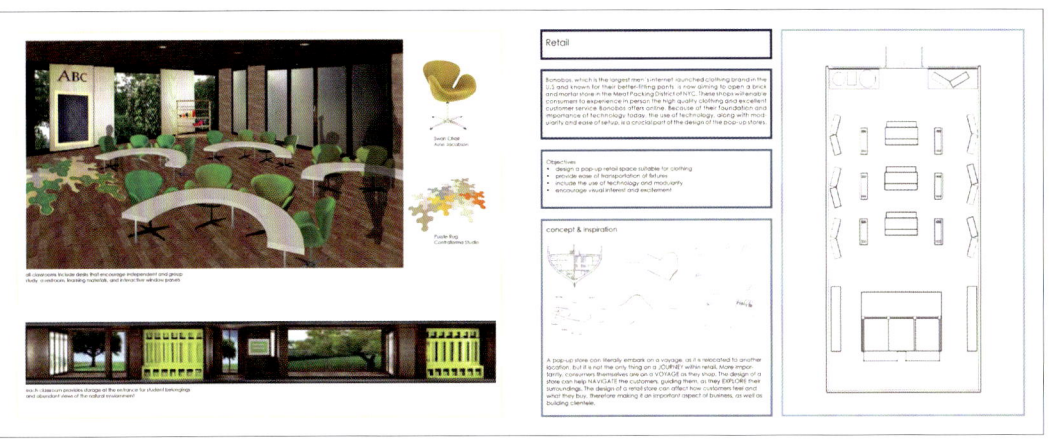

CREATING DIGITAL IMAGES

Incredibly vast, the digital realm continues to generate new trajectories within the field of interior design. Unlike analog approaches, the digital realm provides an almost fantastic condition of manipulation to formal constructs within the work. Void of the specific conditions, the digital image remains in a continuous state of change and provides an almost acrobatic flexibility when developing your work. Reliance on photographic technique now takes center stage within the digital space. Today, it is becoming increasingly common for work to be created and published in the digital space. This trend from physical to digital drawing and modeling is not so much because it is easier or faster, but rather that digital programs can now offer many more opportunities in the design process and output production. Design work can more easily be edited and updated in digital space—without having to start the drawing or model from scratch. Incredibly complex forms and geometries created in digital forms are complicated and cumbersome to calculate manually. It is common for students working in digital space, however, to become disconnected from the physical world, such that designs created in digital space are difficult to translate into the material world and its laws of physics. It is important and needs to be stressed again: The interior designer works in both physical and digital realms as well as the transitions between.

When discussing the software programs accessible in architecture-related fields, it is important first to distinguish their different purposes in education and professional practice. In design education, project work is primarily focused on the front-end of the design and construction process. As such, the amount of technical information and detail required in the work tends to be lower. For education purposes, digital software programs that are lighter and less clunky in manipulating design forms are preferred. Rhino is becoming an increasingly popular digital software for students because it enables 3D modeling, as well as the extraction of 2D views and line work from the digital model. Manipulation of forms is relatively intuitive and straightforward, without having to get into the specifics as to what it is, or how it is composed. Some separate plug-ins can also be installed, such as Grasshopper and V-Ray, that can further expand the capabilities of the software. Additional software includes 3D Studio MAX and Maya, both of which have gained popularity as innovative design and animation tools.

In professional practice, however, more detailed and accurate information is required for the construction process, which would then need to be communicated to others also working on the project. Building information modelling (BIM) excels in this area. It is a common misconception that BIM is only necessary for digitally modeling buildings and for extracting the architectural drawings from the model. In actuality, it is so much more powerful than that. The advantages of BIM reside in its ability to store an incredible amount of detailed information about the model and about every component of a structure, which can then be quickly scheduled and communicated to the necessary people. The higher level of information contained within the model allows any mistakes and inconsistencies to be caught earlier in the design process, as opposed to beginning construction and discovering it on-site. Revit is currently the only significant software program able to support the BIM workflow, and is becoming incredibly popular in professional practice; more firms are requiring that their staff be skilled in the software. It is not commonly taught in design schools, however, as the higher levels of detail needed in the model can inhibit or slow down the design process for students.

Regardless of which digital modeling software is used, traditional architectural line drawings and three-dimensional views (in perspective or parallel projections) can be extracted from the model. Depending on what software is used and how it is exported, these drawings will require some additional editing, so that the drawing can more clearly or effectively communicate its intentions.

Digital graphic software can be used to edit images extracted from a digital model or to create pictures entirely drawn in digital space. In Adobe Photoshop, found images can be collaged together to portray an idea or to create views of a fully new space. Adobe Illustrator can be used to create informative graphics or branding logos. Digital images (created by both modeling and graphic software programs) can also be compiled and used to create animations or videos. Adobe After Effects and Adobe Premiere Pro are great programs for this, as they allow a greater degree of control in the editing process.

It is important to note that the digital images described above will be one of two types of images: "raster" or "vector" images. These different file types are important to know, as they have different strengths and weaknesses that may be more appropriate to specific outcomes. These differences will be discussed in more detail in the next section, including the selection of most suitable software programs.

Before transitioning to what is considered, in both academia as well as the industry, as "post-production," there needs to be a simple re-definition of this term. If we consider the portfolio as a design problem, then we must treat it with the same rigor of development as the work it contains. Therefore, each technique executed and representation selected must further an aspect of the work! This exchange and cross-pollination of mediums shows the interior designer's unique ability to leverage advantageous relations within spatial conditions. Post-production can now be re-defined as a working drawing rather than a finishing piece, pushing the work beyond what it was conceived to be.

"A portfolio is so much more than a record of your work. It conveys your character, communicates your creativity, confirms your abilities, and speaks to clients and employers alike. In addition to demonstrating the breadth of your design capabilities, it foremost features your design process, starting with your concept. A new employer can send you to train on the newest software, but they can't teach you to think creatively, design innovatively, and produce results that will serve your client's needs beyond their initial expectations. Your portfolio needs to communicate the substance of your design education and the potential of your design capabilities."

– **SANDRA REICIS**, ASSOCIATE PROFESSOR, INTERIOR DESIGN, VILLA MARIA COLLEGE, BUFFALO, N.Y.

6 DIGITAL PRESENTATIONS

Gisella Allen

As an undergraduate at the University of Texas at Austin School of Architecture, with a major in Interior Design, Gisella designed this spacious layout (figures 6–10 to 6–15) to take distinct advantage of negative (white) space while emphasizing her substantial talents in visual communications, including sketching, drawing, photography, and illustration. She used the Adobe Creative Suite predominantly throughout the design of her book. She used an 80# cover stock and a commercial print service for a professional result. A black wire coil was used to bind the book to achieve minimal distraction for the book. She made two books: one with a chronological order to the sequence of projects for academic applications, and the other in a condensed version for application for an internship and employment opportunities after school. The portfolio was a gratifying learning experience providing important opportunities to take stock of her work and the task of organization. She learned how to work through multiple kinds of documents to bring them together into a unified and coherent presentation. Photographs were adjusted in Photoshop. Drawings needed unity to bring various attempts of cropping images into a coordinated package.

She remarks, "I spent much time researching portfolios throughout the Internet such as ISSUU, Blurb, and Lulu. The entire effort was highly successful in landing a position as an intern with Gensler and Associates." Her interview was online. She believes that an aspiring interior designer should prepare for both a digital portfolio presentation and a print version depending on the preference of the firm. The firm had her portfolio opened up on a screen as the interview was conducted during a video phone call.

6–10 to 6–15 Gisella's portfolio is a fine example of merging interior design and architecture. She demonstrates this not only in the materials and structure, but in the fenestration as well. The opening graphic form on her cover page supports her concept. The transitional structures of the entrances of her projects are also supported by spatial and material concepts. She closes with a well-developed graphic page that highlights one of her winning designs. The dark negative spaces of the portfolio layouts also support the dark passageways of her projects, bringing the viewer into the light of the project. She challenges structure and surface throughout her projects and calls it out in a title on one two-page spread. This is a good example of continuity within a portfolio form. Gisella Allen, University of Texas at Austin School of Architecture, Austin, Tex. 8.5" x 11".

Creating Digital Images

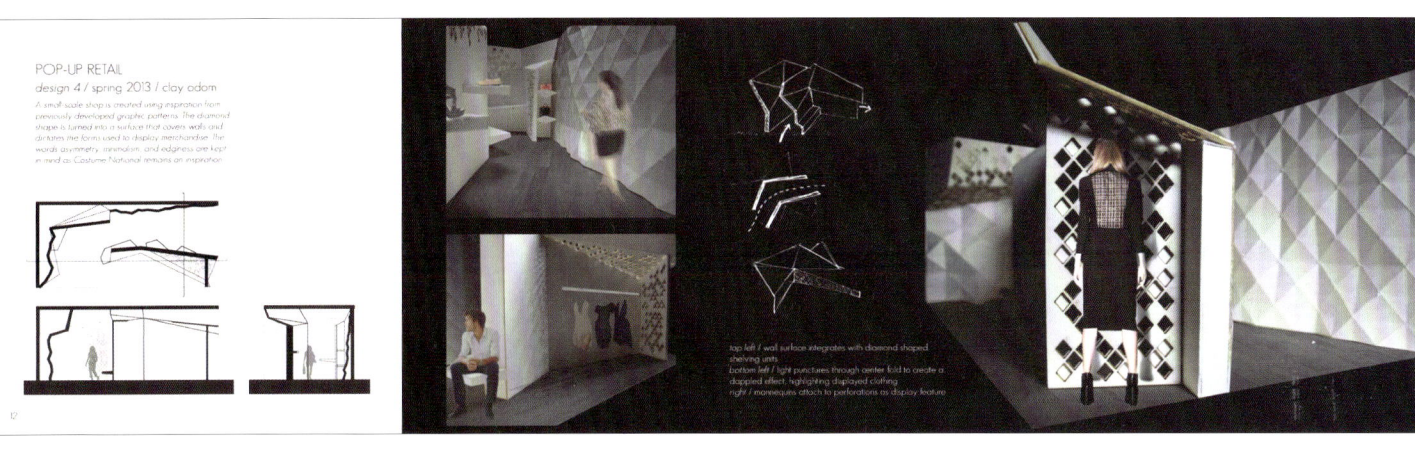

POP-UP RETAIL
design 4 / spring 2013 / clay odom

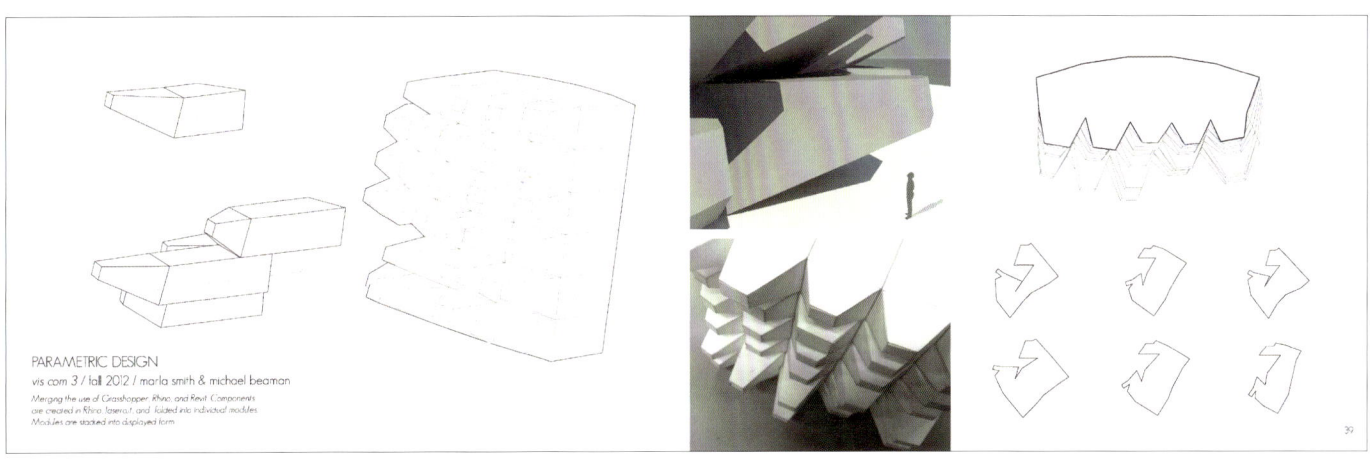

PARAMETRIC DESIGN
vis com 3 / fall 2012 / marla smith & michael beaman

WINDOW STUDY
design 5 / fall 2013 / allison gaskins

143

" A portfolio is a source of pride, and should be seen by the designer as an extension of themselves—their experiences, outlook on life, capabilities, and work methodologies. The portfolio, through the imbedded graphics and content, is the most effective way to communicate how a designer hopes to shape the world around them and the importance of design thinking for the advancement of the design profession into all aspects of society. A portfolio is an organic, living entity, made up of many fine details. It is a piece of artwork, like a sculpted piece of marble or a line of poetry."

— **AARON KADOCH**, AIA, ASSISTANT PROFESSOR OF INTERIOR ARCHITECTURE, THE UNIVERSITY OF WISCONSIN, STEPHENS POINT, WI.

EDITING DIGITAL IMAGES

The Renaissance artist scans the scene, preparing for the first unpredictable stroke on the canvas. Anticipation turns to passion, violently striking the page, interpreting the performance of a world unfolding before him; like an artist, we too wield our mouse. History is an important aspect to recall when observing the attributes of digital tools. Software is developed to aid or assist in an existing analog process that otherwise would prove time-consuming and laborious. Most computational tools are grounded in classical techniques. Why do we use a perspective, why do we choose a black and white image, or why do we use a paint brush versus a pen? All of these are questions the interior designer should be conscious of while editing the digital image and while choosing the software to achieve its effects. The same techniques that comprise a successful Renaissance painting hold faithful to the digital image. Light and shadow, contrast, composition, tension, directionality, and focus all come into play while editing the digital image and should be utilized by the various tools. The interior designer only needs to be conscious of these techniques and the work will already be improved before the program or image type is ever selected.

There are two types of digital images, raster or vector files, and understanding both is necessary for determining the best software to edit them. Raster images are created from a series of tiny dots or pixels, which are aggregated to form the overall image. If you zoom into a raster image, you can see the small squares or pixels that compose the image. The number of pixels that the picture is made from determines the resolution of the image, and so the greater the number of pixels, the sharper the image. Photographs and scanned images are raster files. Vector images, however, are created from a series of paths, which are assigned different color values. These paths allow the image to be resized and scaled without jeopardizing the resolution or quality of the image. When you zoom into a vector image, the information of the paths will be maintained, and so the edges and details will remain crisp; no pixilation will be visible. It is of particular importance for text graphics that require sharp clarity, or images that will need to be resized or scaled frequently. Vector images can only be drawn in specific software like Adobe Illustrator, Corel Draw, or other CAD programs.

RASTER IMAGES

When editing raster images, Adobe Photoshop is by far the most popular software program, as it allows for a greater degree of control and ease in the process. Some of the most useful tools in Photoshop are the adjustment layers, which enable different aspects of the image to be adjusted quickly and easily, without being permanent. Specific areas of the picture can also be selected and applied as a layer mask to the adjustment layers, such that the adjustments only affect the selected areas. The adjusted properties are number values, which then allows for copying into multiple similar files. The following are typical properties that can be adjusted:

- Exposure. Exposure refers to the tonal values in the image. There are three controls—exposure, offset, and gamma—that can adjust the highlights, mid-tones, and shadows separately. The exposure setting mainly affects the highlights; the offset setting adjusts the shadows and mid-tone values; and the gamma setting deals with the mid-tone values and can help to embolden any contrasts in the image.
- Hue/Saturation. The color of the picture can be altered using these three variables: hue, which can completely change the colors in the image; saturation, which can reduce the colors to grayscale or make them bolder; and lightness, which controls the amount of white cast upon the image.
- Photo Filters. This tool applies a color layer over the image, which is very effective at correcting subtle color errors, as well as creating a particular ambiance within the image. The color can be applied at various opacities, which is controlled by a percentage scale; the higher the percentage, the more solid the color layer.
- Transform. This tool offers a variety of ways to manipulate an existing image. Transformation tools become incredibly useful when the original scale, shape, or style of the image does not coincide with the desired portrayal of the work within the portfolio. Things to keep in mind while using these tools include image integrity and resolution. Multiple transformations performed on an image can reduce its initial resolution, and inversely if the existing image resolution is low these transformations will further degrade the work. Safe practice requires a minimum resolution of 150 dpi while utilizing these tools.
- Selection. Sometimes adjustments to the work require masking or selecting different aspects of the work for precise manipulations. This task can occasionally become meticulous and time-consuming depending upon the nature of the region to be selected. Utilizing the save selection function under the layers option provides a history of previous selections, which sometimes may take several minutes to achieve. Recalling selections continuously without reproduction accelerates the editing process and provides precision within the edited work.

Scanned images will typically require a fair amount of cleaning up before you can place them in your portfolio. Sometimes little marks or dust will be left on the scanner bed, which will then appear in your scanned image. If you are using Photoshop, you could use a combination of the magic wand and polygonal lasso tools to select areas of the image and delete or fill the selected areas to make them the same as the surrounding context. Scanned images are also typically more washed out than the original and may need their contrast to be increased. Increasing the gamma in the exposure settings will also embolden the darker colors. If the scanned color does not match the original, the hue/saturation scales can be modified or different photo filters could be applied to different percentages to alter the tint.

Make sure to save a copy of the original images at a high quality, preferably in a non-compressive file format, such as a tagged image file format (TIFF). Compressed image files, like joint photographic experts group (JPEG) files or portable network graphics (PNG), enable smaller file sizes, but also lose a small amount of data; this becomes especially noticeable after multiple editing operations have been applied. Depending on the portfolio format, smaller image files may be required, but it is best to extract these from the high quality "original." One essential quality of note regarding PNG file types is their ability to provide transparency. While JPEG file types read "white" as a solid, PNG file types read white as void, which becomes critical when layering information within Photoshop.

6 DIGITAL PRESENTATIONS

VECTOR IMAGES

Vector image files are composed of a series of line paths, which can only be created using a particular digital software. In architecture-related disciplines, most vector images are created in CAD software like Rhino, AutoCAD, and Revit, then edited in a graphic software program like Adobe Illustrator. Vector image files are ideal for drawings that require crisp and accurate line work, as well as for images that will frequently be re-sized. Text should also be inserted into a vector image, as vector shape graphics are much better at maintaining sharp and crisp text edges, and editing the text is much simpler. Regardless of the image resolution, rasterized text will often be slightly blurred at the edges, and may need to be entirely replaced if any changes are made. Vector images are also typically smaller in file size.

When combining raster and vector images, it is important to note that raster image editing software programs will automatically convert an image into a raster file. The best way to use the strengths of both raster and vector images would be first to edit the raster image in a software program like Photoshop and then place or link the raster image into a vector graphic program like Illustrator for the overlaying of text and other shape graphics. This way, the raster image remains rasterized, and the vector graphics remain as vectors. PDF (portable document format) files can save the image file as either a raster or vector image file. It is important to note, however, that if a vector PDF file is opened in a raster image editing software like Photoshop, the PDF file will immediately become a raster image file.

Regardless of whether your drawing is a raster or vector image file, there are some key points to consider when editing your work. Image editing programs provide a large number of tools and combinations of commands that can be used to enhance your work; however, the multitude of tools available can become a trap of wasted time if you just need to make minor adjustments. Remember, the artist would not spend his time on a detail that will not be perceived by his audience. Before you start editing your image, make sure that you evaluate and identify the essential features of the work to be enhanced. Develop a hierarchy of the image, determining what needs to be bolder and what needs to recede. Continuously look at examples of work that you admire, question the medium, and examine its mode of representation to gain inspiration on different techniques that could work well for you. Have an overall idea or concept of how you want the work to proceed, and keep referring to it, to ensure that all your development decisions are in support of your end goals.

All in all, image editing is the most significant step in preparing your work for a wider audience, and thus takes a great deal of time. Make sure to leave enough time for this process, as it is difficult to determine ahead of time how successful a technique will be. It is often helpful to ask other students and advisers to critique your work during this process, as a fresh set of eyes can help to identify aspects that are favorable or distracting. With experience, the process will get faster, and you will develop an intuition as to what is working, but it will never consistently be a simple and quick process. Paint rather than edit, and explore rather than adjust.

Once your work has been prepared for the digital environment, it is now time to consider how your portfolio will be collated and compiled. As described in Chapter One, a storyboard of your portfolio should already be outlined; now that you have a greater understanding of the particular strengths and weaknesses in your work, it is a good time to pause and re-evaluate this outline against the purposes and intentions of your portfolio.

Terry Londy

Terry is a multi-talented designer with a diverse educational background in architecture, interior design, and graphic design. He created his portfolio (figures 6–16 to 6–21) as an undergraduate at Eastern Michigan University with a purpose

6–16 to 6–18 Terry has created a very comprehensive portfolio that includes key legends, details, and an actual RCP that is well thought out. We think this is to his advantage since he shows the effect of light in most of his rendered drawings. We also like the way he works hand sketching together with the computer rendering. It does support his branding that he talks about in developing this book. The views of his perspectives are well thought out as well; they are dramatic and pull you into his work and design. The yellow circles with drop out typography may have to be made a bit darker since it is unreadable on the screen. Yellow is difficult both onscreen and in printed matter, but we do realize how enticing it can be to work with! Terry also has an interesting way of working with color against the gray background. He also gives us an idea of scale by placing shadowed people in his interiors and trees on his exteriors. His nice compositional layouts, attention to detail and well-drawn narrative all contribute to a very good representation of a passionate interior designer. Terry Londy, Eastern Michigan University, Ypsilanti, Mich. 8.5" x 11".

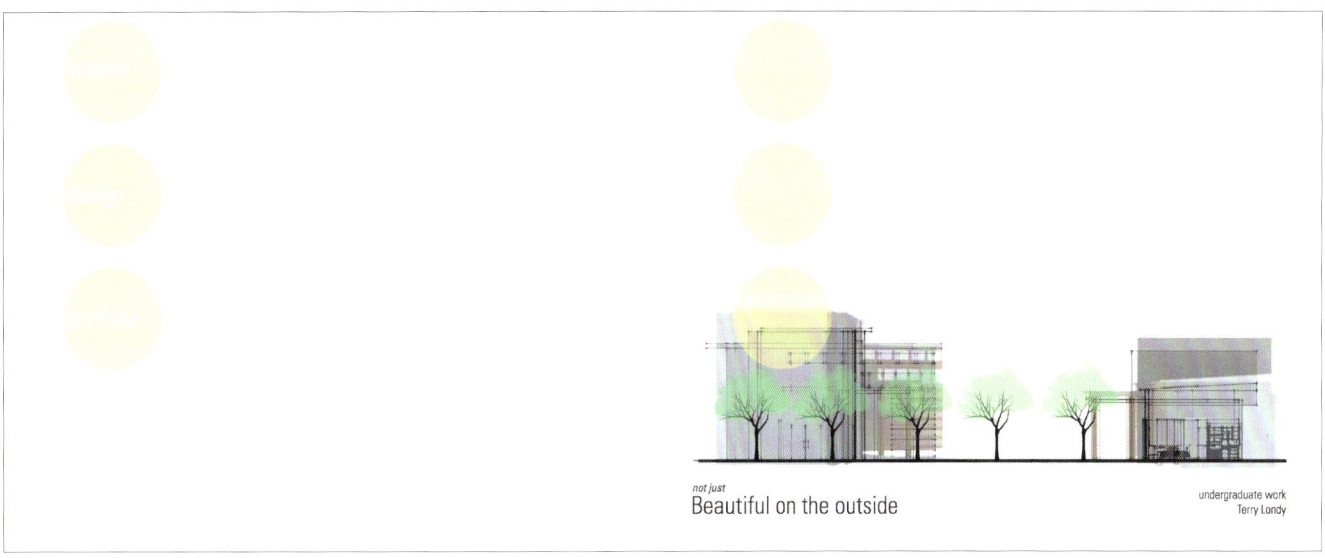

not just
Beautiful on the outside

undergraduate work
Terry Londy

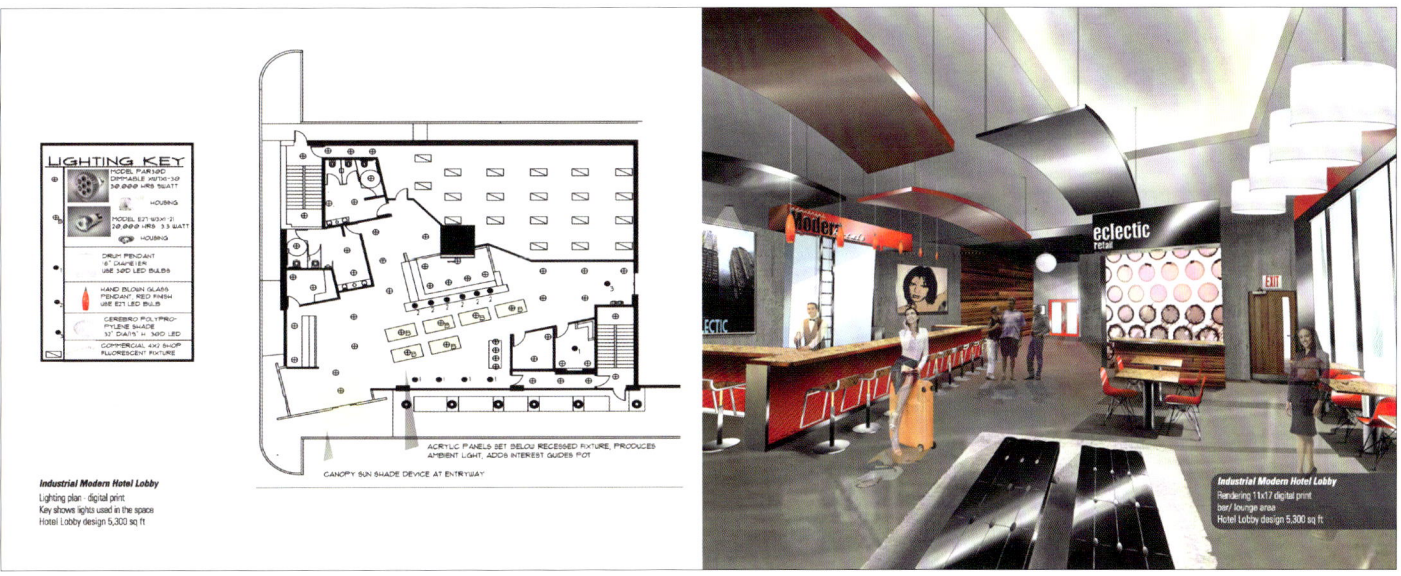

6 DIGITAL PRESENTATIONS

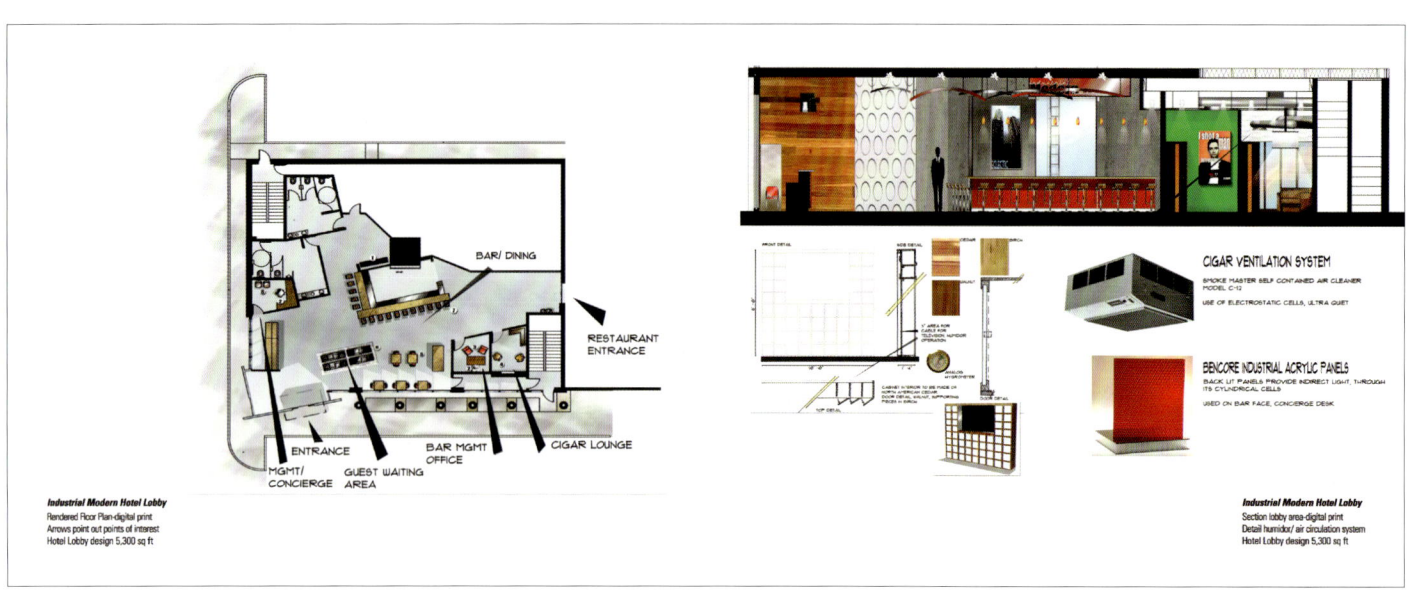

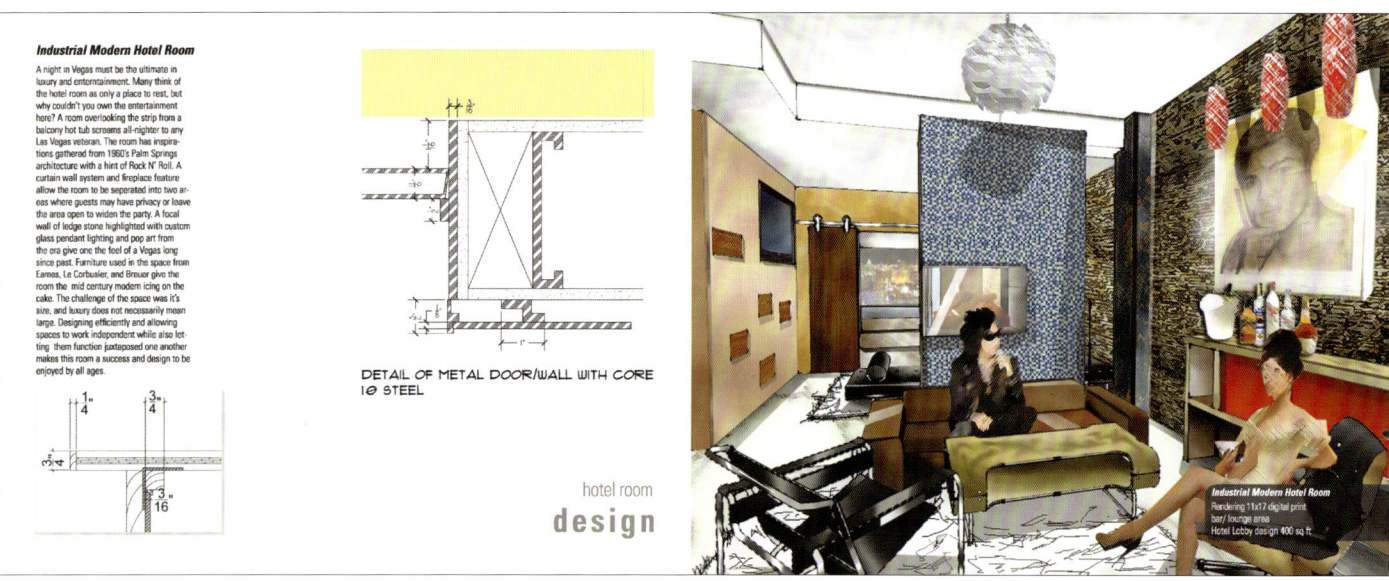

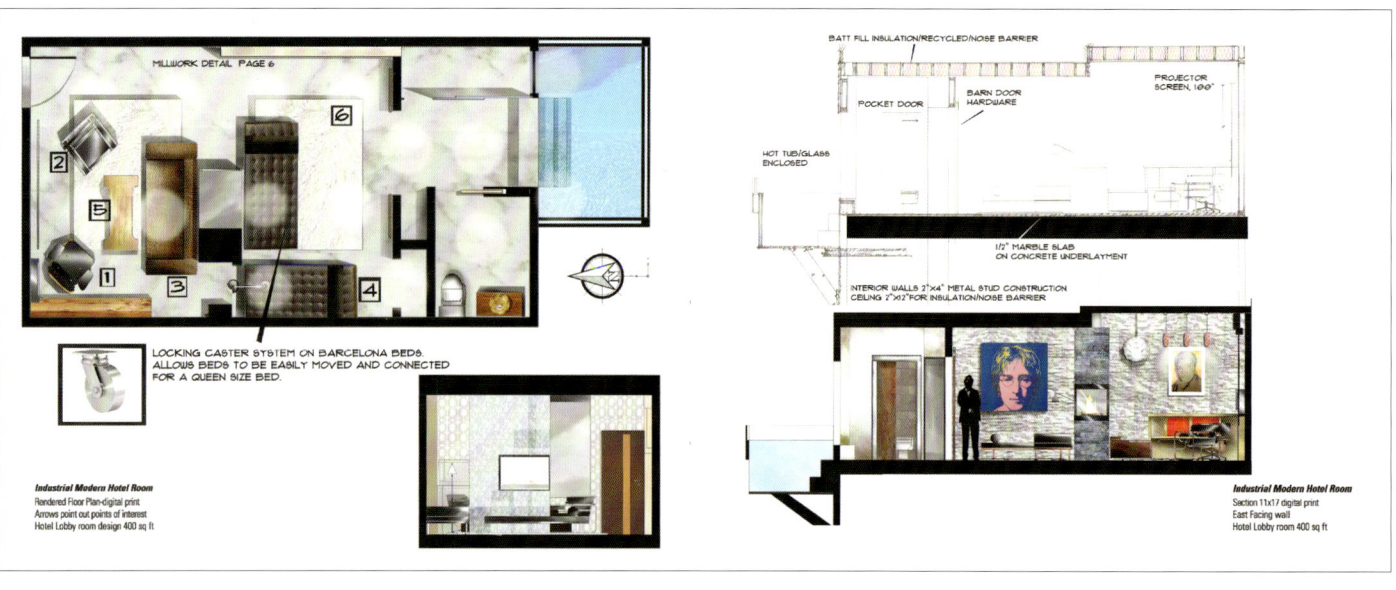

148

6–19 to 6–21 Terry has created a very comprehensive portfolio that includes key legends, details, and an actual RCP that is well thought out. We think this is to his advantage since he shows the effect of light in most of his rendered drawings. We also like the way he works hand sketching together with the computer rendering. It does support his branding that he talks about in developing this book. The views of his perspectives are well thought out as well; they are dramatic and pull you into his work and design. The yellow circles with drop out typography may have to be made a bit darker since it is unreadable on the screen. Yellow is difficult both onscreen and in printed matter, but we do realize how enticing it can be to work with! Terry also has an interesting way of working with color against the gray background. He also gives us an idea of scale by placing shadowed people in his interiors and trees on his exteriors. His nice compositional layouts, attention to detail and well-drawn narrative all contribute to a very good representation of a passionate interior designer. Terry Londy, Eastern Michigan University, Ypsilanti, Mich. 8.5" x 11".

to document his work and influences and seek employment after graduation. The Adobe Creative Suite was the main software used for the design of his portfolio along with AutoCAD. The book was printed professionally at a local print bureau and perfect bound as a soft cover edition containing all of his projects as spreads. Terry created ten copies at an expense of $100.00. The entire project, including curating all of his projects, printing, and binding, required 2 months of work during his senior year at Eastern with a full load of courses. The main purpose was to demonstrate the range of his design experience and numerous skill sets, which proved to be very successful, as he found employment in the Chicago market.

Looking at portfolios and brochures created by successful design firms for their practice and client prospecting is one of the most useful influences toward attaining successful results. Terry learned how to create his brand and demonstrates through his book what he does well. He went on to complete a graduate degree and now designs professionally in the Chicago region. Another important dimension in the preparation of his portfolio was a pervasive attitude toward trial and error which enabled him to move beyond early versions to reach a professional result. "Develop a brand as a signature of yourself, believe in it, and make it work!"

DESIGNING THE LAYOUT

What purpose other than telling a story does the portfolio hold for the interior designer? It is a unique world comprised within several pages, more similar in spirit to a poem than a novel—light whimsical movements across the pages with the ferocity of a flame. The interior designer should craft their narrative, hone their prose, and curate their works. The portfolio holds a tremendous opportunity to explore the way we communicate the passionately complex ideologies surrounding our work. The way these works unfold and their carefully articulated choreography is up to you. Whether it is a performance or an improvisation, each action requires a degree of preparation and understanding to be executed. Revisit earlier sketches, examine previous layouts, and once again question before answering. Begin the narrative and let it resonate with both the physical nature of the work as well as the way you wish it to be seen by the world.

The narrative should be clear throughout the body of work as a whole and communicate the ideals held by you as a designer. These narratives can vary widely, but it is important to identify them, in order to tie your portfolio together as a cohesive whole and to evaluate how your portfolio is satisfying its prescribed purposes (for school, job, grant applications, etc.). These narratives will then help to determine the portfolio format that will most effectively communicate them. For example, if demonstrating a persistent interest or sequence of development is important, then a linearly organized format is desirable. A favorite example of this is the printed book, which can be customized to highlight your personal strengths and interests. If your work is more varied and diverse, a collection of plates, booklets, or a website may be more efficient at organizing the range of work, while also tying them together in an overarching design ideal.

With this in mind, you may then choose to use the digital media that is most appropriate for producing your desired outcomes. Adobe InDesign is the most popular software application for compiling page layouts for books or linear presentations. Adobe Illustrator could be useful for creating separate, non-linear plates (or artboards) within a single document. Numerous software and website companies support website creation. If you are unfamiliar or unable to write code for web building, Adobe Muse offers web design layout tools (that are similar to InDesign), while websites like Cargo Collective, Squarespace, or Wix offer customizable templates that you can insert your work into. If you prefer to build your website from scratch and write your code, you can write your code in Notepad (Windows) or Typepad (Mac) and save it as an HTML document, or use software applications like Adobe Dreamweaver, which could help you to visualize your code more easily. Regardless of what software program you decide to use, it is important to remember that the platform may influence, but should certainly not dictate, the design of your portfolio.

When laying out each page of your portfolio, it is important first to set up consistent margins and an organizing grid. Adobe InDesign and Muse allow you to create master pages, where you can create guides dividing the page into any number of partitions or grids. These master pages can then be applied to any page in the document, which allows consistency in format throughout the whole document. Although you may not want to adhere strictly to the grid layout, it is important that it is there as a guide. It will unify each page within the collection as well as encourage you to align all images and text in a precise and careful manner. If you intend to print pages with full bleed (where the image is printed all the way to the edge of the page), you should include bleed margins to ensure that the image fills the page completely and that there are no white strips at the edges. These little details may seem unimportant, but say a lot about the care you give to your work. When these details are taken care of, they are barely noticed, but when they are not, they are glaringly obvious.

Depending on the purpose and brief restrictions applied to your final portfolio, you may need to curate carefully the work that you choose to include. A good portfolio will portray a clear narrative, and you should only include work that effectively adds to your overall intentions. Do not be afraid to rework and improve on old drawings; you want to present yourself in the best light possible. In the end, your curated portfolio and layout design should serve to support and present the work in its best light, as opposed to distracting from and undermining the quality. You are telling a story, and you are creating an experience. The degree to which the viewer engages with your portfolio is dependent upon the clarity of the work you decide to include, and the manner in which your layout presents them; however, the immediacy of the published format can provide some very significant first impressions, which will be discussed shortly.

Joshua Brewinski

The tour de force, technologically fused illustrative and design portfolio shown in figures 6–22 to 6–26 was created while Joshua was studying design at Colorado State University as a capstone thesis project. It was created as a course requirement with the purpose of seeking employment. He used the Adobe Creative Suite, Autodesk, AutoCAD, Revit, 3D Studio Max, and SketchUp. It was produced on a large format plotter with heavyweight paper. All designs and images included were created digitally.

Joshua states, "The process was ongoing from the beginning to the end of the semester. I was very happy with the outcome as the entire process was a learning experience in and of itself." He believes that he learned a lot in the process. He achieved his goal to package each completed design project in a total digital folio presentation. Joshua continues, "You have to know your audience and be highly selective in choosing only those projects that you believe will bring a positive reaction." Joshua's portfolio resulted in an internship in his junior year and a full-time position upon graduation from college with the same firm.

6–22 to 6–24 If you look at Joshua's projects, you notice he uses line as an integral graphic design element as well as a component of form making. The overall portfolio design utilizes the same linear theme but improvises in different ways. The text "bars" are strong and the thin outlines define his spaces well. He emphasizes the product or surface with a linear definition. This portfolio is a great balance between legends, which are well developed down to the complete RCP and Luminaire schedule giving credit to important designers such as Ingo Maurer, and has overall good spatial design perspectives. We really like the way he uses entourage to give the spaces life and action! Joshua Brewinski, Colorado State University, Fort Collins, Colo. 11" x 17".

Designing the Layout

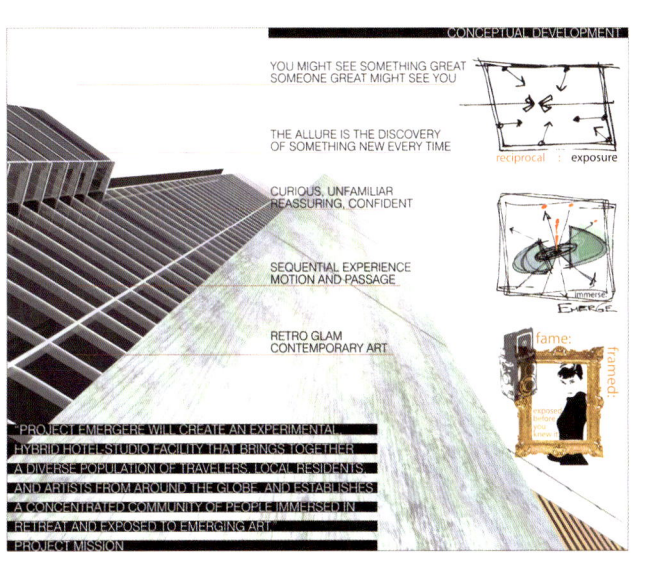

6 DIGITAL PRESENTATIONS

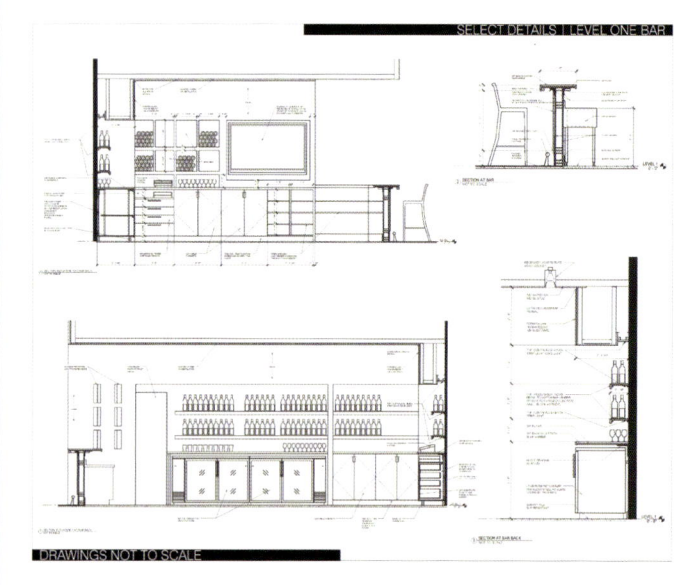

6–25 to 6–26 If you look at Joshua's projects, you notice he uses line as an integral graphic design element as well as a component of form making. The overall portfolio design utilizes the same linear theme but improvises in different ways. The text "bars" are strong and the thin outlines define his spaces well. He emphasizes the product or surface with a linear definition. This portfolio is a great balance between legends, which are well developed down to the complete RCP and Luminaire schedule giving credit to important designers such as Ingo Maurer, and has overall good spatial design perspectives. We really like the way he uses entourage to give the spaces life and action! Joshua Brewinski, Colorado State University, Fort Collins, Colo. 11" x 17".

EXPORTING FOR PUBLICATION

Each embodiment of work deserves a unique stance. If there were a singular system that existed to generate a multitude of designs, we would cease to exist as interior designers. In this same spirit, the selection of a publication platform deserves a distinctive position; there is no one-trick pony. A book should be approached differently than a website, just as a website should be approached differently than paper. This is all to say that the platform chosen for your work needs to be approached in a unique and particular way. This does not mean there are not commonalities that can be leveraged between mediums to save time, but rather, each publication should have the opportunity to affect the work with its distinct qualities. Again the shift between publication platforms holds design opportunities, latent, waiting to be discovered.

Depending on the final format of your portfolio book, the format and settings for export will vary. For physical/print publications, it is important that the exported files are of high quality and resolution. Digital presentations and websites should be much smaller file sizes, but be careful that the image quality is not jeopardized when viewed on large screens. The following section will describe some important settings to keep in mind.

Any publishing that is intended to exist in print needs to be aware of bleeds. Not the warm crimson liquid that exists within a closed system of veins and arteries, but the way an image terminates on a page. Most online publishing resources provide clear descriptions for how to account for this printing phenomenon. Programs such as InDesign also provide options to view these parameters visually within its formats. As a student, the concern will be image resolution. For an image to extend to the edge of the printed page, it needs to be larger. An increase in size always affects resolution. A simple trick to avoid most complications in resolution is to create any image with a 150 dpi resolution, which is a typical submittal requirement for competitions and graduate school applications.

Good practice would also recommend formatting any image to the size in which it will be presented. If the image is to be printed in an 11" x 17" book, then that image should be constructed, formatted, and edited for that size. If the image is to be projected onto a screen within a lecture hall, then the image should be formatted for the scale it is to be seen. In smaller publications, such as books, monographs, and portfolios, this will typically reduce the file size of the overall composition. However, for larger formatted presentations students should be warned that this good practice may result in enormous file sizes. Tests should always be performed no matter the format to find a balance between file size and format.

Programs such as CAD and Illustrator treat image resolution and format differently. These differences relate to whether the program is vector based or raster based. But here is the trick: although a program may be vector based (typically scalable to any format), their outputs are raster based. Many students will produce a plan, print to PDF, and then wonder why it is pixelated on the screen. This problem is most commonly due to formatting and can be quickly resolved by appropriately scaling the vector image within the program before exporting it as a raster image. This way the crisp lines you see on your screen will remain consistent in whatever medium the work is presented. Resolution is a common problem for both the interior design professional as well as students. A basic knowledge of software inputs and outputs should be understood before generating an

Here's a TIP:

You would not attempt to reduce the totality of a Shakespearean play into a single verse; you would not tell the same story to a child as you would an adult, and similarly, you would not force the ferocity of a poem into a single insignificant word.

6 DIGITAL PRESENTATIONS

image for publication. This knowledge will curb most issues surrounding resolution for the interior designer and can be leveraged to make a compelling composition of work within your portfolio.

Whether you are exporting for print publications or digital presentations, the PDF file format is becoming the most popular and reliable for several reasons. Firstly, the PDF file format can support both raster and vector images on a single page. It is vital to keeping text and shape graphics sharp alongside raster images. Second, PDF files can be opened on both Mac and Windows computers with the free Adobe Reader software program, so there is no concern that another computer is unable to open your file. Third, PDF files can be saved at much smaller file sizes without any noticeable loss in quality, which is particularly important when sending files to print or viewing online. Fourth, fonts and images can be embedded into the file, so even if another computer does not have access to your fonts or images, it is not a problem.

Concerning print publications, the quality of the PDF file needs to be very high. In Adobe InDesign, go to File > Export and save your PDF (Print) file. In Adobe Illustrator, go to File > Save As > Adobe PDF. A dialogue box will then appear, and there will be some preconfigured settings for "Press Quality" and "High-Quality Prints." If you will be printing your portfolio professionally, the "Press Quality" setting is preferable. The following settings can be used as a guideline, but make sure to check if they are appropriate for your particular printer:

- Compatibility: Acrobat 4.0 (PDF 1.3) is the only version that saves transparencies.
- General: Check "Optimize for Fast Web View"; uncheck "Preserve Illustrator Editor Capabilities" if you need to reduce the file size.
- Compression: Color/Grayscale Images with Bicubic Downsampling to 300 ppi, JPEG Compression, Maximum Image Quality; Compress Text and Line Art; Crop Image Data to Frames.
- Marks and Bleeds: Confirm with printer for appropriate settings.
- Output: Convert to Destination (Preserve Numbers); Destination Document CMYK.
- Advanced: Transparency Flattener; High Resolution.

When using PDF for digital presentations, it is important to export the PDF at a reduced file size, to minimize any time lag when moving from one page to the next. The resolution on a digital screen or projection is 72 ppi, so any image resolution that is higher is redundant. To avoid any low-resolution images, begin with the document page dimensions of a moderately large screen (1920 x 1080 pixels) or bigger. In Adobe InDesgin, go to File > Export and save a PDF (Interactive) file. Use the following settings as a guideline:

- Layout: Single Page Continuous.
- Presentation: Open in Full Screen Mode.
- Image Handling: JPEG Compression; JPEG Quality Maximum; Resolution 72 ppi.

Here's a TIP:

Do not let the tools shape your work, but rather develop the tools to your own creative ends.

Exporting for Publication

"Allow events to change you. You have to be willing to grow. Growth is different from something that happens to you. You produce it. You live it. The prerequisites for growth; the openness to experience events and the willingness to be changed by them."

– **BRUCE MAU**, *AN INCOMPLETE MANIFESTO FOR GROWTH*

Digital PDF presentations are becoming more common for job applications, particularly when emailing digital work samples with a resume and cover letter to prospective firms. As such, it is important that the total document file size is no more than 10 MB. Otherwise, potential employers may not receive the email, or if they do, they may become frustrated with your email clogging up their inbox. There are many things to consider when sending out images. First of all, you may need to edit your hard copy portfolio or you may wish to send full two-page spreads that are organized similar to your complete portfolio. At any rate, you will need to compress files and send as a PDF, or you may wish to send them by way of Dropbox, WeTransfer, or Google Drive, which many interior design students are using now. You want to make it easy for any firm large or small to be able to open them with ease, and they should be organized in such a fashion that they are easy to scroll through, similar to online portfolio sites such as ISSUU or Behance.com. When there is a lot of scrolling to do, however, you risk the possibility that people will not go through the entire set of images you have sent, so you will still need to make decisions as to what goes up front and what is left for the end. You may also want to consider sending images as separate attachments that do not require any scrolling but instead require clicking and opening up thumbnail images. That said, there are a lot of design decisions to make, including accessibility, when changing your hard copy book to anything online.

Online publishing is becoming a popular choice for portfolio production within academia as well as within the profession. Sites such as Blurb, Adorama, ISSUU, and Lulu position portfolio production as a "click away," but what appears as a seemingly simple procedure is, in fact, a concrete structured process that demands attention if the intended results are to be reached. Each of these sites typically has a set of constraints associated with their online publishing services. Predefined page sizes and file types are common, and each site varies regarding these parameters. A student pursuing an online self-publishing production of his or her portfolio should begin with research. Determine the available parameters the website provides, acceptable file types for submission, recommended dpi for images, suggestions for both raster and vector submittals, bleed constraints, as well as time constraints on upload and production. Understanding these parameters will generate a smooth workflow and save time while you are producing the portfolio. Online self-publishing tools are no different than those used in the production of the portfolio's content. It is a tool, and as such, should not dictate nor steer the directionality of the work's overall intent. A common mistake seen amongst interior design students is a creation of self-imposed rules based on the technology they either know well or are comfortable using. If you have the appropriate tools, use them; if you do not, find them. At the end of the day, if they do not exist, invent them!

6 DIGITAL PRESENTATIONS

John McHenry

From undergraduate school at Philadelphia University, John made a successful application to the graduate MFA program in interior design at New York School of Interior Design. John's intention in designing the portfolio shown in figures 6–27 to 6–34 was to showcase his best work and his range of skills and abilities. In the production of the portfolio and creating the work that went into it, he used 3D Studio MAX, AutoCAD, InDesign, and Photoshop. The book was printed on card stock 80# semi-gloss with a laser color printer. He bought a Shrapnel Design screw-bound portfolio in aluminum, for a total expense of $200 printing and $200 binding. The design and production required about 10 weeks and several significant lessons were learned, including allowing the book to expand by adding work and then allowing time to edit down, going back and forth until a cadence is achieved. He kept a sharp focus on both quality of the overall projects and ensuring the quality of the internal content of each project.

6–27 to 6–30 This is a beautiful portfolio with nice opening descriptions. This book shows a comprehensive study of interiors on so many levels. There is a clear understanding of program and client on the hotel's opening pages. The book notes square footage and scope, information often left out by interior designers when working on their portfolios. His opening page showcases his skills on the computer, and the portfolio clearly shows those skills and how they have been developed at a high level. There is a strong concentration of light in this portfolio. It draws you into the depth and detail of each space. Every page addresses framing systems that envelop the rich textures and deep tones of the skins this designer chooses. His portfolio also demonstrates his understanding of mixing historical and contemporary references. John McHenry, Philadelphia University and NYSID, N.Y., N.Y. 8.5" x 11".

Exporting for Publication

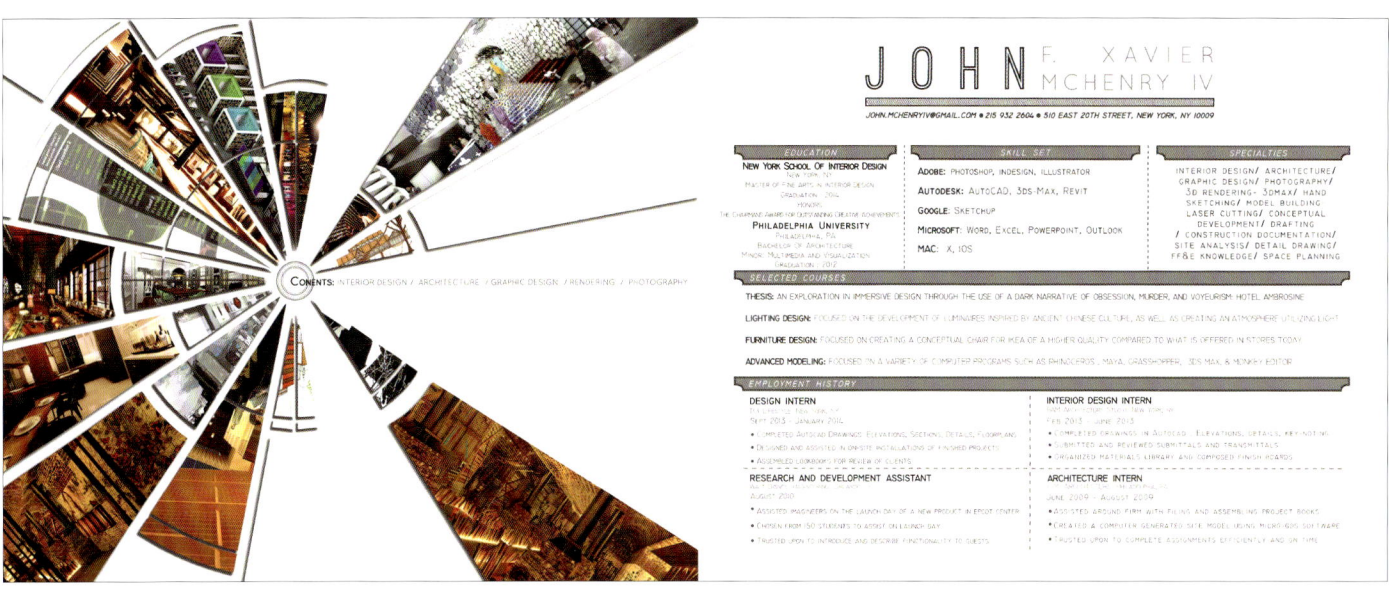

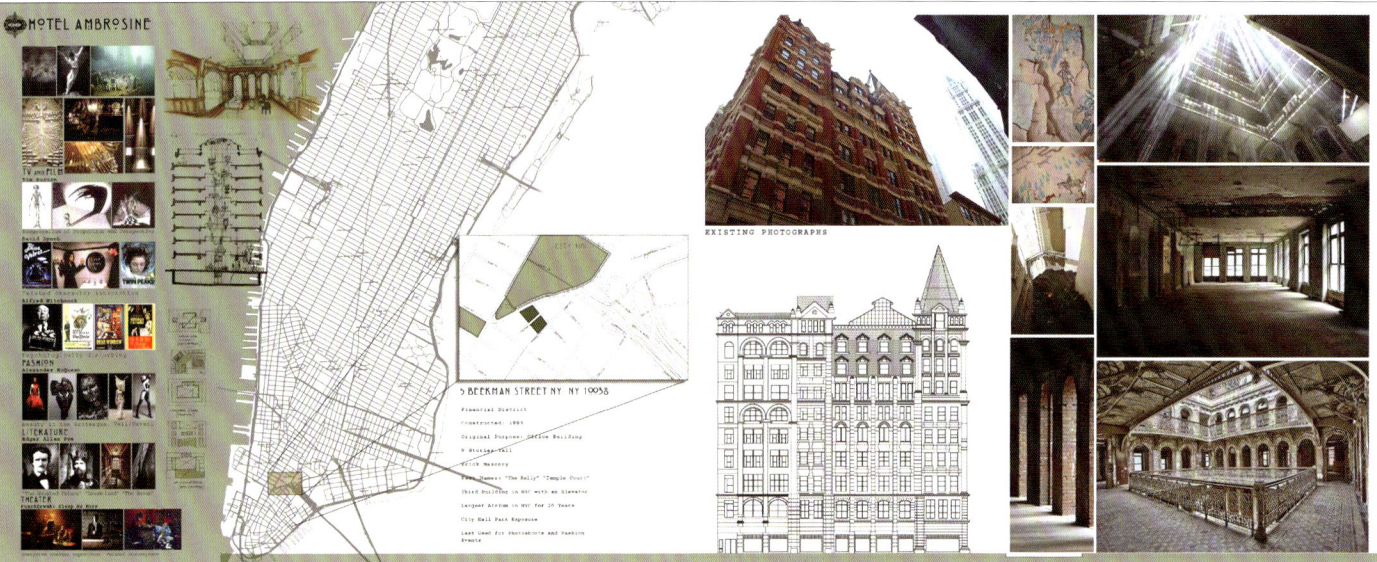

6 DIGITAL PRESENTATIONS

6–31 to 6–34 This is a beautiful portfolio with nice opening descriptions. This book shows a comprehensive study of interiors on so many levels. There is a clear understanding of program and client on the hotel's opening pages. The book notes square footage and scope, information often left out by interior designers when working on their portfolios. His opening page showcases his skills on the computer, and the portfolio clearly shows those skills and how they have been developed at a high level. There is a strong concentration of light in this portfolio. It draws you into the depth and detail of each space. Every page addresses framing systems that envelop the rich textures and deep tones of the skins this designer chooses. His portfolio also demonstrates his understanding of mixing historical and contemporary references. John McHenry, Philadelphia University and NYSID, N.Y., N.Y. 8.5" x 11".

A Few Final Thoughts

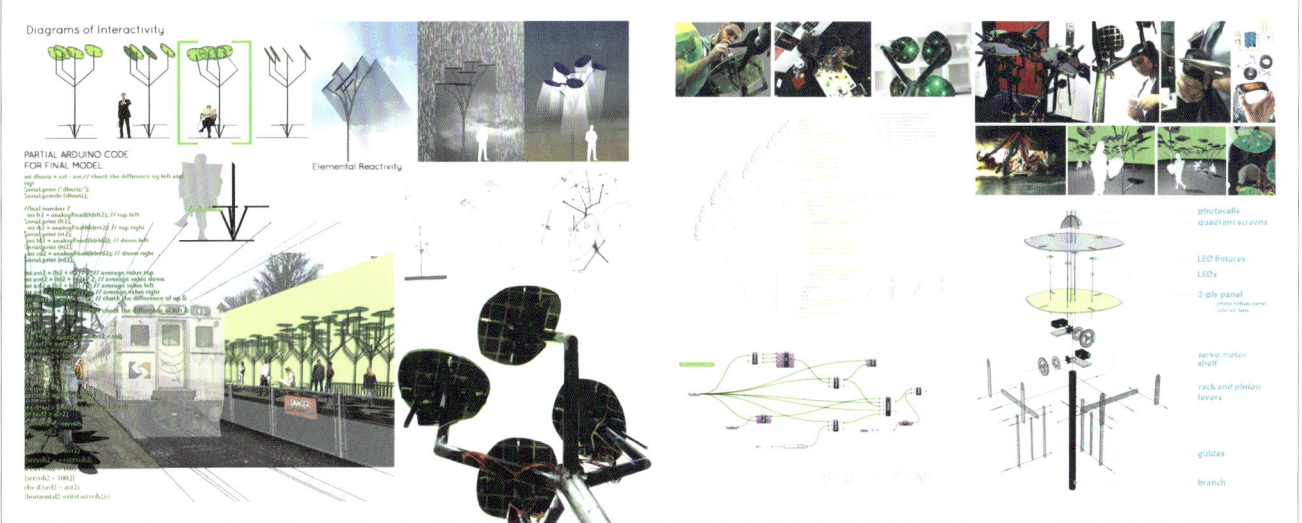

A FEW FINAL THOUGHTS

Remember, you control the way your interior designs are viewed by the world. Your portfolio should instigate conversations and question conventions. The techniques and processes laid out in the previous chapters only provide a sampling of tools that you as the interior designer can begin exploring regarding the way your creative work is disseminated to a broader audience.

Instances of misrepresentation within digital media consistently occur when tools are misused. This goes back to the artist: mastery of technique ultimately opens the doors to much more vast terrain that the interior designer may explore. The portfolio is magic; it creates unexpected encounters and new trajectories that otherwise would lay dormant within the work. It is an opportunity for growth and a galvanization of ideas. Be courageous, take risks, and ultimately let this process affect your work!

7
CRITIQUES
& CONVERSATIONS

"The essence of interior design will always be about people and how they live. It is about the realities of what makes for an attractive, civilized, meaningful environment, not about fashion or what's in or what's out. This is not an easy job."

– ALBERT HADLEY

OVERVIEW

Albert Hadley was a renowned interior designer whose brave and creative eye, distilling both classic and contemporary styles, made him the standard-bearing decorator for the rich and powerful in American society. His taste was relatively spare and modernist, but he was willing to mix ideas, drawing on a deep knowledge of design history and reflecting his own moderate temperament. He had a keen sense of how much was too much and how much was not enough.

In this chapter, we have invited several of the country's distinguished interior design professionals to review a sampling of exemplary portfolios from five outstanding interior design students whom we suggested would benefit. Here you will discover the exemplary accomplishments of five students (both undergraduate and graduate) from leading design schools throughout the country and Canada. These works are not perfect in all ways. They do, however, demonstrate accomplished designs that embody novel and interesting solutions with admirable qualities of writing, page layout, image creation, narrative, concept, and more.

We specifically requested that our review team not hold back from a realistic assessment of the overall skills evident from the qualities demonstrated in the students' books. More importantly and more realistically, we implored the reviewers to give our readership a fair and balanced picture of the across-the-board abilities inherent in the student portfolios and aside from being complimentary, provide insights into areas for future growth and development.

Each professional was paired with a student portfolio based on the authors' instincts regarding which student was appropriate for which professional, taking into account the trajectory of a student's expressed ambitions, goals, and accomplishments. The reviewers are to be commended for their diligence and fortitude in making a careful review of five extraordinary student portfolios. We did not wish to make their job easy, but instead, we provided each reviewer with a top-flight book and challenged them to probe deeply to understand the work and the content of the studio experience as well as the way the book was put together to reflect the goals and aspirations of each of the students.

The reviewers' reactions are based on numerous years of practice in the field. Interviewing and hiring designers at their firms, serving on juries for competitions, reviewing CIDA accreditation applications for interior design schools, visiting as a studio design critic, and serving as admissions reviewers for candidates making application to graduate programs are all essential attributes of our teams' professional backgrounds. More than this, we hope these reviews will serve as inspiration for our readership. These exceptional portfolios provide a unique window onto how you can accomplish your goals and ambitions for a rewarding career in design.

We know you will discover multiple solutions to everything we have addressed in this book. Throughout this book, you will find the impetus to evolve your original portfolio designs. You will be inspired by the work of others to jump into the process. You will see a style and method that upon experimentation enables and transforms your job. In addition to looking at all of the 400+ images included here, it pays to further your research by exploring the work of other portfolios from allied design and fine arts.

7 CRITIQUES & CONVERSATIONS

There are more and more examples finding their way into publication and posted on a growing number of online sites. Keep your eyes open to general design trends by exploring the Internet through websites like Blurb.com, Lulu.com, ISSUU.com, or Behance.com and making frequent trips to the library to peruse contemporary magazines and journals. Seek the reactions of faculty regarding your portfolio design. Be aware that all of your student colleagues are undertaking a similar challenge and exchanging ideas and information might prove helpful to your project. By all means attend important exhibitions in cross-discipline areas at museums, collections, and libraries. If you are not in a large metropolitan city, perhaps make plans with friends to visit a special exhibit and make a weekend of the journey, seeing several shows across the disciplines of design and fine arts.

The patterns, procedures, and standards set by every portfolio shown here, along with every guideline and caution detailed in the preceding pages, can be overturned if you feel compelled to do so because of the nature of the material you are presenting. Rejecting and rethinking, tearing down and building up—these are precisely the processes by which radical new ideas become tried-and-true traditions.

Portfolio design offers enormous scope for original ideas, and reviewers will appreciate a bold leap of imagination; however, they will also be looking for originality tempered by maturity and a realistic outlook, and attention to detail. Never forget that most professional offices undertake projects as a team and that we are in a collaborative business, and you will want therefore to demonstrate that your boldness is not arrogance and that you can summon the discipline to function as a team player.

No matter how good your portfolio is, it will inevitably mean different things to different audiences. A design firm will react differently to your work than an architectural engineering firm, a planning office, or a graduate school review panel. Put in the time and the effort needed to research the companies or institutions you are planning to show your portfolio. To the degree possible, gear your presentation to mesh with their interests. In these days of digital design, making the modifications necessary to achieve this is easier than ever before because you can create and maintain multiple versions of your work. Consider presenting your work as an extension of their mission statement.

It is also appropriate to say that as authors of this book and studio faculty, as well as professionals with several decades of experience working in the field of art and design in addition to teaching portfolio design for several decades in architecture, interiors, and the allied design disciplines, we are impressed with the accomplishments of all those students who submitted work for this book from around the country and Canada. You constitute the next and new generation of professional designers who will carry on this responsibility and who will help to groom many more classes of aspiring and talented interior design professionals who understand the significance of professional development and especially presentation of one's background and work.

It is always a good idea to let someone whose opinion and objectivity you respect review your portfolio before you present it to an admissions or awards committee or a prospective employer. You need to know if something in your portfolio isn't clear, doesn't make sense, or needs additional explanation. A third-party perspective is an invaluable test. Of course, you must learn to review yourself, endeavoring to be as objective as possible and evaluating each element and how it works (or fails to work) with every other component. Ask yourself five basic questions:

- Is the portfolio well organized?
- Does it clearly illustrate my strengths and technical abilities as a designer?
- Does it show how my ideas develop and how I solve problems?
- Does it present a focused vision?
- Are the graphics and titles polished, addressed in a hierarchy, and consistent?

Next, review the overall layout, photography, typography, and reproduction methods. Ask:

- Are the pages in mint condition or have they become worn after frequent reviews? It is out of your control if the former reviewer just ate pizza for lunch and did not wash their hands.
- Are the images presented sharply and clearly, with adequate contrast?
- Is the text consistently legible?
- Are the projects included up to date, reflecting my best and most recent work?
- Do the views of my work make sense, and do subsequent pages expand upon and make the preceding pages more clear?
- Will the reviewer understand the material if I am not physically present to explain it?

FEATURED PORTFOLIOS

Anne Aristya

Anne's portfolio (figures 7–1 to 7–10) is a comprehensive collection of thought, process, and development. The graphics are polished and make the *reading* of her work highly accessible. There are so many layers to this portfolio, including large full-bleed site images artistically presented in black and white. The conceptual diagrams help the reading of her final presentation. There is a wonderful balance of 3D and 2D thinking shown by this designer. Working in tandem, her skillful hand drawings support the computer-generated work. Every page is a balanced composition utilizing large images against small support drawings, while white space allows it all to breathe.

7–1 to 7–2 Anne Aristya, graduate of the New York School of Interior Design, presented a dynamic concept for *Bold Magazine*'s community workspace. It is an open and interpretive environment that nurtures the workforce to seek their own identity. Anne Aristya, New York School of Interior Design, N.Y., N.Y. 8" x 8".

7 CRITIQUES & CONVERSATIONS

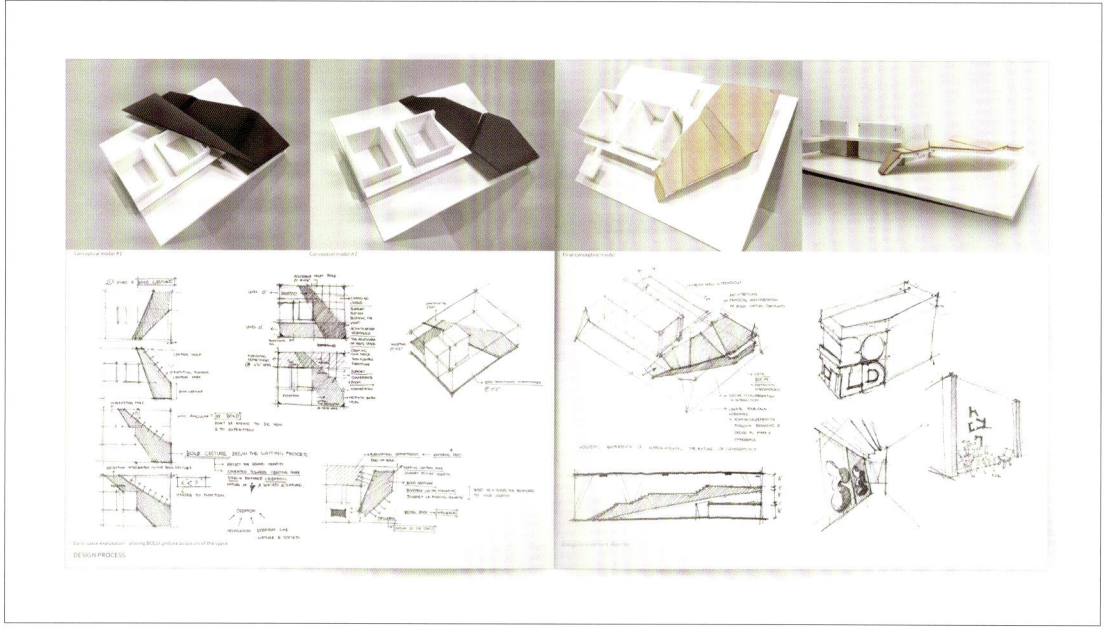

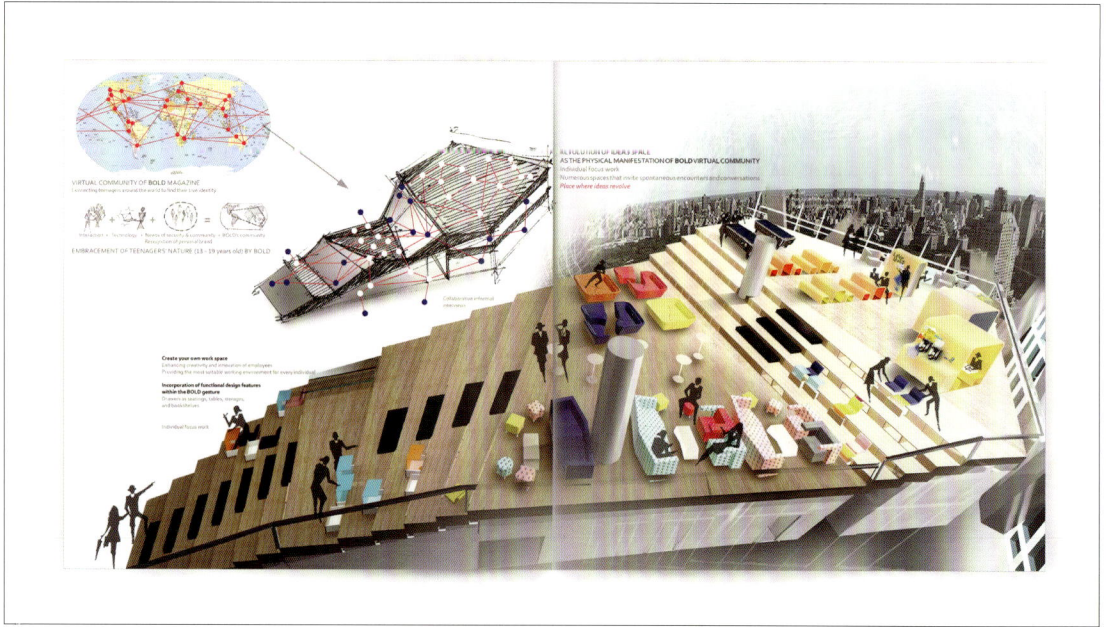

Featured Portfolios

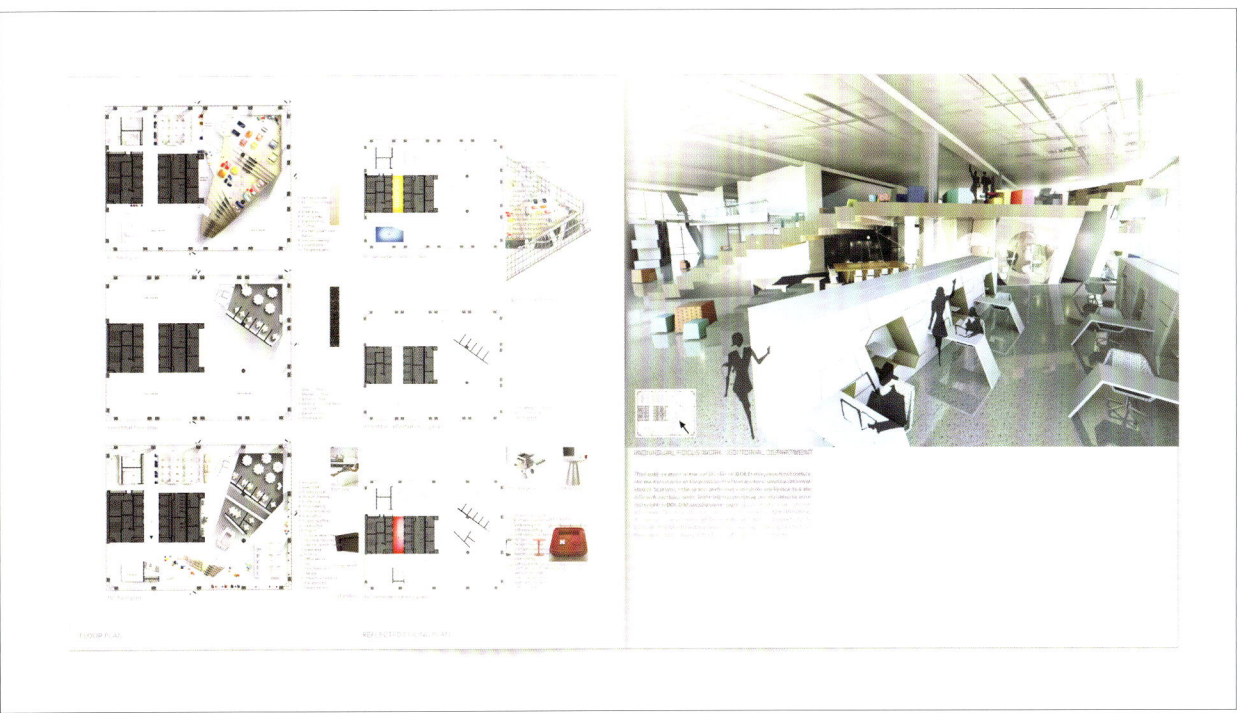

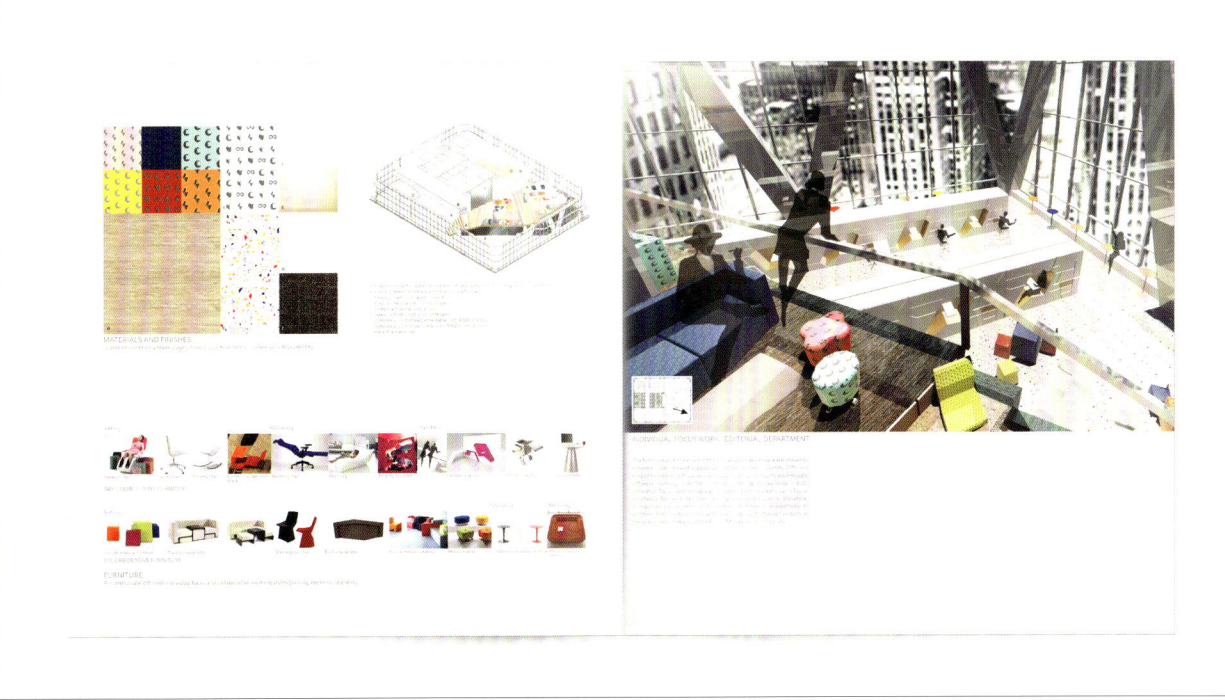

7–3 to 7–7 Anne Aristya, graduate of the New York School of Interior Design, presented a dynamic concept for *Bold Magazine*'s community workspace. It is an open and interpretive environment that nurtures the workforce to seek their own identity. Anne Aristya, New York School of Interior Design, N.Y., N.Y. 8" x 8".

7 CRITIQUES & CONVERSATIONS

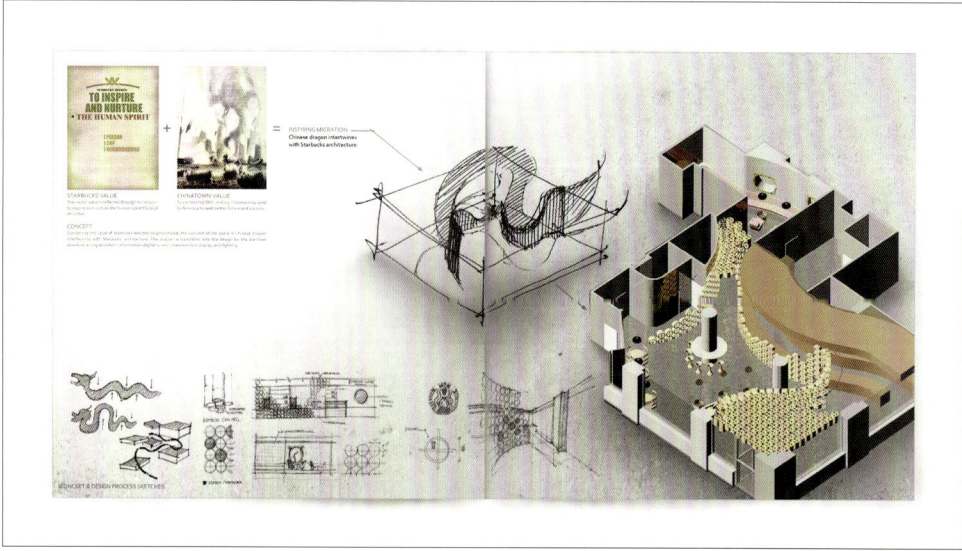

7–8 to 7–10 As an urban site design project, Anne was challenged to design a new and exciting Starbucks store that reflected the brand and its environment in Chinatown. Anne Aristya, New York School of Interior Design, N.Y., N.Y. 8" x 8".

Anne designed her book at the close of her junior year without including her senior year thesis project. Her purpose was to begin looking for employment as early as possible or to find an internship with an opportunity for employment following graduation. A class in portfolio development proved to be instrumental to her success; she discovered a hierarchy and graphic design system that would greatly enhance the presentation layout of her work. The design process required a semester and a half to complete but the results were entirely worth the sweat equity invested in the work.

Anne mentions, "I think a portfolio is about trial and error; to me, the whole development is about an exploration of understanding myself as a designer. The whole process made me reflect on each of my individual projects, and on each project's strengths and weaknesses; good portfolios allow each project's strength to be highlighted, and each project's weaknesses to be covered by its strength."

Anne Aristya Portfolio Review
by Lawrence Chabra

There are many elements that make this such a winning portfolio. First of all, the design work itself, exhibited in each project, is outstanding. The designer displays an aesthetic sense that is compelling without being overwhelming or overdone. Secondly, the images clearly convey the design intent. The designer clearly demonstrates the ability to create compelling images in a variety of techniques and mediums. The images range from rough black-and-white sketches to photorealistic 3D renderings, sometimes combining two or more techniques in the same image. Finally, there are the overall presentation skills that combine all of the elements into a cohesive and compelling narrative that clearly communicates the vision for each project. Graphically the typography and layout not only contribute to the clarity of each narrative, but also further demonstrate the designer's aesthetic sensibilities.

I include a few tips on details for this advanced design student that are intended to help with future refinements to her book. Attention to detail will play an increasingly important role in office work. Photo captions copied from one layout to another and text have not been updated. While this is an attractive book, paying attention to small things will reflect the importance of this point—an attention to detail. Employers wonder what kind of details might be missing when designers have responsibility to execute architectural plans while on the job. Writing clear and concise descriptions of professional projects and their contribution to the work is another important skill similar in importance to defining one's role on a team-driven design project. Not every graduating student has professional work to show to prospective employers. Therefore, this dimension of one's book should be presented as clearly as all the other student work. It is important not to have to guess as to the overall scope of professional projects and the student's contribution.

Anne's portfolio demonstrates numerous attributes of successful design in studio projects, graphics, design solutions, and portfolio layout design presentation. The layout design of her book is especially exciting and well executed. This book has great editorial energy and reflects strong expectations for future growth and professional development.

About the Reviewer

Lawrence Chabra, Associate, has been with Robert A.M. Stern Architects since 2009. He has been involved in the interior design and project management of academic projects including Schwarzman College at Tsinghua University in Beijing, China; the renovation and expansion of Ozark Hall at the University of Arkansas in Fayetteville, Arkansas; and two new residential colleges at Yale University in New Haven, Connecticut. His residential projects include the Marco Polo Hotel, the Residential Villas on Mountain Court, a residential development at 31 Conduit Road, and a private residence, all in Hong Kong, as well as a private residence in Toronto, Ontario. His retail experience includes the Tiffany Mezzanine Jewel Salon on Fifth Avenue in New York City. Prior to joining Robert A.M. Stern Architects, Mr. Chabra worked in broadcast graphics in New York and New Jersey. He received his Bachelor of Fine Arts degree from the New York School of Interior Design.

7 CRITIQUES & CONVERSATIONS

Emily Fike

Emily's drawing and sketching skills (figures 7–11 to 7–18) exhibited throughout her book are an outstanding example of a student showing a life of design and thinking. Her drawings pull you into the process. The gray tones used throughout the graphics of the book support and amplify the color used in the individual projects. Her opening statement is strong and written with conviction. The graphics and shapes used throughout her layouts are sensitive to hierarchy and make the book easy to page through and to understand.

As an undergraduate student in Interior Design at University of Tennessee, Knoxville, Emily produced her portfolio with the idea in mind to seek employment upon graduation from school. Her intent was to represent the full range of skills she acquired while at school, while designing the book as an object and hopefully making it as intriguing as possible. She used Photoshop to edit every photograph in her book, including specific drawings and other image types. She used AutoCAD for various design projects and InDesign for the layout of the overall book. It was printed on a laser color printer, including the mat board cover.

She made two complete portfolios. Including all trial studies and test printing, the expense for two books was $160.00. The development required 3 months of continual work and testing ideas. Her portfolio was showcased in the 66th Annual Student Art Competition at UTK and won Best of Show in the ASID/IIDA Interior Design Showcase. Most important, her portfolio contributed to her securing employment directly following graduation from UTK.

Emily confesses, "Making a book or portfolio is much harder than it appears. It takes time, effort, and a lot of creative thinking." Referencing past students' portfolios was extremely beneficial. She also benefited from seeing which strategies were successful and which were not. She realized the importance of owning a library of examples and has begun adding to her inventory of examples whenever she can.

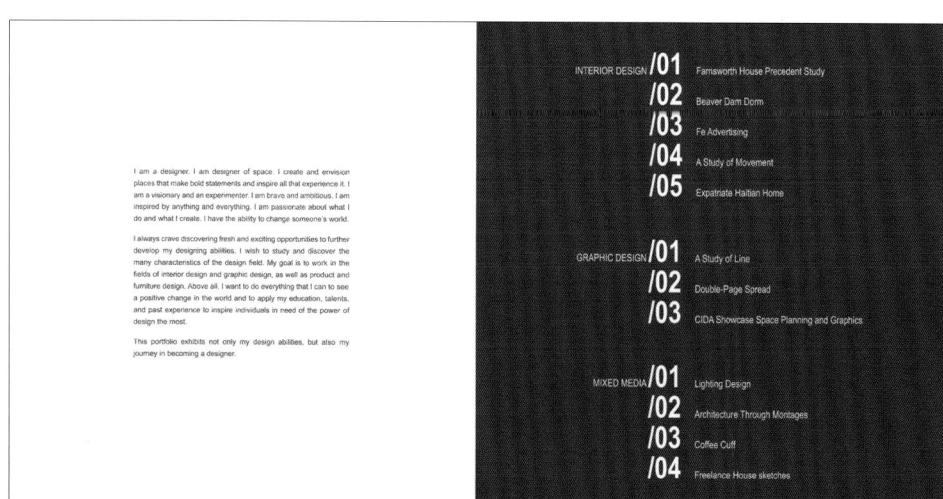

Featured Portfolios

7–11 to 7–15 Emily Fike, graduate of the University of Tennessee, designed an award-winning custom square portfolio with a spacious layout that gained added strength from beautiful hand drawing balanced by clear, full-color perspective illustrations. The Beaver Dam dorm space is testimony to opportunity and to making the most of your schooling. Emily Fike, University of Tennessee, Knoxville, Tenn. 8" x 8".

7 CRITIQUES & CONVERSATIONS

7–16 to 7–18 For Fe Advertising, Emily transformed a vacated high school building of 29,000 square feet into a cool, sleek agency that caters to especially contemporary creative thinking. Emily Fike, University of Tennessee, Knoxville, Tenn. 8" x 8".

Emily Fike Portfolio Review by Jan Bast

Emily Fike prepared her portfolio as a senior in the College of Art and Design at the University of Tennessee, Knoxville. Her stated purpose was to create a collection that embodied her "personality and design aesthetic." She sought to showcase a range of skills in which she was proficient and to building a portfolio that "was as intriguing as the projects that it encased." Her collection of work was shown at the 66th Annual Student Art Competition at UT College of Architecture and Design and won Best of Show in the ASID/IIDA UT Interior Design Student Showcase. In multiple interviews, Emily was told her portfolio was "creative, eye-catching, and memorable."

The portfolio was created using AutoCAD, Adobe Photoshop, and InDesign and featured mat board front and back covers printed on a laser printer. The cover is black with a tone-on-tone graphic on the left side, and Emily's contact information on the right. The next page is a statement of her design philosophy and the rationale behind the design of the portfolio in black type on white, with the table of contents on the right in white lettering on a black background. It is organized into three categories: interior design, graphic design, and mixed media, with page numbers and project names. The use of contrasting background colors is striking and visually pleasing. It is apparent to the viewer that graphic design is also one of her strengths.

Each category is introduced into the same list of projects as in the table of contents, again in white on black. She begins with a hand-sketched/rendered project and describes her design process. The sketches include perspectives, floor plans, and process diagrams; her hand-sketching skills are exemplary and provide an artistic introduction to her work, which then becomes more technical as one progresses through the portfolio.

For the second project, the Beaver Dam dorm, Emily discusses the development of her concept and how she applied this concept to the design of a dorm room. Visuals for this project include a combination of AutoCAD and hand sketching which clearly illustrate her design solution. This small-scale, residential project is followed by a larger commercial project, the Fe Advertising Agency. Deliverables for this project are all digital and include concept photos as well 3D renderings and floor plans.

The final section of the portfolio, graphic design, begins with a study of a line as a "negative gap or a positive mark." For the second project, she includes a two-page spread she designed using an existing article from an architectural publication and re-designing it in a style that matches the featured project. Finally, she provides photos of the exhibit of student work for a CIDA accreditation review that she was asked to curate.

In the mixed media category, Emily presents the design of a light fixture using found objects and the design of a combination wooden bracelet/coffee cup sleeve which she designed and then built using thin sheets of plywood. An architectural collage is also included in this section. She closes the portfolio with hand-sketched pen and ink drawings of a house, one of many that she has done.

As an educator and practitioner for 30 years, I have reviewed a lot of portfolios, and this one is easily in the top ten that I have seen. Emily Fike's portfolio not only showcases her many talents, from hand sketching to computer-generated plans and perspectives, but shows a mature sense of what design is and what it can do. Her passion for design is evident in the work. She has an excellent graphic sense. Her portfolio is graphically bold, yet spare; she has edited her work down to the most important points and presented them simply but completely. Each project showcases a different skill, and as a whole, we get a clear picture of her range of talents. The illustrations are easy to read with enough detail but not too much.

I would caution Emily and design students in general that there is an over-reliance on spell check and grammar check. While these have value, they also have limitations and therefore, it is far more important for students to have what they write for their portfolios (or anything else) be proofread by someone who is a skilled writer. In summary, I feel that Emily has, indeed, created a portfolio that was "as intriguing as the projects it encased."

7 CRITIQUES & CONVERSATIONS

About the Reviewer

Jan Bast is a past president for NCIDQ. She brings to NCIDQ more than 20 years of design experience. Jan was a partner in Bast/Wright Interiors for 15 years, providing programming, space planning, contract document writing, and project administration for both commercial and residential projects. During those years Jan operated her business, she taught a variety of subjects at Design Institute, which is accredited by the Council for Interior Design Accreditation.

Jan is a professional member of ASID, IIDA, and the Interior Designers Educators Council. She served as President of the San Diego Chapter of ASID in 1992–1993 and has been a member of ASID's National Education and Training Advisory Committee. In 2006, she was selected as an ASID Fellow.

In the late 1980s and early 1990s, Jan met with California legislators to promote interior design legislation in the state. She applied for California self-certification upon passage of the laws in 1992. She regularly represents NCIDQ at legislative coalition meetings and continues to monitor the legal situation in California. Many students in California have benefited from Jan's considerable passion for promoting NCIDQ as the path to professionalism. In 2007, she made more than 20 presentations around the state. Jan received a Bachelor of Arts in Art from San Diego State University and had done post-graduate work in Special Needs Design there. She is a certified interior designer in California.

Tak Imoto

Tak focuses on the design of finished perspectives for his portfolio rather than detailed drawings and technical documents (figures 7–19 to 7–28). His drawings, however, are

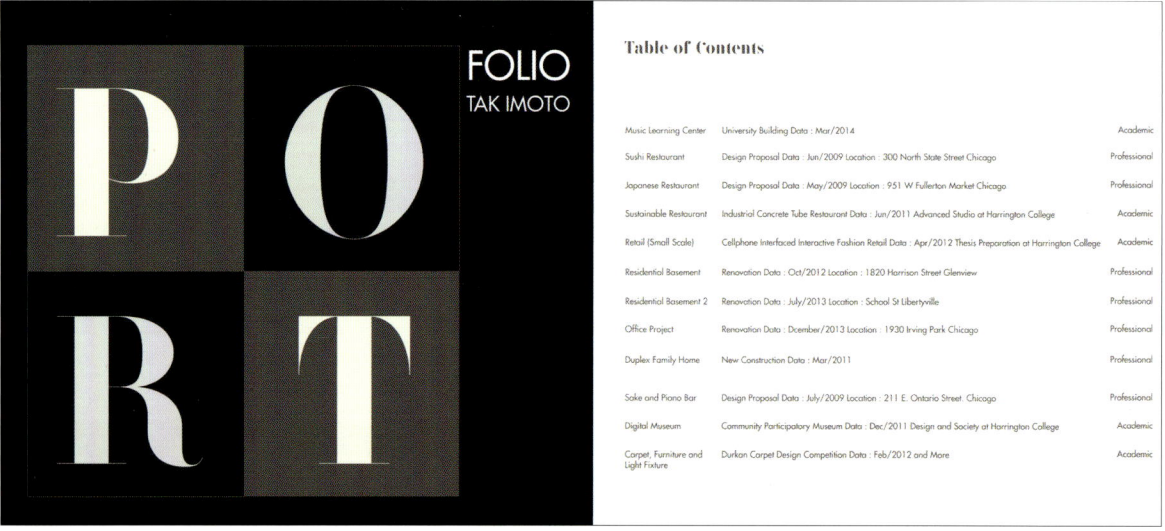

Featured Portfolios

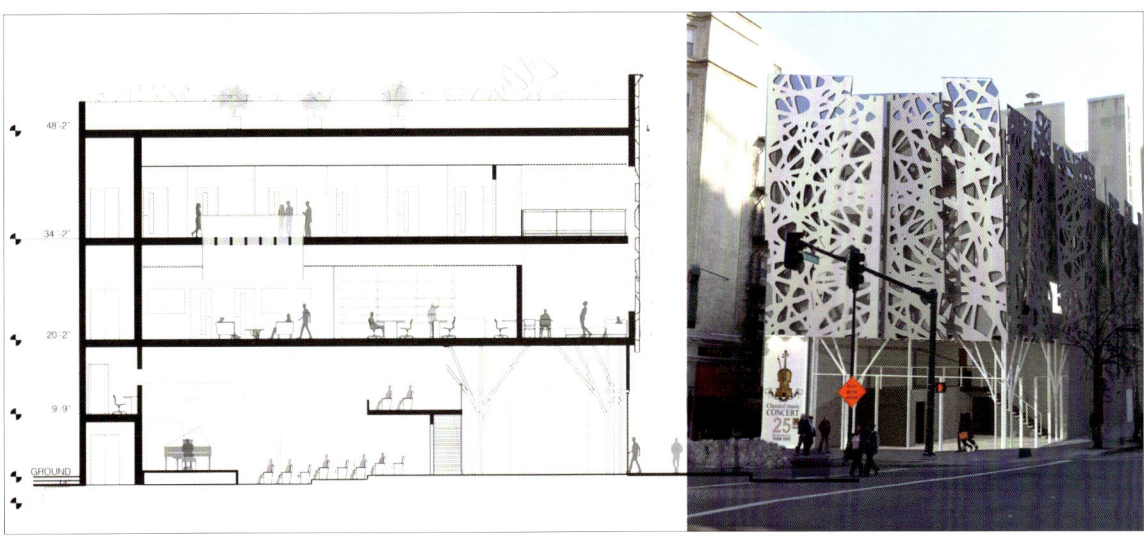

7–19 to 7–23 Tak Imoto's design for the Northeastern University Music Building delights in the metaphor of an organic, transparent façade as an expression for luminance and sound emanating from within the interior. Tak Imoto, Harrington College of Design, Chicago, Ill. and Boston Architectural College, Boston, Mass. 8" x 9".

7 CRITIQUES & CONVERSATIONS

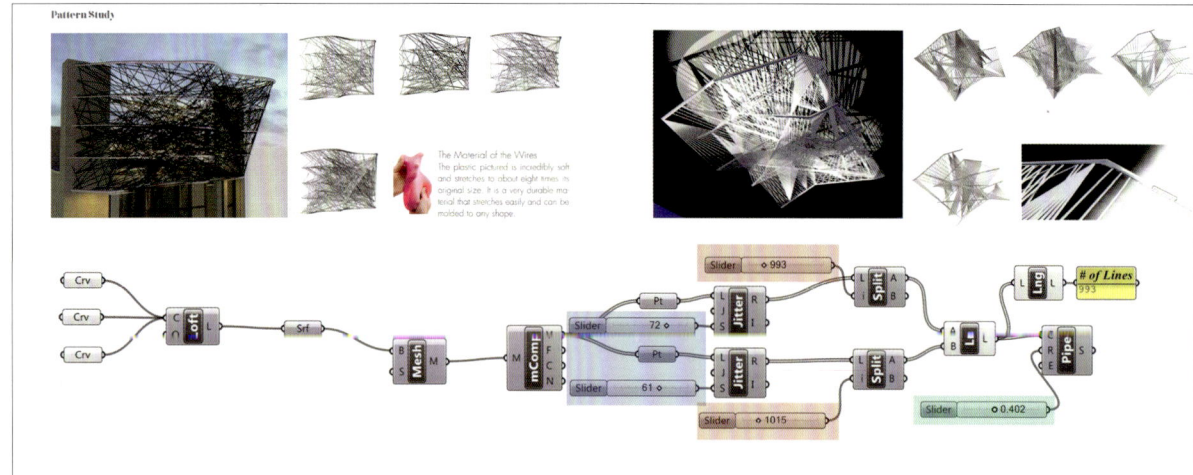

7–24 to 7–28 Tak's design for an interactive fashion retail store which integrates state-of-the-art smart phone technology. The store interior synchronizes with your personal data via your cell phone, taking into consideration your size, style preferences, and colors. Tak Imoto, Harrington College of Design, Chicago, Ill. and Boston Architectural College, Boston, Mass. 8" x 9".

Featured Portfolios

enticing and his sketches of ideas demonstrate the fluidity of his process and skill. They both demonstrate his design process in a refreshing way. It is a clear portfolio based on image and less on technical skill. The assumption is that to get to this stage of drawing, one must have the innate skill to produce such material. He has chosen to interweave academic and professional work labeled in his table of contents.

Tak's portfolio was created at the graduate level with the purpose of seeking employment following undergraduate school at the Harrington College of Design and graduate school at the Boston Architectural College. It was produced predominantly with InDesign and Photoshop and with special emphasis on interior architecture and focus on strong conceptual interests underpinning each project in his book. Tak felt his search for employment would be a national effort so he produced 20 bound copies at $50.00 per book. The entire process required 2 full months of work. Perhaps the aspects most helpful to the design and production were taking a graphic design course and watching many tutorials on related subjects on YouTube.

Tak Imoto Portfolio Review
by Vanessa Deleon

Every year I review a handful of portfolios as part of the hiring process at our firm. Since first impressions are important, the portfolio should be a masterpiece. I look for balance in the presentation; it should be well organized and cohesive, as a portfolio can speak volumes when it is fine tuned. Many students tend to leave out page numbers or use their brand only on a couple of pages, leaving the rest to guess work. Although Photoshop, PowerPoint, SketchUp, Revit, and so on, are content areas students need to master, it is crucial that they concentrate on the basic 101 organization skills of creating a portfolio.

Tak Imoto's portfolio is very well prepared. Greater emphasis, though, on pattern design would be helpful on every page of his portfolio to reinforce his brand identity. Here are some additional tips that would further distinguish an already accomplished body of work.

When building a brand, it should be irreparably clear whether he is "Tak" or "Takimoto." It is advisable to simplify to the use of one name. While his primary emphasis is on the perspective illustrations, which are quite impressive, the use of section elevations are equal in importance with the graphics. Tak's annotations need to be prominent. The lack of identification on several of the pages is inefficient and may lead the reviewer on an empty search for them throughout the book. The portfolio would benefit if the renderings and floor plans had greater visibility, keeping in mind that floor plans take a higher priority over the perspectives.

Tak's creative planning phase, however, displays well, incorporating thoughtfully detailed drawings on a large scale. Tak also demonstrates excellence in hand-rendering skills and his inspirational drawings are exceptional. It is evident that Tak is proficient in using quality material applications in his work. It is essential to the design scheme to hone in on all the design elements such as rhythm, emphasis, harmony, scale, and balance to create a masterpiece of a portfolio.

It has been a pleasure to have had the opportunity to review the portfolio of this accomplished and emerging design professional. Through his work I can see that Tak has remarkable passion in everything he does as well as great enthusiasm for growth and professional development.

About the Reviewer

Vanessa Deleon is a New York–based interior designer and television personality with offices on the Gold Coast of New Jersey and in the SoHo neighborhood of New York City. She was previously featured on the Food Network program *Restaurant Impossible* and her extensive television credits also include HGTV's programs *Generation Renovation*, *Designer's Challenge*, *Bang for Your Buck*, and *Design Star*.

She is a previously featured designer on the hit Food Network program *Restaurant Impossible*, helping turn around failing restaurants around the country. In 2007, Vanessa was named a Rising Star of Interior Design by the International Furnishings and Design Association. Her expertise and projects have been featured in numerous publications including *New York Spaces*, *Design NJ*, *(201) Home*, *Latina*, *Time*, *Entertainment*, *ASPIRE Metro*, and *Cosmopolitan*.

Coleen O'Leary

Coleen has a spacious, clear vision of design (figures 7–29 to 7–37) that is reinforced by the way she created her book with strong white space and delicate color. She emphasizes two sections in her book: studio work and other work that supports her life as a designer. Her pages have engaging layouts with a nice mix of materiality, color, and technical drawing. She has created a zone that floats in the middle of each page surrounded by white space. It gives her delicate drawings a credibility and sense of power.

Coleen graduated in Interior Design from the University of Tennessee, Knoxville. She felt the most important purpose behind the design of her book was to showcase work from school and present it in such a way that is clean, beautiful, and reflective of her personality. She used Adobe InDesign for the full layout of her book. It was printed on an 80# smooth text paper using four-color offset printing for production. The book was saddle-stitch (staple binding) so that images that extend across spreads would appear as continuous with minimal interruption. She made two portfolios at a cost of $40.00 per book.

Coleen worked continuously over a period of 4 months creating multiple drafts and adding new work until she was

Featured Portfolios

7–29 to 7–31 Coleen O'Leary designed her portfolio with ample white space and sensitivity to color forms. In Provisions Café, the ambiance provides a warm welcome while the asymmetric interior arrangement of seating is intended to instigate social interaction in unexpected ways between residents. Coleen O'Leary, University of Tennessee, 10" x 10".

7 CRITIQUES & CONVERSATIONS

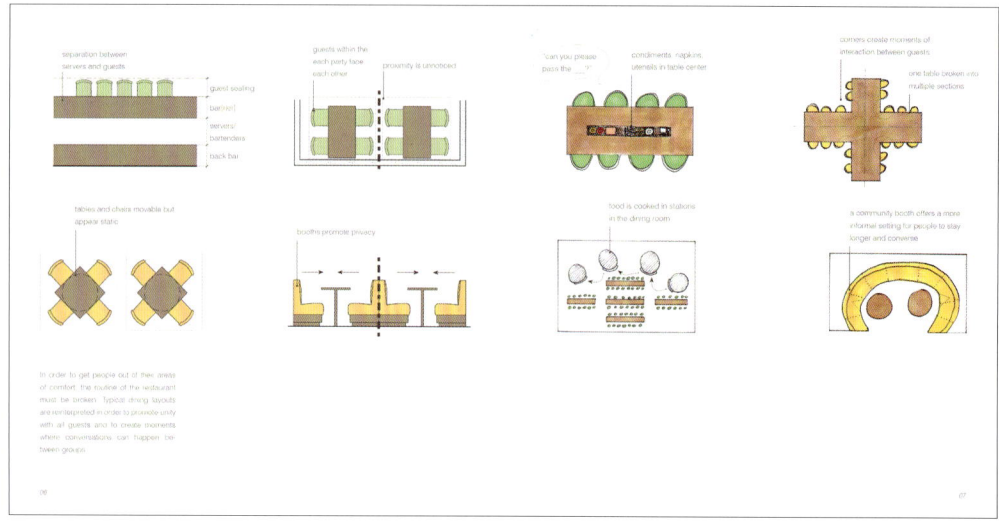

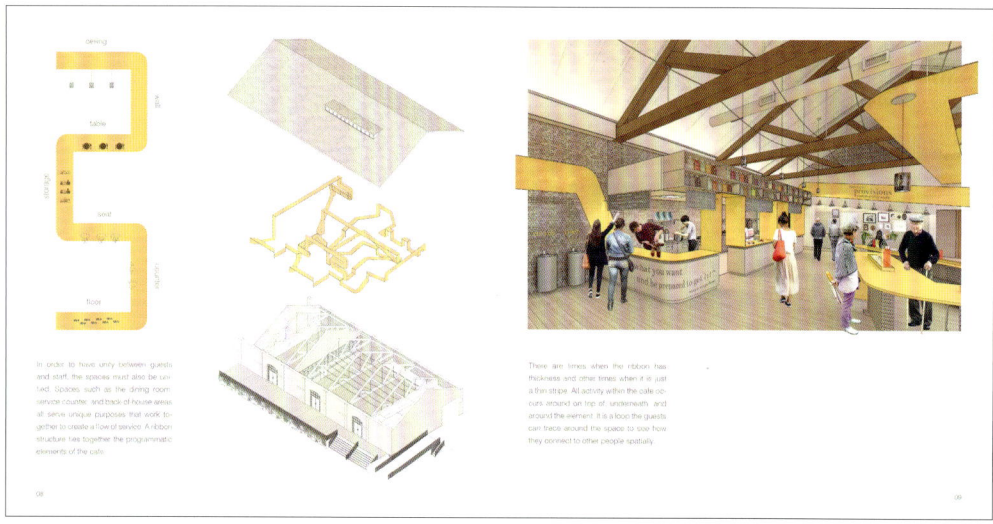

7–32 to 7–34 Coleen O'Leary designed her portfolio with ample white space and sensitivity to color forms. In Provisions Café, the ambiance provides a warm welcome while the asymmetric interior arrangement of seating is intended to instigate social interaction in unexpected ways between residents. Coleen O'Leary, University of Tennessee, 10" x 10".

7–35 to 7–37 Coleen's "Enchanted Loom" plays on the idea of the think tank and neuroscience charting pathways of how the human brain processes information. Almost like an incubator business, spaces are available to lease for short durations of 6 to 8 months for exploring innovative projects and business planning. Coleen O'Leary, University of Tennessee, 10" x 10".

7 CRITIQUES & CONVERSATIONS

happy with the final product. She was supported by feedback from her design professors and commentary from the faculty in the interior design department. One of the most important lessons learned from the process was that a portfolio is never complete. She plans to continuously update and delete work as she goes along. ISSUU was a great resource for her book production. Her involvement in a presentation design class helped enormously in understanding hierarchy, the importance of white space, and how to properly use text. She was eventually offered an internship in an interior design department of an architecture firm and her employer mentioned how impressed they were with her portfolio and how much her talent shined through!

Coleen O'Leary's Portfolio Review
by Nancy Kwallek

Coleen O'Leary's portfolio reflects a solid foundation in design thinking and builds her designs from the design concept. Such ability comes from a studio background that allows her to think and design creatively. More interest could be generated in her portfolio by including a greater variety of design work. Hand drawings, study and finished models, along with explanations of projects created inside and outside the classroom would further enrich this already substantial presentation.

Of the four interior design projects provided in Colleen's portfolio, I wish to offer initial comment especially on the Incubator Office Space project which clearly shows development of design concept, especially in the ceiling design, chair and table designs, and in the floor plans with moveable parts being put away—all with an unfolding theme. As for the final Conch Shell project, the design concept is clearly explained and its relationship to the abode is described for the viewer. Curves in plan and furniture show the inspiration without literally being overdone. This is also true for the color palette used.

Tips for the future: I am happy to offer the following tips as suggestions regarding further refinements and aspects for future consideration. It would be nice to see a first page that introduces the designer in a broader, more exciting way; herein, the first page is a table of contents rather than something more exciting to entice an employer to delve further into this student's work. An exciting introduction/enticement to this portfolio would tell the reader that this is an innovative portfolio to review. A resume of who she is with background, education, and experience is vital, too.

All in all, this is an ample presentation with evidence throughout of the student's substantial design abilities. Certainly, there is always room for more that could be done. In the NEXT project, including study models and illustrations of how the design concepts develop into the final design would more clearly show the linkage of the brand to the concept terms presented. And for the TN Orthopedic Clinics, accessories in that space would make it more inviting. The concept of using cool and warm colors in patient areas is mentioned and may be more clearly depicted. Possibly more can be done with the "joint" in design development—it is presented but not developed.

Overall, I commend Coleen for a successful presentation that grows out of a comprehensive studio background. Her work amply demonstrates a trajectory of undergraduate professional development that will stand her in good stead as she competes for employment in a variety of interior offices that do diverse kinds of work from residential, commercial, and specialized projects.

The reader should realize that comments offered relate to a juror's critique of the individual interior design projects presented. Included here are design issues that a prospective employer would certainly evaluate, not only the graphic design work of the presentation. Students should be encouraged to make corrections in their designs after their jury reviews, a lesson all designers are aware of, but time can be a constraint.

About the Reviewer

Dr. Nancy Kwallek directed the undergraduate and graduate Interior Design programs at the University of Texas at Austin (UT) from 1983 until her retirement in 2015. Upon retirement she was named the Gene Edward Mikeska Endowed Chair Emeritus for Interior Design in the School of Architecture. Since its inception in 1999, the $1 million Chair endowment generates thousands of dollars yearly for the program and interior design research.

After earning her Ph.D. at Purdue University and throughout a long career in higher education, she has contributed significantly to the advancement of interior design through course development, service, and research. Recognized as an international expert on the effects of interior color on humans, she has published scholarly articles and presented her research to numerous audiences. Her color research discoveries have reached the scientific community (in Nature and The Scientist newsletter) as well

Featured Portfolios

as popular websites (e.g., Discovery Channel, CNN, *The New York Times*, *The Wall Street Journal*). Such exposure of research in interior design helps promote respectability for and the value of interior design. Currently she is completing an elected four-year term as the USA representative on the Association Internationale de la Couleur's (AIC) Executive Committee and will represent the United States in Chile this year and Korea next year.

Having been awarded numerous honors and awards during her career (a Lifetime Achievement Award from Kent State University and Media and Merit Awards from the Interior Design Educators Council and the Council for Interior Design Accreditation), her career achievements have recently been topped off by the naming of a new $1 million endowment in the School of Architecture, the Dr. Nancy Kwallek Endowed Chair for Design and Planning. The significance of these two chairs for and inclusive of the Interior Design program are unique in the history of the discipline in the United States.

Melissa Vasconcelos

Melissa's portfolio demonstrates great strength in research and process (figures 7–38 to 7–47). She has created titled zones to the left-hand column on introductory pages to signify important steps to her design development. This clearly shows that she understands that there are many stages to developing a real project. Several pages focus on the design concept with ample diagrams. The shapes of the perspective renderings are also carefully constructed. It is important to note that she includes entourage in her presentation drawings to show how humans *use* the space. Complete materiality, well-illustrated spaces, and careful design research and analysis make this portfolio outstanding.

Melissa designed this portfolio in her final year of the graduate program in Interior Design at the University of Manitoba, Winnipeg, Manitoba. The central purpose was to demonstrate her various abilities to prospective employers. She used InDesign CS5 to do the layout design and printed it on a heavy white bond paper. She created a

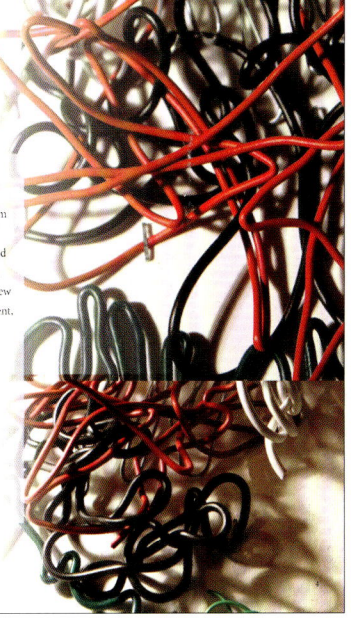

7–38 Melissa Vasconcelos explores music and interior space in this beautifully designed portfolio presentation of research and innovative thinking. The open form of the layout design, the clarity of graphic illustrations, and successful organization make for a comprehensive presentation of great breadth and depth. Melissa Vasconcelos, University of Manitoba, Winnipeg, 9" x 22".

7 CRITIQUES & CONVERSATIONS

variation of the book for her graduate thesis and had it published on Blurb.com as a hardback book. Blurb is an online self-publishing platform that prints and binds your portfolio like a traditional book. She created seven copies of her book at an individual cost of $70.00. The entire process of design required a full non-stop week of design and additional time for binding. The result was completely successful as it marked the completion of her graduate thesis. Her portfolio was exemplary and an inspiration for other students, and resulted in her being offered an attractive job by a local architecture firm.

One of the most important lessons that Melissa learned was that finding the right layout to complement her work required the greatest investment in time and experimentation. Her advice to others is to sample numerous layout options before settling on one. She also suggests using resource books to help understand graphic and layout design and as a boost to good results.

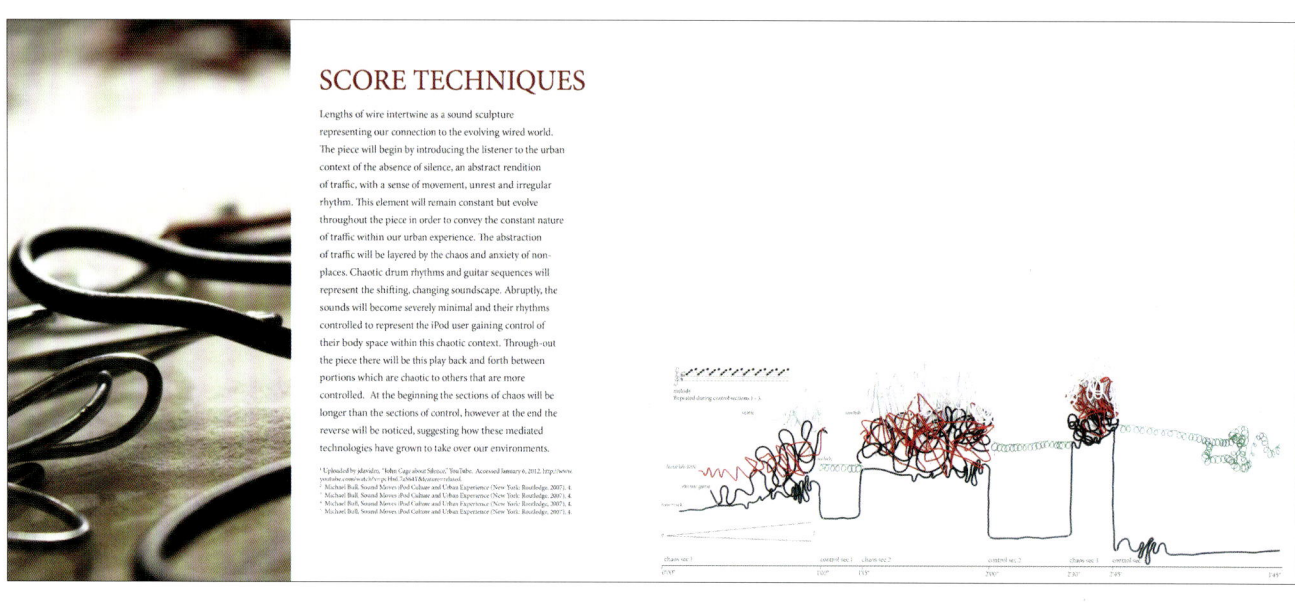

7–39 to 7–43 Melissa Vasconcelos explores music and interior space in this beautifully designed portfolio presentation of research and innovative thinking. The open form of the layout design, the clarity of graphic illustrations, and successful organization make for a comprehensive presentation of great breadth and depth. Melissa Vasconcelos, University of Manitoba, Winnipeg, 9" x 22".

Featured Portfolios

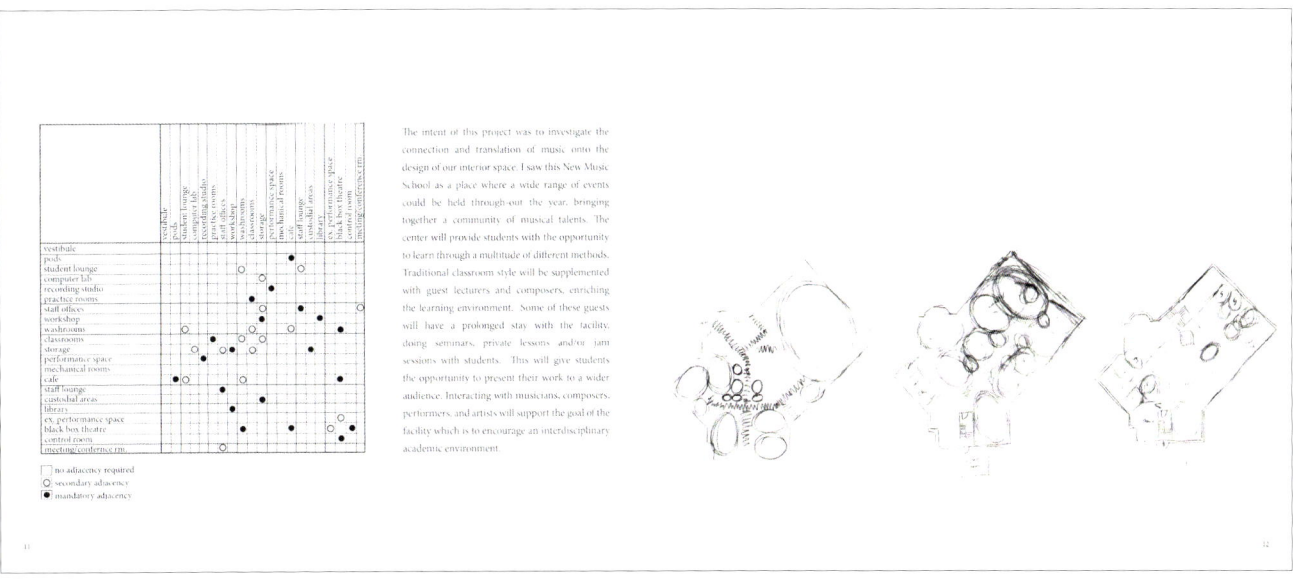

The intent of this project was to investigate the connection and translation of music onto the design of our interior space. I saw this New Music School as a place where a wide range of events could be held through-out the year, bringing together a community of musical talents. The center will provide students with the opportunity to learn through a multitude of different methods. Traditional classroom style will be supplemented with guest lecturers and composers, enriching the learning environment. Some of these guests will have a prolonged stay with the facility, doing seminars, private lessons and/or jam sessions with students. This will give students the opportunity to present their work to a wider audience. Interacting with musicians, composers, performers, and artists will support the goal of the facility which is to encourage an interdisciplinary academic environment.

I began by overlaying our composition Absent Silence onto the original plan. This developed into creating forms that represented chaos and control. My plan was to integrate seating pods into my design which would act as moments of control over one's environment. As for how I laid out the music on my plans, I saw the main entry and exit points of the building as the most chaotic as they would have the most traffic flow. I automatically recognized the design of my space as a progression, as our piece, Absent Silence would have been characterized similarly. As I was developing my translation it informed my decisions as to where extensions on the original building needed to be placed. I also began developing how my translation of music could be further enhanced through the ceiling plane. In the sketch below you can begin to see the development of my ceiling panels that enhance the feeling of chaos and order in sections of the space.

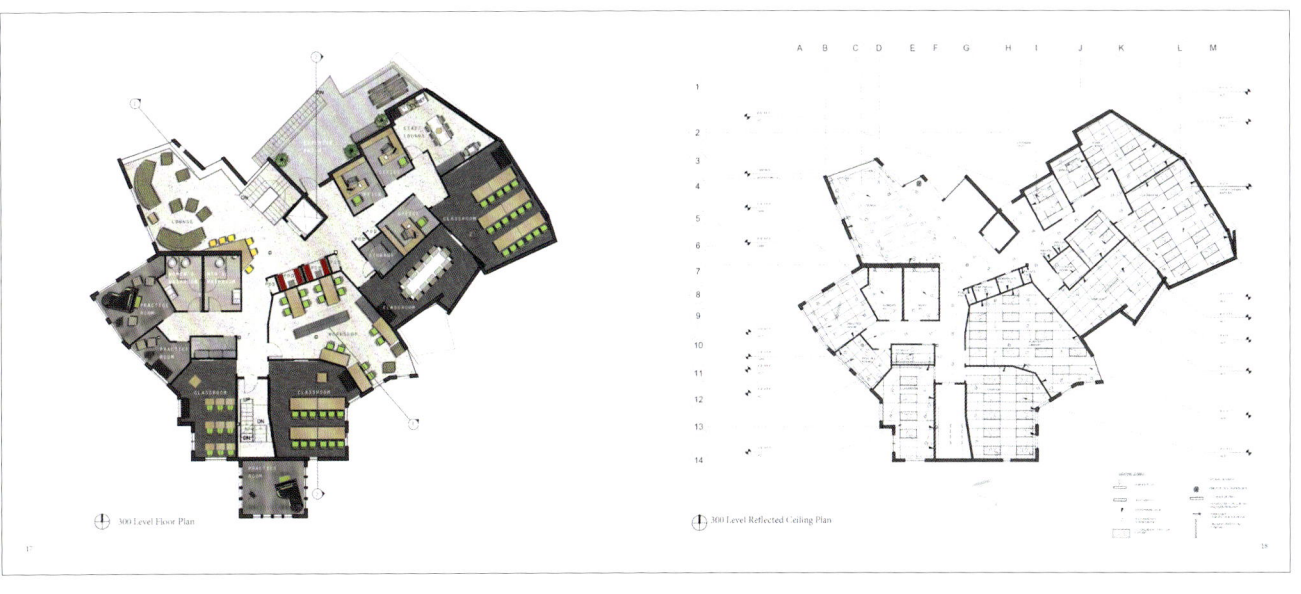

300 Level Floor Plan

300 Level Reflected Ceiling Plan

7 CRITIQUES & CONVERSATIONS

3. 200/300 Level - Stairs and theatre entrance
4. 200/300 Level - Lounge & stair elevation
5. 200 Level - Theatre elevation

200 Level - Lounge
200 Level - Cafe & theatre entrance

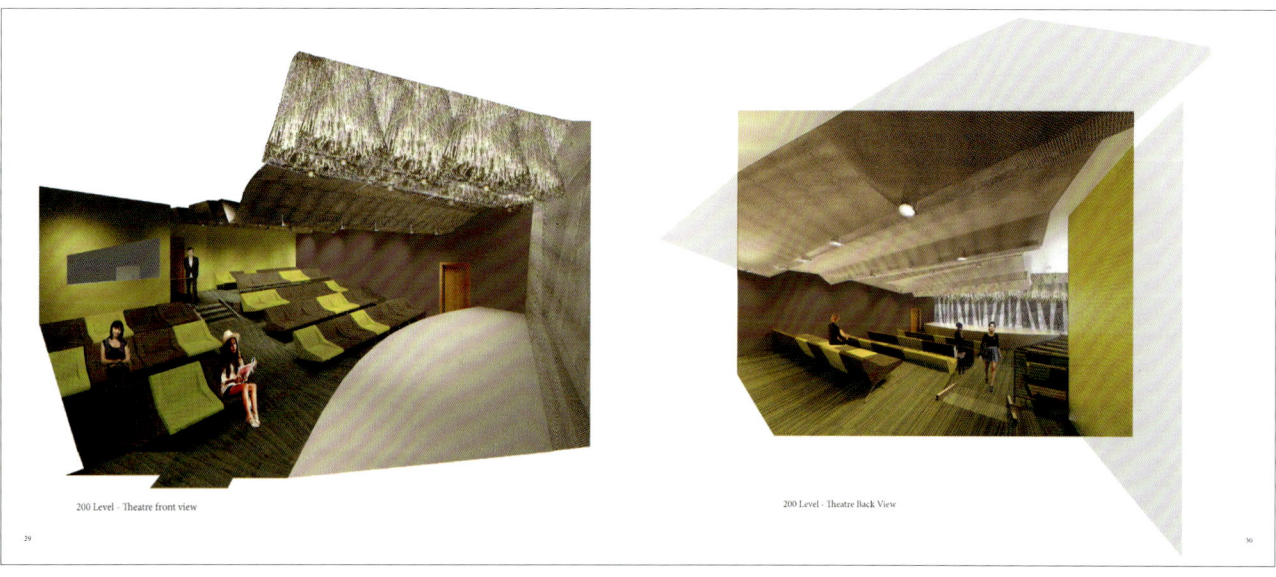

200 Level - Theatre front view
200 Level - Theatre Back View

Featured Portfolios

7-44 to 7-47 Melissa Vasconcelos explores music and interior space in this beautifully designed portfolio presentation of research and innovative thinking. The open form of the layout design, the clarity of graphic illustrations, and successful organization make for a comprehensive presentation of great breadth and depth. Melissa Vasconcelos, University of Manitoba, Winnipeg, 9" x 22".

Melissa Vasconcelos Portfolio Review by V. Mason Wickham and Edwin Zawadzki

This graduate portfolio is very successful at its primary objective. It sets up a simple, clear layout design to document two projects in depth with logical and rational development and without extraneous or redundant information. The text and drawings are well presented, and their content is legible so the reader can focus on the work. As with advanced portfolios of substance, we examine the successful qualities inherent in its design and suggest ways to further refine it in the future.

Basic Organization

The primary organization is straightforward. There are two sections in the portfolio containing one project each. Both have a double title page with a solid, olive green background color and white type. The muted earthiness of the green chosen for the title pages appears to be connected to the color palette of the renderings in the first section and remains neutral in the second section.

The first section is called "Master Studio" and explores the relationship between music and space. The second is called "Practicum" and investigates the evolution of the museum typology. The divisions are graphically clear. These projects leave us wanting to see more than two large projects. They pique our curiosity to see more work that has been done in the curriculum and that would broaden our understanding of the student's education and abilities. Perhaps another portfolio would be forthcoming in an interview situation.

The designer states that the portfolio graphics will change as they relate to concepts. This is a nice idea and is well executed on the pages diagramming "Absent Silence" and "Scoring Techniques." These pages, again, really piqued our interest right from the start. The subsequent information is clear, and the unique and strong voice and confident hand creates interest and adds to one's engagement in the work.

Cover

On the cover, the subject and object are composed of three different graphic elements. These typographic elements are working harder than they need to be to achieve the overall effect, which is still simple and elegant.

Section One

The first section starts off with a simple "photo-graphic" of what looks like speaker wire in full bleed alternating from the left and right margins. This imagery was a sophisticated abstract representation of the design concept and a catchy graphic all in one. It would be even more efficient if the designer found connections and transitions for this technique further along and throughout the portfolio.

After these first pages, a different series of graphic styles begins, unified by the content. The project is thoroughly represented. However, the graphics from page to page can be jarring. Within the book, there are several strong sets of paired facing pages. This strategy is a strength through to the end of the section.

Reviewer Tips

While the overall presentation strategy is simple and efficient, alternative design considerations could include pairing the rendered floor plans with reflected ceiling plans; and not formatting text and diagrams to hold the pages as strongly as the pages before and after. Key plan icons are great at showing the viewer where one is located, but they float all over the place instead of being logically placed from page to page. They should never (or always) overlap the image; decisions regarding when to contain a picture on the page and when to allow a full bleed appear random. The contained image pairs tend to be stronger, although the bleeds could be used more efficiently if they were deliberate. Cropping of the 3D renderings into vignettes is interesting at first—hip and dynamic—but in the end, no logic appears to rule where the cropping is done, so they are weaker than more standard framing would be.

Section Two

This section, like the first, has a robust combination of representational materials and overall is visually lively and appealing. Most of the same comments from Section One apply regarding decisions of image position and bleeds. The graphics in this section are quite different from the first part. So again in coordinating the design, a neutral or tertiary color for the title page helps to distinguish the front matter from the other pages. The bands of dark olive green with large font headers in white labeling the contents of the sub-sections like "project scope" and "public space" are a strong and simple way to keep the viewer on the "path." (Is the author consciously mimicking museum signage so the graphic is conceptually linked in? Might this explain why this technique was not used in the first section?) There are a couple of pages where the header system disappears, just as it did in Section One, but it should be on every left margin here, even if blank or didactically repetitive, to keep the pages tied together and not have the left margins shifting back and forth. This would also help enliven the visually dull pages of charts. There are some pages with too much blank space. We admire the discipline to not fill the white with padding, but perhaps some of the process work that does not always fill its pages well could have been formatted to accompany some of the final images floating alone on the page.

Micro-Organization

In general, the palette and graphics communicate effectively. There could be a little more work with alignments, fonts, and devices like bleeds, margins, and frames. The more consistently these techniques are employed, the clearer the work is, and the more the viewer trusts the content and author. To its credit, this portfolio is very sober and humble in its use of graphics. Even more attention to graphic rules would make it quieter and stronger still.

Summary

Overall we found the portfolio to be energetic and filled with quality. Both the layout design and content held our interest and at times made us wish for a larger representation of studio work. That's what happens when an intriguing body of work is designed beautifully into a portfolio—it stirs the reviewer and kindles one's desire to see more, more!

About the Reviewers

In Situ Design is the alter ego of partners Mason Wickham and Edwin Zawadzki who met while slaving away at Perkins+Will and decided to run off to Paris to start their own very-much-not-corporate design studio. In Situ Design has since gone on to complete a range of projects from homes to hotels, restaurants to dot coms in several countries and languages. The studio has won some awards and been published in some perfectly respectable magazines and blogs, such as *Interiors* magazine. The reviewers have long since removed to NYC but still look to the world for ideas.

BEYOND THE PORTFOLIO

In Chapters Eight and Nine, we want to get you thinking and motivated to review the written communications in your book and to prepare for using your portfolio as a tool for advancement. The goal of the portfolio may not be to get a graduate placement, a grant, or a job, but could be a stepping stone to scheduling an interview leading to one of these. So let's assume your portfolio or teaser images were sent out via email and succeeded in winning you an interview. What next? What should you expect?

A typical interview lasts a half-hour or more and is usually conducted by a member of the faculty or administration or, in a practice office, by a member of the design team, a partner, project manager, or personnel officer. Expect to be asked questions about your education, your previous employment, and the projects you have completed, as well as, possibly, questions about your personal goals.

Almost certainly, you will be asked why you chose your field of study and how you see yourself fitting into the position. Make sure you know your portfolio and the projects in it well and be prepared to talk about them forcefully. This is one good reason proper labeling and concept statements are beneficial in the layout of the portfolio. If you sense that a reviewer is unclear about some aspect of your presentation, offer help. Make the necessary explanations and clarifications—and learn from the experience. Address any problem areas revealed in your portfolio before your next interview. Be aware that not everything the interviewer wants to know may be solicited through formal, cut-and-dried questions. The less-formal conversation in which you and the interviewer engage reveals much about your personality, attitude, interests, and personal and professional goals.

The most important questions may be those you ask. Always come to a job interview with some thoughtfully prepared questions of your own. The worst answer you can give in an interview is "no" when you are asked "Do you have any questions?" Unless you demonstrate curiosity about a company and your prospective position within it, the interview is unlikely to interest either you or the interviewer(s). And if the interview fails to generate interest, it will almost certainly fail to produce an offer.

Obvious questions to ask include how the office is structured, how design teams operate, and how employees advance in responsibility. To arm yourself with more specific questions than these, you will need to do some advance research on the company—the more, the better. You need, for example, to learn as much as possible about the kind of work the firm does: Commercial? Residential? Institutional? Some combination of these? Is there traveling involved and do you speak other languages?

Whether the interview in question is for your dream job or a "safety" or "fallback" position, you should approach the interview with wholehearted enthusiasm and a display of earnest eagerness to learn more. Nothing is more appreciated than a demonstration of sincere interest and engagement. Focus less on yourself and your needs than on the needs of the interviewer. Interviews are about what you can do for the company, not what the company can do for you. Be open to an interviewer's interest in the skills they see in areas of your portfolio and in your background that you haven't considered. Balance creativity and communication. And don't automatically reject an offer for employment in an allied field, for example, as a graphic designer or webmaster.

Don't be afraid to express yourself and your individual style. Your portfolio is a product of self that must speak to others. Your mission in preparing your portfolio is to balance two functions. It is a creative act that exhibits your skills and your imagination, but it is also an act of communication, a tool for promoting yourself to others. Demonstrate originality and inventiveness, but accept the restraints and conventions of professionalism. Do this successfully, and you will show that you can get your ideas across in terms that working architects, designers, clients, and graduate faculty will understand. Practice achieving this balance between creativity and practicality until it comes naturally to you—or, at least, seems to.

A portfolio may break all the rules but, if it is to succeed as communication, it must be clear and comprehensible to the viewer by following its *own* set of rules. You will engage in the contest between invention and convention throughout your entire career as a designer, and the portfolio presentation shows that you can balance these organically, efficiently, and beautifully. This is the most compelling evidence of what you are capable of achieving in your chosen field.

8
RESEARCH
& WRITTEN COMMUNICATIONS

"The portfolio design process is hard work. But in the end you want your book to feel relaxed and not labored. Learn to ruthlessly edit text and visuals, continuously reinventing versions of things that make incremental improvements up and down the book's contents."

– **SCOTT AGELOFF**

SUMMARY OF START-UP INTERIOR DESIGN FIRMS: WHAT MATTERS?

Interior design firms are in the business of obtaining clients and projects and producing satisfactory solutions. Customers want to know how you are going to support their needs before hiring you. Although they know you have an education in interior design and are pursuing employment as an interior designer, design firms need to find out if you will add value to their business. Also, they want to understand better what unique qualities you bring to their team, especially in relationship to other new designers.

8 RESEARCH & WRITTEN COMMUNICATIONS

Lauren Vella

Lauren studied interior design at NYSID and created a striking highly visual undergraduate portfolio in the form of a PowerPoint presentation to mail on CD as well as a bound 5" x 7" booklet that she could show in person at an interview (figures 8–1 to 8–5). To create interest in her book, she made the print portfolio a small custom size to convey an unusual form on first impression. She used screws, washers, and nuts to bind the booklet and made three copies as backups. With each new project in the book, she added a material page to convey a tactile sensory experience and another sense of conceptual thinking and design for the viewer. She worked on it over a period of one semester, and her design studio work and portfolio were created with AutoCAD, PowerPoint, and Photoshop.

Lauren received positive feedback from interviewers as she walked them through the booklet discussing the concept for each design and her solutions. Since graduation, she has expanded her repertoire of software abilities and believes her next version will be more expansive and flexible using an even broader approach to print and online presentation strategies. Most importantly, she believes it was wise to have hard copy and CD versions to work with as each employer has a different approach to looking at work. She was successful in interviewing with her book and did acquire employment.

Summary of Start-Up Interior Design Firms: What Matters?

8–1 to 8–5 Contract Design II: Chop. The objective for this project was to design a hair salon. Lauren's inspiration was drastic change. In the floor plan the angled walls created abrupt obstructions in the flow—as if the plan was "chopped." This also influenced the materials utilized. She chose metal in both rust form and polished. In the waiting area, the client is exposed to the rough and unmaintained nature of the rust (representing the state of the client's hair). Inside the angled walls is the area where transformation would take place. The finishes in the space were polished and contrasted in the waiting area. The material insert on this page was an image of rust representing change. Lauren Vella, New York School of Interior Design, N.Y., N.Y. 5" x 7".

Researching a design firm provides many insights into the business of being a design firm and aids the aspiring interior designer by offering a summary of the goals, values, and aspirations of the emerging or well-established design office. It makes perfect sense to review as much available background information on those firms that you wish to pursue. What you learn from a search online or by networking can be substantial and aid you in gearing your presentation and interview in strategic ways to best accomplish a successful introduction and discussion. Consider what kinds of designers a startup firm, for example Bright Interiors, needs during the initial three years of growth in operations and what types of specific skill sets they will most likely be looking for as part of their employee search during that time. Try putting their hat on and see what new revelations occur that you can use to understand better another person's perspective and needs!

Bright Interiors offers comprehensive interior design services for homes and offices in the Washington, D.C. area. Bright Interiors provides products and services to complement their successful design consulting business including furnishings, both new and antique, fabric, lighting, fixtures, and home and office accessories. Personalized services are their hallmark and what the target market desires. From concept to implementation, Bright Interiors offers a unique, customer-friendly service appreciated in the community.

Recent market research indicates a specific and growing need in the D.C. area for interior design consulting services and products. Bright Interiors proposes a market strategy based on a conservative business model approach to reach this clearly defined target market. Although the population of metropolitan area of Washington D.C. is over 2,500,000, the market has a significant quantity of relatively wealthy households that are conscious of the appearance and feel of their homes and offices.

The approach to promote Bright Interiors will be through establishing relationships with key organizations and people in the community and then through referral activities once a significant client base is established. Design solutions by Bright Interiors originate with the customer's taste, budget, use, and goals for the space and style. Value-based pricing will differentiate Bright Interiors from the other options in the area, as will selection, accessibility of products, design services, and more.

Total revenues for the first year are projected to exceed $246,000. Profits in years two and three along with revenues are expected to climb to almost $800,000. This interior design business plan outlines the concept, implementation, and details regarding the first three years of this venture.

Bright Interiors needs to hire designers with technical design skills demonstrated in their portfolio; this is among the most important considerations when hiring a new design team. Floor plans, elevations/sections, AutoCAD drawings, perspective sketches, reflected ceiling plans, lighting/electrical plans, and 3D computer illustration and design are all outstanding professional abilities that firms look for when interviewing a candidate for a new position and verify by following an interview with calls to your references. Character traits are important as well, with a focus on professional sincerity, honesty, ethical and moral character, good work ethic, professional etiquette, good manners, and being a polite team player. Other qualities related to successful performance on the job discerned by an interview and reference check include your eagerness to grow and learn, time management skills, whether you are a good fit for the firm, professional appearance and attire, outgoing personality, and passion and enthusiasm for design. Much of this is evident in the written documents and visual artifacts in your portfolio as well as during an initial interview.

Macy Hale

Macy created her portfolio (figures 8–6 to 8–10) as an undergraduate in interior design at the University of Tennessee, Knoxville. Her purpose was to use the portfolio and interview for employment. She used InDesign to produce the layout design for her book, and Revit, AutoCAD, and FormZ for the specific projects included in her book. She printed the book on an 80# text white opaque paper stock and bound the book by saddle stitch. She produced two books at $40.00 per book.

8–6 to 8–8 Macy effectively uses call-out words via contrasting colors in opening concept statements, which help to orient the viewer's attention to her design direction. This approach highlights her thought process and calls attention to what she feels is important in the project. Her digital renderings are sensitive and relate well to her palette of materials and colors. She has allowed the white space surrounding the drawings to support her delicate renderings and quality of light in her interior design spaces. Macy Hale, University of Tennessee, Knoxville, Tenn. 8.5" x 11".

Summary of Start-Up Interior Design Firms: What Matters?

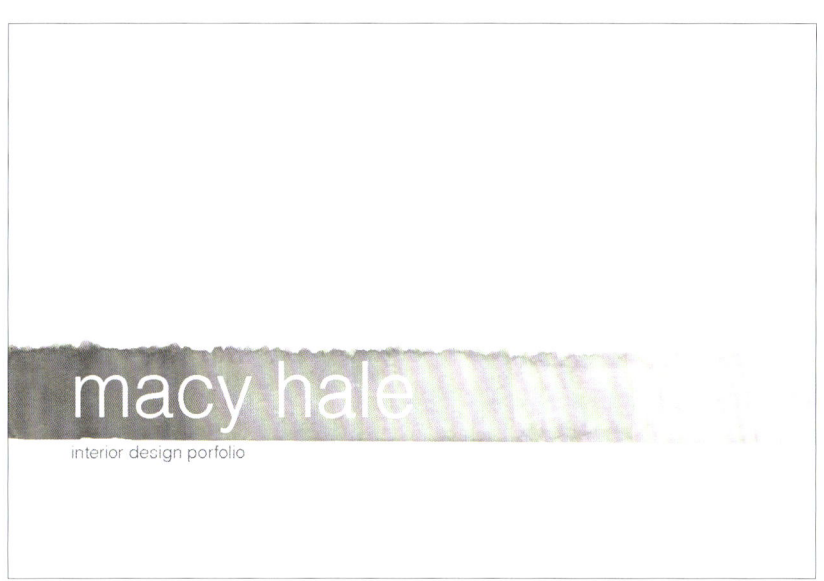

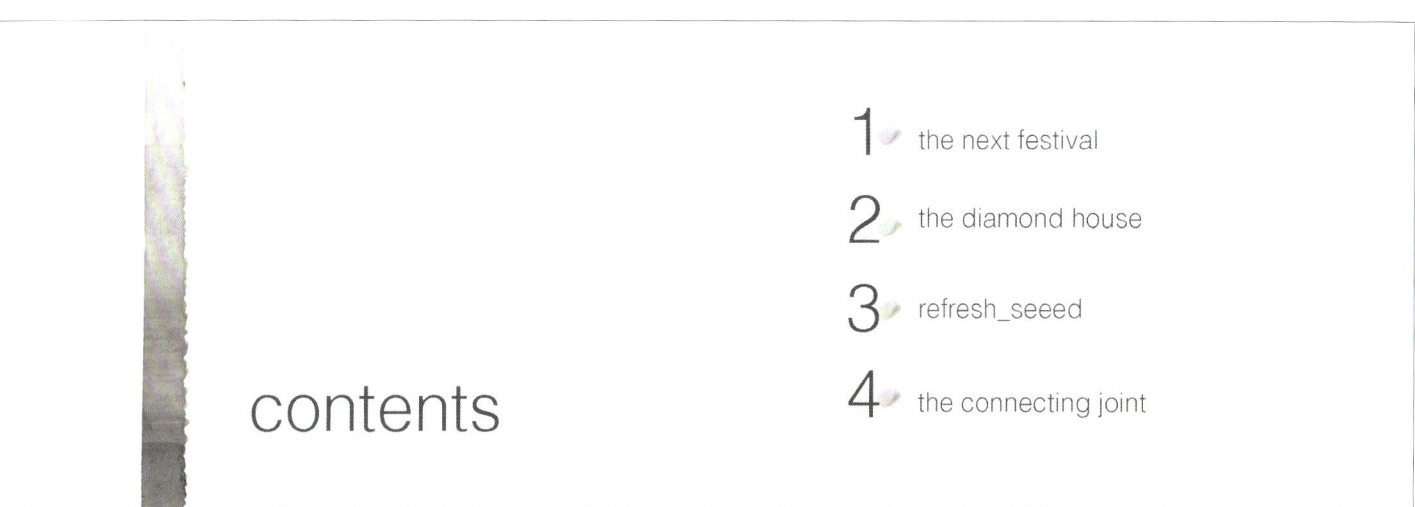

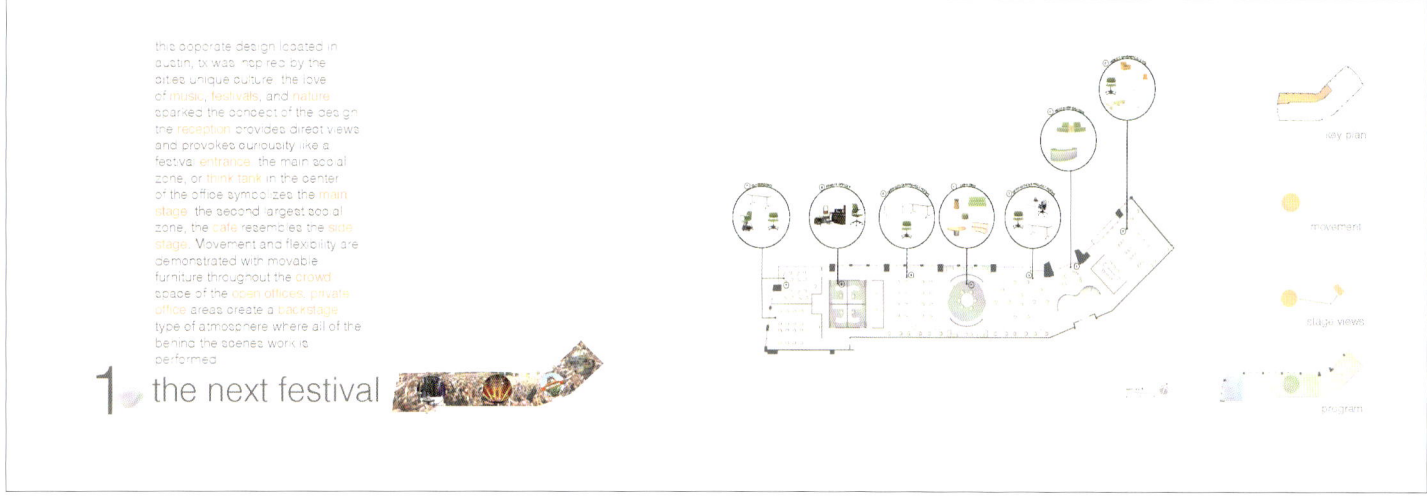

8 RESEARCH & WRITTEN COMMUNICATIONS

Her portfolio was designed over the course of a full academic semester, devoting several hours per week over a prolonged period of time. She gained awareness by studying portfolios available on ISSUU. She also gained awareness throughout the process of the importance of demonstrating design process in your work and in your portfolio. She also understood the significance of being comprehensive in representing your skills and abilities. Upon graduation, Macy found employment in Knoxville, Tennessee.

The investment a firm makes in a new employee is considerable. Not only is salary a significant factor, but also, other employees frequently perform training time along with their current responsibilities. Growth into new and future responsibilities is integral to the ongoing achievements of the firm. Still other important skills and attributes employers look for in a portfolio and interview are organization, strong communication skills (especially verbal), positive/friendly attitude and demeanor, outgoing personality, time management skills, and an appropriate curiosity demonstrated by asking good questions.

Employers hire new designers based on the right combination of exhibited qualities and abilities. Often this basket of qualifications includes prior work experience, confidence, ability to sell oneself and one's work, professional appearance and work ethic, good language skills, communication and presentation skills, good people skills, realistic expectations and knowledge of career path, ability to work with others and be a team player, appropriate sense of accomplishment, humility, and practical (how-to) design knowledge. As you compile your portfolio, think of it not just as a collection of discrete exercises but a way to tell a story about your work and your approach to design. What does the story entail? Be confident in what you are presenting. Discuss the project from beginning to end. List the challenges and the design solution. Showcase your knowledge on the subject.

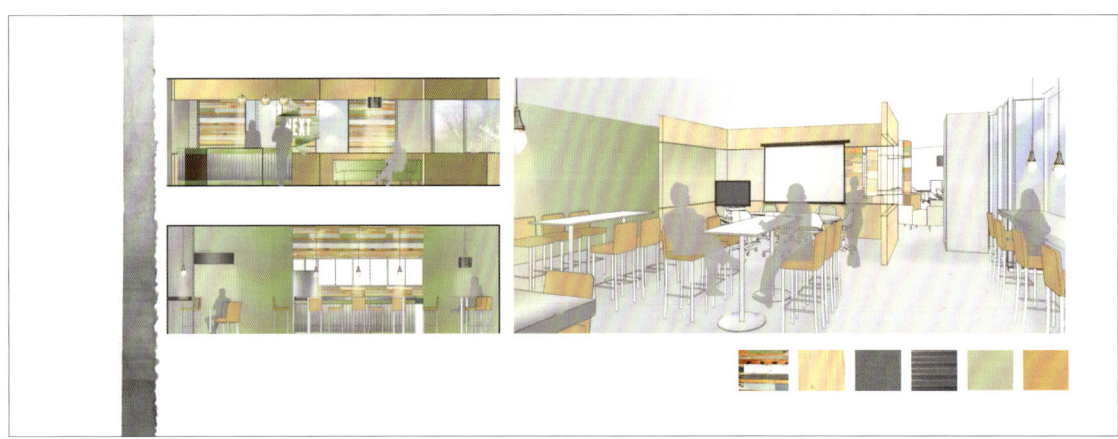

8–9 to 8–10 Macy effectively uses call-out words via contrasting colors in opening concept statements, which help to orient the viewer's attention to her design direction. This approach highlights her thought process and calls attention to what she feels is important in the project. Her digital renderings are sensitive and relate well to her palette of materials and colors. She has allowed the white space surrounding the drawings to support her delicate renderings and quality of light in her interior design spaces. Macy Hale, University of Tennessee, Knoxville, Tenn. 8.5" x 11".

RESUME AND COVER LETTER

Your resume and cover letter are your gateways to a prospective employer. They must be coherent, well-written statements in everyday language that is easy to understand. Interviewers want to know if the applicant is serious about his or her work and is passionate about the profession of interior design. You must communicate these qualities through both the information you provide and the clarity of your materials.

Think of the purpose of these documents as dominoes. The purpose of the cover letter is to make the reviewer want to review your resume, and the purpose of the resume is to help gain an interview to show your portfolio. Provide the employer with a description about you to determine if you will meet his or her needs. Relevant information for writing a resume includes:

- Education/degree type
- List of design skills
- List of technical skills, including technology skills
- Design-related course work
- Internship experience

Other desirable information includes a list of projects or project work, a brief statement of a career objective, work experience (other than design internships), and membership in professional organization(s). Information about study abroad, volunteer experience, or extracurricular activities is of less importance.

Sergio Mondragon

Sergio's portfolios were created while an undergraduate at California State University, Sacramento. His purpose was to create a foundation portfolio (figures 8–11 to 8–13) that captured his entry-level experience in basic design followed by a full undergraduate program portfolio reflecting his comprehensive design experience (figures 8–14 to 8–18). Both of these books were entirely successful! He received his first job offer at Gensler. The entire design and production process for the undergraduate portfolio took about 3 months. Sergio comments, "I learned the craft of editing. I made sure to include the best work I had available and would not change anything as a result." Important to the

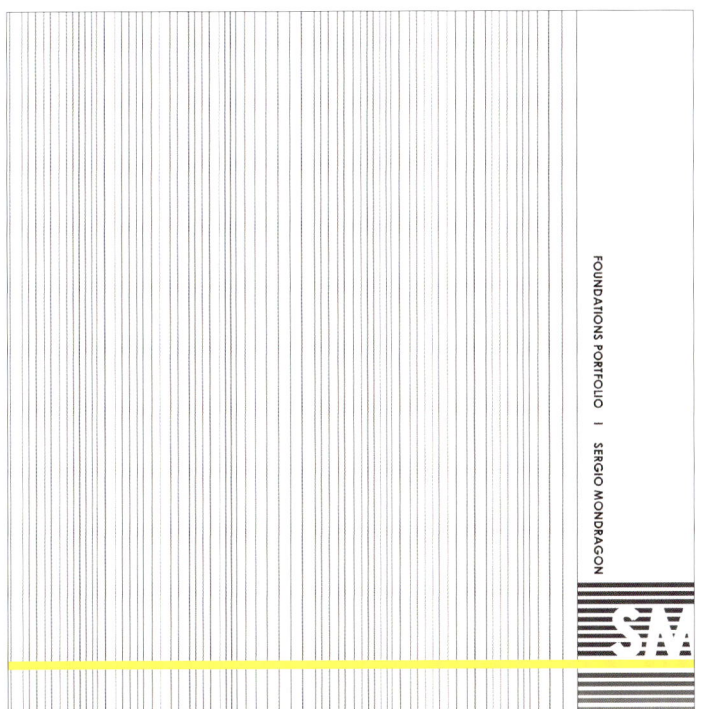

8–11 Sergio's foundation portfolio formed the successful groundwork for a progression of growth and design development leading to a far more involved and comprehensive undergraduate portfolio used for employment interviews and applications to graduate schools. Sergio Mondragon, California State University, Sacramento, Calif. 8.5" x 8.5".

8 RESEARCH & WRITTEN COMMUNICATIONS

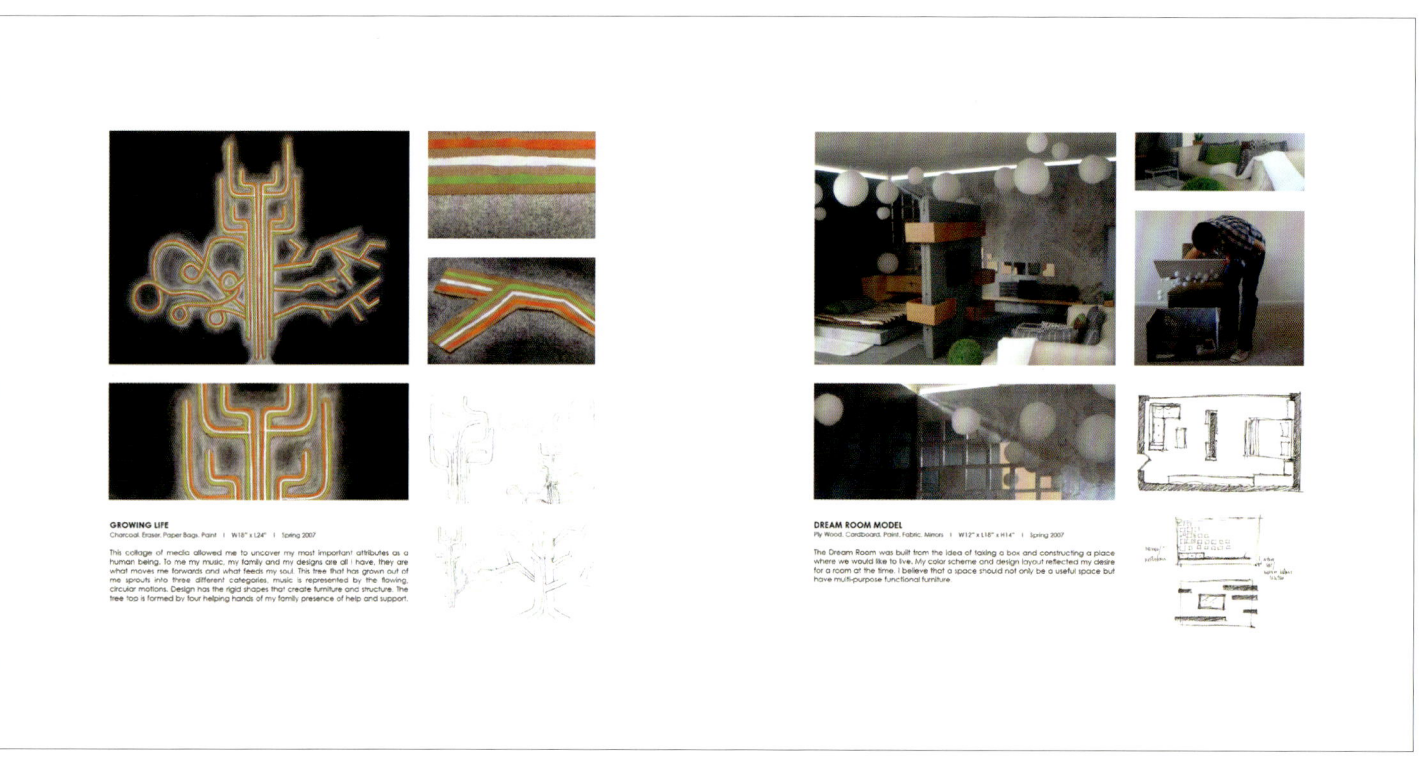

8–12 to 8–13 Sergio's foundation portfolio formed the successful groundwork for a progression of growth and design development leading to a far more involved and comprehensive undergraduate portfolio used for employment interviews and applications to graduate schools. Sergio Mondragon, California State University, Sacramento, Calif. 8.5" x 8.5".

Resume and Cover Letter

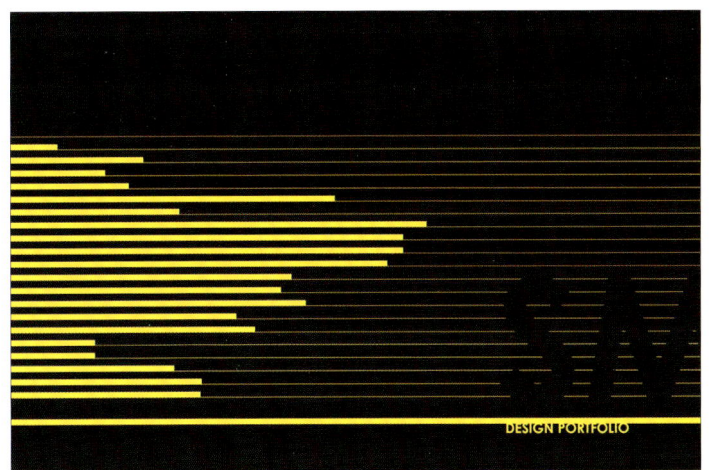

8–14 to 8–16 In Sergio's undergraduate portfolio, designated zones for showing his "layering process" and planning methods are effective. The use of lines is an organizing theme for his table of contents page and carries through all of his project presentations. The black zones with process sketching reversed into white are an effective way to demonstrate the design thinking underlying every project presented. The play of positive and negative space works well to isolate what was thought and what is reality. We appreciate his conceptual cover and the meaning it has for Sergio. The use of the yellow line both as a conceptual tool for his cover and also as a cut tool for his sections works well within the plan without disturbing the order. We like that he used the ground line at the right side of the page for the typography of his categories, such as residential, hospitality, and corporate. Sergio Mondragon, California State University, Sacramento, Calif. 11" x 17".

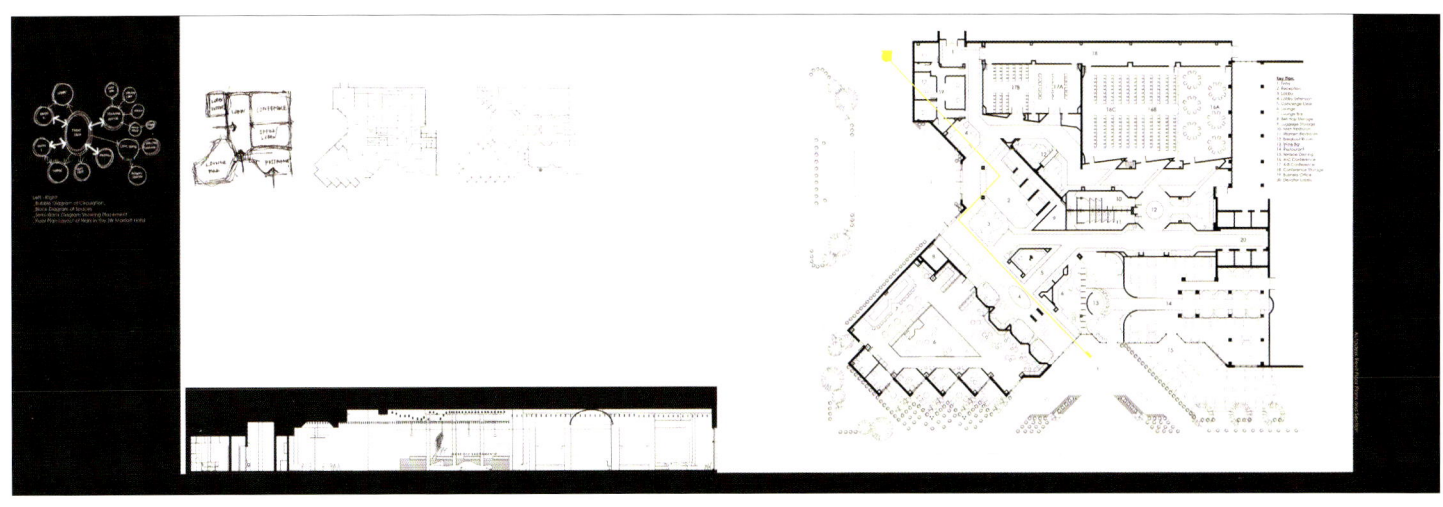

8 RESEARCH & WRITTEN COMMUNICATIONS

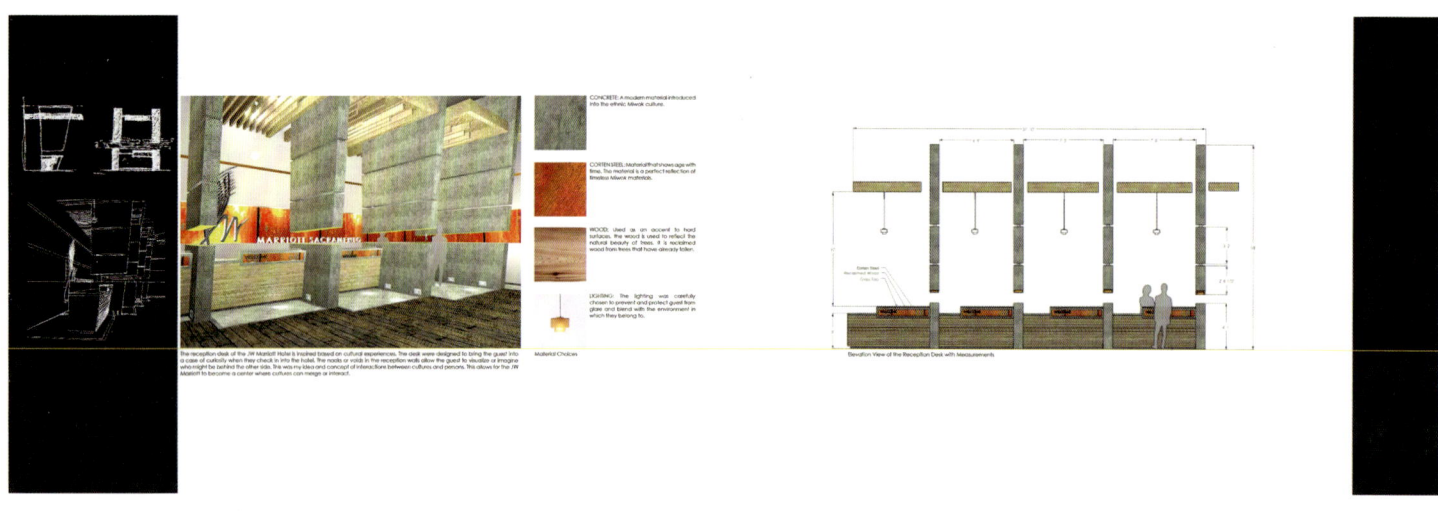

8–17 to 8–18 In Sergio's undergraduate portfolio, designated zones for showing his "layering process" and planning methods are effective. The use of lines is an organizing theme for his table of contents page and carries through all of his project presentations. The black zones with process sketching reversed into white are an effective way to demonstrate the design thinking underlying every project presented. The play of positive and negative space works well to isolate what was thought and what is reality. We appreciate his conceptual cover and the meaning it has for Sergio. The use of the yellow line both as a conceptual tool for his cover and also as a cut tool for his sections works well within the plan without disturbing the order. We like that he used the ground line at the right side of the page for the typography of his categories, such as residential, hospitality, and corporate. Sergio Mondragon, California State University, Sacramento, Calif. 11" x 17".

creation of these books were the Adobe Creative Suite, AutoDesk, Revit, and Google SketchUp. He used an Epson Stylus photo 1400 inkjet 11" x 17" printer with scored kraft paper. Sergio was accepted into graduate school at Parsons, The New School of Design, Rhode Island School of Design in Masters of Architecture, and California College of the Arts, San Francisco.

What employers often look for in your book:

- Professionalism, meaning efficient and understated work
- Originality and creativity (but not overdone)
- Concise, precise, correct grammar and spelling
- Clear visual presentation of the work with coherent organization
- Simplicity and legibility in the selection of fonts
- Neutral tones in the choice of paper stock (or bright white-satin, glossy, or matte)
- Technical and physical skills throughout the presentation
- A listing of computer skills; Adobe Creative Suite, AutoCAD, Revit, and Microsoft Office Suite are among the most in demand.
- Quality graphic design layout and appearance of the resume.

Laura Taylor

Laura created this high-contrast professional presentation as an undergraduate at Utah State University in order to find both a summer internship and a full-time position at Rapt Studio, San Francisco (figures 8–19 to 8–24). She used the Adobe Creative Suite for image correction, layout design, and creation of specific design images. The page spreads were printed at 11" x 17", then trimmed and bound similar to a magazine format. The magazine-like booklet was then placed into an open-faced custom-made birch box with a card stock sleeve to secure it within the box. She chose ISSUU to display the portfolio online.

Laura worked through four drafts before settling on the final layout design. She spent approximately $200.00 on the entire process including preliminary drafts and final reprints. The entire project required 1 1/2 months including 60 hours of content revision and digital formatting. In addition, she spent 30 hours on printing, critiques, and assembly. It worked! She was offered a 9-week full-time paid internship at Rapt Studio following a successful interview and offers from her "plan B" firms as well! Laura reflects on her result, stating, "I learned there are a million ways to make a great portfolio. The most important thing is to find the balance between representing your aesthetic and appealing to a professional firm." The book reflects a remarkable effort investing great energy into the portfolio. She invested the greatest proportion of time and revisions on representing her design content and evidence. This has been her best design project to date.

An effective resume needs to:

- Demonstrate clear organization of thought
- Present the information in a clean, clear layout design
- Adhere to acceptable business style
- Include employer, positions held, and dates of employment under work experience

The portfolio, rather than the resume, is the place to demonstrate your design skills. Sans serif or serif fonts are most familiar and legible. Use one or two typefaces at the most. Avoid or minimize the use of graphics in the resume (figures 8–25 to 8–28).

8–19 to 8–24 Laura is focused on interviewing with Rapt Studio in San Francisco. She introduces and designs the cover of her portfolio as a cover letter to the firm itself. She has no problem taking a stand. Her red lips on the image of herself demonstrates a young woman with conviction. She chooses singular colors in the Beta Hotel project, such as the vivid green chair, not unlike the red lips on her own image. She also displays images that have sharp contrast with strong black-and-white forms throughout the portfolio. We feel she is most successful with typographic layouts using flush left as opposed to a justified paragraph format, which in final design aids overall legibility of her book. The book itself has a nice blend of gray-toned textures and strong black-and-white graphic imagery that challenges the formality of the orthogonal grid. When she makes a statement it is big and strong. You get a clear sense this is a person who can take charge. Laura Taylor, University of Utah, Salt Lake City, Utah. 8.5" x 11".

Resume and Cover Letter

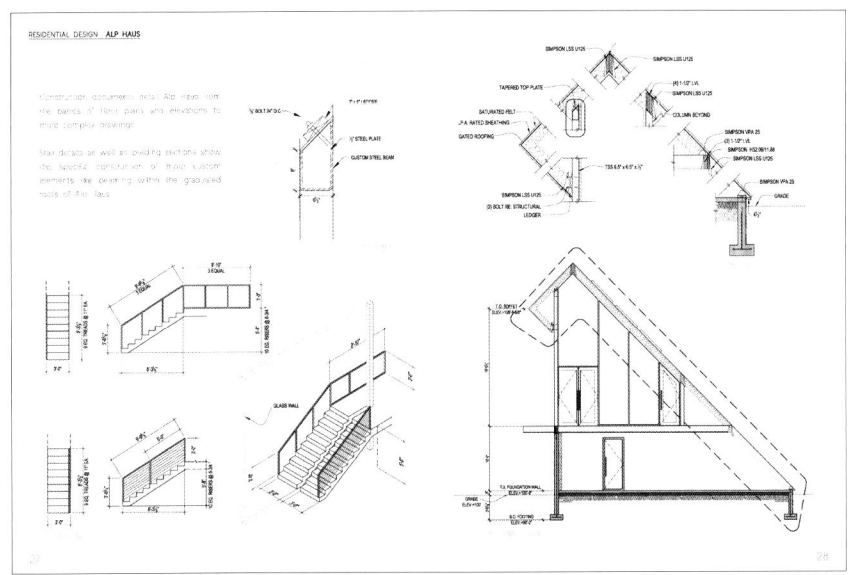

8 RESEARCH & WRITTEN COMMUNICATIONS

macy hale

1631 queen anne way
knoxville, tn 37916
mhale8@utk.edu
(615) 775 -1375

education
university of tennessee knoxville | august 2010 - present
expected graduation | may 2015
current cumulative GPA | 3.55
current design GPA | 3.64

honors
manfred & fern steinfeild scholarship recipient | 2014
house and garden exhibition | 2014
university of tennessee dean's list | 2011 - 2013
selected to represent ut in steelcase next competition | 2013
college of architecture and design, interior design showcase | 2014
tn hope scholarship recipient | 2010 - present
hendersonville women's club/arts council scholarship recipient | 2010

experience
lauderdale design group | intern | 2014 -present
mill agent fabric and upholstery | sales associate | 2012 - 2013
robins nest interiors | design assistant | 2009 - 2012
portrait artist | 2010 - present
nanny | 2009 - 2010
cages bend swim club | lifeguard | 2008

skills
hand sketching | portraiture, architectural, illustration
drafting
design development & research
spatial & program planning

computer skills
autocad
revit
formz
photoshop
illustrator
indesign
lightroom
powerpoint
word
imovie

HANNAH PIERROU LEED AP

hpierrou@gmail.com PHONE 574.286.7423
31554 SIX RIVERS COURT TEMECULA, CA 92592

ENTREPRENEUR.

HANNAH PIERROU PHOTOGRAPHY // temecula. california // jan 2010 - present
{PHOTOGRAPHY STUDIO}
FOUNDED LIFESTYLE PHOTOGRAPHY STUDIO
CREATED ALL BRANDING, GRAPHICS & WEBSITE DESIGNS
MAINTAIN FINANCES, ADVERTISEMENTS, & ALL CLIENT INTERACTIONS
ALONG WITH BEING A FREELANCE DESIGNER
THIS HAS FULLFILLED A MAJOR CHILDHOOD DREAM
APPLY PROJECT MANAGEMENT & DESIGN EXPERIENCE TO RUN BUSINESS
BALANCE MY TECHINICAL & CREATIVE SIDES

CORPORATE.

DECORWARE INC. // chino. california // dec 2009 - june 2010
MARKETING & DESIGN TEAM
DESIGNER OF VARIOUS PRODUCTS & PRICING FOR SPECIFIC MARKET
IMPLEMENTED MARKETING STRATEGY
DESIGNED PRODUCT LINES FOR KOHL'S, MICHEALS, & MORE

DESIGNS OF THE INTERIOR // temecula. california // feb 2009 - aug 2009
HEAD LEED AP & EDUCATOR OF SUSTAINABLE DESIGN
HIGH-END RESIDENTIAL FURNISHINGS & DECOR
SALES TEAM & HIGH END FURNITURE EXPERTISE
INCREASED LEED AWARENESS, SALES & CUSTOMER SERVICE

CSO ARCHITECTS // indianapolis. indiana // may 2007 - may 2008
HIGHER EDUCATION & RESEARCH STUDIO
SPECIFIED MATERIALS & INVOLVED IN 5 MAJOR LEED PROJECTS
PROVIDED SOLUTIONS FOR SUSTAINABLE DESIGN IN
53,177 SQ FT RESIDENCE HALL THAT WAS PROMPTLY
OCCUPIED BY HUNDREDS OF STUDENTS AT MARIAN COLLEGE
CREATED ARCHITECTURAL & INTERIOR RENDERINGS & SPECIFICATIONS
FOR **LEED GOLD** PROJECT: NOTRE DAME, GEDDES HALL, 65,600 SQ FT
PARTICIPATED IN DAILY TEAM MEETINGS
PERFORMED PROPOSED DESIGNS TO CLIENTS & TEAM LEADERS
IMPLEMENTED LEED WORKSHOPS
DISPLAYED PROFESSIONAL ATTITUDE & ARCHITECTURAL KNOWLEDGE
PROFESSIONAL CLIENTS
PURDUE UNIVERSITY // ROCHE DIAGNOSTICS // ELI LILLY
NOTRE DAME // MARIAN COLLEGE // BALL STATE UNIVERSITY

OFFICE INTERIORS, INC. // granger. indiana // may 2006 - dec 2006
{HERMAN MILLER DEALERSHIP}
CO-OP INTERIOR DESIGNER
TEAMED WITH EXPERIENCED INTERIOR DESIGN TEAM
PROJECT MANAGED ALONG SIDE OF OWNER
SOLE PROJECT MANAGER ON VARIOUS PROJECTS
AUTO CAD + TECHNICAL RESPONSIBILITIES
UTILIZED CAP STUDIO 20/20 FOR SPECIFICATION
GENERATED VARIOUS TYPES OF COMMERCIAL FURNITURE PLANS
EXPLORED JOB SITES + FIELD MEASURING
CLIENT ENVOLVEMENT + PRESENTED DESIGN PROPOSALS
SPECIFIED FINISHES + CREATED FINISH BOARDS
PROFESSIONAL CLIENTS
NOTRE DAME // INDIANA UNIVERSITY SOUTH BEND-ELKHART
TRINITY UNITED METHODIST CHURCH // SOUTH BEND ORTHOPAEDICS
MEMORIAL HOSPITAL // DEL PILAR // DR. MACRI

FREELANCE.

UNIVERSAL CUSTOM DISPLAY // elkgrove. california // apr 2013 - present
DESIGNED CUSTOM RETAIL SPACES & DISPLAYS FOR DOMESTIC & GLOBAL COMPANIES
COLLABORATED WITH SALES & ENGINEERING TEAM TO DEVELOPE COST EFFECTIVE
DESIGN BUILDS FOR MAJOR CELLULAR COMPANY
GENERATED HIGH QUALITY DESIGN PROPOSALS FOR SALES PRESENTATIONS
BRANDED INNOVATIVE SOLUTIONS FOR PRODUCT DISPLAY AND MARKETING
CREATED ORIGINAL TABLE DESIGNS FOR WELL KNOW JEWERY & ACCESSORIES COMPANY
EXCEEDED EXPECTATIONS AND DELIVERED BEYOND REQUIREMENTS & PRESENTATION
DEVELOPED GRAPHICS FOR PIZZA COMPANY DISPLAYS & SIGNAGE INSTALLED IN DOZENS
OF GROCERY STORES IN CALIFORNIA.

DLZ // evansville. indiana // may 2013 - present
RENDERED MULTIPLE 3D VIEWS OF PROPOSED BRIDGE OVERPASS, HUNTINGBURG. IN

Oasis (church) // granger. indiana // may 2009 - present
DESIGN CONSULTATION FOR CHURCH REMODEL & EXPANSION TO BE COMPLETED 2013
GENERATED PRESENTATION BOARDS TO CAPTURE CHURCH'S DESIGN VISION

PRETZEL TWISTER // jacksonville. north carolina // may 2008 - sept 2008
DRAFTED CONSTRUCTION PLANS AND SPECIFICATIONS FOR PRETZEL TWISTER REMODEL
TO INCREASE STORE FRONT APPEARANCE AND REBRAND COMPANY IMAGE

BODY GLOVE // hawaii // july 2006
RENDERED & ASSISTED IN YACHT DESIGNS FOR BODY GLOVE YACHT

EDUCATION.

PURDUE UNIVERSITY, C.I.D.A.
BACHELOR OF ARTS in INTERIOR DESIGN (WITH CO-OP DEGREE)
GRADUATED WITH DEANS LIST + HIGH HONORS
AUGUST 2003 - MAY 2008

AWARDS/ACCOMPLISHMENTS.

LEED ACCREDITED PROFESSIONAL
2009 PUBLICATION IN FALLBROOK,VILLAGE NEWS (Southern California)
DESIGNED FOR 5 MAJOR LEED CERTIFIED/REGISTERED BUILDINGS
SEEKING LEED AP WITH SPECIALTY CREDENTIAL ID+C FALL 2013
IIDA & ASID LOCAL CHAPTER ENVOLVEMENT
2006 TO 2007 ASID STUDENT CHAPTER PRESIDENT
2007 IMI DESIGN COMPETITION : HONORABLE MENTION
2006 IIDA STUDENT DESIGN COMPETITION TOP 10
2003 BEST MENTAL ATTITUDE AWARD SCHOLARSHIP
2003 GOLF STATE CHAMPION TEAM - PENN HIGH SCHOOL
GOLF TEAM CAPTAIN

TECHNICAL EXPERTISE.

MICROSOFT OFFICE 2013 ILLUSTRATOR CS6
PHOTOSHOP CS6 SKETCHUP HAND RENDERING
3D STUDIO MAX 20 20 CAP STUDIO HERMAN MILLER Z-AXIS

PERSONAL INTERESTS.

FAMILY // PHOTOGRAPHY // LEED + SUSTAINABILITY // GRAPHICS + VISUAL COMMUNICATIONS
FURNITURE DESIGN // MARKETING // 3D RENDERING // SKETCHING // TEACHING
MENTORING // COMMUNITY SERVICE PROJECTS // GLOBALIZATION
SCRAPBOOKING // GOLF // BIKING // RUNNING // CREATIVE WRITING

REFERENCES.

CINDY HEIGL, NATIONAL SALES DIRECTOR
UNIVERSAL CUSTOM DISPLAY PHONE 574.225.2004

TERRY WONG, CUSTOM DESIGN PROJECTS COORDINATOR
UNIVERSAL CUSTOM DISPLAY PHONE 916.541.1812

8–25 to 8–26 The following successful resumes from Macy Hale, Hannah M. Pierrou, H.K. Han, and Iryna Carlson reflect the important information to include and essential categories in presenting your background accomplishments.

8 RESEARCH & WRITTEN COMMUNICATIONS

8–27 to 8–28 The following successful resumes from Macy Hale, Hannah M. Pierrou, H.K. Han, and Iryna Carlson reflect the important information to include and essential categories in presenting your background accomplishments.

Cover Letter: Content and Format

Your cover letter should consist of a single page and, preferably, one or at most two paragraphs. State clearly and succinctly the reasons why you believe you are a good fit for the firm. Email or mail your cover letter with an attached resume.

Quality Control

Be sure to carefully proofread. Many employers receive resumes and cover letters that contain numerous spelling and grammatical errors. They simply discard them without hesitation or further reading. One of the best resources for writing for designers is *Writing for Design Professionals* by Stephen A. Kliment, published by W. W. Norton and Company Inc., New York. Spell check and grammar check are not the best solutions for the review and correction of your writing. It is best to ask one or two people skilled in writing to go over your resume and cover letter for you.

THE INTERVIEW

The interview includes discussion and demonstration of what you have learned and your abilities. Questions will focus on areas that help the prospective employer determine if you fit in with the firm, have good work habits, and use good judgment.

Knowledge About the Firm

- Who we are—owner, designers, values/culture, size, time in business
- What we do—projects, clients, competitors, awards
- Why we do it—philosophy, vision, goals

Most Frequently Asked Questions

- What are your strengths and weaknesses?
- Why do you want to work here?
- What talents will you provide to the business?
- What are your aspirations?
- What has been your biggest mistake/challenge so far and what did you learn?
- What has been your greatest accomplishment so far?

Design Questions

- Describe your design process. Where do you begin?
- Why are you an interior designer?
- Tell me about your marketing skills and business skills.
- What projects in school were least enjoyable and why?
- What sets you apart from other designers?

Interpersonal Questions

- How would you handle a difficult client?
- Tell me about your people skills.
- Describe your work ethic.
- Do you feel comfortable presenting a project in a room full of strangers?
- Is there work that you prefer not to do or would consider beneath you to do?

Whitley Semrow

Whitley created this portfolio in one semester while an undergraduate student at Kendall College of Art and Design (figures 8–29 to 8–34). She knew she was going to need it to interview for employment positions. Distinctive ideas about the book's design include a wood cover that provides firmness and protects it from bending. She used Adobe InDesign for the book's layout with a goal in mind of a simple, clean layout that would attract the reader by virtue of its valuable dialogue of positive images and negative space. She created the book for her portfolio design capstone course. She states, "The value of a portfolio design studio course in our curriculum was the continual presentation of student and professional portfolios by the instructor, which provided innumerable examples to learn from."

8 RESEARCH & WRITTEN COMMUNICATIONS

8–29 to 8–34 Whitley Semrow's portfolio is strong in organization. She has designed a storyboard for her narrative, supported by her opening image that appears like TV screens. The narrative is told in a linear manner with graphic dotted lines that are easy to follow. She even has included a graphic clock timeline of her daily design routine on one page. The storyboard continues to the rest of the portfolio with developed screenshots of her design perspectives. It is a thoughtful, cohesive portfolio that also exhibits with words her excitement of her career in interior design. Whitley Semrow, Kendall College of Art and Design, Grand Rapids, Mich. 8.5" x 11".

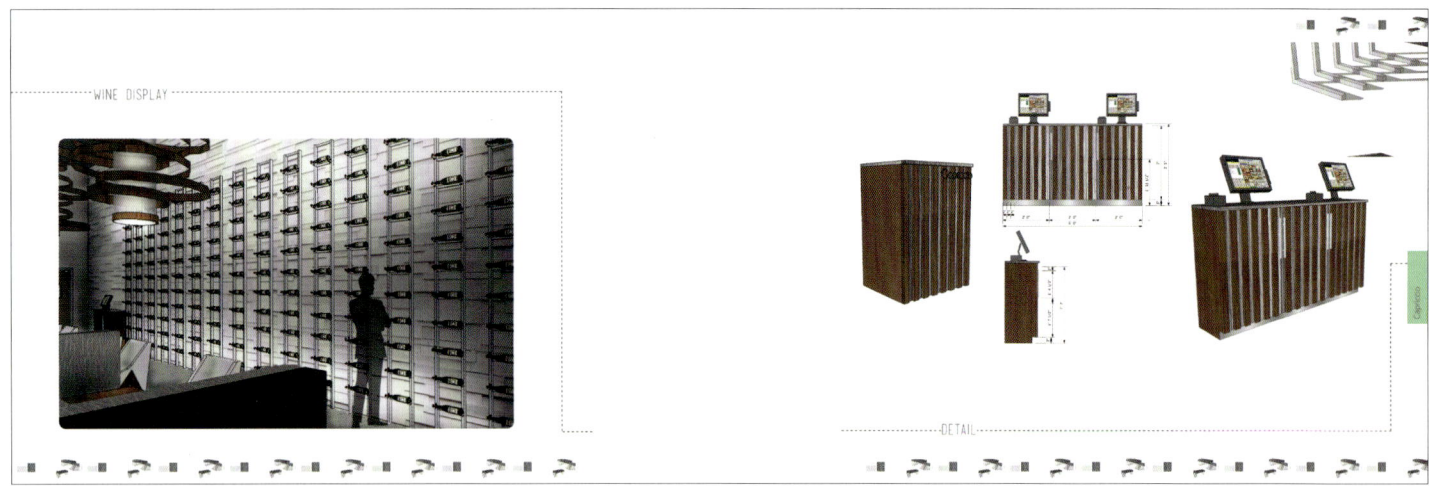

The Interview

8 RESEARCH & WRITTEN COMMUNICATIONS

ADVICE ON HOW TO SHOW A PORTFOLIO/PROJECT

- Use note cards only to rehearse what you're going to say. Establish all the key points that you will mention during the interview. (Tattoo them on your wrists and forehead so the interviewer can prompt each topic in the order you prefer.)
- Animate the story. What did you do? What did you learn? Engage the interviewer—and ask for comments.
- Be brief in your description of each project: present the concept and solution. Explain how your solution met the needs of the client.
- Communicate clearly. Be enthusiastic and confident.
- Show only your most accomplished work. Emphasize growth in your projects in a variety of ways and areas. Make sure your portfolio is neat. Do not point out mistakes or errors. Always position page layouts in one direction, so you never have to rotate your book to show a project right side up.

GENERAL ADVICE

Have enough knowledge of the firm so that you can connect your remarks back to the firm's goals. Smile, have a firm handshake, look people in the eye, remember names, wear professional dress, be prompt—in fact, come a little early. Come prepared with questions for the interviewer.

I Almost Got the Job!

Don't hesitate to express a positive attitude and interest in working your way up from the bottom. Be honest and respectful. Always be a self-starter. Know what you want from a job and what sets you apart from other candidates. Select only those companies you want to work for; have patience and don't give up. Don't take a job you don't want—you and the firm will both be unhappy. Be enthusiastic and show you are willing to work hard to be successful.

Advice for Candidates Who Have Been Seeking a Position for Some Time

Stay active in the profession, including taking an unpaid internship or volunteering with your professional association or on a community service project. Keep abreast of industry developments. Don't be afraid to look for employment in a related field so that you are never without a job and have no gaps on your resume; consider the furniture industry, both wholesale or retail, home improvement stores, or working as a homebuilder, contractor, or manufacturer. Learn new skills, like SketchUp or Revit. Update your portfolio. Remain positive and confident; focus on your abilities and strengths.

DESIGN STATEMENT

The design statement is an introductory summary of one's interests, abilities, and direction in design. The increasingly specialized and competitive world of professional interior design requires true creativity to express a client's vision through the cultivation of appropriate intellectual and practical skills. Conceptual thinking must be tempered by an informed response to function and fabrication. I believe that the contemporary design firms demand an intense, sustained involvement to successfully bring a project to fruition. The design process also demands a heavy workload of analysis for diverse projects which together offer comprehensive experience of the discipline. Many successful design firms are deliberately small, with between ten and twelve designer-employees. I believe that a small cohesive and dynamic group works better and achieves more regular success with clients because they are able to better service clients in contrast to large, 50+ employee firms. Small groups also allow staff to form a clear perception of individual client needs in order to achieve the client's vision and aspirations.

All full- and part-time designer-employees are actively engaged in multi-disciplinary practices offering a complementary range of specialist experiences, including furniture design, materials expertise, computer drafting, and professional management services. All employees bring supplementary experience of major specialist activities, such as in retail, leisure, hospitality, health, exhibition, or theater design. Because interior design also regards the

Design Statement

revitalization and enrichment of buildings and the creation of exciting, enjoyable—and working—environments, updating old buildings with new functions must be an important dimension of today's successful practices. Designing an interior involves making a personal statement. It is important to reach a shared understanding between designer and client of the social and architectural conventions that gives developers and those who use their buildings a common language. Interior design is a vibrant profession with a proven record for the improving the quality of life and generating business success. It has a well-established professional structure which allows graduates the opportunity to gain invaluable experience at various levels of responsibility before establishing either independent practices or taking leading roles in established studios. I look forward to achieving an entry-level position and to add value to a relatively small or mid-size design firm.

Kelsey DeBree

Kelsey DeBree created an undergraduate portfolio in the senior year of her interior design program at Rochester Institute of Technology to achieve an internship leading to employment following graduation (figures 8–35 to 8–39).

8–35 to 8–36 Kelsey chose to use a diagonal slice in her portfolio layout that cuts into her perspectives and provides a dynamic edge to position her content. She has used green materials throughout her design. In the Hive Village Project for affordable housing she found a successful way to layer the logo over a veil of white in the perspective image. This page also shows diagrammatic schematic adjacencies and beautifully rendered figures populating the spaces within her designs. The material descriptions in this project amply demonstrate where finishes are to be used. The lighter gray typography supports the drawing and also allows the black line plans to remain dominant and the most important object on the page layout. Kelsey DeBree, Rochester Institute of Technology, Rochester, N.Y. 8.5" x 11".

8 RESEARCH & WRITTEN COMMUNICATIONS

8–37 to 8–39 Kelsey chose to use a diagonal slice in her portfolio layout that cuts into her perspectives and provides a dynamic edge to position her content. She has used green materials throughout her design. In the Hive Village Project for affordable housing she found a successful way to layer the logo over a veil of white in the perspective image. This page also shows diagrammatic schematic adjacencies and beautifully rendered figures populating the spaces within her designs. The material descriptions in this project amply demonstrate where finishes are to be used. The lighter gray typography supports the drawing and also allows the black line plans to remain dominant and the most important object on the page layout. Kelsey DeBree, Rochester Institute of Technology, Rochester, N.Y. 8.5" x 11".

She used InDesign and Photoshop for the overall design of her portfolio. Her goal was to format the project as a bound book with printing on both sides. She used a high-quality laser printer to achieve professional print results, and a wire coil binding with a clear acetate cover.

Experimentation between the 11" x 17" and the 8.5" x 11" formats to judge legibility, flow through the narrative of her work, and image sharpness and clarity, proved to be important to the final decision to adopt the smaller format because it was more portable and easier to handle. Kelsey's portfolio underscores the strength of a solid foundation and those key principles that guide competent design. It was a success that earned an offer of employment. Portfolio design for Kelsey is an ongoing learning experience that continues to evolve to this day. Her inspiration comes from looking online at what other designers are doing to project themselves and their work into the public sector. Above and beyond all else, she believes that her book should continue to maintain a simple, clean presentation emphasizing her brand as an eminently employable design professional. Kelsey could not be more adamant in saying, "It's good to have a variety of projects represented and have all your design evidence on hand so you can work efficiently to find ways and places to integrate process studies, sketching, and developmental sequences throughout as many of your projects as possible."

MEETING WITH CLIENTS, DESIGN BRIEF, AND ANALYSIS

The starting point for any project is a clients' portfolio with their profile and design needs. From it, one learns about the age, profession, and likes and dislikes of the client, as well as the scope of work. One needs to analyze, understand clients' personalities, and make conclusions based on their habits, the way they dress and live. For example, a client, Mr. Bright, is an investment banker. He wears expensive clothes and smokes cigars. One concludes that he appreciates solidity, quality of materials, and an expensive look. In no case would one suggest to him a design in shabby chic style or cheap furniture. For the design analysis, one digs into the client's personality and character. A picture is worth a thousand words—so an exploration widely uses images (cuts from magazines and print outs) to illustrate clients' taste.

CONCEPT BOARDS

The concept is the starting point of any interior design project. A concept is delineated through a visual presentation, of style, mood, and color of the future space. Clients looking at a concept board must be able to understand the overall feel and look of the room. It doesn't show the concrete furniture, finishes, or accessories yet, so the designer has freedom when working further on the project. You could say that the concept shows the climate for the design inspiration. Here are some important steps for creating an exciting concept board:

- Elements of lighting
- Color range and coordination
- Texture and manufactured materials
- Spatial experience
- Furnishings
- Aspects of scale

TRANSITIONS AND EVOLVING NEW DOCUMENTS

Even seasoned designers need to re-evaluate their portfolios and written documents periodically. The design world is constantly evolving and changing along with advances in computer technology and the building industry in general. It makes sense to review and sometimes rethink your brand as you grow and develop in the profession. Perhaps your brand concept in school is no longer a realistic summary of what you have evolved into in the world of professional practice.

8 RESEARCH & WRITTEN COMMUNICATIONS

Kyle Wessling

Kyle had the opportunity to take an undergraduate portfolio development class at Pratt Institute for the School of Interior Design. Kyle quickly learned that continuity throughout the portfolio would be enhanced by maintaining a consistent flow of design content and by structuring the book with design parameters such as using two pages per project and maintaining white or negative space throughout the book (figures 8–40 to 8–46).

He used the Adobe Creative Suite for the book design and AutoCAD, 3D Max, and Maya for editing and bringing the quality up on project evidence. Kyle used a laser jet color printer with two different paper stocks. His book is presented in an envelope with his signature, which communicates his brand in a professional presentation. Much experimentation and testing all the way through the project contributed greatly to its success. The book *Tree Houses, Fairy Tale Castles in the Air* by Taschen piqued his curiosity about designing imaginative habitats with a minimalist aesthetic. Kyle spent at least 60 hours on the project over several weeks. The overall budget was $250 inclusive of the full production and packaging of the book. If he had it to do all over again, he would make it more interactive.

8–40 to 8–42 Kyle has used a blocking method to create his portfolio utilizing positive and negative space to his advantage. Even his title page separates positive and negative space with his name becoming the dividing element. Texture and form is obviously important to Kyle and his photo of the chipboard model clearly celebrates this by allowing you to be in the space. The shapes he uses for zones within the portfolio support his architectural view of design and form. The photo of the person using his 32-square-foot stool shows that he understands the human form at the same time! Kyle Wessling, Pratt Institute, School of Interior Design, Brooklyn, N.Y. 8.5" x 11".

Transitions and Evolving New Documents

01 ANIMAL SCIENCE PRODUCT

WOOD & METAL | SCULPTURE >

A CREATION BASED ON NATURE, "ANIMAL SCIENCE PRODUCT" AS IF THE FISH IS MOUNTED ON A PEDESTAL SOMEWHERE BETWEEN SCIENCE AND ART.

04 OYSTER BAR SALOON

CORK HARVESTING | MODULE ^

THE CORK WALL DELAYS THE MOVEMENT OF OPPOSING FORCES AS THEY ENTER THE FEELING OF PRESSURE ON THE OCCUPANTS FROM AFAR. ONCE INSIDE THE INTERIOR, THE OCCUPANT IS FREE TO BEHAVE, AS THE ENVIRONMENT CREATES THIS EXPERIENCE. PRESSURE AND RELEASE COMBINE TO INFORM THE EXPERIENCES AND RELATIONSHIPS OF INHABITING ADJACENT SPACES.

8 RESEARCH & WRITTEN COMMUNICATIONS

07 THE VANS SHOE STORE

08 THE 32 SQ FT CHAIR

Transitions and Evolving New Documents

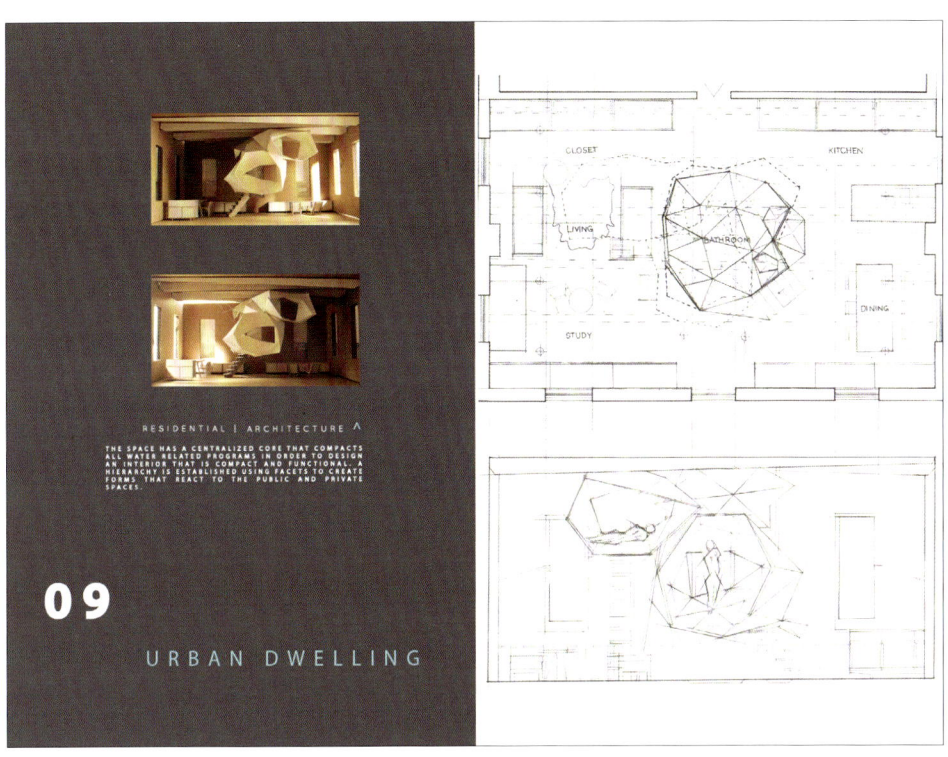

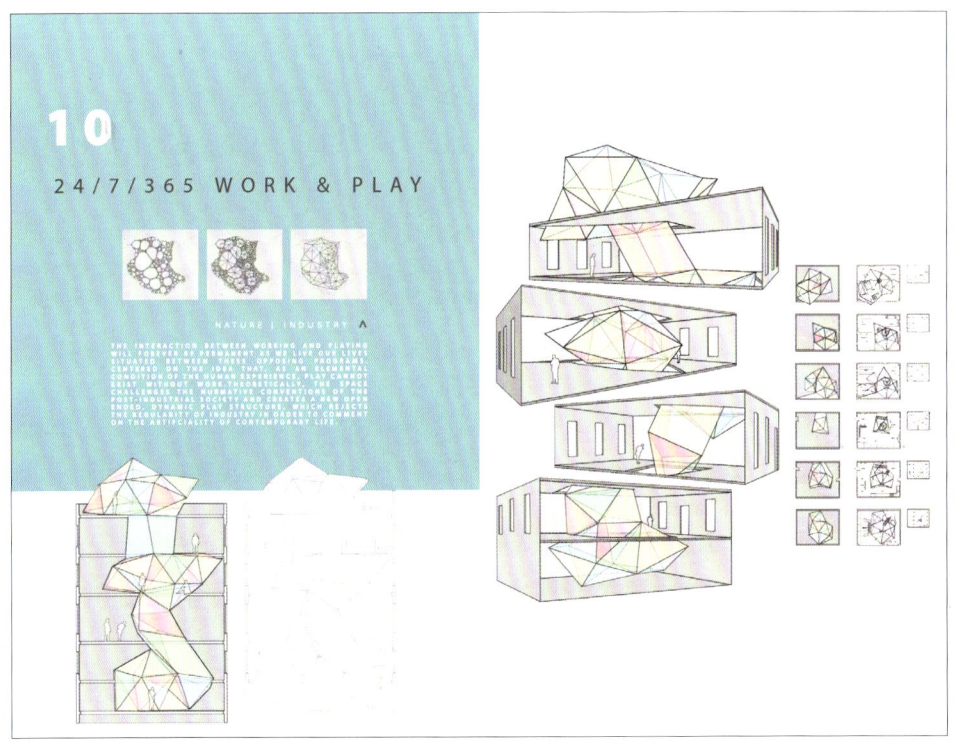

8–43 to 8–46 Kyle has used a blocking method to create his portfolio utilizing positive and negative space to his advantage. Even his title page separates positive and negative space with his name becoming the dividing element. Texture and form is obviously important to Kyle and his photo of the chipboard model clearly celebrates this by allowing you to be in the space. The shapes he uses for zones within the portfolio support his architectural view of design and form. The photo of the person using his 32-square-foot stool shows that he understands the human form at the same time! Kyle Wessling, Pratt Institute, School of Interior Design, Brooklyn, N.Y. 8.5" x 11".

THE UNDERLYING HUMAN EXPERIENCES

The following topics represent areas of design interest today. Your work might touch on and reflect some of them. Your awareness of them might support your interview and conversations with various audiences. The interests of the reviewer, professor, or audience that sees your book may include, but not be limited to, some of these topics, representative of a range of design interests within the field. It is helpful to view these areas as part of a broad involvement in design culture. From the perspective of your interests in the field, these topics are of more than a passing interest to an employer or review panel.

Sense and Sensibilities: Culture, Methods, and Intuition

Design thinking requires a great deal of attention as increasing numbers of innovative organizations succeed in solving complex problems by creative means. In doing so, many of these firms implement specific "design methods" such as observational research, iterative prototyping, and storytelling, alongside more mainstream approaches such as research, scoring, value-action, and performance (RSVP). But as any professional designers will attest, to create value, methods must be applied together with design sensibilities.

Designers use innate sensibilities such as delight, beauty, personal meaning, and cultural resonance. Such subtle qualities are difficult to put into words and thus are discounted in the workplace. Managers schooled in analytic and rational decision making may find the idea of relying on their sensibilities uncomfortable. But when coupled with design methods, design sensibilities create the experiences and outcomes upon which successful businesses capitalize: clear distinction from competitors, lasting market impact, and customer loyalty.

A project involves making multiple judgment calls in order to express both its big key idea and pay attention to the finer details of implementation. Design sensibilities not only guide these decisions, but they also ultimately influence how people experience the resulting product, service, or brand. Will customers just end up getting something that "works," or will they make an emotional connection with it—one that entails personal and cultural relevance and inspires future loyalty?

Conceptual Activities Underscore Most Projects

A successful interior architecture project will marry both formal considerations along with a theoretical foundation. Design thinking combines conceptual activities with form and space-making to arrive at a unified project result. The intellectual activities of a project included in a portfolio will also reveal non-aesthetic design activities. Conceptual issues find ways to integrate with the other factors of design, and the portfolio is the opportunity to demonstrate your understanding of the importance of concept within a project. Conceptual thinking could be elevated in importance by including a well-crafted concept statement page as an introduction to the project. Another approach would be to break down the individual moments in design to demonstrate the concept and its application. Another approach is to show image equivalence in "thought bubbles" or use notes tagging particular places in the project as a reminder that the work reaches beyond the formal expression of design. Including evidence of your creative process demonstrates how you gather together ideas and what it might be like to work with you in an office setting. It also provides clarity as to how you plan in otherwise complex situations.

Unifying Nature with Design

Nature finds its way into a design in many forms. Life is brought to interior design through windows, entry orientation to the site, choice of materials, and interior features such as water features, planters and gardens, and sound. To communicate the elements of design in the layout pages of your portfolio requires a variety of visual strategies. Knowing the orientation of your building to the cardinal points and knowing the seasons for the particular location will help you create an authentic experience for your audience. Window openings will draw in light and create shadows that offer a visual dimension. If mixed-source lighting is appropriate, understand the strength of artificial light in relationship to natural light.

Nature can be our greatest teacher. Designing within the golden mean is a hidden dimension that can be added to any portfolio, down to the size and proportional shape of the book itself! Organic systems of designs can also inspire methods of organization and connections within the book.

When addressing nature and objects, collage might be appropriate. Use your illustration skills and collect images of objects from reliable sources, either online or in magazines, and create a visual interior landscape. Imagine the point of view of your audience and be consistent with perspective. When designing with a focus on sustainable materials, your statement should include the choice of materials. Some natural materials are more visible than others. Develop a visual vocabulary that works consistently throughout your portfolio that clearly identifies your material choices. The use of an index is an appropriate place for project details.

Be a Practical (Pragmatic) Problem Solver

Pragmatic design is sensible and realistic in ways that are based on practical approaches. Whether mandated by the client, a project perspective, or your design ideology, efficient design can display your range of talents. The interior space can be designed to reflect the nature of the use. The interior of a factory or assembly plant will reflect the operations of making or building or assembling. Specific needs will be addressed in the interior design, including lighting and human factors and providing space for human or robotic movement along with considering equipment. Every condition and genre of space making will mandate specific interior consideration. The way the story unfolds on the pages of the portfolio should reveal the obvious connections being addressed by the designer of the function and the "business-like" environment. If the pages communicate the commonsense intention of the design, then your audience will better understand the relationship of the design to the concept.

Adaptive Reuse

Adaptive reuse is one of the most exciting and socially responsible acts of design. It can also be one of most challenging. Rather than demolish a building, there is a multitude of teaching and learning opportunities for the interior architect and design students. Here, the interior architect can demonstrate their knowledge of structures, building systems, materials, such as reclaimed wood so often used in design presentations, along with history and space planning. The interior design student learns to collaborate with the architect regarding the inclusion of critical areas of the building. The portfolio pages should reflect the existing building, with original photographs of both the interior and the exterior, and the site conditions should be included in the project statement.

The Americans with Disabilities Act (ADA)

The Americans with Disabilities Act (ADA) became law in 1990. The ADA is a civil rights law that prohibits discrimination against individuals with disabilities in all areas of public life, including jobs, schools, transportation, and all places that are open to the general public. The purpose of the law is to make sure that people with disabilities have the same rights and opportunities as everyone else. Within the ADA, there are five titles (or sections) that relate to different areas of public life. CIDA (Council for Interior Design Accreditation) requires that aspiring interior design students incorporate the standards for ADA in their studio design research and project solutions. You should address human-centered design factors in the projects in your portfolio.

Communications and Technology

The scope of human activities is defined by the design of interior spaces—the spaces where we learn, work, play, worship, and heal. Today, students and professionals conduct the majority of their design education and professional practice activities on the computer. Students' growing knowledge and skill in design is developed with a growing array of technology devices, online resources, communication tools, image manipulation software, and printing technology. Under the direction of experienced faculty in classrooms, labs, and studios, a design is a thoroughly technological experience.

Visual communications cuts a wide swath through the environmental design arts, including architecture, urban planning, interior design, industrial design, graphic design, illustration, and many other art and non-art disciplines. Students learn how to communicate ideas and information effectively, embracing courses on theory and practice. Studio education now includes collaborative work with students from other disciplines in the classroom, plus community service and extracurricular projects. Many students have an opportunity to spend a summer semester in Europe and conduct much

8 RESEARCH & WRITTEN COMMUNICATIONS

of their research and design activities via a laptop computer as a requirement for the design program. Technology in interior design education and professional practice permeates every aspect of visual communications and development. Every application of design, such as problem-solving and critical thinking skills, are conducted on a computer. Technology embraces vast research capabilities regarding innovations in new design materials, building systems and technologies, lighting, sustainability, green building, factors of human behavior, and more.

Eco-Friendly Design

Being eco-friendly or environmentally friendly is becoming progressively more important in all aspects of life. The simplest way to define what being "green" means is to say that it is the act of living with intent. The purpose is to avoid harming the environment, that is, to prevent damage from occurring to the environment through your interactions with it. How do you express being eco-friendly? Make plans to demonstrate your sensibility regarding the environment through your work.

Within each project, the concept and design criteria should be followed by the revealing of your design thinking. The components of the project set up each step of the process, starting with precedent studies, thumbnail drawings, material studies, site photographs, and all the other support material for the final design.

It is equally impressive to begin with the final design solution and allow your audience to peel away or reverse engineer the process. Public interaction offers the opportunity to place content selectively on pages following the final project with elements of the project becoming part of a narrative.

Sustainability

Sustainability is the endurance of systems and processes. According to the Government Services Administration (GSA), the goal while designing is to reduce adverse impacts on the environment, and contribute to the health and comfort of building occupants, thereby improving building performance. There will be a day when this will be the "normal" and the word "sustainable" will be intrinsic to design. But until then, sustainability could be a yet another strategic approach or emphasis for your portfolio. If your design work or the purpose of the portfolio is to emphasize sustainability, then it is necessary to demonstrate your knowledge and application of that knowledge. Mechanical systems, light and lighting, materiality, space planning, and the relationship of the parts to the whole (both specific to the project and globally) all play a part in sustainability. It is critical to consider a hierarchy of information both conceptually and visually while laying out and pacing the projects in the portfolio. Also, the origin of the materials, re-purposing of materials, and your sources play a significant role in the conversation of sustainability. Additional pages or a place in the index can serve to identify important details that might not be used in the particular discussion of each project.

LEED (Leadership in Energy and Environmental Design) was developed by the U.S. Green Building Council to be an excellent guide for the building and interior design industry. LEED offers a rating system for designers and building construction properties. The ratings include Certified, Silver, Gold, and Platinum based on a point system. It addresses interior components that allow us to breathe easier, especially given the fact that we, as humans, spend 90 percent of our time indoors! Be sure to address elements in your portfolio such as paint with low VOC (volatile organic compounds, or solvents that get released into the air as the paint dries). Many students will be interested in working for firms that are LEED certified, as this is considered the future of the industry, and will require that you be approved as well. Noting these components in your portfolio will prove to be beneficial on many levels.

Luminosity (Qualities of Color, Light, and Space)

A key design function of the built environment is to provide the appropriate quality and quantity of light. A strategy for a portfolio could be to concentrate on how light, both natural and artificial, were integrated and helped form the guiding concept of the design. Designing with light can turn a building inside/out and bring the outside in. This also affects one's perception of color, both intrinsic to the materials of the architecture and type of light specified. You can also coordinate the orientation of the project and the time of day. There are a multitude of opportunities to highlight "light" in a portfolio. Renderings, photographs, technical details, specifications, design narratives, and scientific data along with local and seasonal sun movement diagrams are just a few ideas to include in your portfolio. These can be placed in prominent locations on a page layout and/or identified in a table of contents, index, or appendix.

Overlays can also be useful for demonstrating light and its effect on an interior. For instance, printing RCP drawings (reflected ceiling plans) on transparent sheets can overlay a plan view page with direct correlation. Diagrams with light studies showing direction and effect of the light on a plan or elevation view is also helpful in demonstrating your understanding of light as a task and ambient source in your projects. Keep in mind that the portfolio itself can express these ideas of light and value. Dark adverse backgrounds, medium grays, and white space all contribute to the idea that light and value play an important role in the development of an original interior.

Tectonics

The definition of tectonics is "the science or art of construction, both in relation to use and artistic design," and it is the designer's role in the activity that raises this construction to an art form. The inter-relationship of an interior space with the building envelope and materials should always be considered. Therefore, it is a suitable strategy to place an emphasis on the tectonics of your design decisions. Tectonics cannot stand alone but can be highlighted. If you are graduating from a design program that is both technically and conceptually grounded in design, then this strategy makes sense. Diagrams and visual details placed strategically on a page within a portfolio will support your desire to be viewed as someone capable of designing with tectonics in mind. This would also be an opportunity to demonstrate your ability to converse with engineers, because this is where design and science meet. Supplemental working drawings and millwork details can be "chapters" within your portfolio as well. They can also be subsidiary complete portfolios that focus on your ability to illustrate a design to completion, such as a complete set of working drawings for a kitchen or bath.

Following the Trends

With the value of real estate property and space escalating at a rapid pace along with the current trend of the entrepreneurial spirit, there are opportunities to explore trendier areas of temporal design. These may include research in styles of the moment or retrospective movements, driven by nostalgia and profit. Such projects are typically found in retail or other consumer-based space making, and trends in interior design follow taste-makers. Examples include set design for awards shows and pop-up retail, restaurant, and entertainment establishments. Locations could include theaters, performing arts stages, urban sidewalks, empty neighborhood lots, airport terminals, shopping malls, atriums for hotels, and many others.

9

USING YOUR PORTFOLIO
AS A TOOL

"I do not try to dance better than someone else, I only try to dance better than myself."

– **MIKHAIL BARYSHNIKOV**

OVERVIEW

In this chapter, we wish to discuss practical strategies for using your book as an integral part of a successful interview. In doing so, we couple the portfolio with the written documents, such as the cover letter, resume, statements of design philosophy and design interests, review of abilities, and future directions you wish to pursue as an interior design professional. In previous chapters, we spoke of your portfolio as an instrument useful to talking about yourself and your work. In this chapter, we wish to focus more specifically on your book as a tool and how to use your ingenuity with demonstrated skills during the give-and-take of the interview process.

Your resume expresses your work mainly through written communication. A portfolio reveals your work visually with only the most necessary words. We refer to "portfolio" as any designed text and visuals (and other related media) that present your work to potential employers, academic programs, and other interested people. Five milestones for making an effective portfolio also apply when you are making a careful audit of portfolio content for the presentation of your work in an interview.

1. Visual appeal in portfolio layout design, content, and process

2. Sequencing of projects as a demonstration of consistent strengths

3. Representation of abilities in design development and technology

4. Demonstrated rigorous research and narrative(s)

5. Concisely written, yet detailed text

RESEARCH

Before an interview and before contacting interior design offices, the process of research begins with a broad and realistic view of the type of positions that hold your interest and those that you feel prepared to approach. Start by reviewing position descriptions and firms that are within your geographic region. Examine the sites of those offices that share an affinity with your interests in interior design content and the type of work you wish to practice. Consider looking outside of your comfort zone, because you never really know what new opportunities might await you when you undertake quality preparation. Examine the work from large, mid-range, and small firms that have solid reputations in their professional niche. Never second-guess the outcome of a job search nor pre-judge a potential office's needs, because you might be passing up a golden opportunity for development. If you've got the skills, and the right attitude, you deserve consideration—so let us walk you through some simple but effective concepts and tactics useful for preparing for that design job interview and sailing through it.

9 USING YOUR PORTFOLIO AS A TOOL

Employment is a process. When you join a new office, you meet new people and acquire new responsibilities. The following phases of the employment process offer you a glimpse of what the process entails, before, during, and after the interview. A good understanding of these aspects will suit you well during the entire process. Let's take a look at where a good portfolio and interview can lead as you advance through the interview process and onto employment. Anticipate the following:

- Portfolios and Conversations: Interviewers and office staff will remember your portfolio and its design. They will connect your portfolio presentation with what abilities they anticipate you are bringing to the office in your new position. Be confident in the content of your book and be able to explain your work in response to any question asked about it.
- Remain Open to Modifications: During your research of firms, be prepared and open to modifying certain designs and include or exclude projects as determined by new knowledge of a firm or firms. You are doing research on and gaining feedback about each company's unique attributes, which could quite possibly affect your portfolio's purpose and thematic visual presentation. Your portfolio, as much as is realistic, should be designed to meet the unique goals of each of your academic or office reviews. Graphic designers, binderies, book artists, web developers, photographers, and allied craftsmen offer design support and consultation to help you achieve a custom solution for your portfolio layout. Embrace the possibilities of creating this object in a way that will set you apart from the competition.

Kristian Hinds

Kristian designed this comprehensive portfolio (figures 9–1 to 9–8) during her undergraduate program in interior design at the Savannah College of Art and Design (SCAD). Her intention was to seek employment following graduation. She used the Adobe Creative Suite including InDesign, Photoshop, and Illustrator. The images and renderings were created with various software including Revit, AutoCAD, and Photoshop, and also included hand drawings. The portfolio was printed by a professional print company on a satin finish paper. The teaser package case was made of a silicone-coated, heavyweight paper with a matte finish, and the cards within were printed on satin finish card stock. The portfolio case was bound in a pre-made, stainless steel portfolio. She designed the portfolio case herself out of acrylic sheet. She also designed the teaser package using a heavyweight silicone-coated paper. The teaser insert with contact information was also cut from acrylic sheet.

The large portfolio case and all parts was $450.00 for both printing and materials. Each resume package (including resume papers, teaser package, and packaging) cost $12.00 each. She sent 20 sets in her first round of applications. She designed the entire production and all parts during a 10-week professional portfolio design studio at SCAD. The entire presentation was successful in communicating Kristian's strengths, including attention to detail, as well as her refined yet bold aesthetic, while also expressing her personality. Kristian graduated toward the end of the recession but was able to set up several interviews with large firms based on the strength of her portfolio.

Kristian believes that she learned the importance of designing a comprehensive portfolio package that sets you apart from the competition. Equally important is learning how to work within a budget and not permit costs to escalate out of control. Among the inspirational sources explored were design magazines and product marketing materials including brochures and business publicity materials.

Research

9–1 to 9–3 Kristian uses line and color to her advantage. She has demonstrated that she can complete a total designed package that has continuity and personal branding. Her pink dividing line in her own logo serves as a device not only for her initials but also as an element used in her table of contents. The colored curvilinear line shows up in her designs as well. The separate booklets and leave behind materials have integrated her sensibility and strong graphic sense. She uses white as positive space/form, and black as negative space throughout her books, making vivid colors all the more dynamic and providing for a fascinating progression that has a clear narrative. Kristian Hinds, Savannah College of Art and Design, Savannah, Ga. Boxed set of portfolio materials approximately 10" x 14".

9 USING YOUR PORTFOLIO AS A TOOL

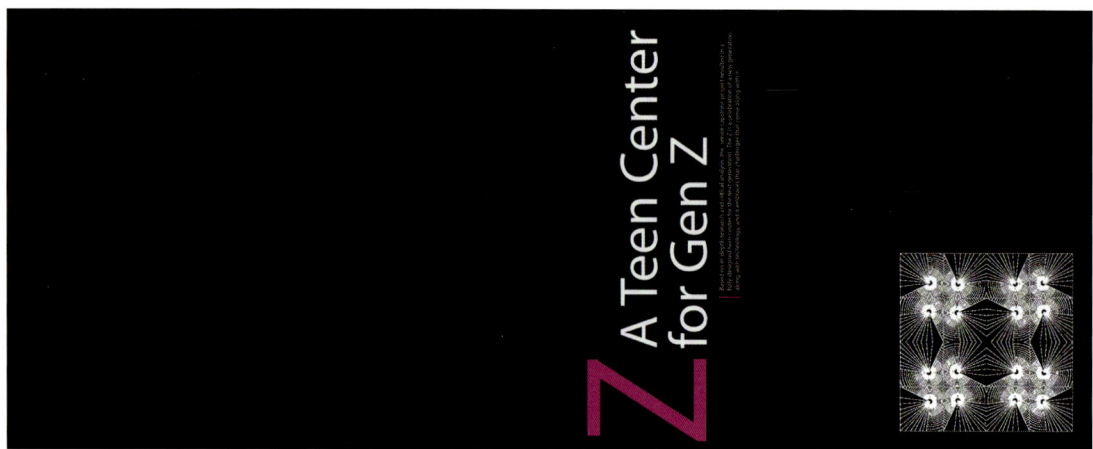

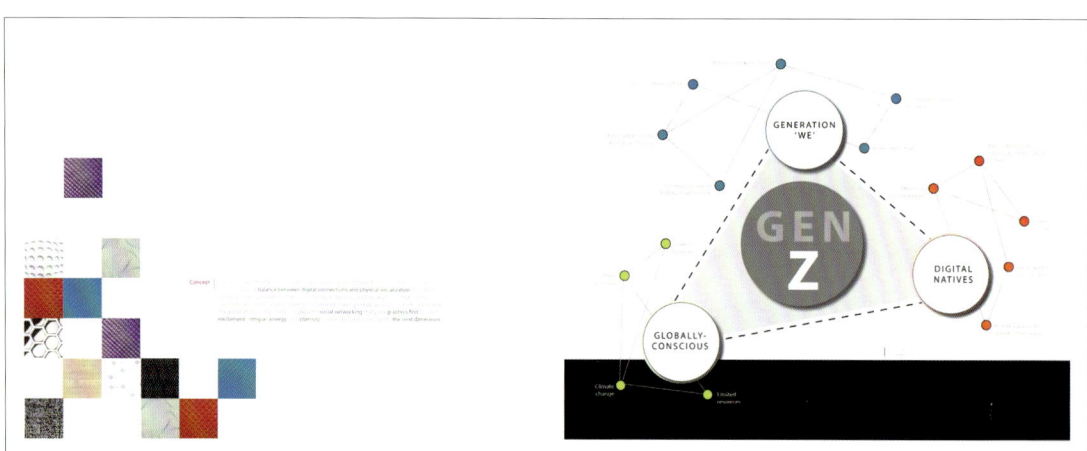

9–4 to 9–8 Kristian uses line and color to her advantage. She has demonstrated that she can complete a total designed package that has continuity and personal branding. Her pink dividing line in her own logo serves as a device not only for her initials but also as an element used in her table of contents. The colored curvilinear line shows up in her designs as well. The separate booklets and leave behind materials have integrated her sensibility and strong graphic sense. She uses white as positive space/form, and black as negative space throughout her books, making vivid colors all the more dynamic and providing for a fascinating progression that has a clear narrative. Kristian Hinds, Savannah College of Art and Design, Savannah, Ga. Boxed set of portfolio materials approximately 10" x 14".

Initial Discussions

INITIAL DISCUSSIONS

Understand the context of business regarding the interview and hiring process. Interior designers and architects interview applicants for a design position with the goal of figuring out if they are a good fit. They have already eliminated most of the prospects and almost (but not quite) know whom they want to partner with (based on a raving recommendation, a specific design philosophy, etc.), and they might skip the initial first interview step with you. They have called you to come back to discuss your work (portfolio) and your background interests in detail.

Firm Goals and Requirements

The reviewers often spend hours with all the books they have received. They sort the books into three categories: hot, medium, and cool. They express their opinions with each other as to which books or candidates seem most qualified from the hot pile. During the interview, the interior designers gather information from the applicant. They work through an outline of what the expectations are for the position and what you will bring to the firm. Are they looking for a fit and something else?

Something Else

Finding a match with a candidate's demonstrated abilities through review of the book has highest priority. The book illustrates one's individual talents by its design, assembly and efficiency, preparation and concept, and graphic design, which are likely to all be important factors under consideration. Your demeanor, how direct you are in answering questions, your knowledge of design, your interest in the firm, how you dress, your positive attitude, collaborative experience, and written and oral communication skills are the something else!

Receiving an Offer

Upon discussion with partners and principles, the interior designers representing their firm can advance the interview process by a phone conversation with you, another call back for an offer of employment, or by mail. Once you have received an offer, the door is open for a conversation about the responsibilities of the position, employment package (salary and benefits), and timetable for ending one position and moving to this new opportunity.

Powers of Ten: Larger Aspirations

What is the firm's reputation in the design market? What is the company's growth potential and where do they see themselves in the next 5–10 years? What kind of work and functions within the firm do you wish to pursue and as the business grows what additional opportunities await you?

Office Introductions

The hiring interior designers should discuss schedules and office functions of their workplace. They will introduce the activities and sections within the office that concern you, including where and with whom will you will be working.

Designers and Community

Designers are often tasked with describing the professional office culture to new hires. Who is the competition and whom is the firm allied with in project partnerships? Discussion ensues regarding the history of projects and alliances. Individual relationships with community and civic leaders, government officials, and business associations are all described in appropriate introductory detail.

Construction

It is important to know the contractors who carry out the work. They help you to make sure you're meeting state, city, and local codes in all of the work that you do. The firm that's offering full-time employment welcomes you into a team of successful professional designers who have worked to build partnerships and relationships in their community.

Administration

Typically, with a project of any complexity, the interior designer retains contractors to review questions, clarify, and administer revisions if necessary. Designers also protect the interests of the client and the integrity of the design. Interior designers rely on business officers within the firm to review the invoices and overall costs, and schedule construction.

Rachel Eggert

Rachel created this portfolio while an undergraduate at the University of Wisconsin, Stevens Point (figures 9–9 to 9–12). Her purpose was to organize and present her most significant projects over the past four years. She used a combination of PowerPoint and Photoshop. It was printed with a laser printer on 80# enamel paper stock at a price of $120.00 per book. Her work was also posted on a self-authored web page at http://racheleggert.weebly.com. The entire production including design required four months to complete. She was pleased with the result as it represented her work and design philosophy in a clean and well-organized design. She found inspiring examples online at ISSUU in particular and is continuing to refine her foundation book with the purpose of finding employment.

Initial Discussions

9–9 to 9–12 Rachel has given the overall design of the portfolio a very friendly, casual presentation. The choice of typography supports this and the color shapes introducing the sections do not take away from the color that she uses within individual projects. She is careful to choose achromatic graphics that allow more intense colors in the renderings to remain the focus in the page layout. The hospitality hotel project has a nice diagram that is highlighted and keyed in color. Her title page also moves from a range of complementary color systems, as do her individual projects. This is one example where the design of the cover supports her overall work. Rachel Eggert, University of Wisconsin, Stevens Point, Wis. 8.5" x 11".

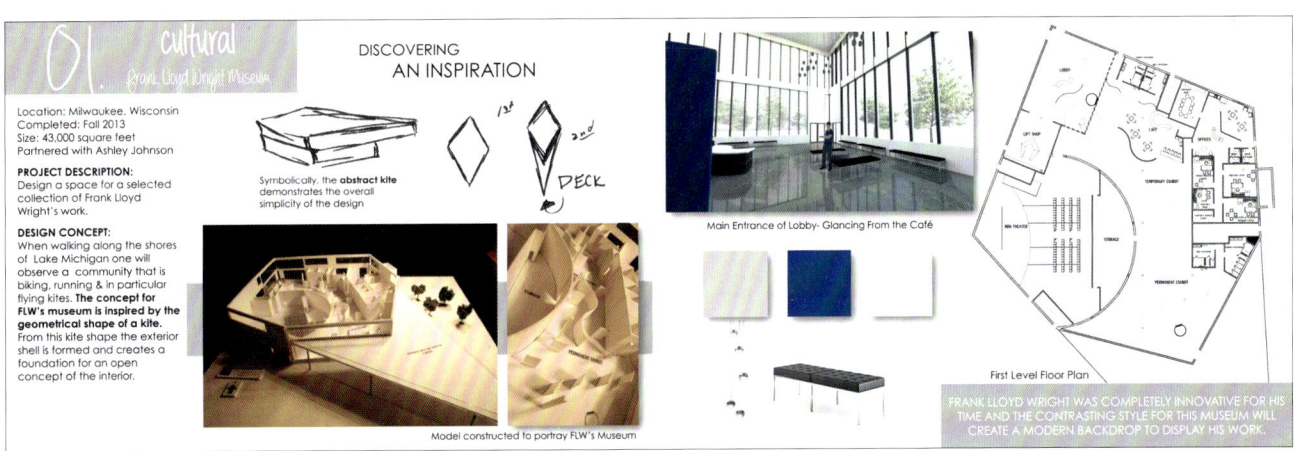

9 USING YOUR PORTFOLIO AS A TOOL

A NEW TEAM

Networking is a multi-dimensional and sophisticated operation. In today's contemporary design office practices, positions are advertised in newspapers, professional journals, and on websites. Do not assume that a resource might not be appropriate to contact. A brief friendly email may be just the thing to prompt someone to keep you in mind. Letting someone know you are on the market is an easy note to write and especially useful as the contact may think of something you haven't. An unpredictable event can lead to a 40-year career—you just cannot predict the outcome of following up on a possible lead. Web communities such as Twitter, LinkedIn, and Facebook enable you to interact with practicing designers while sites such as IIDA, ASID, InteriorDesign.net, and others offer free marketing and support to gain visibility for your work. Use your social network profiles to connect you with new opportunities and human resources. When networking, the golden rule is this: Don't hesitate to request direction and ask about potential employment opportunities from all of your friends, colleagues, faculty, and mentors.

Added value is hard to underestimate. Never assume that creative firms know their next step. Present your background at the right time and you might discover you intersect with the firm's objectives and receive your dream job interview. Creative interior design studios are social environments where designers like to discuss their accomplishments. Blog and tweet, and make insightful comments. Before your next design interview, join one of their interest groups and interact first.

During your research and assessing you'll find interior design firms fall into various categories of specialty such as hospitality, residential, commercial, historic preservation and restoration, and more. Become familiar with a company's staff, history of projects, awards and commendations, and current, ongoing, and future projects. Having an awareness of all this background information is useful. When applying for a job, the goal is not to impress your potential employer with everything you do and how capable you are; this will be self-evident in your book. The goal is to get into a give-and-take dialogue and back-and-forth discussion of their needs and your accomplishments, their achievements and your goals and directions, their needs and your abilities. Never let an interview degrade into a question and answer monotonous exchange. Feel free to mention your aspirations, accomplishments, goals, and directions.

> **Here's a TIP:**
> There doesn't necessarily need to be an actual job vacancy for you to find a job. If your experience and skill set enable a design department to win business, improve its offering, or bring a novel approach to the table, then the reviewer will try to make space for you.

Tactfully use the information to trade professional know-how. Remember that the interviewer realizes you are familiar with their company. The interview dynamic is, therefore, a multi-dimensional knowledge-based exchange that can be exciting, animated, and filled with background slices of experience exemplified through discussion, or related to samples taken from your portfolio. An independent study experience also has essential attributes of design accomplishment on offer to a firm.

Melissa Tennant

As an undergraduate at University of Wisconsin, Stevens Point, Melissa designed her portfolio in one semester with a goal in mind of seeking employment after graduation from the university (figures 9–13 to 9–17). She sought to achieve a carefully organized balance between image, text, and negative space to every spread and yet infuse individuality to each project in the book, especially at its beginning. With advice from faculty, friends, and colleagues, she continually tested the state of the design, encountering some redundancy and overly unique layout designs until she found the compromise between those extremes. She eventually achieved her goal of control with augmentation. Melissa states, "I also learned how critically important it is to take one's time and fix renderings with appropriate software to enhance the entire experience of my work." Inspiration came from numerous sources including websites and online publishers such as ISSUU, Blurb, and Lulu.

A New Team

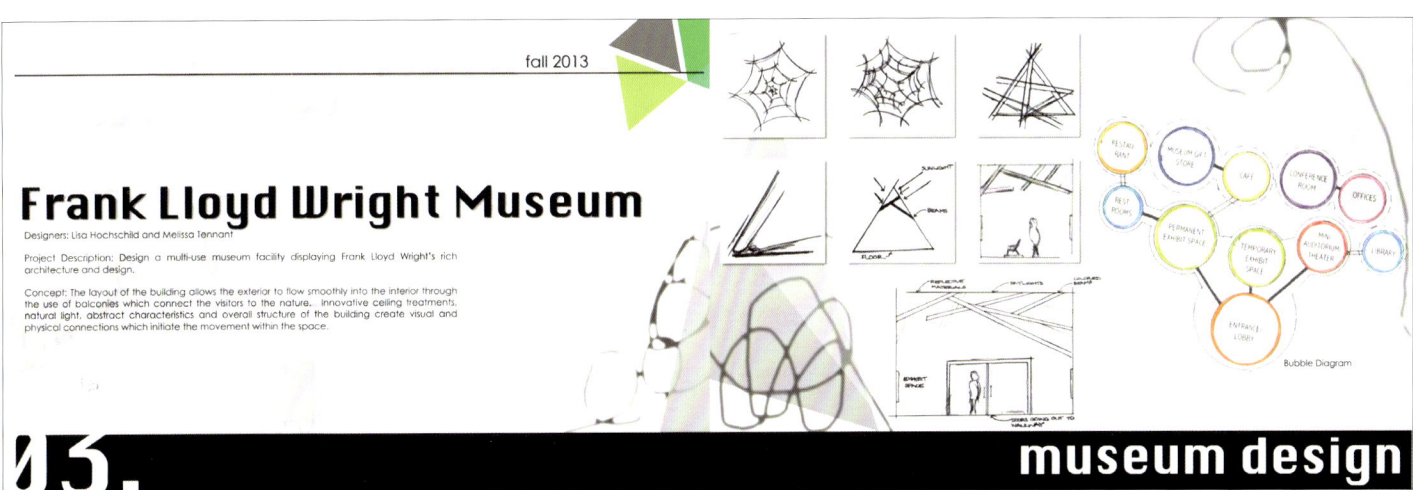

9–13 to 9–15 Melissa's portfolio demonstrates her process and bold thinking. Her shapes are geometric, and her colors and textures are strong. The grid layouts support her orderly design. There is a sense that this is a portfolio that evolved from process in a studio, with her hand at work laying out materials, drawings, and samples. The first page acts as a "snippet" immediately letting the viewer know she can lace color and gestural hand drawing as part of the design process. Melissa Tennant, University of Wisconsin, Stevens Point, Wis. 8.5" x 11".

9 USING YOUR PORTFOLIO AS A TOOL

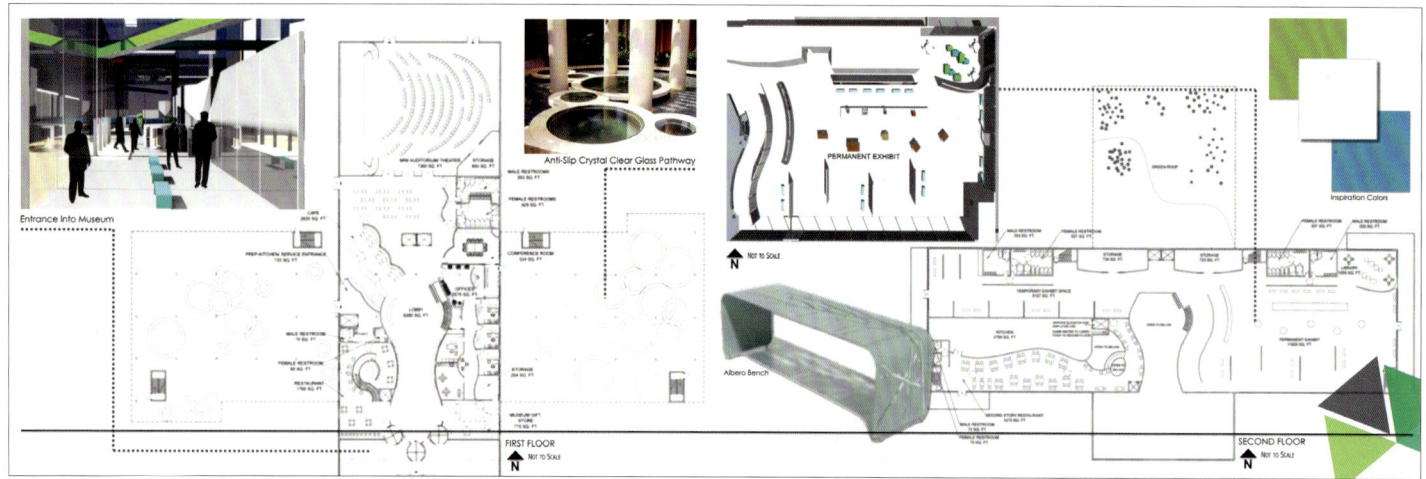

9–16 to 9–17 Melissa's portfolio demonstrates her process and bold thinking. Her shapes are geometric, and her colors and textures are strong. The grid layouts support her orderly design. There is a sense that this is a portfolio that evolved from process in a studio, with her hand at work laying out materials, drawings, and samples. The first page acts as a "snippet" immediately letting the viewer know she can lace color and gestural hand drawing as part of the design process. Melissa Tennant, University of Wisconsin, Stevens Point, Wis. 8.5" x 11".

Here's a TIP:

As you engage a reviewer in an interview, keep in mind that *listening* is the primary facility you bring to an interview. Look to the interviewer to direct the discussion by opening with introductions and initial questions. Follow the pathway of introductions ready to participate in the dialogue with thoughts and questions of your own.

Remember, a canned or scripted response to each and every question from an interviewer is a predictable pattern to avoid. Your response to any matter should be peppered with awareness and interest in what the firm is doing. They are great professionals with a host of significant awards, commendations, and accomplishments interested in expanding the staff of their company. Demonstrate your enthusiasm for their firm by responding in a modest, respectful, and yet confident manner. Following a brief review of your resume, an invitation to open your book and review your work will expand the discussion. By demonstrating experience with relevant content, the conversation widens to encompass the firm's needs, your skills and abilities, your desired design direction, and creative concepts and accomplishments. During the interview, reviewers probe here and there to see how aware you are of the requirements of professional practice and whether you will be able to fulfill them. Do not hesitate to point out relevant projects and office experiences, and how design solutions were achieved and received in studio critique or practice, to send a welcome message to the client or critic.

The design interview process can often seem like an uncomfortable set of challenges that can dampen your interest. Do not allow challenges to thwart your design ambitions. One of the advantages of working within the creative industry is that they are leaders of innovation. Numerous websites can keep you up to date on what's current and breaking. Prepare, review, rehearse, and relax, so that you can be yourself, speak with confidence, and be at the top of your game.

It may sound obvious, but arriving late for an interview creates a wrong impression. Excuses about late-running trains or traffic congestion will not help. Provide enough time in your schedule that you'll be there on time. No excuses!

A common mistake in an interview is to play down your accomplishments. Practice your presentation and don't say "this is only . . ." It's hard if you're nervous, but when you've spent weeks on a piece of work, you must present it in a positive light. How you present yourself is vital.

What to wear? Dressing smart and casual or business savvy makes the most sense. Wear clothes you are comfortable in; this will reflect your confidence in a design interview scenario.

Design firms are always looking for people who can add something new to their business. At the outset of an interview, don't present all of your skills before you have given them confidence in your ability to do the particular job that was advertised. Instead, portray these additional skills as a good way to add value to the business in the future. It is common to be asked to discuss your resume in the interview. Make sure you bring some copies in a proper form and familiarize yourself with your accomplishments and what you're able to do. You will almost certainly be asked to present your portfolio.

Here are a few more things to consider so that you prepare thoroughly. Perhaps your design content refers to a narrow wavelength of project types, such as residential design. Consider the content list of all the classes you've taken and write out all projects associated with design categories, catalog them in a spreadsheet, or put them on index cards or sticky notes. What form does the visual representation of your work take on? Have you performed an appropriate amount of research to understand the nature of the work conducted by the firm you wish to present a portfolio to? Is it best to show a PDF, a printed book, a website, a laptop or iPad/reader, or something else? What design evidence have you been collecting? What makes a good portfolio presentation—does your work make your reviewer think? A thorough demonstration of the process throughout the portfolio supports the content in your job. It can underscore research, different solution studies, precedents in design, a survey in the context of the building, analysis of the site, the study of space-form compositions, the evolution of a design concept, and structural systems adopted for the building. The following documentation enables your process in design to be revealed, reviewed, and responded to in comment and follow-up questions.

PROCESS PRESENTATION IN YOUR BOOK

Visual attributes of process presentation in a portfolio include:

- Sketching
- Rendering
- Modeling/CAD
- Looks like/works like prototype
- Alternative studies
- Precedents
- Context, research, analysis

Among other attributes, a good portfolio includes much of the following:

- Pleasing aesthetics in layout design and typography
- A variety of different types of projects
- Projects from internships
- Projects created on your own
- Projects that show initiative
- Projects that target a company you wish to interview
- A variety of individual and team/group projects
- Projects that show personal interests
- Projects that show personality/creativity beyond academics

GUIDING THE RESUME

Clearly state the specific objective and goal of your search at the top of your resume. Here are some variations on the theme:

Seeking an Interior Designer position at Smith and Wesson Interior Planning where I may be able to apply my creative energy, skills in technology, and depth in office planning to meet project goals regarding excellence in design and execution.

Seeking a position as Interior Designer with Smith and Wesson Team Design using proficiency in 3D rendering programs along with strong interior planning ideas.

To work for Smith and Wesson Designs as an Interior Designer where I can use my outstanding graphic presentation skills to manage the performance of design projects for the company.

To add value to the Smith and Wesson Organization as an Interior Designer utilizing creativity and promoting and maintaining the highest level professionalism.

Desire a position as an Interior Designer with Smith and Wesson Architects and Interiors, offering excellence in design strategies along with a keen sense of elemental colors and schemes.

To obtain an Interior Designer position with Smith and Wesson where I can apply my strong knowledge of design processes and outstanding multi-purposeful presentation skills.

More information can be found at the following link: http://theundercoverrecruiter.com/cv-vs-resume-difference-and-when-use-which/

Be careful about going out on a design limb, such as resumes written on wrinkled paper or arriving in the form of a jigsaw or playing cards, when you're working in a mainstream business and design environment. We have all seen giant resume posters, inflatable resumes, and resumes crafted using origami or delicate and intricate paper engineering. Naturally these resumes linger in the mind, but they also seem like novelty resumes, too, so if you choose to go down this route, it's a calculated risk. On the one hand, you might appear to be a creative thinker, on the other it might seem pretentious and excessive. It depends on the recipient. Relevant categories to include on the resume are education, employment, skills and abilities, professional memberships and organizations, and other interests.

INTERVIEWING (RESUME, PORTFOLIO, IPAD, LAPTOP, AND URL)

The design interview process can be an intimidating maze of challenges and frustrations that can inhibit you from applying in the first place. However, that should not deter you from pursuing your design aspirations. With preparation and the right attitude, you can make every attempt to compete for the design interview and win the position.

Sarah Vogel

Sarah's purpose for her undergraduate portfolio (figures 9–18 to 9–21) was to use it to find employment upon graduation from the University of Wisconsin, Stevens Point. She used PowerPoint for the layout and Photoshop to adjust some of her images. IRender nXt was helpful for rendering SketchUp images. It was printed at a local print shop on 100# semi-gloss paper. Sarah decided not to bind the portfolio into a book, but rather to form a plate portfolio so she could add plates in the future. She made two

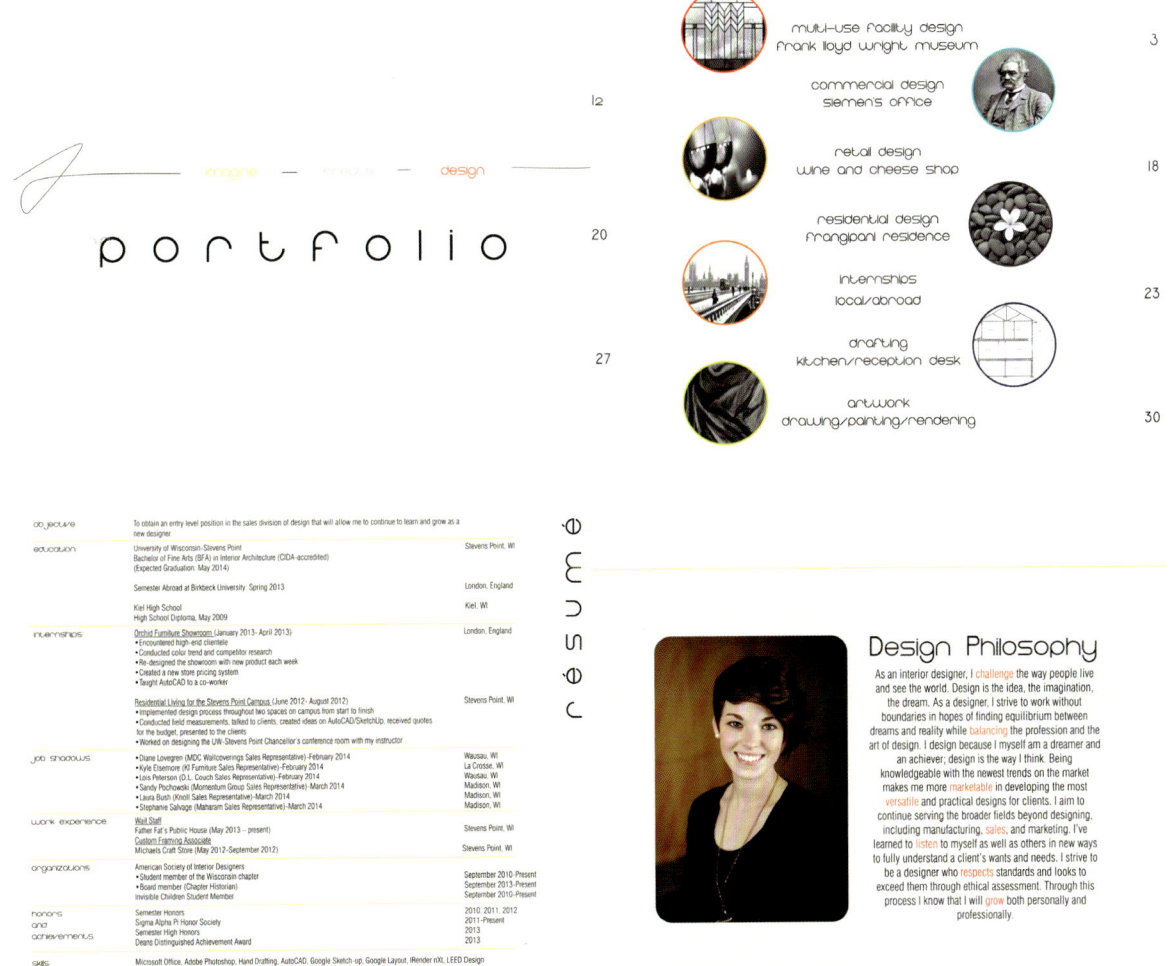

9–18 to 9–19 Sarah's graphics are strong and her process of thinking is clearly laid out not only in her resume, but with the opening to her design process with the Frank Lloyd Wright Museum in Wisconsin. She also has included a photo of herself smiling that is a welcoming addition to her exuberant portfolio. Sarah Vogel, University of Wisconsin, Stevens Point, Wis. 8.5" x 11".

9 USING YOUR PORTFOLIO AS A TOOL

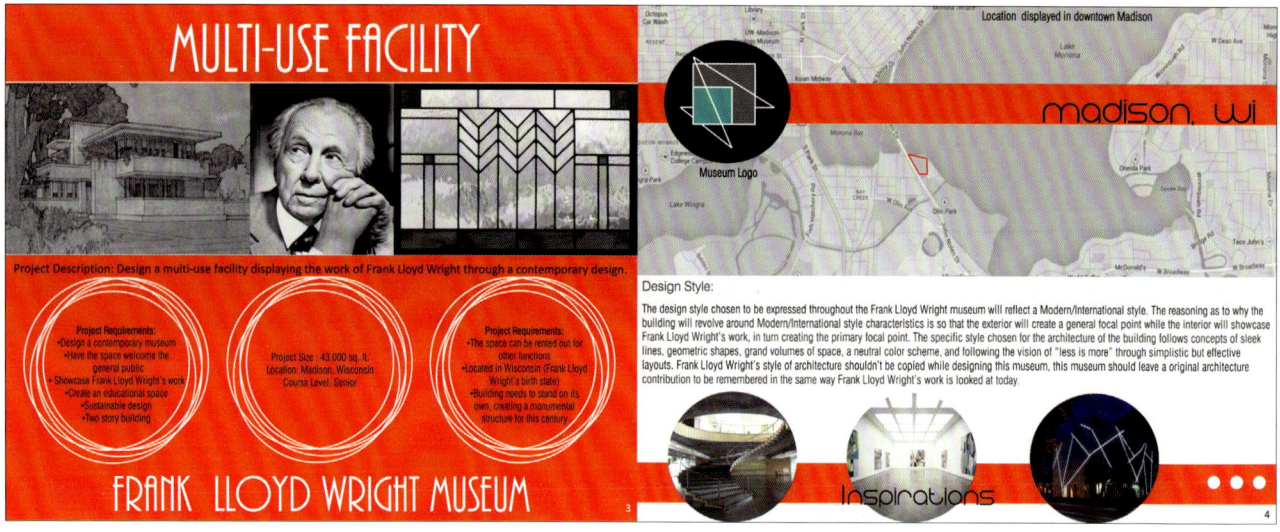

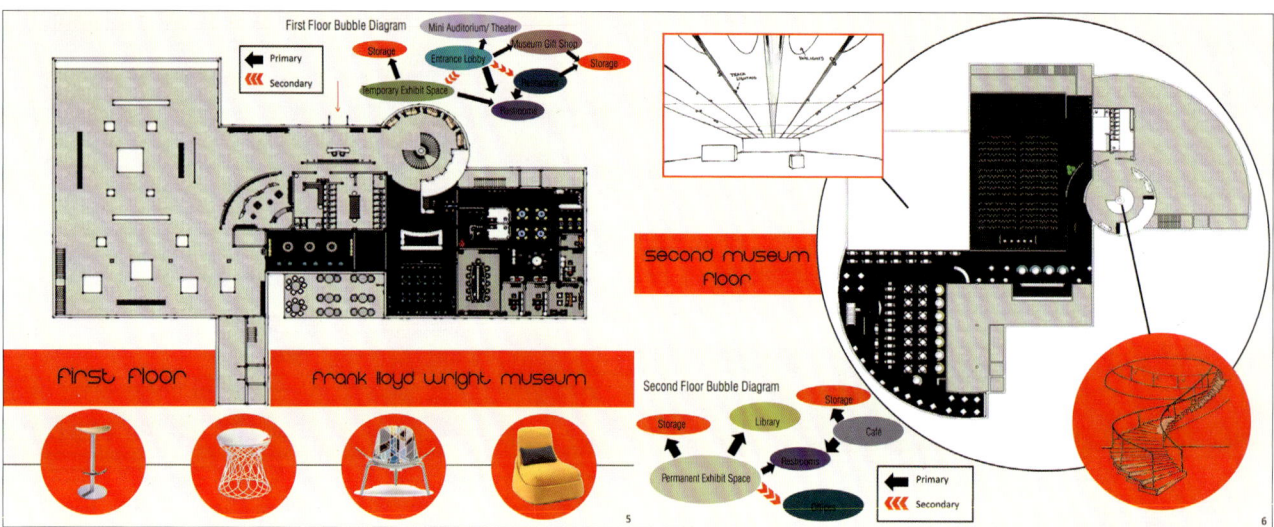

9–20 to 9–21 Sarah's graphics are strong and her process of thinking is clearly laid out not only in her resume, but with the opening to her design process with the Frank Lloyd Wright Museum in Wisconsin. She also has included a photo of herself smiling that is a welcoming addition to her exuberant portfolio. Sarah Vogel, University of Wisconsin, Stevens Point, Wis. 8.5" x 11".

portfolios at a cost of $25 per portfolio plus a case to hold all the plates, which was an additional $60.00. She spent 3 1/2 months working on the project and testing ideas that she knew would elicit a response from a reviewer. Sarah learned that it's a long process and the best thing to do is allow far more time to work through all the issues of design in order to get the best results. She found employment based in part on her portfolio which was well-received and paved the way for a very positive interview.

Here are a few more tips for networking and getting the job of your dreams.

1. Don't be bashful, diffident, farouche, timid, sheepish, reserved, reticent, introverted, retiring, self-effacing, withdrawn, timorous, mousy, nervous, insecure, unconfident, inhibited, repressed, self-conscious, embarrassed, or *shy*. Design students are always mapping ways to connect to designers through social networks, colleagues, friends, family, professors, and employers. You have made it this far in your education and practice. Now is the time to put some muscle behind your accomplishments and attack all of the possible employment outlets with a ferocity reserved for wolverines. Post links to social network profiles to help connect you to as many avenues toward interviews as possible. Until now, connecting with people may have been difficult. You haven't had to step in front of lots of audiences to sell yourself. Quite the contrary, you have been nameless and unknown. I will say it again: When connecting with people, don't be bashful, diffident, farouche, timid, sheepish, or reserved. Be bold!

2. Don't wait for advertisements. Pretend that all of the design firms in your region are all looking for new hires. Now you don't have to wait for a formal invitation. Although a few design companies may post new position descriptions on the web or in professional journals, why to wait to introduce yourself, your qualifications, and your availability? Make it easier for a firm to know you by finding the time and opportunity to introduce yourself, at a time when a manager or principal has a free moment to hear about a new face in the crowd. There doesn't need to be a position open. If your experience and skill set will help a design department win business, improve its offering, or bring an innovative approach to the table, then it will try to make space for you. Do not underestimate how often people come and go in the world of design practice. Creative firms are busy places. If your details hit the right screen at the right time, you could make someone's life easier and bag your dream job interview.

3. Get into the thick of it. Creative design studios are beehives of activity. Interior design practices exist within architecture firms, environmental design groups, and all the small to large diversified private practices. You can characterize design agencies as social yet business-oriented environments. Designers enjoy sharing knowledge and stories about their accomplishments. Don't randomly try to link with people you don't know on LinkedIn; join one of their groups and interact first. Read their blogs and tweets, and make insightful comments by way of an introduction.

4. Stay up to date. It's easy to see that the creative industry views itself as working on the leading edge of innovation. Good websites can keep you up to date with what's new and what's brewing. You don't have to look too far, and it's all online related to a fast-paced design industry allied to your interests. Staying up on the latest developments makes you look savvy in an interview.

5. Be punctual. It may sound obvious, but arriving late creates a bad impression, and feeble excuses about late-running trains or traffic congestion just won't impress anybody. Leave enough room in your schedule that you'll be there in plenty of time and without sweat pouring off you.

6. Practice Investigation 101. Take a close look at the company's site and search the creative press for stories about them. Become a corporate culture historian in one hour. Cruise the Internet perusing articles and points of interest related to the staff and accomplishments of a given design firm. Do not make assumptions one way or another; just absorb all you can to seem in touch, interested, and knowledgeable about the company and who is who.

7. Be modest. It's okay to be self-effacing, self-deprecating, humble, unpretentious, unassuming, unpresuming, unostentatious, and unflashy. However, sometimes to be modest about the abundance of talent demonstrated in your portfolio is underselling your actual skill sets and abilities. A common mistake in an interview is to play down one's work too much. Rehearse your presentation. Present your projects in a realistic and positive light.

8. Dress to impress. Not everyone wears the same style or garb when attending an interview. A business presentation is probably the most acceptable way to dress for an interview. No flip-flops. Clean underwear is a must. My rule of thumb is to dress smart-casual.

9. Identify how you add value. Identify those attributes of your work that demonstrate prowess in skill sets, conceptualization, and process, or find a few elements that are individual standouts in your book. You know this because when people see your work, they identify you as being adept in one area or another in design. Portray your particular strengths and additional skills as good ways to add value to the business in the future.

10. Take resume action. Be prepared to walk and talk the interviewer through your resume. Bring a few clean copies in case there is more than one person involved in your interview or a post-interview referral. Be completely familiar with what you say you've done and what you're able to do. You will almost certainly be asked to demonstrate those abilities in the context of the interviewer reviewing your portfolio with you.

11. Put yourself in their position. Interviewers' temperaments vary, however they are all looking for something tangible in your work that they can help to cultivate. They want to help your development and also enable their firm to grow and succeed. How do you tell just such a story efficiently (in a few minutes)? Your story should convey your interest in working for that firm, and also put yourself in a position of having substance they will wish to acquire. A mission, philosophy, or design statement outlines the chronology of your development, including your interests, abilities, and direction in design. Your statement is usually found at the beginning of the portfolio after the title page and close to the contents page.

12. Digital or printed? Having a digital and a printed portfolio is helpful. The latter can be a basic mailer or a bound brochure of your work. It can be viewable on an iPad/reader or an online portfolio. It should follow the idea to Keep It Simple, Stupid (KISS), because if it's not simple in its navigation and design, the interview may be shorter than expected.

13. Put your best foot forward. Have projects of various lengths and complexity in your book. Include a few brief exercises and longer multi-page complex projects. Position the strongest three or four projects so that there is one at the beginning, middle, and closing of your book. These are called the posts or main projects. The rails are connecting shorter projects that enable you to move confidently from short to longer projects as the interview draws to a close. If you leave your book with the interviewer, they will have the opportunity to spend more time with your work as well as show it to others who may have an interest in the new hire.

14. Know that brilliance is relative. The world of interior design is full of plans, priorities, and approved practices. The presentation of your portfolio should be respectful of a diversity of viewpoints in design and performance but also provide an impression of you as an individual with emerging talent and skills. You are hoping that the reviewer will spend more time exploring your work. For this to happen, you have to excite the reviewer, yes, but also make his or her job as easy as possible.

15. Less is less and more is more. Although the amount of work included in anyone's portfolio will vary from person to person, that doesn't mean you should cram it full with the kitchen sink. Remember that a portfolio is an instrument to demonstrate you have something that others want. Designers see through fluff in a heartbeat.

Interviewing (Resume, Portfolio, iPad, Laptop, and URL)

Claire Shoemaker

Claire created this undergraduate portfolio (figures 9–22 to 9–25) while studying design at the Kendall College of Art and Design. Her purpose was to use the result to help her find employment. She spent two semesters creating and refining the book. It was a challenging prospect to understand how to brand herself and create a convincing document that represented the full range of her skills and abilities. Her abilities really shine in her book. She reflected strength on many levels, which played well in interviews because it showed that she was not a candidate that needed to be instructed heavily. Instead, it showed that she had the right array of design experiences and skills and was ready to go to work.

9–22 to 9–23 Claire made sure to show projects which used software programs from Revit to SketchUp. The project for Higher Education was nicely laid out with good blocking and spacing between images. The statement is simple and to the point. She included sketches and diagrammatic studies. Choosing image size is as important as choosing hierarchy of typography. The grouping and clustering of these images relates nicely to her block image of her name on the front cover. She also shows a variety of color systems that support each and every design problem. These decisions show that she is flexible with design solutions that reflect an in-depth understanding of the given problem. Claire Shoemaker, Kendall College of Art and Design, Grand Rapids, Mich., 8.5" x 11".

9 USING YOUR PORTFOLIO AS A TOOL

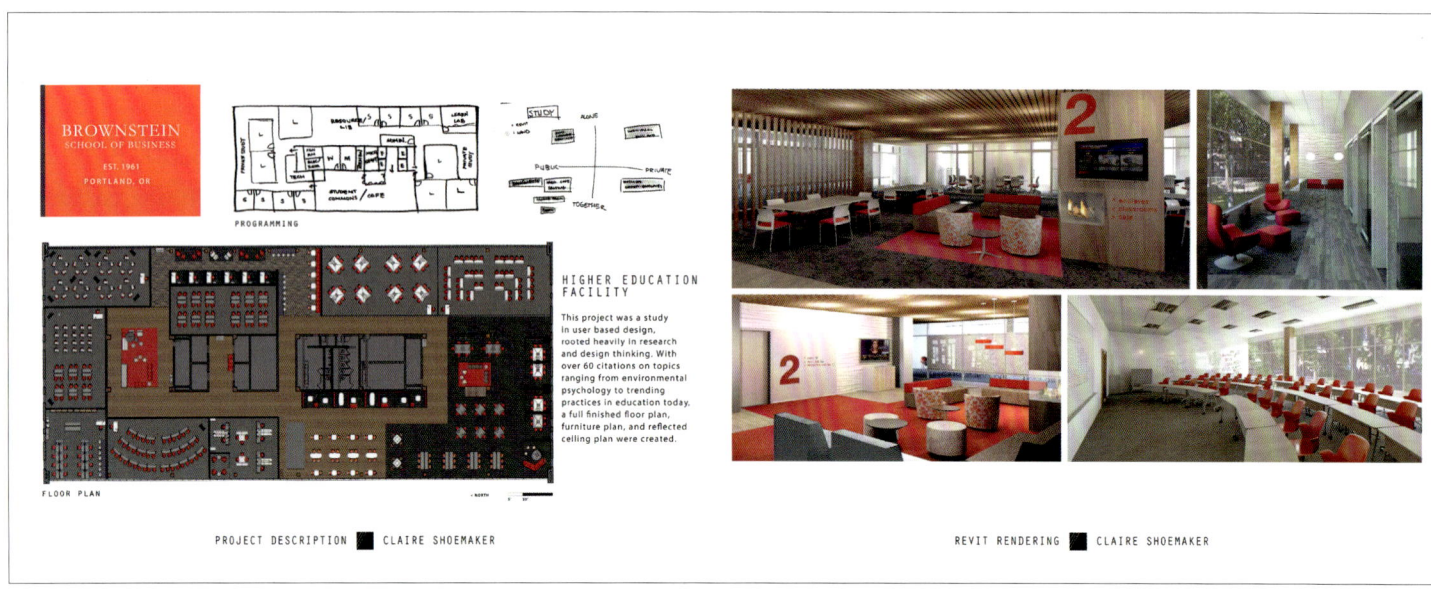

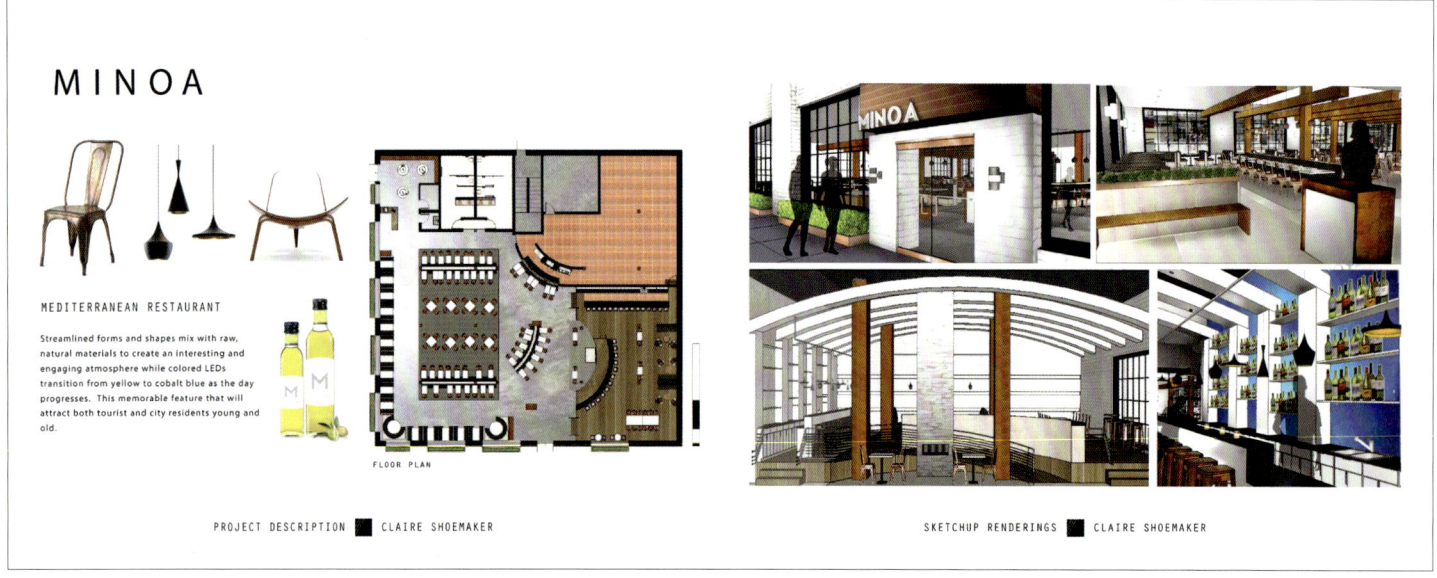

9–22 to 9–23 Claire made sure to show projects which used software programs from Revit to SketchUp. The project for Higher Education was nicely laid out with good blocking and spacing between images. The statement is simple and to the point. She included sketches and diagrammatic studies. The hierarchy of images in the office think tank project is also well executed. Choosing image size is as important as choosing hierarchy of typography. The grouping and clustering of these images relates nicely to her block image of her name on the front cover. She also shows a variety of color systems that support each and every design problem. These decisions show that she is flexible with design solutions that reflect an in-depth understanding of the given problem. Claire Shoemaker, Kendall College of Art and Design, Grand Rapids, Mich., 8.5" x 11".

LEAD WITH CONFIDENCE

You have done your homework and then some. Now is the time to sleep on all of your preparations and begin the next day with a renewed sense of self-confidence and enthusiasm. Almost everyone has faltered during a job interview at some point—arriving late, stumbling over an answer, tripping over a rug, and so on. Candidates have little control over certain blunders, yet others are preventable. A survey taken by Design Intelligence found that the most common interview mistakes are not the result of circumstances or bad luck but stem from thoughtlessness and poor etiquette. Here are five faux pas to watch for and how to avoid making them.

1. Deep-six your phone. Nothing should take your attention away from the hiring manager. When you check messages or answer a call during the job interview, you're sending a not-so-subtle signal that you aren't serious about the position. What to do instead: Turn off the phone and put it away before the interview starts. Even silencing it may not be enough. If the phone vibrates and you respond to it, you could lose your train of thought or, worse, alienate the hiring manager.

2. Don't be late—and apologize if you are. Many interviewers realize that sometimes there's not much you can do about running behind. However, there's no excuse for being casual about it. A majority of design managers would immediately discount interviewees who don't at least acknowledge their late arrival. Be safe and build in extra travel time. If your interview is half an hour away, leave the house 45 minutes to an hour before it starts. Keep the hiring manager's phone number handy so that if the train is delayed or you get stuck in traffic, you'll be able to get in touch. If you don't arrive on time, briefly explain the reason and sincerely apologize.

3. Get yourself organized. You've researched the potential employer, practiced responses to tough interview questions, and googled the directions. But before you head out the door, double-check the interviewer's instructions. Creative managers responding to the survey were equally annoyed by candidates who didn't have everything they were asked to bring as by those who weren't concerned about arriving late. In addition to the usual preparation, reread the email inviting you for an in-person meeting. If you're asked to bring a physical portfolio or list of references, have them ready and by the door. You also should bring several hard copies of your current resume.

4. Don't look unprofessional. While some creative agencies have casual dress codes, a job interview is not the place to flaunt your laid-back look. On the other hand, there's a risk of looking too stuffy and not fitting in with the company culture. Blend your professional and personal style. Do a little research to see what most employees wear by exploring the company's website or asking people in your network; then pick an outfit that's a touch more formal. Above all, choose attire that makes you feel confident and comfortable.

5. Play up your soft skills. You may have worked for some real jerks, but 62 percent of survey respondents said speaking poorly of a former employer or job is an immediate turnoff. During an interview, one of your goals is to demonstrate your soft skills, such as the ability to collaborate and get along with a wide range of personalities. Besides, in the close-knit creative world, the hiring manager may like and respect the person you just dissed.

Watch everything you say, especially when the interviewer asks why you left a previous position. It's best to not go into ugly details, but rather to speak in general terms about how the company was going in a different direction or you were looking for a new challenge. In today's competitive environment for creative jobs, one wrong move can knock you out of the running. To increase your odds of advancing to the next step of the search process, know what interview mistakes are deal breakers for hiring managers—and do your best to avoid them.

9 USING YOUR PORTFOLIO AS A TOOL

Adrianna Costanza

Adrianna designed her demonstrative portfolio during her senior year as an undergraduate in interior design at Utah State University (figures 9–26 to 9–31) and with a purpose of finding an internship. She acknowledges that she has a strong visual style that attempts to balance graphics with interior content. She used Photoshop and Illustrator for design software. She used a thin matte-finished paper at approximately 60 lb with a professional laser color printer, and bound it with a basic saddle-stitch. Her inspiration sprang from reviewing fashion magazines and style books. Three portfolios were created at an approximate expense of $100.00 total. The book was received well and she found an internship in New York City. She realized as a result of the design process and research how much the industry relies on exceptional graphics; however, you do not want to be overpowered by them, but rather use them to enhance the portfolio and present concepts in a professional manner. Adrianna is inspired by the energy and enthusiasm of fashion to always remain highly creative in every way.

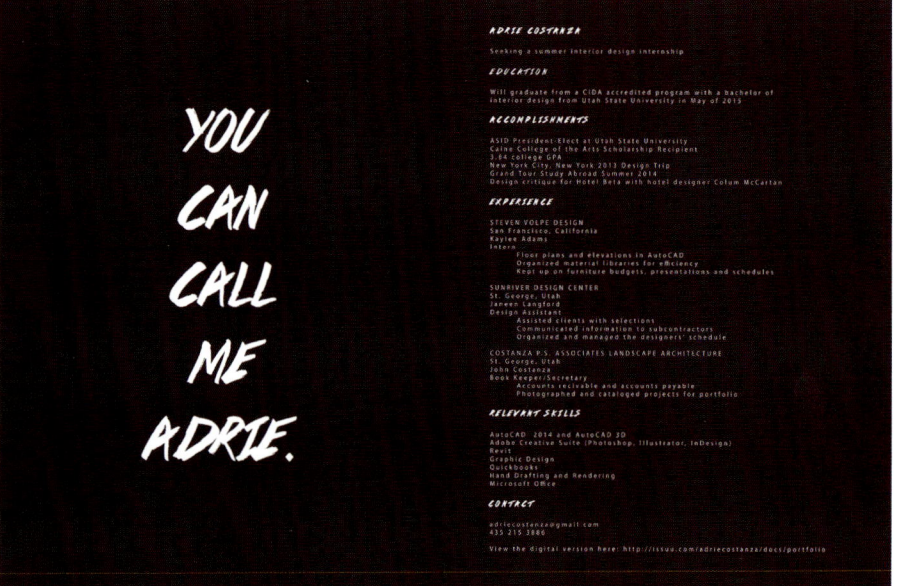

Lead with Confidence

Here's a TIP:

Final tip from Adrianna. Never call the interviewer from their office to thank them for the opportunity!

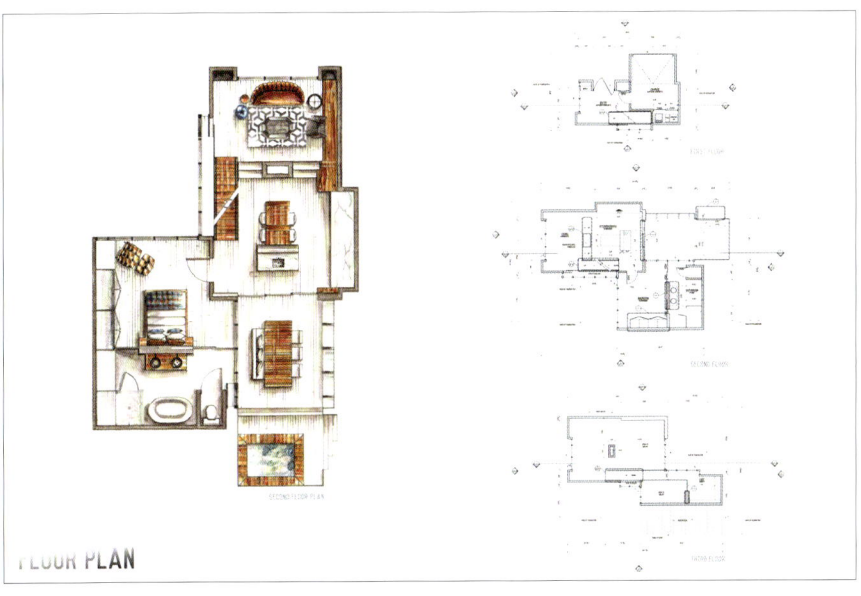

9–26 to 9–31 Adrianna invites you to look at her personal portfolio. She welcomes you to call her by her nickname. She boldly designs her titles, straight-forward and unapologetic. Her materials are strong and layered and her renderings are sensitive to her understanding of materiality, light, and surface. She also uses positive and negative space to push and pull you through her projects. The use of diagonal shapes prompt you to look forward to the next page and to the next project. Although she brands herself with a strong image, it does not get in the way of designing the individual spaces. Adrianna Costanza, Utah State University, Logan, Utah. 8.5" x 11".

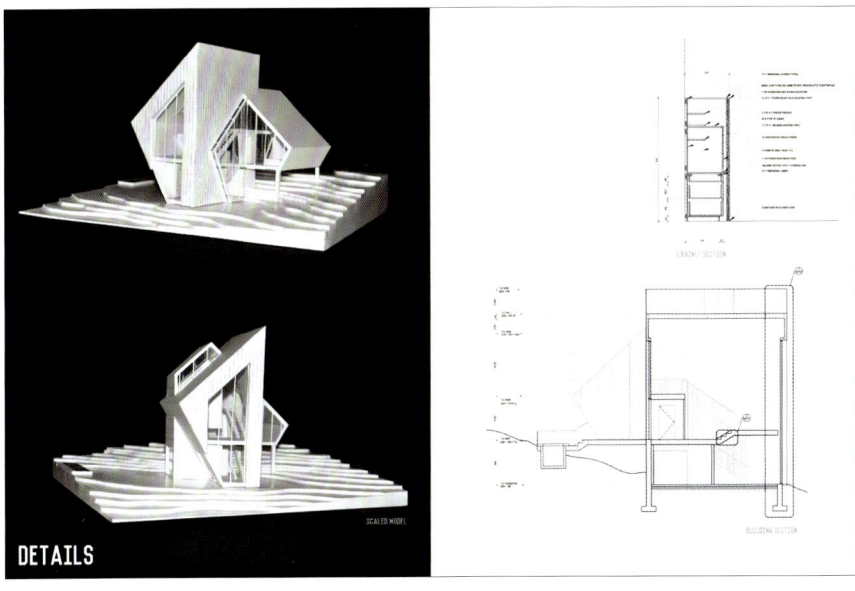

10
PORTFOLIO
OF INTERIOR PORTFOLIOS

"I try to give people a different way of looking at their surroundings. That's art to me."

– MAYA LIN

The purpose of this book has been to demonstrate the process of portfolio development in interior design and to visually inspire the reader by discussing examples of how design ideas and materials can be organized into portfolio presentations. In our final chapter, we wish to close with significant examples of guiding concepts for the layout design of your portfolio. More than polished graphics of floor plans, elevations, sections, details, and perspectives for interior design projects, the plates and spreads included here inspire further study of innovative ways of problem-solving, sketching, and using various techniques and methods to plan solutions for the layout design of interior design portfolios.

ALEXANDRA SEAGER: SUCCESSFUL LAYOUT AND GRAPHIC DESIGN

Alexandra studied interior design at the School of Visual Arts in New York. She designed her undergraduate portfolio to showcase her recently completed senior thesis and simultaneously use her book for job interview purposes. The Adobe Creative Suite was instrumental to designing her portfolio as well as AutoCAD and 3D MAX for studio projects, and includes plenty of evidence of quality hand sketching and model making. She printed the pages for her book on a card-stock-weight paper and bound it simply with a wire coil. From beginning to end, the design and production of her book required 40 hours of intensive layout and graphic design work. The effort was evidently worth the time as she was offered a job at her first interview. Alexandra feels that investing in graphic design skills and software knowledge was worth every minute of her time.

At this point, you should be on your way toward planning the design for an impressive array of documents. With your hardcopy portfolio, online website or CD version, and peripherals, you are ready to make application to an advanced degree program or engage in an employment interview regarding your abilities, experience, and fit within a firm. You are well aware that the portfolio is the single most important document that an interior design student has to demonstrate his or her expertise. Portfolios created by young professionals working at a high level of design production convey a refined visual process; sophisticated technical methods; an ability to program, analyze, and organize diverse types of visual and text information; problem-solving skills; and ability to work in various forms of historic, contemporary, and innovative styles or genres of design.

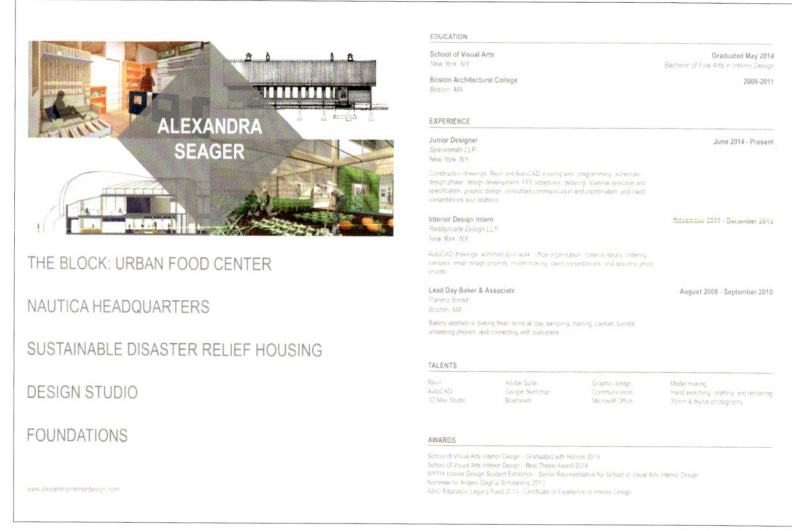

Alexandra Seager: Successful Layout and Graphic Design

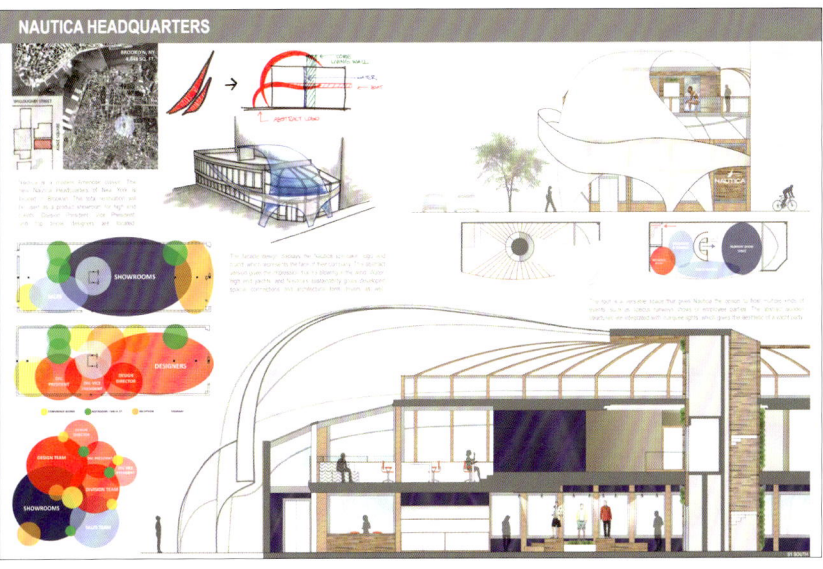

10–1 to 10–5 Alexandra's portfolio uses a gray title bar for each project as an architectural cap to each page. She includes well-organized, colored transparent diagrams of her space planning and with many sections that show interconnected volumes and space from level to level. She even includes fast sketch studies of these relationships. The diagrams demonstrate that she is a designer who is able to navigate people and human activity and sight lines through interconnected spaces. Her projects also include well-developed renderings of her design solutions. The foundation page also sheds light on her skills beyond design. Her initial page with contents and resume also demonstrates a passionate young designer who is ready to face the challenges of the design industry. Alexandra Seager, School of Visual Arts, N.Y. 8.5" x 11".

10 PORTFOLIO OF INTERIOR PORTFOLIOS

10–6 to 10–11 Alexandra's portfolio uses a gray title bar for each project as an architectural cap to each page. She includes well-organized, colored transparent diagrams of her space planning and with many sections that show interconnected volumes and space from level to level. She even includes fast sketch studies of these relationships. The diagrams demonstrate that she is a designer who is able to navigate people and human activity and sight lines through interconnected spaces. Her projects also include well-developed renderings of her design solutions. The foundation page also sheds light on her skills beyond design. Her initial page with contents and resume also demonstrates a passionate young designer who is ready to face the challenges of the design industry. Alexandra Seager, School of Visual Arts, N.Y. 8.5" x 11".

Alexandra Seager: Successful Layout and Graphic Design

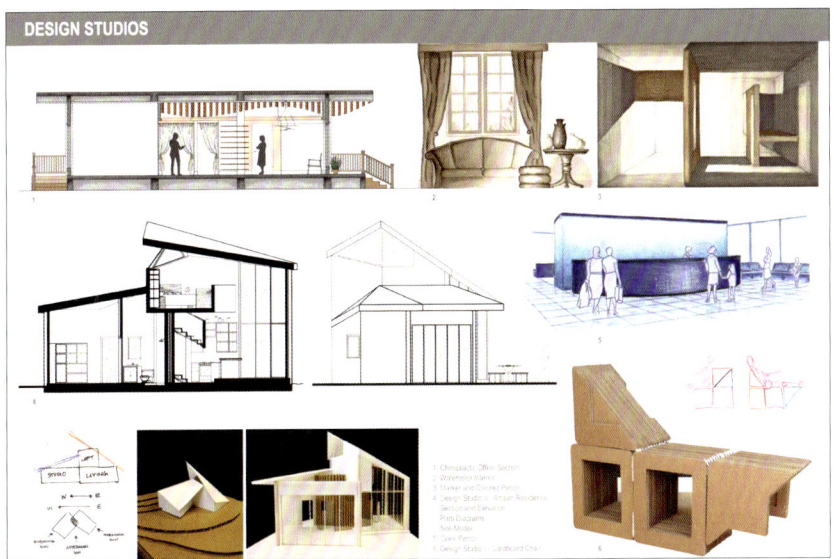

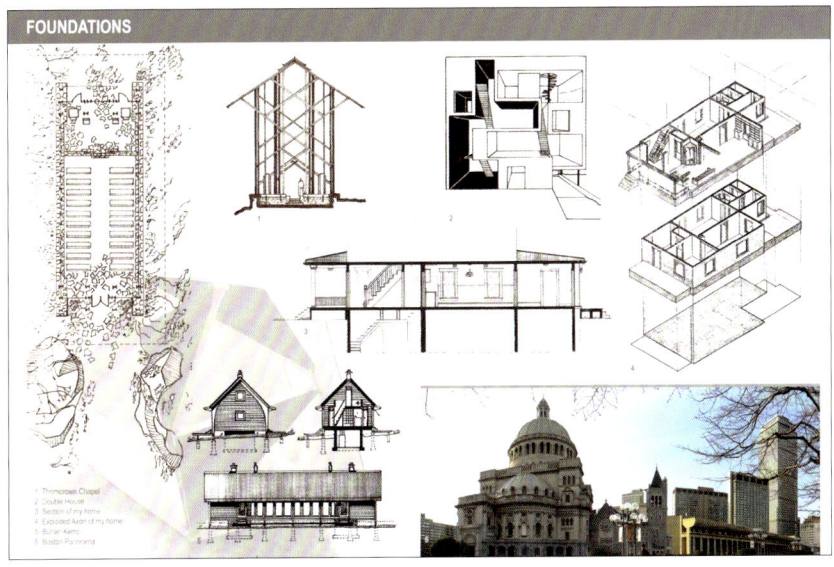

CHAD ZUMBAUGH: DESIGNING WITHIN LIMITS

Chad's portfolio was designed completely in PowerPoint. Creating a portfolio was a requirement of the interior design program at Central Michigan University. Chad was not satisfied with the first round of printing and continued to revise and upgrade the production until it was as professional as possible. He printed the book on a medium-weight card stock paper and slipped the pages into a ready-made binder with 24 acetate inserts. Total cost for printing and the binder was approximately $100.00. Chad admits, "I am a perfectionist and spent way more time than I probably should have, about 60 hours. My attention to and appreciation of design kept me revising drafts until the layout reflected a far better grasp of graphic design than at the outset. My suggestion to others is to think outside the box but also pay attention to design principles. The biggest source of inspiration was looking online for professional examples. I used my portfolio at interviews and was offered a position a week before graduation. All the work I invested in my book was critical to a successful interview and job offer."

The design studio classroom has transformed itself into a laboratory for technological experimentation and exploration. The most extraordinary aspects of this process are focused on the creation and manipulation of images, text, content, and perhaps motion and sound. There is no *universal* type of successful portfolio. The ubiquity of high-quality digital output has made it increasingly more important for young professionals to distinguish their work through a demonstration of skills in traditional and new media along with strong conceptual design background and abilities. Innovations in imaging technology ultimately impact all design-related professions, redefining the methods and processes of visualization and communication in most industries.

Chad Zumbaugh: Designing within Limits

10–12 to 10–16 Chad designed a portfolio that includes a well-drawn narrative in brackets throughout his book. It literally walks you through the spaces in concise language. The colors used on the contents page reflect those used in each individual project so that you always know where you are in the book. The renderings are strong saturated color and pop out of each page layout. All other material, including the cover, are underplayed with softer tones and quiet colors. This strategy and formal use of hierarchy keeps the focus on his finished designs. He repeats the rectangular shapes throughout his book, including white space. This creates a harmonious feeling to the overall layout. Chad Zumbaugh, Central Michigan University, Mt. Pleasant, Mich. 8.5" x 11".

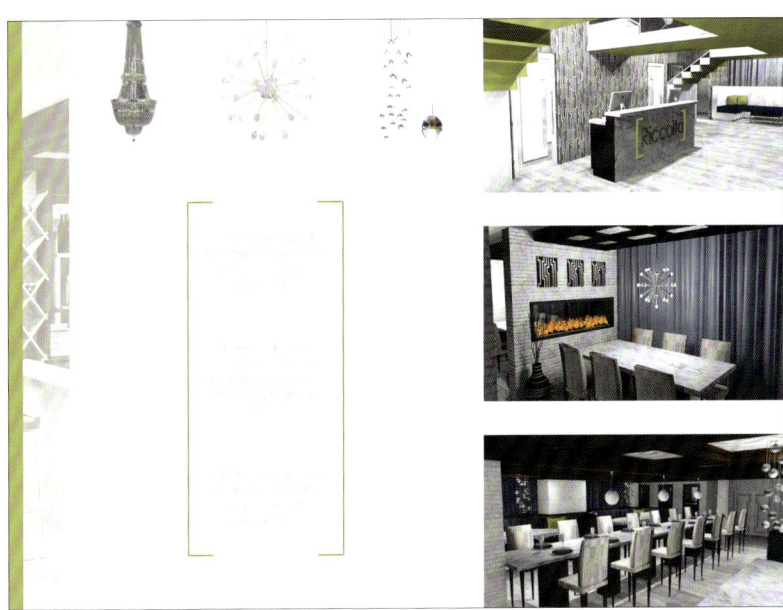

10 PORTFOLIO OF INTERIOR PORTFOLIOS

10–17 to 10–21 Chad designed a portfolio that includes a well-drawn narrative in brackets throughout his book. It literally walks you through the spaces in concise language. The colors used on the contents page reflect those used in each individual project so that you always know where you are in the book. The renderings are strong saturated color and pop out of each page layout. All other material, including the cover, are underplayed with softer tones and quiet colors. This strategy and formal use of hierarchy keeps the focus on his finished designs. He repeats the rectangular shapes throughout his book, including white space. This creates a harmonious feeling to the overall layout. Chad Zumbaugh, Central Michigan University, Mt. Pleasant, Mich. 8.5" x 11".

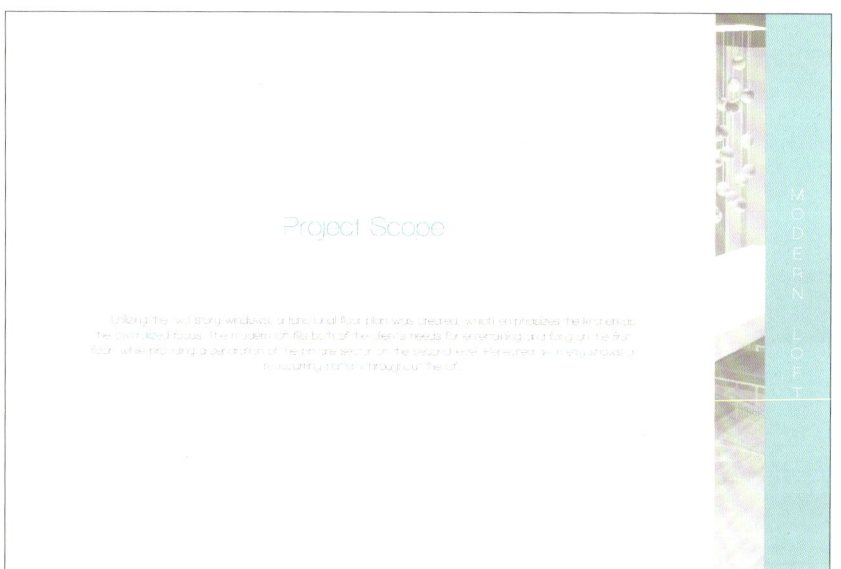

Chad Zumbaugh: Designing within Limits

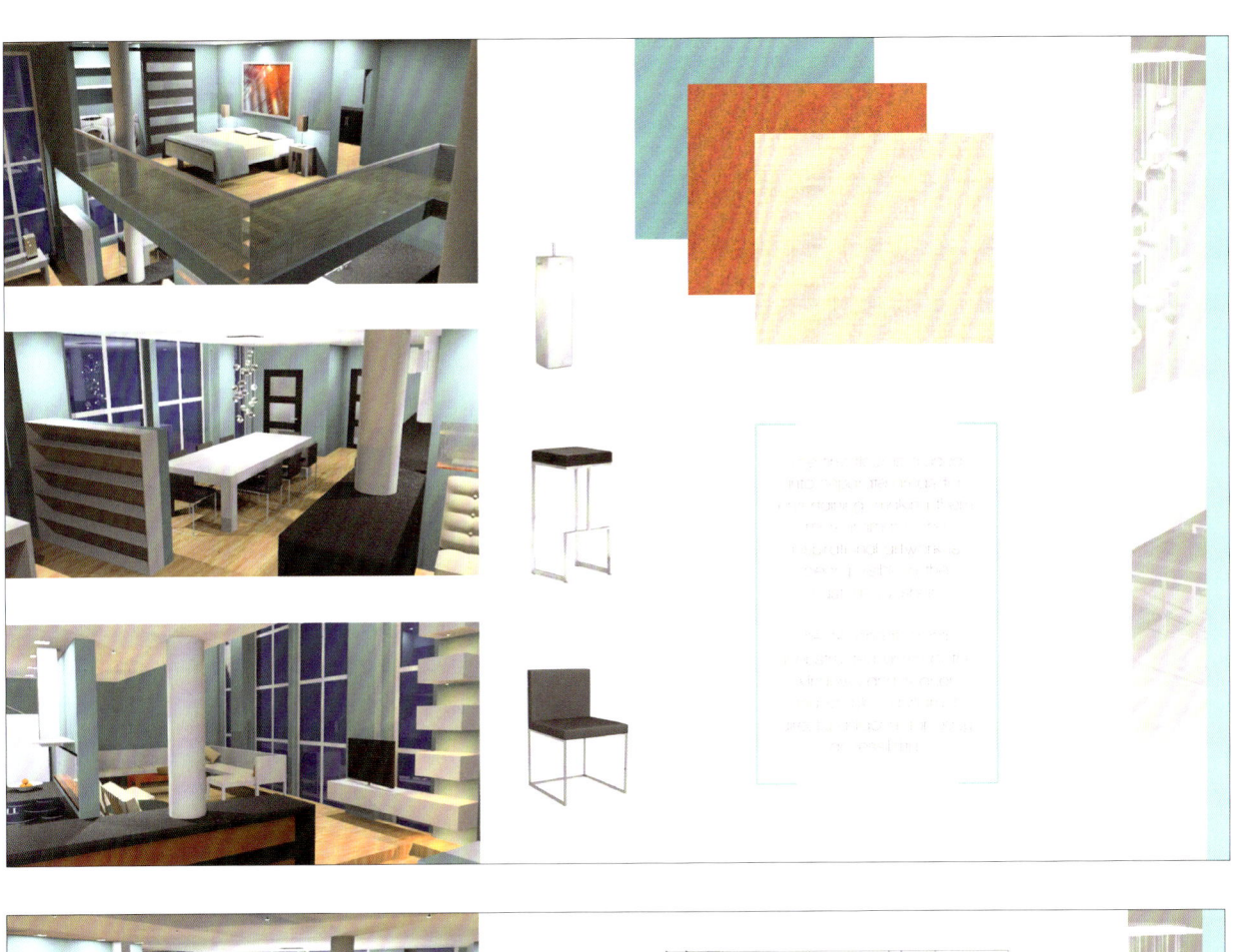

10 PORTFOLIO OF INTERIOR PORTFOLIOS

KIRSTEN STOVER CESSNA: CUSTOM SIZE BOOKS HAVE PERSONALITY

Kirsten studied interior design at the University of Missouri, Columbia and created her portfolio as a capstone course assignment, a showcase for her work and internship experiences, and as a tool to interview for employment after graduation. Adobe InDesign was the main software used for layout design. The book was printed on a semi-gloss paper at a format size of 8" x 8". She found the size to lend an air of individuality to her work; she created just one portfolio and provided PDF samples of her pages as leave behinds. She worked on the design and production for well over a month using every moment of available time to organize and create a successful layout design. She received three interviews and two offers of employment thanks to a successfully designed book. She found advice from graphic designers to be some of the most enlightening information useful to the project.

A reviewer is just as curious to see your best work as you are to express your interests and ask about the reviewer's academic program or design firm. The reviewer does not make a decision based solely on the creativity you display. A portfolio demonstrates multiple skill sets that reviewers make mental or written notes about to eventually weigh in relation to the competition and in tune with the firm's needs. Similarly, an academic reviewer determines who they believe would be a dynamic fit for the student body of their program.

10–22 to 10–24 Kirsten's Bear Creek Prairie co-housing project is designed to float on a gray background. She chose to organize her colored renderings as large thumbnails to the right of each page layout. Her design process drawings are larger and to the right of each page. This causes the viewer to focus on the overall detailed drawings, elevations, sections, and floorplans of this complete design project. She reverses the usual hierarchy of putting the large renderings front and center, while giving large white space to the technical drawings and overall space planning of her design. Kirsten Stover Cessna, University of Missouri, Columbia, Mo. 8" x 8".

Kirsten Stover Cessna: Custom Size Books Have Personality

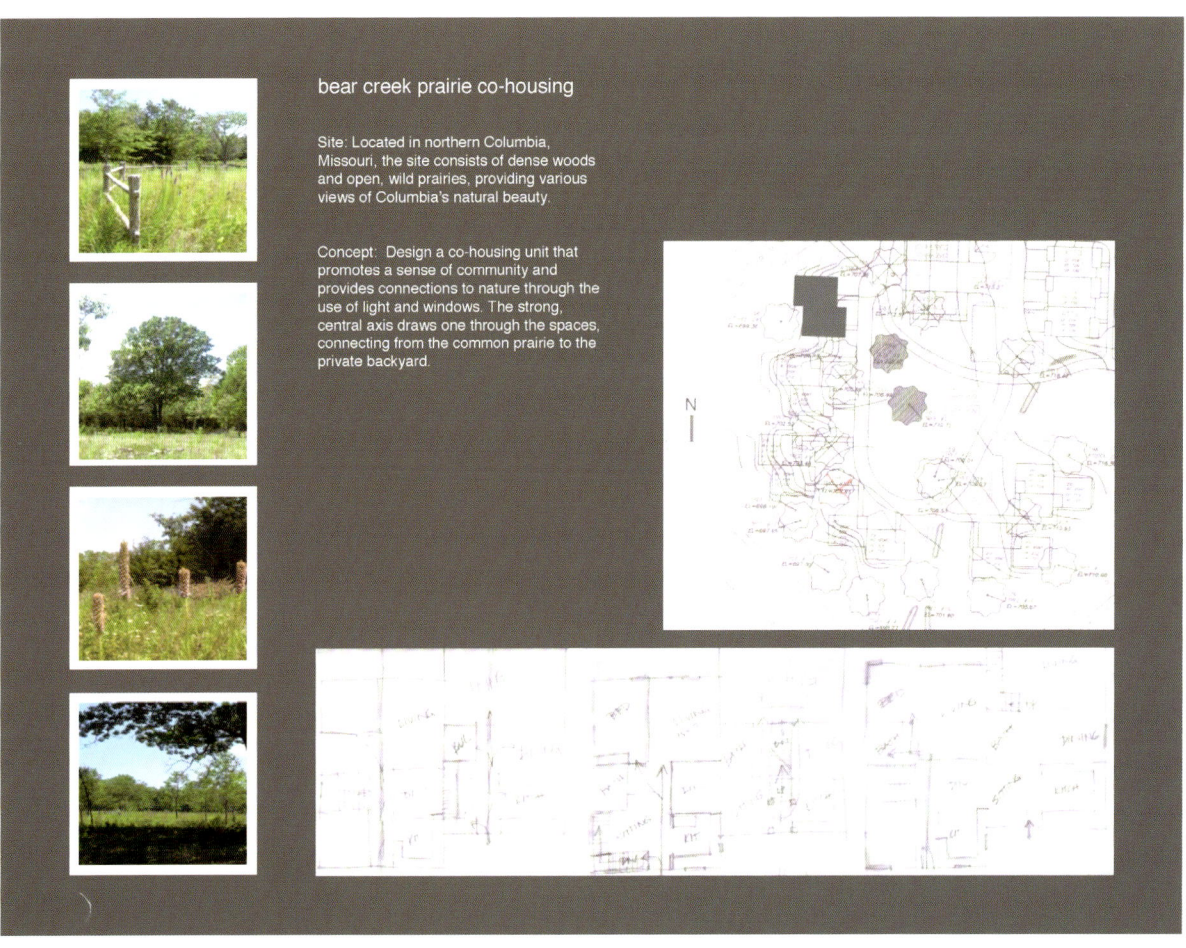

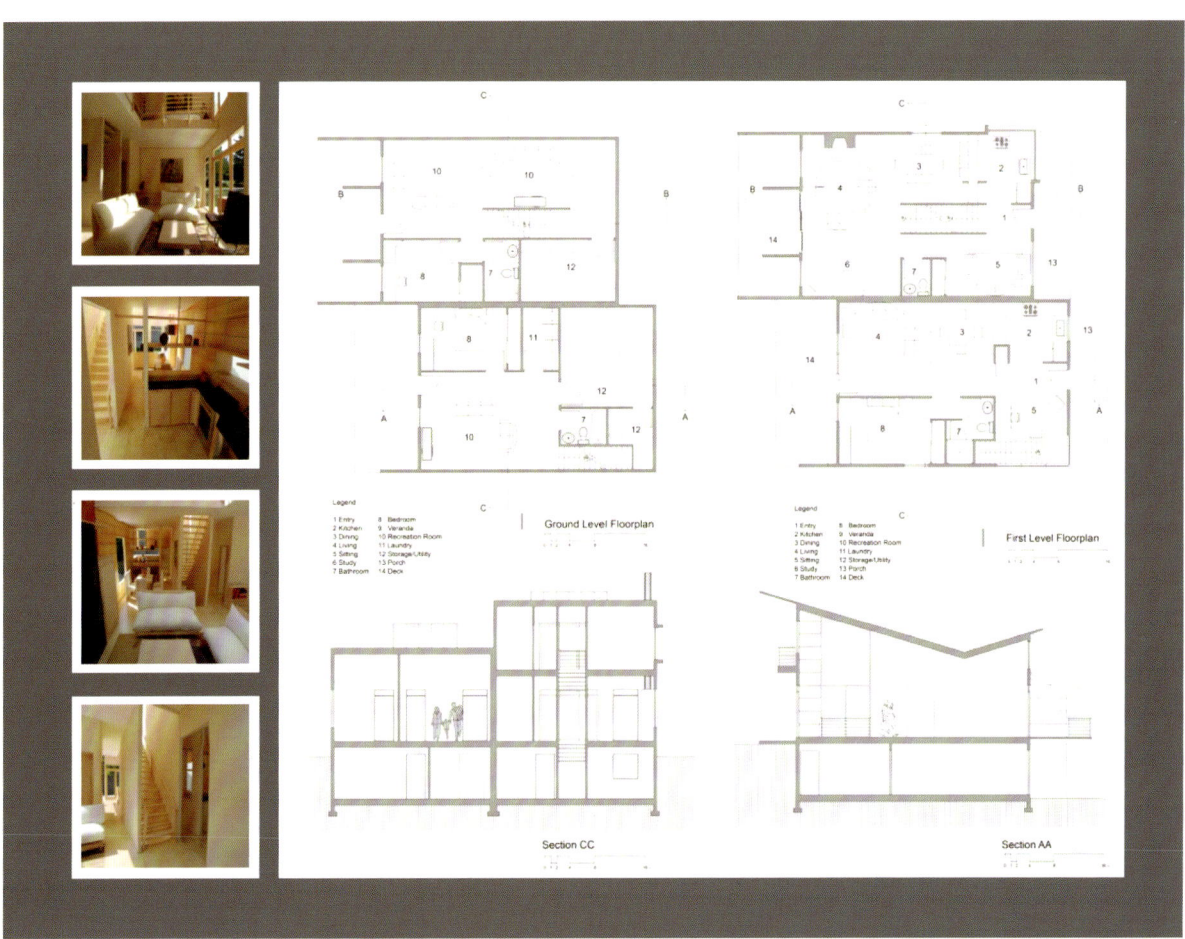

10 PORTFOLIO OF INTERIOR PORTFOLIOS

Hand Model with Photoshop

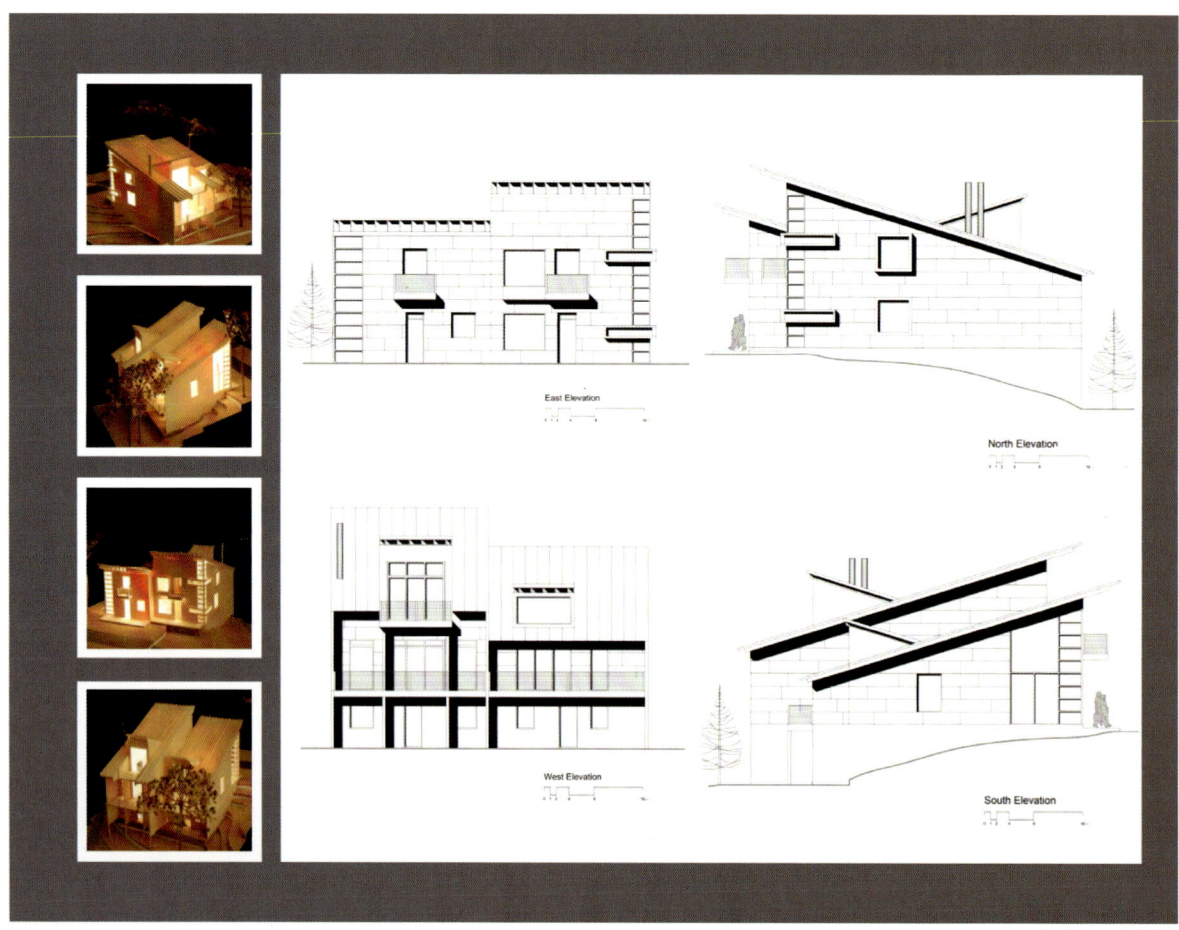

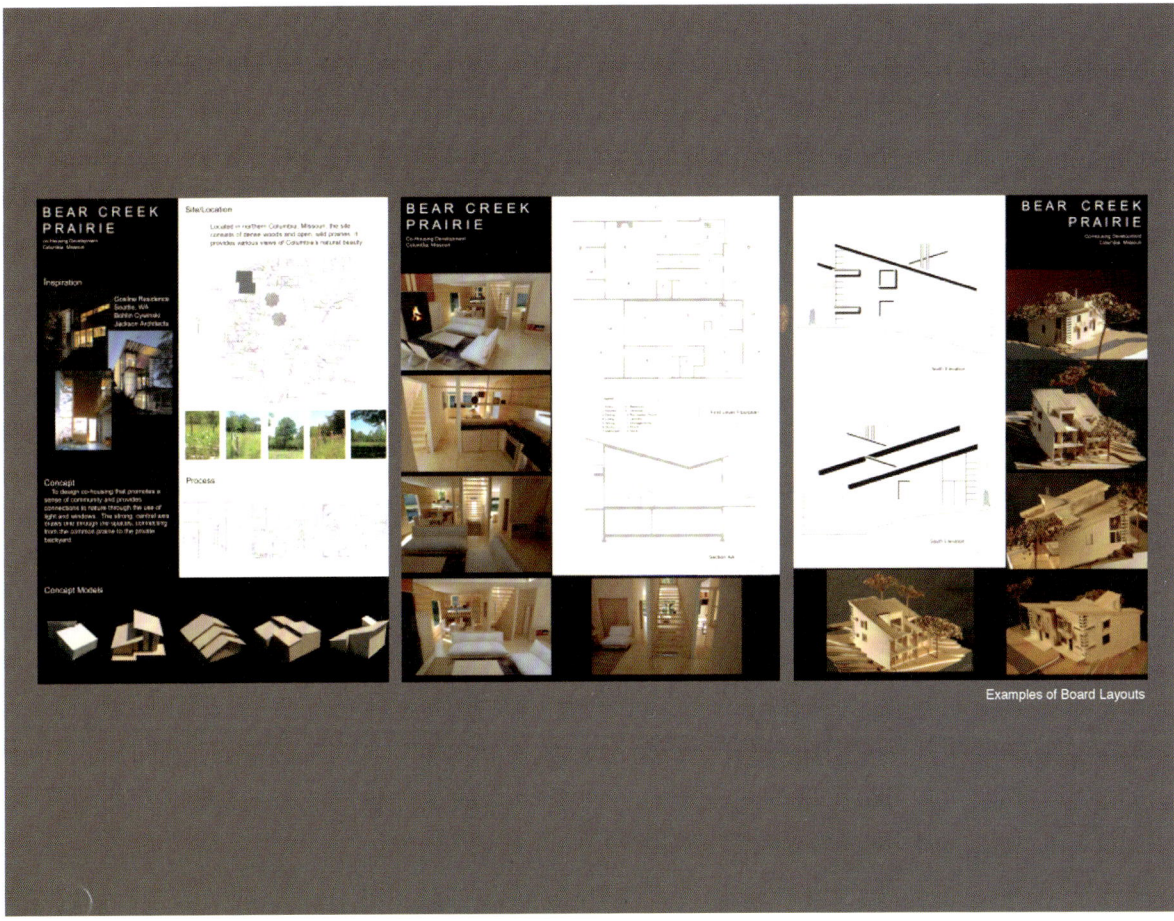

Examples of Board Layouts

10–25 to 10–27 Kirsten's Bear Creek Prairie co-housing project is designed to float on a gray background. She chose to organize her colored renderings as large thumbnails to the right of each page layout. Her design process drawings are larger and to the right of each page. This causes the viewer to focus on the overall detailed drawings, elevations, sections, and floorplans of this complete design project. She reverses the usual hierarchy of putting the large renderings front and center, while giving large white space to the technical drawings and overall space planning of her design. Kirsten Stover Cessna, University of Missouri, Columbia, Mo. 8" x 8".

SHIZUKA NAGAYA: LAYOUT DESIGN REFLECTS INDIVIDUALITY

Shizuka studied interior design as an undergraduate at the New York School of Interior Design. Assembling all of the imagery useful to each project in the book required searching through various project files for just the right content to demonstrate process, technology, and design development for each project. Having your files organized saves an enormous amount of time and frustration.

The Adobe Creative Suite was instrumental in successfully creating the design of this portfolio. The book pages were a heavyweight dull enamel stock that reflected the work without too much glare. Shizuka feels that test printing several different kinds and weights of paper were instrumental in eventually settling on the right one for his portfolio. The portfolio was successful in leading to interviews and achieving employment soon after graduation.

He discovered inspiration by looking at marketing books, graphic design books, and infographic books and journals.

All applicants show creative skills in a variety of media and project types. As a student interested in interior design, you probably already have several examples of your art and design work that can form the basis of a good portfolio. Do not be afraid to demonstrate your talent, aspirations, and dreams. If you are applying to a design school, your interests should visually demonstrate a desire to create something unique that will touch many people around you. Students without academic background or experience in design-related fields are often counseled to take a beginning level design and drawing studio course to see if they have the inclination to study further and in what areas of design.

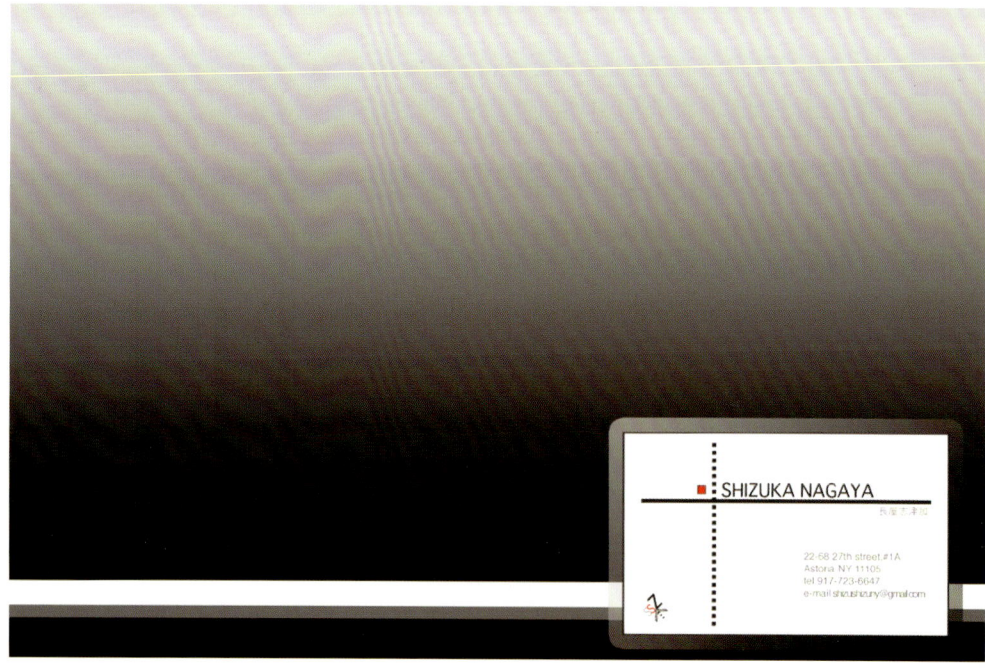

Shizuka Nagaya: Layout Design Reflects Individuality

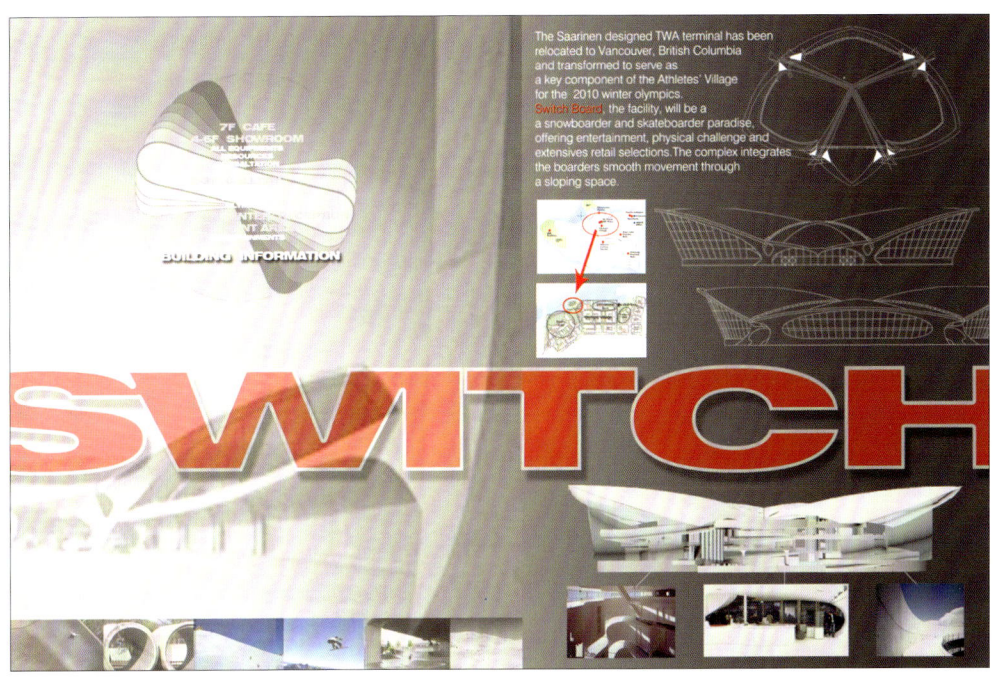

10–28 to 10–30 Shizuka has designed a dense portfolio that fills each horizontal layout with rigorous design and interesting graphics that relate to the overall redesign of the TWA terminal in NYC. He includes models and drawings that exhibit his 3D spatial thinking. We think this is a good example of an enthusiastic and engaging layout that shows his strength of 3D work and interior design. The bold use of color and repetitive shapes in his furniture design layouts also make it easy to become a part of his world in design. Shizuka Nagaya, New York School of Interior Design, N.Y. 11" x 17".

10 PORTFOLIO OF INTERIOR PORTFOLIOS

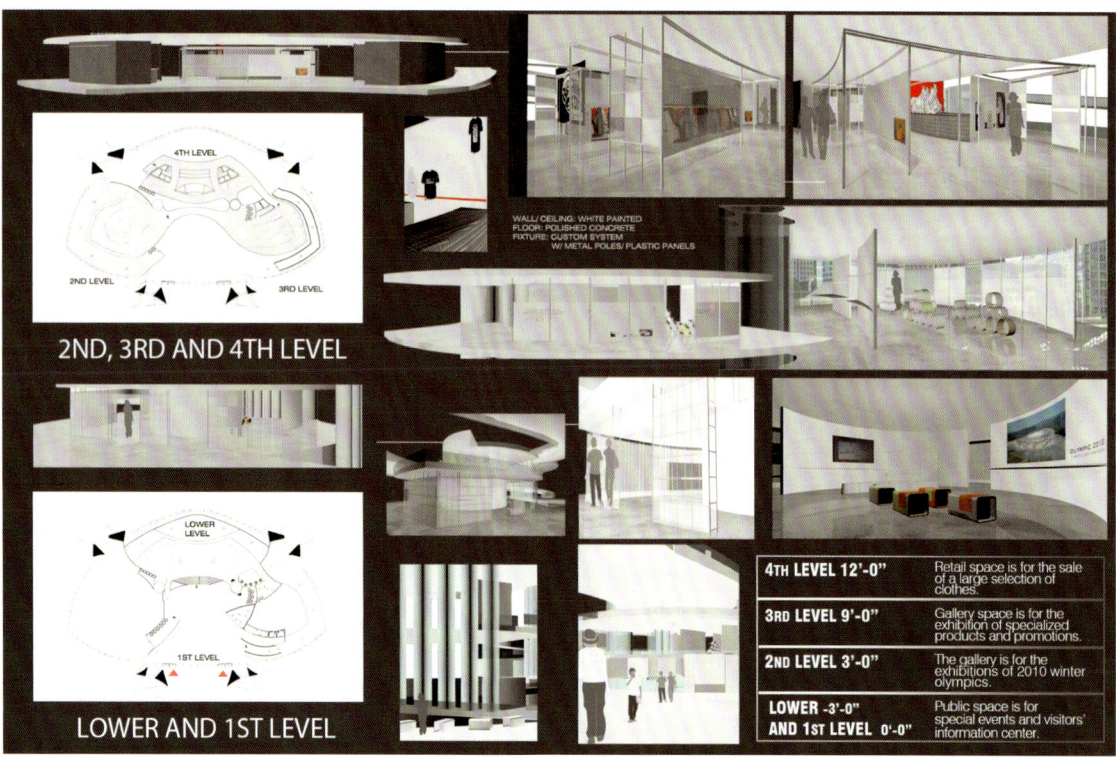

Shizuka Nagaya: Layout Design Reflects Individuality

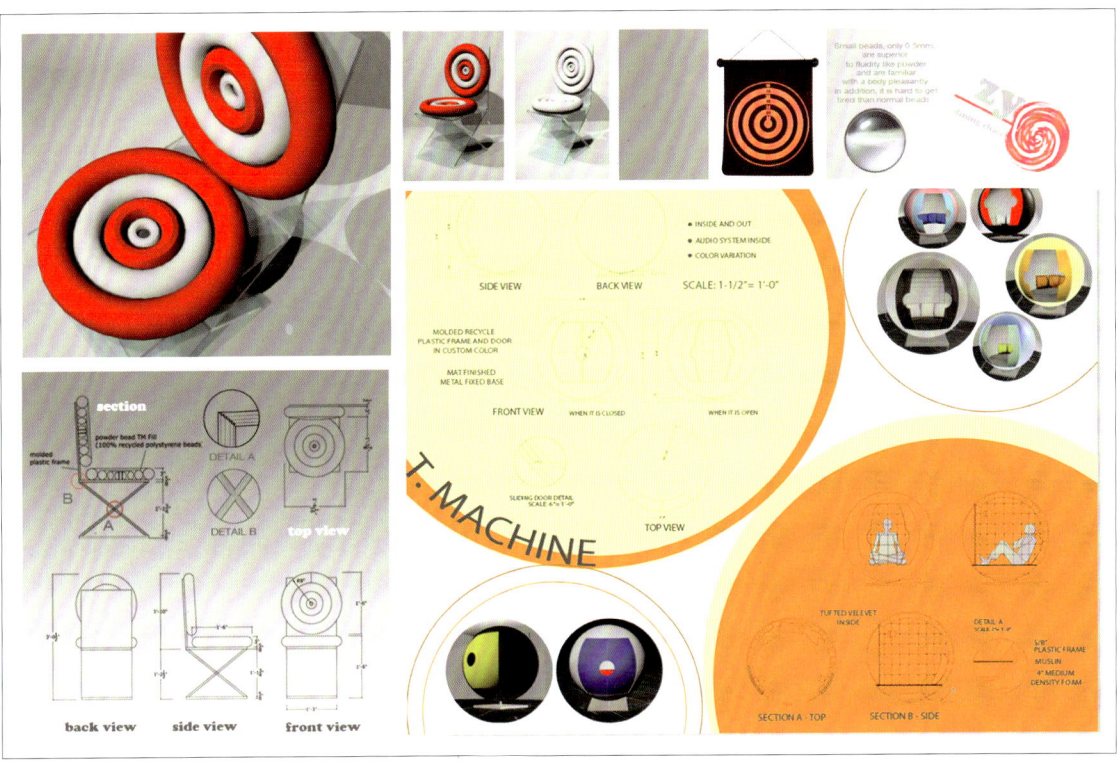

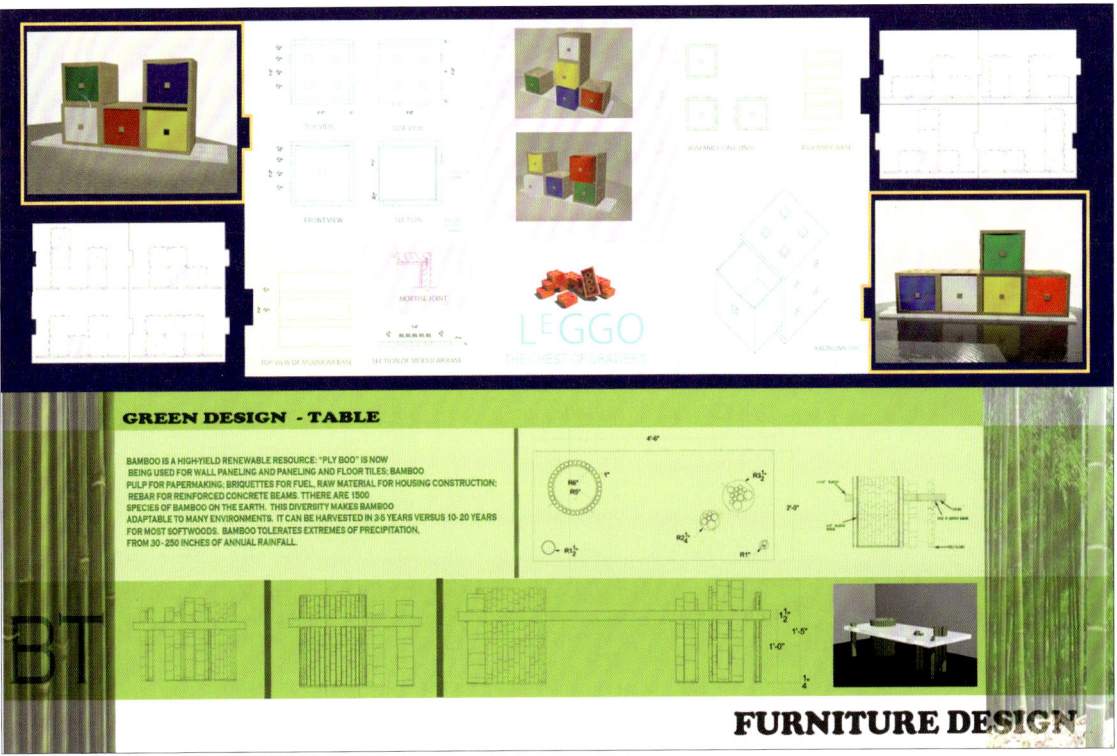

10–31 to 10–34 Shizuka has designed a dense portfolio that fills each horizontal layout with rigorous design and interesting graphics that relate to the overall redesign of the TWA terminal in NYC. He includes models and drawings that exhibit his 3D spatial thinking. We think this is a good example of an enthusiastic and engaging layout that shows his strength of 3D work and interior design. The bold use of color and repetitive shapes in his furniture design layouts also make it easy to become a part of his world in design. Shizuka Nagaya, New York School of Interior Design, N.Y. 11" x 17".

KALIE HENDRICKS: ORGANIZING PROCESS AND PRODUCT

Kalie designed her interior design portfolio as a program requirement at the University of Wisconsin, Stevens Point. She used Photoshop and PowerPoint for the design of her portfolio as well as Autodesk and SketchUp predominantly for her projects. She spent a total of 80 hours in design and production over the course of her final semester. She believes that starting early is critical to success and making a thorough inventory of all her work was instrumental to working efficiently. The inventory helped her decide what to use and what to discard, and to feel confident in the overall level of quality expressed in the final version of her book.

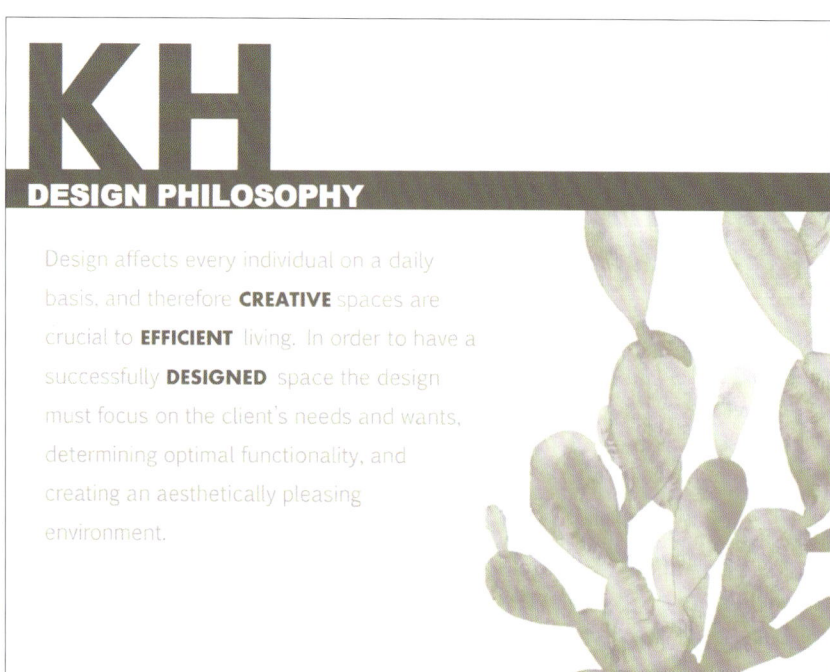

Kalie Hendricks: Organizing Process and Product

10–35 to 10–39 Kalie has a bold format for presenting her projects. She opens her book with a design statement and fuses color–form as a graphic tool to move you from page to page. It is exciting to look at and to page through her individual projects. Rather than using a lot of open white space, she fills the page with bold graphics and exuberant renderings and marker schematic sketches. She balances this bold use of color and form by keeping her titles and narrative in a soft gray that does not undermine her rigorous design of each presentation. Kalie Hendricks, University of Wisconsin, Stevens Point, Wi. 8.5" x 11".

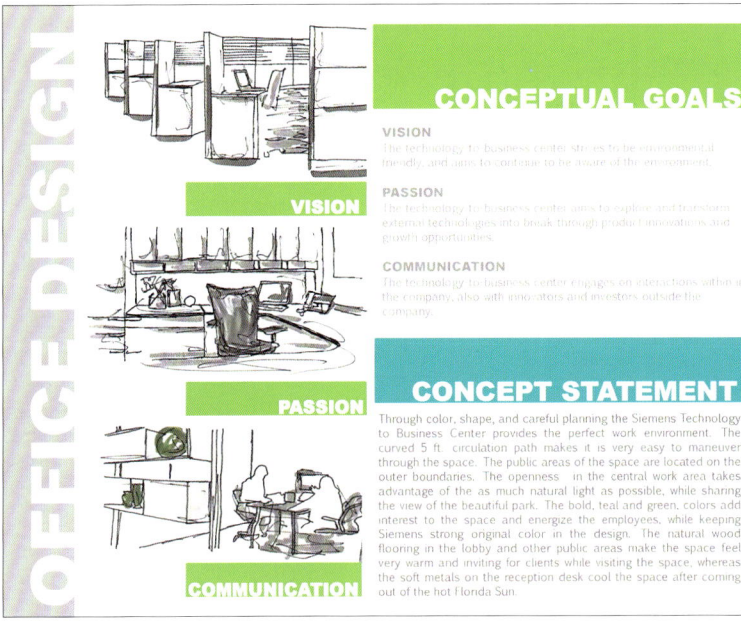

261

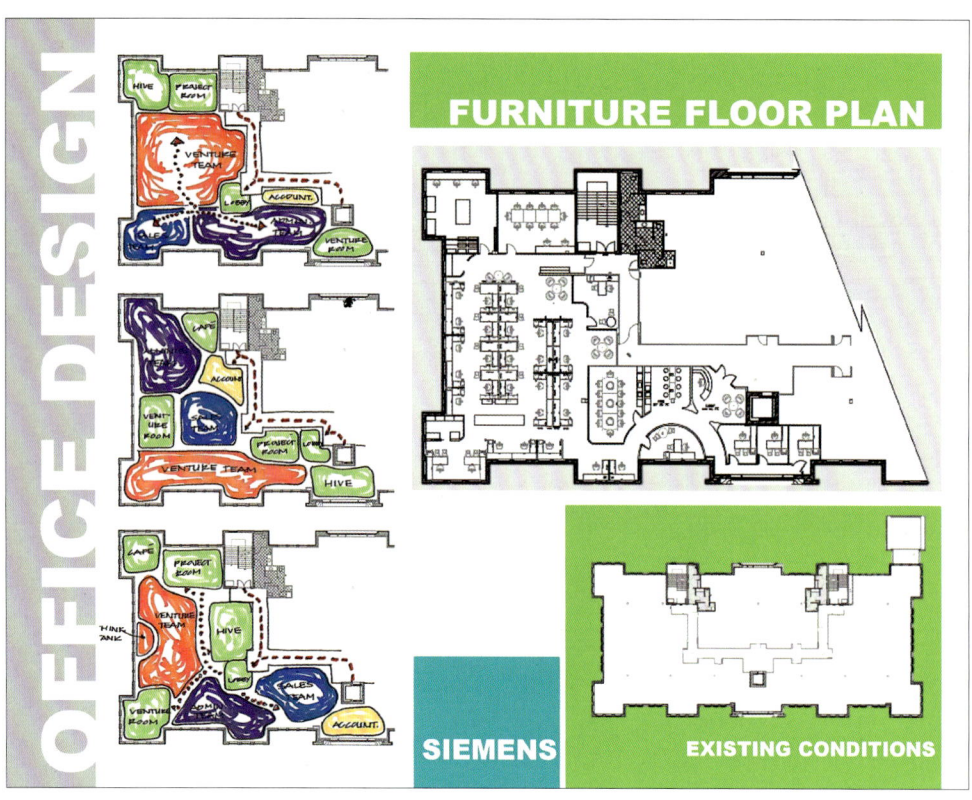
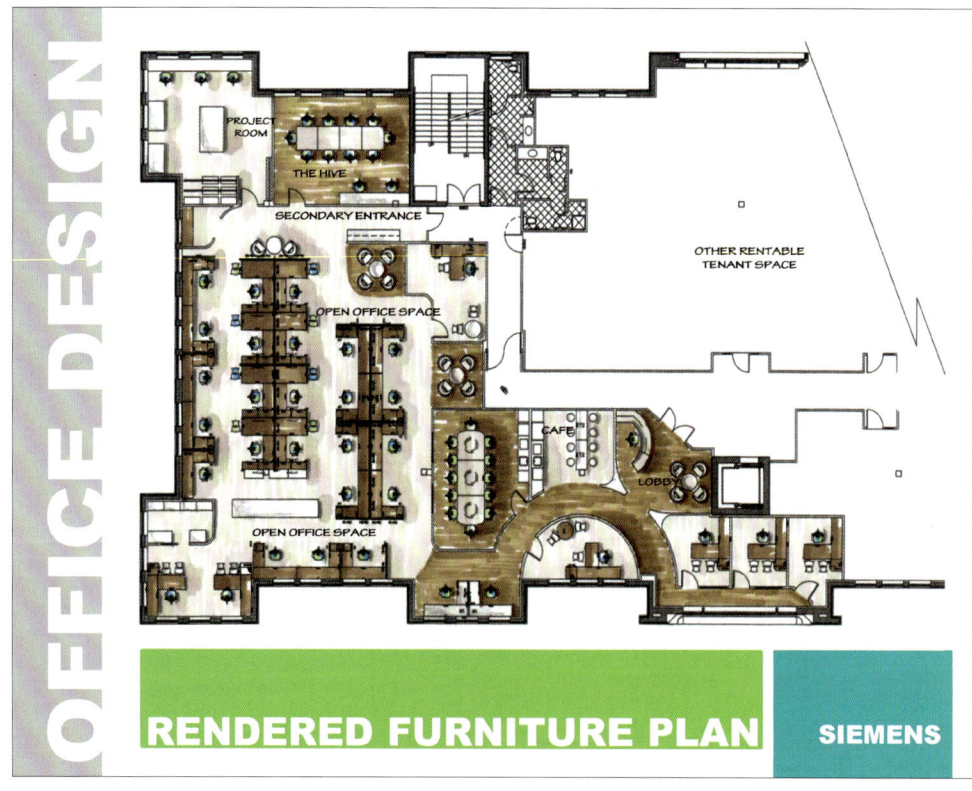

Kalie Hendricks: Organizing Process and Product

10–40 to 10–43 Kalie has a bold format for presenting her projects. She opens her book with a design statement and fuses color–form as a graphic tool to move you from page to page. It is exciting to look at and to page through her individual projects. Rather than using a lot of open white space, she fills the page with bold graphics and exuberant renderings and marker schematic sketches. She balances this bold use of color and form by keeping her titles and narrative in a soft gray that does not undermine her rigorous design of each presentation. Kalie Hendricks, University of Wisconsin, Stevens Point, Wi. 8.5" x 11".

KELSIE LALLY: PROJECT BRIEFS SPEAK VOLUMES ABOUT CONCEPT AND IDEATION

Kelsie studied interior architecture at the University of Wisconsin, Stevens Point, and feels that she had excellent instruction in design and in the creation of her interior design portfolio. Her purpose was to showcase her most successful projects throughout the program with an eye toward seeking employment following graduation. Kelsie created a sequence of brief presentations one after the next that underscored the nature of creative conceptualization, a strength in her work and portfolio. She used Photoshop for the design of her portfolio, printed it on 11" x 17" paper, and trimmed it down to 8" x 14" to accommodate her layout design, especially of the visuals. She laminated the front and back covers and had the project coil bound so the pages would lie flat as one paged through the book.

She made one portfolio at a total cost of $50.00. She spent approximately 160 hours on design and production combined. She spent 16 weeks designing the book averaging 10 hours of work per week. She enjoyed the process of design development that afforded her time to change things as she went along. She learned how important time management is to a large project such as a portfolio. Some of the most inspiring examples that influenced her book came from looking at *Vogue* and *Elle Décor* magazines. She applied to three design firms and was accepted at two of them.

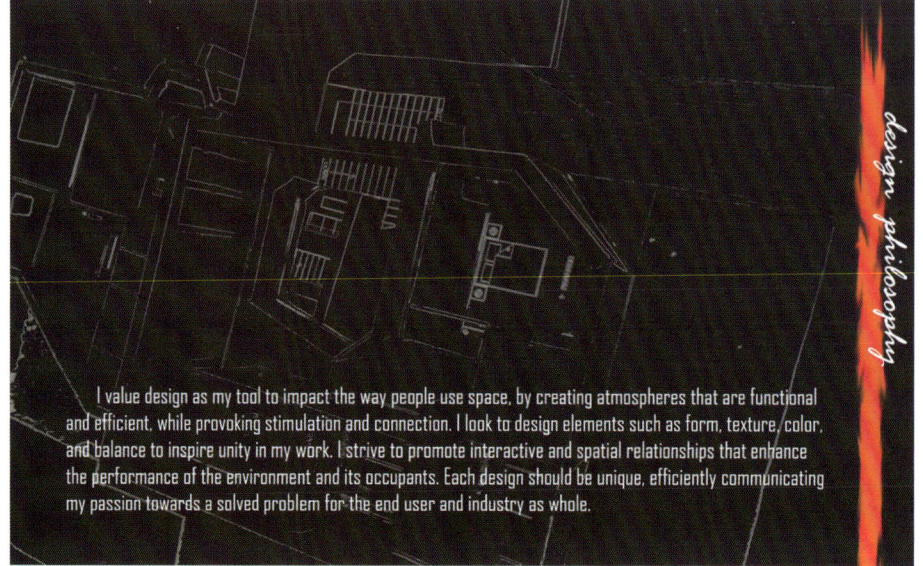

Kelsie Lally: Project Briefs Speak Volumes about Concept and Ideation

10–44 to 10–48 Kelsie included an entire page in gray to illustrate her design philosophy at the beginning of her portfolio. She also uses a line drawing style to introduce the title of each project. It is at an angle as if it is laying on a work table. This is a great idea to introduce you to how line drawing becomes form and reality during her working process. She includes a narrative that is designed within a gray field at the beginning of each project and within each project that articulates an objective and solution to the given problem. Her colorful lines at the bottom of each page are like a brush stroke of her thinking and provide an energetic gesture to what is developed in each and every project. Kelsie Lally, University of Wisconsin, Stevens Point, Wis. 8" x 14".

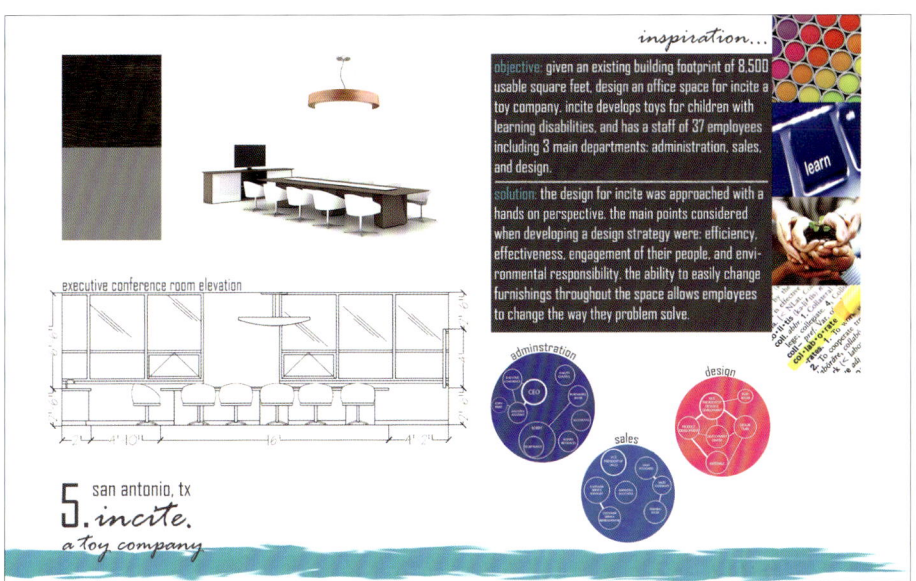

CONCLUSION

In review, consider the following as you now embark on planning the design for your portfolio. Can a portfolio story demonstrate a progression of creative projects that serves as a profile of your creative interests and abilities? What are the types of work that best represent your multiple artistic abilities and simultaneously draw attention to the type of design you wish to study or practice? How will you make the final selection of your best work? When and how will you emphasize certain technical or creative conceptual aspects of your work?

What are the best methods to demonstrate a foundation in three-dimensional forms and space, composition, and basic understanding of light/shadow, depth, and color through sketches, drawings, photography, crafts, sculptures, and so on? What methods can I employ toward editing my work in a clear, concise, and legible manner? How many are too many projects? How do I form an intelligent progression of projects in my book? How do I show how early projects build on one another? Or, are they standalone projects that show my diverse talents?

The answers to all of these questions are important. Hopefully, you have found relevant materials throughout this book that provoke answers to these questions. A portfolio is a self-presentation tool that creatively communicates a student's design outlook and level of development through a variety of media and skill sets. The portfolio should include a selection of works with at least one example of your design work in the area of your professional interests.

> "If you have total freedom, then you are in trouble. It's much better when you have some obligation, some discipline, some rules. When you have no rules, then you start to build your own rules."
>
> — **RENZO PIANO**

Conclusion

What are the evaluative criteria that will be used to review and judge my work?

1. Ability to develop convincing visual narratives through graphic and 3D presentation methods and written descriptions that convey the design development process, i.e., research and inspirational material, concept generation, study models, and drawings that demonstrate process/thinking and an excellent final presentation of the design solution.

2. Demonstration of fundamental abilities to conceptualize and communicate design solutions using two- and/or three-dimensional representation skills in any media (digital, hand drawings, sketching, drafting, modeling) as they relate to research, diagramming and schematics, programming, plans, elevations, sections, perspectives, models, space planning, and lighting, as well as layouts, forms, colors, materials, and finishing aspects.

3. Demonstration of an understanding of functional and experiential issues related to the process of creating interior design/architecture, built environments and/or artifacts, such as structural, environmental and building systems, spatial generation, organization, perception and design solutions, and specific project results reflecting contextual and programmatic demands.

4. Ability to effectively and flexibly organize the graphic design, typography, and visual communications of the overall portfolio, including titles, styles, page composition, written materials, references, and information hierarchies.

5. Expansive portfolios demonstrate examples of skills and experience outside of your specific education/training (photography, paintings, sculptures, music, etc.) that will help set you apart from other applicants. Oftentimes, these abilities find a way to be integrated into the content of given projects inside your portfolio projects so that a final section on fine arts or foundations is redundant.

6. Does this applicant or candidate have office experience that would make in-house training easier for the firm?

7. Are the interests of the applicant in tune with the breadth and depth of the firm's project history, design niche, and business interests?

8. Does the applicant possess those personal and professional traits that would be in harmony with the design team and staff, and also clients?

9. Does the applicant exhibit a strong sense of motivation, and would he or she be a self-starter?

10. Are the longer-term professional aspirations of the applicant in harmony with the firm's future and strategic planning?

Most importantly, our best wishes toward achieving your goals through a rigorous plan for your interior design portfolio!

BIBLIOGRAPHY

Baron, Cynthia L. *Designing a Digital Portfolio* (2nd Edition). Berkeley: Peachpit, Pearson Education, 2004.

Bender, Diane M. *Design Portfolios: Moving from Traditional to Digital*. New York: Fairchild Books, 2008.

Berryman, Greg. *Notes on Graphic Design and Visual Communication*. Los Altos, CA: William Kaufmann, 1979.

Cohen, Jonathan. *Communication and Design with the Internet*. New York: W. W. Norton, 2000.

Eisenman, Sara. *Building Design Portfolios: Innovative Concepts for Presenting Your Work (Design Field Guide)*. Gloucester, MA: Rockport, 2006.

Foote, Cameron. *The Business Side of Creativity*. New York: W. W. Norton, 1996.

Hoffmann, Armin. *Graphic Design Manual*. New York: Van Nostrand Reinhold, 1965.

Kliment, Stephen A. *Writing for Design Professionals*. New York: W. W. Norton, 1998.

Linton, Harold. *Marketing for Architecture and Design*. New York: W. W. Norton, 1998.

Linton, Harold. *Portfolio Design* (4th Edition). New York: W. W. Norton, 2012.

Luescher, Andreas. *The Architect's Portfolio: Planning, Design, Production*. London: Routledge, 2010.

Marjanovic, I., Rüedi Ray, K., Lokko, K. N. N. *The Portfolio: An Architectural Student's Handbook*. Burlington, MA: Architectural Press, an imprint of Elsevier, 2003.

Mitton, Maureen. *Portfolios for Interior Designers*. New York: John Wiley & Sons, Inc., 2010.

Rowe, R., Will, G., Linton, H. *Graphic Design Portfolio Strategies for Print and Digital Media*. Upper Saddle River, NJ: Prentice-Hall, 2009.

Waldrep, Lee, W. *Becoming an Architect: A Guide to Careers in Design*. New York: John Wiley & Sons, Inc., 2006.

INDEX

3D interior space, 72

A

Ageloff, Scott, 188
Algonquin College
   Rempel, Caleb, 44
   Sanchez, Mark, 114
   Soltani, Nazli, 15
Allen, Gisella, 142, 143
Allied interests, role of, 74
Americans with Disabilities Act (ADA), 217
Ammidon, Callie, 5
Ando, Tadao, 52
Aristya, Anne, 163–167
   featured portfolio, 163–166
   portfolio review by Chabra, 167
Art Institute of Austin, Jenkins, Jennifer, 94
Art Students League, Rand, Paul, 29
ASID, green design, 69

B

Bakhash, Lillian, 110, 111
Baryshnikov, Mikhail, 220
Bast, Jan, 171, 172
Bear Creek Prairie co-housing project, Stover Cessna, Kirsten, 252–255
Beaver Dam dorm space, design by Emily Fike, 169, 171
Betesh, Stephanie, 84, 85
"BE WHAT YOU SEEM TO BE" lighting design, 77–78
Bold Magazine, concept by Anne Aristya, 163–165
Bollvik, Asa, 80, 81
books. *See also* Portfolio
   custom size, 252–255
   going full size, 12
   living sequences, 14
   portfolios, 2, 8
Boston Architectural College, Imoto, Tak, 173–175
boxes. *See* Portfolio

Brewer-Cantelmo, 8
Brewinski, Joshua, 6, 7, 150, 151, 152
Bright Interiors, interior design firm, 192
building information modelling (BIM), 140

C

California State University, Mondragon, Sergio, 195–199
capturing images, 108, 112
Capuano, Michael, 30, 31
Carlson, Iryna, 8, 9, 59, 204
Central Michigan University, Zumbaugh, Chad, 248–251
Chabaud, Audrey, 33
Chabra, Lawrence, 104, 167
Chambers, Jenna, 56, 57
Chaminade University, Clemente, Beverly, 42
Cheng, Chu Yen, 34, 35
CIDA (Council for Interior Design Accreditation), 217
Clemente, Beverly, 42, 43
color, 3D interior space, 72
color temperature, images, 113
Colorado State University, Brewinski, Joshua, 7, 150–152
combining images, 123
communications
   design interview process, 231–232
   networking, 228, 235–236
   technology and, 217–218
competition, among designers, 100
comprehensive design projects, 60
computer inventory, 54
concept, 29–30
   big idea, 39
   boards, 211
   layout design, 93
   lead, 102
   lighting and temperature of images, 113
   origins of, 79
   project briefs, 264
   sketches, 58
   umbrella concept, 92

continuity, portfolios, 16
Costanza, Adrianna, 240, 241
cover letter, 195, 200, 205
creating digital images, 140–141
creative process
   collecting images for form board, 32
   concept of big idea, 39
   engaging audience, 44
   inspiration, 37–38
   perspective to step back, 30
   preliminary budget, 48–49
   reading your form board, 34
   robust research, 46
   testing materials and ideas, 48–49
   thinking out loud, 48
   titles and problem statements, 41–42
critiques
   basic organization, 185
   beyond the portfolio, 187
   cover, 185
   interviews for, 187
   micro-organization, 186
   portfolio by Anne Aristya, 163–167
   portfolio by Coleen O'Leary, 176–181
   portfolio by Emily Fike, 168–172
   portfolio by Melissa Vasconcelos, 181–185
   portfolio by Tak Imoto, 172–176
   portfolios, 161–162
   reviewer tips, 186
Cuellar, Sarah Elena, 74, 75

D

Danckaert, Thomas, 14
Davis, Amanda, 5
DeBree, Kelsey, 209–211
Deleon, Vanessa, Tak Imoto portfolio review, 176
design, 79. *See also* Portfolio design
   adaptive reuse, 217
   conceptual process for layout, 93
   designing within limits, 248–251
   eco-friendly, 218

INDEX

design *(continued)*
   evaluative criteria, 267
   layout and visualization, 96–97
   layout reflecting individuality, 256–259
   luminosity, 218–219
   origins of concepts, 79
   personality of custom size books, 252–255
   planning, 266
   pragmatic problem solver, 217
   role of process, 89
   sustainability, 218
   tectonics, 219
   unifying nature with, 216–217
designers. *See also* Interior portfolios
   Allen, Gisella, 142, 143
   Ammidon, Callie, 5
   Aristya, Anne, 163–167
   Bakhash, Lillian, 110, 111
   Betesh, Stephanie, 84, 85
   Bollvik, Asa, 80, 81
   Brewinski, Joshua, 6, 7, 150, 151, 152
   Capuano, Michael, 30, 31
   Carlson, Iryna, 8, 9, 59
   Chambers, Jenna, 56, 57
   Chaubaud, Audrey, 33
   Cheng, Chu Yen, 34, 35
   Clemente, Beverly, 42, 43
   competition with other, 100
   Costanza, Adrianna, 240, 241
   Cuellar, Sarah Elena, 74, 75
   Davis, Amanda, 5
   DeBree, Kelsey, 209–211
   DeVries, Leah, 22, 23
   Eggert, Rachel, 226–227
   Epelbaum, Evgenya, 36, 37
   Fike, Emily, 168–172
   Flynn, Phylicia, 6
   Hale, Macy, 192–194
   Han, Hyun Kyu, 20, 21
   Hashizume, Shunsuke, 65, 66
   Hendricks, Kalie, 260–263
   Hinds, Kristian, 222–225
   Hong, Jun, 126, 127, 128
   Imoto, Tak, 172–176
   Jenkins, Jennifer, 94, 95
   Kaner, Robert, 106, 107, 120
   Kasick, Jennifer, 72, 73
   Klein, Amanda, 62, 63
   Lally, Kelsie, 264–265
   League, Lisa, 118, 119, 120
   Li, Shiqi, 16, 17
   Liao, Ming Chen, 41–42
   Lin, Wei Tsun, 103
   Londy, Terry, 146–149
   MacDonald, Courtney, 5
   McHenry, John, 156, 157, 158
   Miles Pierrou, Hannah, 2, 3, 203
   Mondragon, Sergio, 195–199
   Nagaya, Shizuka, 256–259
   O'Leary, Coleen, 176–181
   Pickett, Carlita, 46, 47
   Pierrou, Hannah M., 2, 3, 203
   Ravhon, Reut, 60, 61
   Rempel, Caleb, 44–45
   Rohey, Michael, 40
   Rosenberg, Vivi, 134–136
   Sanchez, Mark, 114, 115
   Schultz, Jillian, 138, 139
   Seager, Alexandra, 244–247
   Semrow, Whitley, 205–207
   Shoemaker, Claire, 237–238
   Soldan, Ilijana, 98, 99
   Soltani, Nazli, 14, 15
   Spohn, Tarah, 128, 129, 130
   Stafford, Chelsea, 100, 101
   storyboarding, 10–12
   Stover Cessna, Kirsten, 252–255
   Struthers, Renee, 124, 125
   Taylor, Laura, 199–201
   Tennant, Melissa, 228–230
   Todd, Sarah, 4, 25–26
   Vasconcelos, Melissa, 181–185
   Vella, Lauren, 190–191
   Vogel, Sarah, 233–236
   Wessling, Kyle, 212–215
   Wierzbicki, Courtney, 70, 71
   Wong, Laura-Anne, 89–90, 91
   Wong, Topaz, 12, 13
   Wyllie, Kevin, 4
   Yang, Joe Hynn, 67, 82, 83
   Zhou, Mia, 52, 53
   Zumbaugh, Chad, 248–251
design statement, 208–209
desktop organization, portfolio materials, 55
DeVries, Leah, 22, 23
digital images, 133, 159
   creating, 140–141
   designing the layout, 149–150
   editing, 144
   exporting for publication, 153–155
   preparing physical work for, 137–138
   raster images, 145
   vector images, 146
dossier, 19
Driftwood on the Ocean (Montauk, NY), Bakhash, Lillian, 110

E

Eastern Michigan University, Londy, Terry, 146–149
eco-friendly design, 218
editing
   digital images, 144
   images, 124
   raster images, 145
   vector images, 146
Eggert, Rachel, 226, 227
Einstein, Albert, 32
employment
   design interview process, 231–232
   initial discussions, 225–226
   portfolio and interview, 222
   tips for getting dream job, 235–236
Enchanted Loom, design by Coleen O'Leary, 179
engaging audience, 44
envision vs. revision, fresh approach, 24–26
Epelbaum, Evgenya, 36, 37
expressing, images, 109, 128

F

Fashion Institute of Technology
   Bollvik, Asa, 80
   Ravhon, Reut, 60, 61
Fe Advertising, design by Emily Fike, 170, 171
Fike, Emily
   portfolio of, 168–170
   review by Jan Bast, 171
   reviewer Bast, 172
Flynn, Phylicia, 6
Focused skills, research, 68–69
form board
   beginning of project, 92
   collecting images for, 32
   perspective to step back, 30
   reading your, 34
Fox, Diane, 49
full size, 12

G

Gehry, Frank, 52
George Mason University, lighting studio at School of Art, 121
George Washington University, Carlson, Iryna, 8, 9, 59
Government Services Administration (GSA), 218
graphic design, layout and, 244–247
green design, 69

INDEX

H

Hadley, Albert, 160, 161
Hagner, Rachel, 97
Hale, Macy, 38, 192–194, 202
Han, Hyun Kyu, 20, 21, 204
Harrington College of Design, Imoto, Tak, 173–175
Hashizume, Shunsuke, 65, 66
Hendricks, Kalie, 260–263
hidden factors, portfolio design, 18, 20–21
Hinds, Kristian, 222–225
Hong, Jun, 126, 127, 128
House of Portfolios NYC, 8
human experiences, 216–219
human factors, images, 113, 131
hybrids, portfolios, 8

I

idea
   concept, 29–30
   concept of big, 39
Illinois Institute of Art, Pickett, Carlita, 46
images. *See also* digital images
   capturing, 108, 126
   capturing, with purpose, 112
   color temperature, 113
   controlling editing process, 124
   cultivating sensibilities, 126
   design thinking, 112
   expressing, 109, 128
   human factors, 113, 131
   interior setup, 120
   lighting, 113
   lighting studio, 121–122
   materials, media, and studio lighting, 116–117
   models, 120
   presentation strategies, 123
   scanning, photocopying, and combining, 123
   sensing, 105, 108
   understanding your strengths, 126
Imoto, Tak
   portfolio, 172–175
   review by Vanessa Deleon, 176
Incubator Office Space project, design by Coleen O'Leary, 179, 180
industries, organizing materials for, 64
inspiration, creative process, 37–38
inspired layout design, 77–78
Interactive Fashion Retail Store, design by Tak Imoto, 174, 175
interior design. *See also* interior portfolios
   portfolio development, 243
   start-up firms, 189
interior portfolios. *See also* designers
   Hendricks, Kalie, 260–263
   Lally, Kelsie, 264–265
   Nagaya, Shizuka, 256–259
   Seager, Alexandra, 244–247
   Stover Cessna, Kirsten, 252–255
   Zumbaugh, Chad, 248–251
interior setup, images, 120
interior space, 3D, 72
interview, 205
   design firms, 228, 231–232
   employment, 222
   initial discussions, 225–226
   portfolio leading with confidence, 239
intuition, design thinking, 216
inventory
   computer, 54
   organizing materials, 51–52

J

Jenkins, Jennifer, 94, 95

K

Kadoch, Aaron, 144
Kaner, Robert, 76, 106, 107, 120
Kasick, Jennifer, 72, 73
Kendall College of Art and Design
   Klein, Amanda, 62
   Semrow, Whitley, 205–207
   Shoemaker, Claire, 237–238
   Stafford, Chelsea, 100
   Wierzbicki, Courtney, 70
Kenney, Jim, 137
Klein, Amanda, 62, 63
Kwallek, Nancy, 180–181

L

Lally, Kelsie, 264–265
layout design
   digital media, 149–150
   inspired, 77–78
   portfolio design, 102
   reflecting individuality, 256–259
   and visualization, 96–97
League, Lisa, 89, 118, 119, 120
leave behinds, portfolios, 10, 272
LEED (Leadership in Energy and Environmental Design), 218
lenses, images, 116–117
Li, Shiqi, 16, 17
Liao, Ming Chen, 41–42
lighting
   images, 113
   luminosity, 218–219
   materials, media, and studio, of images, 116–117
   studio, 121–122
Lin, Maya, 242
Lin, Wei Tsun, 103
living document, portfolio as, 2, 97
Londy, Terry, 146–149
luminosity, 218–219

M

McCracken, Tara, 64
MacDonald, Courtney, 5
McHenry, John F. Xavier, IV, 58, 156, 157, 158
Maeda, John, 114
materiality, 68
materials, images, 116–117
Mau, Bruce, 155
media, images, 116–117
Miles, Josh, 55
models, images, 120
Mondragon, Sergio, 195–199
music and interior space, design by Melissa Vasconcelos, 182–185

N

Nagaya, Shizuka, 256–259
nature, unifying with design, 216–217
networking, 228, 235–236
New York School of Interior Design
   Ammidon, Callie, 5
   Aristya, Anne, 163–166
   Bakhash, Lillian, 110
   Capuano, Michael, 30, 31
   Chabaud, Audrey, 33
   Chabra, Lawrence, 104, 167
   Cheng, Chu Yen, 34, 35
   Cuellar, Sarah Elena, 74
   Davis, Amanda, 5
   Epelbaum, Evgenya, 36, 37
   Hashizume, Shunsuke, 65, 66
   Hong, Jun, 126
   Li, Shiqi, 16, 17
   Liao, Ming Chen, 41
   Lin, Wei Tsun, 103
   Nagaya, Shizuka, 256–259
   Spohn, Tarah, 128–130
   Rohey, Michael, 40
   Rosenberg, Vivi, 134

INDEX

New York School of Interior Design *(continued)*
    Todd, Sarah, 4, 25, 26
    Vella, Lauren, 190–191
    Wong, Topaz, 13
    Yang, Joe Hynn, 67, 82
NEXT project, design by Coleen O'Leary, 179, 180
Northeastern University Music Building, design by Tak Imoto, 172, 173

O

objects and openings, portfolios, 4–7
Ohio State University, Department of Design, Kasick, Jennifer, 72
O'Leary, Coleen
    portfolio, 176–180
    portfolio review by Nancy Kwallek, 180
online publishing, 155
opportunity for fresh approach, 24–26
organizing portfolio materials
    3D interior space, 72
    comprehensive design projects, 60
    computer inventory, 54
    concept sketches, 58
    desktop organization, 55
    fixing older projects, 58
    focused skills, 68–69
    green design, 69
    materiality, 68
    portfolio design, 82
    role of allied interests, 74
    supplemental categories, 68
    understanding industries, 64
    wish list, 51–52

P

Pallasmaa, Juhani, 132
parallax, 117
Parsons School of Design, Rand, Paul, 29
patterns of success, portfolios, 22
Philadelphia University, McHenry, John, 156–158
photocopying images, 123
photography. *See also* Digital images; Images
    interior, by Lisa League, 118, 119
    lighting studio, 116–117, 121–122
    materials, 116–117
    media, 116–117
Piano, Renzo, 266
Picasso, 37
Pickett, Carlita, 46, 47, 67
Pidgeon, Nadia S., 109
Pierrou, Hannah M., 2, 3, 203
portfolio. *See also* critiques; interior portfolios
    advice on how to show, 208
    books, 2, 8
    boxes, 8
    capturing images, 108
    continuity, 16
    critiques of, 161–162
    design, 1
    digital vs. printed, 97
    employment, 222
    envision vs. revision, 24–26
    evaluative criteria, 267
    fixing older projects, 58
    hidden factors, 18, 20–21
    hybrids, 8
    layout and visualization, 96–97
    leave behinds and teasers, 10
    living document, 2, 97
    objects and openings, 4–7
    opportunity for fresh approach, 24–26
    organizing process and product, 260–263
    patterns of success, 22
    process presentation in, 232
    reading between the lines, 27
    storyboarding, 10–12
    titles and problem statements, 41–42
portfolio as a tool
    guiding the resume, 232–233
    initial discussions, 225–226
    interviewing, 233
    leading with confidence, 239
    process presentation, 232
    research, 221–222, 228
portfolio design. *See also* organizing portfolio materials
    competition among designers, 100
    concepts lead, 102
    designing with typography, 86–88
    inspired layout design, 77–78
    juggling concepts, 103
    layout, 96–97, 102
    organization, 82
    origins of concepts, 79
    road map for conceptual process, 93
    role of process design, 89
    sketching, 102
    storyboards, 102
    umbrella concept, 92
    visualization, 92, 96–97
Pratt Institute
    Han, Hyun Kyu, 20, 21
    Rand, Paul, 29
    Wessling, Kyle, 212–215
preliminary budget, 48–49
presentation. *See also* digital images; images
    images as strategies, 123
    process in portfolio, 232
printing materials, 48–49
problem statements, portfolio, 41–42
professional documents, conceptual process for layout, 93
projects
    comprehensive design, 60
    fixing older, 58
Provisions Café, design by Coleen O'Leary, 177–178
publication
    conceptual process for layout, 93
    exporting digital images for, 153–155
Purdue University, Pierrou, Hannah Miles, 2, 3, 203

Q

quality control, 205

R

Rand, Paul, 28, 29
Rapt Studio, 199–200
raster images, 145
Ravhon, Reut, 60, 61
reading between the lines, portfolios, 27
Reicis, Sandra, 141
Rempel, Caleb, 44–45
research
    advice on showing portfolio, 208
    communications and technology, 217–218
    conceptual process for layout, 93
    creative process, 46
    design firm, 192, 228, 231–232
    design statement, 208–209
    focused skills, 68–69
    general advice, 208
    human experiences, 216–219
    meeting with clients, 211
    portfolio as a tool, 221–222
    robust, 46
resume, 195
    Carlson, Iryna, 204
    Hale, Macy, 202
    Han, Hyun Kyu, 204
    Pierrou, Hannah M., 203
    portfolio guiding the, 232–233
    Taylor, Laura, 200

INDEX

Rochester Institute of Technology, DeBree, Kelsey, 209–211
Rohey, Michael, 40
Rosenberg, Vivi, 134–136

S

Sanchez, Mark, 114, 115
Savannah College of Art and Design, Hinds, Kristian, 222–225
scanning, 77
scanning images, 123
School of Visual Arts, Seager, Alexandra, 244–247
Schultz, Jillian, 138, 139
Seager, Alexandra, 244–247
self-publishing, 49
Semrow, Whitley, 205–207
sensibilities
   cultivating, for images, 126
   human experience, 216
sensing, 104, 105, 108
Shaker proverb, 112
Shoemaker, Claire, 237–238
Siemens, Hendricks, Kalie, 261–263
Sinek, Simon, 94
sketching
   portfolio design, 102
   thinking out loud, 48
skills, researching focused, 68–69
Socratic method, teaching, 1
Soldan, Ilijana, 98, 99
Soltani, Nazli, 14, 15
Spohn, Tarah, 128, 129, 130
Stafford, Chelsea, 100, 101
Starbucks, concept by Anne Aristya, 166
Storyboards, portfolio, 10–12, 102
Stover Cessna, Kirsten, 252–255
Struthers, Renee, 124, 125
Sung Kyun Kwan University, Hong, Jun, 127
supplemental categories, 68
sustainability, 218

T

Taylor, Laura, 199–201
teacher, Socratic method, 1
teasers, portfolios, 10
technology, communications and, 217–218
tectonics, 219
temperature, images, 113
Tennant, Melissa, 228–230
testing materials and ideas, 48–49
titles, portfolio, 41–42
Todd, Sarah, 4, 25–26
Tree Houses, Fairy Tale Castles in the Air (Taschen), 212
trends, 219
Tsao & McKown, 120
typography
   designing with, 86–88
   letterspacing, 88

U

umbrella concept, 92
University of Manitoba
   Struthers, Renee, 124
   Vasconcelos, Melissa, 181
University of Michigan, Wong, S. Laura-Anne, 89, 90
University of Missouri–Columbia, Stover Cessna, Kirsten, 252–255
University of Northern Iowa, DeVries, Leah, 22, 23
University of Tennessee, Knoxville
   Chambers, Jenna, 56
   Fike, Emily, 168–171
   Hale, Macy, 192–194
   O'Leary, Coleen, 176
University of Texas–Austin School of Architecture
   Allen, Gisella, 142
   Betesh, Stephanie, 84
   Kwallek, Nancy, 180
University of Utah, Taylor, Laura, 199–201
University of Wisconsin–Stevens Point
   Eggert, Rachel, 226–227
   Hendricks, Kalie, 260–263
   Lally, Kelsie, 264–265
   Tennant, Melissa, 228–230
   Vogel, Sarah, 233–236
Utah State University, Costanza, Adrianna, 240, 241

V

Vasconcelos, Melissa
   portfolio, 181–185
   review by Wickham and Zawadzki, 185–186
vector images, 146
Vella, Lauren, 190–191
Ventura, Roberto, 19
Villa Maria College, Schultz, Jillian, 138
Virginia Commonwealth University
   Soldan, Ilijana, 98
   Zhou, Mia, 52
visual communications, 217–218
visualization
   layout design and, 96–97
   words, 92
Vogel, Sarah, 233–236
Volchansky, Nadia, 117

W

Wang, Alexander, 50, 51
Wessling, Kyle, 212–215
Wickham, V. Mason, 185–186
Wierzbicki, Courtney, 70, 71
William Hotel, Bakhash, Lillian, 110, 111
Wong, Laura-Anne, 89–90, 91
Wong, Topaz, 12, 13
Wood-Nartker, Jeanneane, 122
written communications
   concept boards, 211
   design statement, 208–209
   resume and cover letter, 195
   transitions and evolving new documents, 211
Wyllie, Kevin, 4

Y

Yang, Joe Hynn, 67, 82, 83

Z

Zawadzki, Edwin, 185–186
Zhou, Mia, 52, 53
Zumbaugh, Chad, 248–251

275